HARRY POTTER AND THE OTHER

Children's Literature Association Series

HARRY POTTER and the OTHER

Race, Justice, and Difference in the Wizarding World

Edited by

SARAH PARK DAHLEN

and

EBONY ELIZABETH THOMAS

University Press of Mississippi / Jackson

The University Press of Mississippi is the scholarly publishing agency of
the Mississippi Institutions of Higher Learning: Alcorn State University,
Delta State University, Jackson State University, Mississippi State University,
Mississippi University for Women, Mississippi Valley State University,
University of Mississippi, and University of Southern Mississippi.

www.upress.state.ms.us

The University Press of Mississippi is a member
of the Association of University Presses.

Portions of this work appeared in altered form in
a forum section of *Rhetoric Review* 36, no. 4 (2017).

First printing 2022
∞

Library of Congress Control Number: 2022935069
Hardback ISBN 978-1-4968-4057-8
Paperback ISBN 978-1-4968-4056-1
Epub single ISBN 978-1-4968-4055-4
Epub institutional ISBN 978-1-4968-4054-7
PDF single ISBN 978-1-4968-4053-0
PDF institutional ISBN 978-1-4968-4052-3

British Library Cataloging-in-Publication Data available

To minispark, who fills our life with magic every day.
—Sarah Park Dahlen

To fandom, and all those who dream, hope,
and long for more inclusive storyworlds.
—Ebony Elizabeth Thomas

Contents

Acknowledgments

First, we'd like to thank the University Press of Mississippi team for believing in this anthology and bringing it into the world. We are also grateful to our reviewers, whose comments helped sharpen each chapter. A very big thank you to all St. Catherine University Master of Library and Information Science Program graduate students who worked on the project at various stages: Kallie Schell, Sierra Pandy, and Maria Becker, and an especially big thank you to Maria Becker for her careful copy editing and proofreading of each chapter.

We are indebted to other scholars who led the way in examining race and difference in Harry Potter and for the scholarly communities that nurture us both intellectually and socially, including the Children's Literature Association, the Association for Asian American Studies, the National Council for Teachers of English, and the American Library Association. And as we read, research, and write in an increasingly public, socially mediated environment, we offer our gratitude to the thousands of readers whose tweets, Facebook posts, and other communications have helped us to learn, unlearn, and reconsider our own perspectives.

Special thanks are due to *The Lion and the Unicorn* and New York University Press for allowing reprints of two of our chapters, and the *Harvard Educational Review* for the figure on page 000. Thank you to the artists who granted Kathryn Coto permission to include their artwork in chapter 6.

We could not have completed this anthology without the love and support of our families: Sarah's husband Jeff, daughter, parents, brother, and sister-in-law; and Ebony's mom Susan, sisters Danielle and Lorri, brother-in-law Alex, and niblings.

Finally, we thank each of our contributors, whose essays are pushing forward necessary discussions as they relate to the wizarding world. We are so honored that you have trusted us with your essays.

HARRY POTTER AND THE OTHER

Introduction

Sarah Park Dahlen and Ebony Elizabeth Thomas

Who We Are in the Wizarding World

When Sarah and Ebony met in 2006, we were huge fans of the wizarding world of Harry Potter. Sarah began reading the *Harry Potter* series in the early 2000s, just as she was beginning to study children's literature. Meanwhile, Ebony began her Hogwarts journey as a fifth-grade teacher in Detroit, when an unknown person left a copy of *Harry Potter and the Chamber of Secrets* on the threshold of her classroom right before winter break in 2000. Six years later, we were both anticipating the final book and movie, having enjoyed midnight book release parties and fan conferences, engaging in fandom squees and fandom wars, and sharing the adventures of Harry, Hermione, Ron, and their family and friends with the young people in our lives.

Back then, we were twentysomething graduate students. After finishing our PhDs, multiple moves, tenure, grieving losses (both of us), marriage and a daughter (Sarah), health challenges and niblings (Ebony), and the joys and stresses of life, we are now fortysomething associate professors.

We have changed. And so has our perception of the *Harry Potter* series and its author.

We write these words with heavy hearts. As scholars of children's literature, as women of color (Sarah—Korean American; Ebony—Black American), as advocates for diversity, equity, inclusion, and justice in children's and young

3

adult literature, and as citizens of the world, we have found ourselves puzzled, dismayed, and angered by the words of a billionaire bestselling fantasy series author who uses her platform in ways that are harmful.

The wizarding world of our young adulthood is now under siege because the author who created it chooses not to see everybody as whole persons.

Yet, we both contend, this refusal to see every reader has always been a signal feature of the *Harry Potter* series, which led to our desire to curate this collection of essays in the first place.

The impetus for this volume was spurred by J. K. Rowling's Pottermore (now called Wizarding World) announcement that there were wizarding schools on the continent currently known as North America and other places around the world. In 2015, Rowling tweeted that "[Indigenous] magic was important in the founding of the school. If I say which tribes, location is revealed."[1] Scholar activist Adrienne Keene, enrolled member of the Cherokee Nation and writer of the *Native Appropriations* blog, wrote, "I'm nervous about 'Indigenous magic' and specific tribes being associated with the wizarding school."[2] The school, which dates back to the "early 1600s,"[3] was established at a time when there was intense, violent conflict between Indigenous peoples and white settlers. Scholar-activist Debbie Reese, enrolled member of Nambé Pueblo, read the first short story, then blogged that "each paragraph of that short story was laden with troubling misrepresentations of Native peoples."[4]

We share the concerns of Indigenous peoples regarding the wizarding community in the United States. The worldbuilding of that wizarding community took liberties with those existing Indigenous cultures; Rowling made stuff up. In 2015, Keene explained: "The problem . . . is that we as Indigenous peoples are constantly situated as fantasy creatures. . . . But we're not magical creatures, we're contemporary peoples who are still here, and still practice our spiritual traditions, traditions that are not akin to a completely imaginary wizarding world."[5] After the first story came out in 2016, Keene wrote, "Rowling is completely re-writing these traditions. Traditions that come from a particular context, place, understanding, and truth."[6]

In addition to the problems with #MagicInNorthAmerica, Ebony and Sarah discussed the many ways in which the series fails to attend to issues of diversity, particularly with regard to race, gender, and class, much of which has been addressed by scholars in various disciplines. Existing studies include the relationship between religion and Harry Potter, interracial relationships, J. K. Rowling's social justice agenda, and how young people growing up in the wizarding age experience and interpret the series. Given that Rowling continues to expand and reveal more details about the wizarding world, both at Hogwarts and elsewhere, some fans and scholars are conflicted and concerned about how the original wizarding world—quintessentially white and British[7]—manifests in other worlds, worlds with which Rowling may be less familiar. Therefore, it is a good time to publish an anthology that specifically interrogates representations of race and difference across various Harry Potter media.

Young people who are progressive, liberal, and empowered to question authority may have believed that they were reading something radical, but as the authors in this volume demonstrate, a deeper reading of the series reveals multiple ruptures in our understanding of the liberatory potential of Potter.

Race: Why Race (Should) Matter in the Wizarding World

Race has always mattered in the world of children's literature. In 1919, W. E. B. Du Bois, Jessie Redmon Fauset, and Augustus Granville Dill created *The Brownies' Book* as an antidote for the invisibility of Black children they saw in most media.[8] Librarians of color such as Pura Belpré, Augusta Baker, and Charlemae Rollins made sure the children of color in their communities had books that reflected their experiences. The Council on Interracial Books for Children, established in 1965, questioned the white supremacist world of children's literature, which Nancy Larrick famously wrote about, too:[9] why did picture books taking place in Chicago or on a football field fail to include children of color? Forty years later, in the 1990s, a white writer built an entire world for a children's book series with predominantly white characters. The glaring whiteness of the wizarding world mirrors the all-white world that Larrick criticized in 1965. Rowling's superficial attempts to diversify this world occurred in three primary ways. First, she included nonwhite secondary characters in the Hogwarts student body. Second, she introduced the existence of a global wizarding community represented by Quidditch teams and wizarding schools from other European communities. Third, Rowling built an entire world based on classifications of species and wizarding status, which were then ordered in such a way that the resulting hierarchies paved the way for prejudice, oppression, and enslavement.

Although much of the series criticizes the prejudices built into the third category, we must contend with the fact that the racial diversity of the wizarding world does not match—or even come close to—that of the real world. Black characters such as Angelina Johnson and Dean Thomas, though memorable, are hardly integral to the story. The Patil twins, the only obviously South Asian students at Hogwarts despite the school being located in the country that colonized India, are most interesting when they accompany Ron and Harry to the Yule Ball. And Cho Chang, with her stereotypically orientalist name, is a brief crush and later exists as a foil to Ginny, the white student who ends up marrying the white hero. As Ebony writes in *The Dark Fantastic*, "race in the Harry Potter series almost seemed like an afterthought."[10]

It remains that characters of color do not play significant roles in moving the series forward, especially when compared to Harry, Ron, Hermione, and all the Hogwarts teachers and employees at the Ministry of Magic. The hypervisibility of the white trio and white adults in positions of authority, and the relegation of the people of color to the background, uphold white supremacist views that people of color are not essential, even in a fantasy world built in the imagination.

Justice: What Readers, Fans, and Audiences (Can't, and Shouldn't Have to) Do

When the *Harry Potter* series appeared in the late 1990s, it was applauded as a story that was explicitly against bigotry (see Jackie C. Horne's chapter in this volume). Given the dearth of diverse speculative fiction for youth and young adults at the time, Potter's themes of blood magic, and its inclusion of secondary and tertiary characters of color, seemed groundbreaking. However, the generation that grew up and came of age reading Harry Potter were not satisfied with marginalia and metaphor. Instead, they demanded to be centered in this and other fantastic worlds (Ebony Elizabeth Thomas, in this volume). In response to social media discourses and demands, starting with 2007's declaration that the Hogwarts headmaster, Albus Dumbledore, was gay,[11] Rowling began making postcanon remarks in interviews that diversified characters at the center of the narrative. After reader interpretations of Hermione Granger as Black gained social media momentum during the early to mid-2010s, Rowling sanctioned Black girls' reading of canon, tweeting, "Canon: brown eyes, frizzy hair and very clever. White skin was never specified. Rowling loves black Hermione."[12] At the time, this was applauded and very much in keeping with the Potter franchise's multicultural (some would say neoliberal) view of cultural inclusion in fantastic storytelling.

Ironically enough, it was the postcanon platform for the expanded wizarding world, Pottermore, that led to fans questioning who was truly included in Rowling's worldbuilding and who was not. Six years after the platform was released, the Ilvermorny School of Witchcraft and Wizardry appeared in a short story on Pottermore. Native and First Nations scholars, critics, fans and their allies pushed back using the aforementioned #MagicInNorthAmerica. That sparked conversations about the limits of demands for diversity, equity, and inclusion within mainstream science fiction and fantasy, as well as whether fans of color and Native fans could truly repair broken, stereotypical, Eurocentric stories and genres through transformative works (fan fiction, art, video, meta). When the source material tells a single story about race and difference, reading and writing the self into existence is work that readers, fans, and audiences should *not* have to do, especially when this often comes at the expense of new insider narratives written from myriad perspectives. Additionally, Rowling's stature within the literary world, and the place that the storyworld she created holds in the hearts of millions, carry extra responsibility—responsibility that hateful remarks striking at the heart of young readers' trans and nonbinary identities abdicate.

In deciding whether to proceed with this critical volume, we sought to listen to, and center, the perspectives of Black trans and nonbinary authors and scholars. As award-winning author Kacen Callender writes:

> It was difficult to come to terms with the fact that this came from the same author who had saved my life, who had offered so much hope during the years when I'd wanted to die, who made me feel powerful, and who had taught an entire generation empathy and love. There was outrage, rightfully, and calls for readers to denounce the Harry Potter series. While I immediately knew I could no longer support Rowling, I initially had a harder time untangling my emotions from Harry Potter. I'm still here, at least partly, because of the series. I'm an author because of those books.[13]

Callender and many others have called for divestment from the *Potter* series, and in this volume, Tolonda Henderson provides ethical clarity in their discussion of Rowling's 2020 essay about her transphobic comments:

At the same time, we should absolutely hold You-Know-Who responsible for her bigotry and the harm that she continues to cause. There is early evidence that people are buying fewer of her books since her 2020 essay was published. . . . I do not say (or write) her name anymore—partly a symbolic gesture that will never harm her directly but mostly a way of maintaining my own dignity as a nonbinary person. Taking her name out of my vocabulary is a form of resistance that helps me to remember that I am not powerless in the face of her extremely large platform. In the end, it is up to each person how they want to navigate this tension; I hope that this essay will help people to make an informed decision.

We concur with Callender and Henderson. It is our hope that this critical volume will assess Rowling's record on race, justice, and difference and help readers come to an informed decision about what diversity in the wizarding world of Harry Potter will mean going forward. Young readers, fans, and those who love fantasy shouldn't *have* to grin and bear discriminatory remarks from a beloved author in order to feel at home at Hogwarts.

Difference in the World of Harry Potter

Our volume opens with chapters that consider issues of "Race, Gender, and Gender Identity" in the wizarding world. Jackie C. Horne's "Harry and the Other: Multicultural and Social Justice Anti-Racism in J. K. Rowling's *Harry Potter* Series" places the wizarding world into current considerations of antiracist education and traces how antiracism operates throughout the series. In "Realism and Race: The Narrative Politics of Harry Potter," Karin E. Westman raises the question of genre, noting that, given the realistic elements of the wizarding world, readers expect that Rowling's handling of race and racial politics also be grounded in realism. In Christina M. Chica's "The Magical (Racial) Contract: Understanding the Wizarding World of Harry Potter through Whiteness," the whiteness of Hogwarts, generally unmarked throughout the series and the postcanon, is analyzed through the framework of the racial contract. Sarah Park Dahlen and Kallie Schell's chapter, "'Cho Chang Is Trending': What It Means to Be Asian in the Wizarding World," illuminates the stakes of the question by considering the way that race informs both Rowling's worldbuilding and her characterizations—Cho Chang's name, background, and (unsatisfying) storyline being a case in point. In "When the Subaltern Speak Parseltongue: Orientalism, Racial Re-Presentation, and Claudia Kim as Nagini," Jennifer Patrice Sims addresses the challenges that actresses and other creatives of color—in this case, South Korean model-actress Claudia Kim—face when embodying diverse problematic fantastic transmedia narratives like Potter.

This section continues with the role of transformative works in racial justice—in this case, racebent fanart—in Kathryn Coto's "Racebending Potter: How Fan Artists Are Recoloring the Wizarding World." Lily Anne Welty Tamai and Paul Spickard provide insight into the role of mixed-race identity in history, contemporary society, and the wizarding world of Rowling in "Half-Blood: Mixed-Race Tropes Old and New in Harry Potter's World." This section concludes with Tolonda Henderson's "Chosen Names, Changed Appearances, and Unchallenged Binaries: Trans-Exclusionary Themes in Harry Potter," a powerful analysis of the contradiction that lies at the heart of the *Potter* series: an author and a world that make the tacit promise of fantastic escape for the marginalized, all while the author inscribes exclusion and bigotry within the wizarding world—as well as with her public words.

The next section, "#BlackHermione," sheds new light on the contested racialization of the main girl character in the series, Hermione Granger. In "Hermione Is Black: Harry Potter and the Crisis of Infinite Dark Fantastic Worlds," Ebony Elizabeth Thomas traces her personal journey with the *Harry Potter* series through the assumption that Hermione *could* be Black alongside the reality that Angelina Johnson is the only *definitively* Black female character in the series. Sharing her experience as a writer of fanfiction from the perspective of Angelina, Thomas questions the possibilities and limits of being Black both in fiction and in fandom, and the potential of restorying to write new worlds. Peter C. Kunze, in his chapter "#NotMyHermione: Authorship and Ownership in the *Harry Potter and the Cursed Child* Casting Controversy," explores the casting of Black actor Noma Dumezweni, extending the question of Hermione's Blackness beyond the books; Dumezweni was cast to play Hermione in the play *Harry Potter and the Cursed Child*. Given how Pottermania has exploded outside of the books, Kunze asks about the "specific constraints and attendant cultures that come with media franchises," particularly as they relate to race. Similarly, Florence Maätita and Marcia Hernandez take up the subject of Black Hermione in their chapter, "Racism, Canon, and the Controversy Surrounding #BlackHermione" by interrogating the social media fallout that ensued after the casting announcement. Maätita and Hernandez contend that this fallout, specifically with regard to whether or not Hermione can and should be played by a Black actress, brings into relief questions regarding control of the canon and J. K. Rowling's role in rupturing the continuity of the whiteness of the original series.

The volume closes with chapters on "History, Pedagogy, and Liberation." Jasmine Wade's "Harry Potter and Black Liberation Movements: Addressing the Imagination Gap with History" places the *Potter* series into conversation with Black American and Black British movements for civil rights and power, helping readers identify contrasts between fictional movements for liberation (such as S.P.E.W. and Dumbledore's Army) and actual, impact-filled movements that have changed the world in which we live. This is one way we can fill the imagination gap that Thomas writes about. In "Teaching Harry Potter as an 'Other': An African American Professor's Journey in Teaching Harry Potter in the College Composition Classroom," Susan E. Howard reflects on her experiences as an African American professor teaching Harry Potter. Similar to how Ebony Elizabeth Thomas's Blackness and Sarah Park Dahlen's Asianness inform their reading of the *Harry Potter* books, Howard's identity as a Black woman informs her pedagogy. She writes, "Teaching Harry Potter in the college composition classroom can be a tool for encouraging students to be agents of social change as they confront and modify their views about difference as it relates to the Other." Sridevi Rao and Preethi Gorecki reexamine the character of Dobby to question whether or not he is truly liberated in "Is Dobby a Free Elf?" In "The Failed Wizard Justice System: Race and Access to Justice in Harry Potter," Charles D. Wilson examines how "[t]he wizard justice system functions as a form of social control dictating who can use magic, what magic they can use, and under what circumstances." The chapters in this section—indeed, all the chapters in the volume—force readers to reckon with how the *Harry Potter* series has shaped how the collective imagination in the twenty-first century positions the Other.

Conclusion

This volume cannot address the many other criticisms scholars and fans alike have made about Harry Potter. We need to look deeper at the way diversity is attended to when the text is adapted for films and other media such as toys, costumes, and coloring books. Related to this, as Joel Taxel writes, we need to examine more carefully "whether children [can] differentiate between, for example, Harry Potter as a brand and Harry Potter as a compelling character worth reading about."[14] There is also much more to be said about the legal and educational systems depicted in the stories, as well as the news media and information systems that keep wizarding communities updated about magical happenings. Thus, we take heart in the flowering of scholarship and criticism from the generation of children and teens who grew up loving and living in the wizarding world—a Millennial generation of adults who are challenging power, privilege, and potential in communities all over the planet.

Some mention the pivotal role that Harry Potter played in this generation's social, emotional, and political development. In a 2016 article for the University of Wisconsin–Eau Claire student newspaper, the *Spectator*, Deanne Kolell notes that Anthony Gierzynski and Kathryn Eddy's *Harry Potter and the Millennials: Research Methods and the Politics of the Muggle Generation* warrants the idea that this young adult generation is much more liberal, empathetic, and open to diversity than those of the past.[15] Gierzynski and Eddy cite an article in the *Journal of Applied Social Psychology* that echoes the same themes of tolerance, yet the title, "The Greatest Magic of Harry Potter: Reducing Prejudice," is bittersweet,[16] for the very narrative that was viewed to be inclusive of every child came from the mind and imagination of someone who is trans-exclusionary and (at the time of this writing) has not been open to changing her views. It is thus with heavy hearts that we must note this recent disappointing development amid the thwarted promises of a series that we as editors, and many if not most authors within the pages of this volume, sincerely enjoyed. While, as scholars, we do not believe that Rowling can revise her storyworlds to attend to issues of *race* and *justice* more carefully, we use this occasion to express our hope that she might reconsider her words about *difference* in the world that we live in—and share together.

As mentioned earlier, we are now fortysomething associate professors who have read, loved, and taught Harry Potter many times throughout our careers. We grapple with how something that was such a formative part of our growth as readers and scholars could also be so hurtful, but we are clear that it is. Our decision to frame this introduction through this current understanding—that neither Harry Potter nor its creator are perfect, and in fact, they promote harmful and untrue ideas about race, identity, and other *others*—testifies to our belief that the author is not dead. Rather, the author keeps speaking. We encourage our readers to approach each chapter here with an open heart and an open mind, one that sees members of under- and misrepresented communities as whole persons with real histories, dignity, and value.

Notes

1. Rowling, "@loonyloolaluna."
2. Keene, "Dear JK Rowling."
3. Wizarding World, "Everything You Need to Know."
4. Reese, "Native People Respond to Rowling."
5. Keene, "Dear JK Rowling."
6. Keene, "Magic in North America Part 1."
7. Shoker, "Harry Potter, Race, and British Multiculturalism"; and Gupta and Xiao, "Harry Potter Goes to China."
8. Johnson-Feelings, *The Best of the Brownies' Book*, 12.
9. Larrick, "The All-White World of Children's Books."
10. Thomas, "Hermione Is Black," 145.
11. Tosenberger, "Homosexuality at the Online Hogwarts."
12. Bennett, "Seeing a Black Hermione"; and Rowling, "Canon: brown eyes."
13. Callender, "Harry Potter Saved My Life."
14. Taxel, "The Economics of Children's Book Publishing."
15. Kolell, "Learning Tolerance and Empathy"; and Gierzynski and Eddy, *Harry Potter and the Millennials*.
16. Vezzali et al., "The Greatest Magic of Harry Potter."

Bibliography

Bennett, Alanna. "Seeing a Black Hermione in 2018 Is a Reminder of What Fandom Can Build." BuzzFeed News, April 26, 2018. https://www.buzzfeednews.com/article/alannabennett/seeing-a-black-hermione-in-2018.

Callender, Kacen. "Harry Potter Saved My Life. J. K. Rowling Is Now Endangering Trans People Like Me." them, June 8, 2020. https://www.them.us/story/kacen-callender-op-ed-jk-rowling.

Gierzynski, Anthony, and Kathryn Eddy. *Harry Potter and the Millennials: Research Methods and the Politics of the Muggle Generation.* Baltimore: Johns Hopkins University Press, 2013.

Gupta, Suman, and Cheng Xiao. "Harry Potter Goes to China." In *Children's Literature: Approaches and Territories,* edited by Janet Maybin and Nicola J. Watson, 338–51. Basingstoke, Hants., England: Palgrave Macmillan, 2009.

Johnson-Feelings, Dianne, ed. *The Best of the Brownies' Book.* New York: Oxford University Press, 1996.

Keene, Adrienne. "Dear JK Rowling, I'm Concerned about the American Wizarding School." *Native Appropriations* (blog), June 9, 2015. http://nativeappropriations.com/2015/06/dear -jk-rowling-im-concerned-about-the-american-wizarding-school.html.

Keene, Adrienne. "Magic in North America Part 1: Ugh." *Native Appropriations* (blog), March 8, 2016. http://nativeappropriations.com/2016/03/magic-in-north-america-part -1-ugh.html.

Kolell, Deanna. "Learning Tolerance and Empathy through the Harry Potter Series." *Spectator* (Eau Claire, WI), November 21, 2016.

Larrick, Nancy. "The All-White World of Children's Books." *Saturday Review*, September 11, 1965, 63–65.

Reese, Debbie. "Native People Respond to Rowling." *American Indians in Children's Literature* (blog), March 10, 2016. https://americanindiansinchildrensliterature.blogspot .com/2016/03/native-people-respond-to-rowling.html.

Rowling, J. K. (@jk_rowling). "@loonyloolaluna However, indigenous magic was important in the founding of the school." Twitter, June 7, 2015. https://twitter.com/jk_rowling/status /607458078427082752?s=20.

Rowling, J. K. (@jk_rowling). "Canon: brown eyes, frizzy hair and very clever." Twitter, December 21, 2015. https://twitter.com/jk_rowling/status/678888094339366914?s=20.

Shoker, Sarah. "Harry Potter, Race, and British Multiculturalism." *The Hooded Utilitarian* (blog), April 2, 2013. http://www.hoodedutilitarian.com/2013/04/harry-potter-race-and -british-multiculturalism/.

Taxel, Joel. "The Economics of Children's Book Publishing in the 21st Century." In *Handbook of Research on Children's and Young Adult Literature*, edited by Shelby A. Wolf, Karen Coats, Patricia Enciso, and Christine A. Jenkins, 479–94. New York: Routledge, 2011.

Thomas, Ebony Elizabeth. "Hermione Is Black: A Postscript to Harry Potter and the Crisis of Infinite Dark Fantastic Worlds." In *The Dark Fantastic: Race and Imagination from Harry Potter to the Hunger Games*, 143–70. New York: New York University Press, 2019.

Tosenberger, Catherine. "Homosexuality at the Online Hogwarts: Harry Potter Slash Fanfiction." *Children's Literature* 36, no. 1 (2008): 185–207, 273.

Vezzali, Loris, Sofia Stathi, Dino Giovannini, Dora Capozza, and Elena Trifiletti. "The Greatest Magic of Harry Potter: Reducing Prejudice." *Journal of Applied Social Psychology* 45, no. 2 (February 2015): 105–21.

Wizarding World. "Everything You Need to Know about Ilvermorny." September 24, 2017. https://www.wizardingworld.com/features/everything-you-need-to-know-about -ilvermorny.

PART I.

Race, Gender, and Gender Identity

Harry and the Other

Multicultural and Social Justice Anti-Racism in J. K. Rowling's *Harry Potter* Series

Jackie C. Horne

An earlier version of this essay appeared in *The Lion and the Unicorn* 34, no. 1 (January 2010): 76–104. © 2010 by Johns Hopkins University Press.

As Farah Mendlesohn notes in her essay "Crowning the King: Harry Potter and the Construction of Authority," "attempting to write a critique of a body of work that is clearly unfinished is a challenge to any academic."[1] Despite such difficulties, literary critics, including Mendlesohn, found the interpretive challenge too tempting when it came to analyzing J. K. Rowling's *Harry Potter* series. Unfinished though it was until 2007, critics could not resist putting forth arguments about Rowling's novels, and the world(s) they depict, long before the final book in the series had been published.

One issue in particular led to vastly different early interpretations of the *Potter* series: the books' stance on issues of race and ethnic otherness. On one end of the spectrum, critics such as Karin E. Westman suggested that the *Harry Potter* novels offer a trenchant critique of "materialist ideologies of difference," a critique that Brycchan Carey argued demonstrates "opportunities for political activism available to young people in the real world."[2] Such critics asserted that Rowling's texts create an implied reader who is

asked to condemn the racism of the wizarding world—not only the distinction between "Mudbloods" and "pure-bloods" voiced by its more extreme
members, but also its limitations of the rights of sentient others and its
dependence on the enslavement of house-elves. On the other end of the
spectrum were scholars such as Mendlesohn, who argued that "Rowling's
world of fantasy is one of hierarchy and prejudice."[3] In the middle, critics
such as Andrew Blake, Giselle Liza Anatol, and Elaine Ostry asserted that
the texts' attitudes toward race are contradictory, simultaneously embracing
both radical critique and conservative traditionalism.[4]

More than a decade after the release of *Harry Potter and the Deathly Hallows*, the final book in Rowling's series, critics are still debating whether or
not the *Harry Potter* books promote anti-racist values.[5] To definitively answer
this race question, I believe, we must look first not at the novels themselves
but at "anti-racism" as a word and a concept. For, as Alastair Bonnett points
out in his history of the term and the various movements that have claimed
or disavowed it, "different forms of anti-racism often operate with different
definitions of what racism is."[6] Different readers can find Rowling's novels
conservative or liberal in their depiction of race relations not because some
are right and some are wrong, but because they draw on different traditions
of thought about what constitutes racism, and what remedies are required
to overcome it.

What are these differing traditions of thought about racism and anti-
racism? And how have these traditions influenced pedagogy and literature?
Bonnett begins his examination with the *Oxford English Dictionary*, which,
while it dates the term "anti-racist" to the 1930s, does not find widespread cita-
tions of the corollary term "anti-racism" until the 1960s, and then primarily
in countries where either French or English was spoken.[7] During the 1960s,
two very different definitions of the concept emerged, definitions that were
from the start in tension with one another. While both definitions agree that
anti-racism centers on "those forms of thought and/or practice that seek to
confront, eradicate, and/or ameliorate racism," they differ in what they label
racism and in what steps should be taken to eradicate and/or ameliorate it.[8]
One line of thought, which has its roots in the European Enlightenment,
argues for *universalism*, "the conviction that people are all equally part of
humanity and should all be accorded the same rights and opportunities."[9]
Those who embrace a universalist approach to anti-racism typically see their
main task as overcoming prejudice; if we overcome prejudice (our own and

others'), we will see how those of a different race are the same as we are, and will thus treat them fairly.

During the same period, however, a different approach to anti-racism developed, one that often conflicted with a universalist approach. This approach to anti-racism, termed *relativism*, also has deep roots in European history, dating back to the writings of the eighteenth-century philosopher Michel de Montaigne. Montaigne wrote of Europeans' encounters with New World civilizations not to point out the superiority of his fellow Frenchmen but to call into question the idea that French manners and norms were natural, and therefore superior. Relativism, then, emphasizes the belief that "truths are situationally dependent" and that "cultural and/or physical differences between races should be recognized and respected; that different does not mean unequal."[10]

In many ways, these two definitions of anti-racism form the two faces of one coin, with the strengths of one pointing to the weaknesses of the other. A universalist approach embraces the idea of emancipation for all but can easily slip into colonialism, mistakenly concluding that culturally specific norms of a dominant group are "universal" and therefore in need of promulgation to other, less enlightened societies or races.[11] A relativist approach would seem to ameliorate this problem, recognizing and honoring difference. Yet focusing on human difference can also easily slip into an antiegalitarian discourse; as Bonnett notes, "respecting difference can easily turn into asserting hierarchy."[12] Respecting racial differences can slide very quickly into respecting racial *inequality*.

Such different beliefs about what anti-racism is, and should be, have led, of course, to very different approaches to anti-racist education and practice. As Bonnett notes, one can "do" anti-racism in "a variety of not always complimentary ways."[13] While Bonnett lists six different types of anti-racism practice, in contemporary educational discourse, anti-racist work is typically "done" using two of the approaches he describes.[14] The most common takes the form of multicultural[15] anti-racism, an approach that affirms the value of diversity as a method of engaging racism. Since the late 1980s, learning about and celebrating other cultures has become a cornerstone of educational practice in many British, Canadian, and American schools. The goal of such multicultural education is not simply to become familiar with the traditions of other cultures but to "enable empathy," to "generat[e] cross-cultural understanding and solidarity," and to "see things from others' point of view."[16] Part of this understanding stems from the creation of "positive racial images";[17] celebrating Black History Month, teaching about the role of Islamic scholars in the development of early mathematics, or learning about the Navajo working as codebreakers for the US Army during World War II would all be examples of such practice. Proponents of multiculturalism believe that by learning about the culture of other races, or learning about positive role models of members of previously ignored groups, students will learn to rid themselves of their prejudices, which in turn will lead to a more egalitarian world.[18]

Less common in K–12 education is what Bonnett terms "radical anti-racism," an approach that focuses less on personal awareness of prejudice and more on developing critical thinking skills in order to confront racism.[19] I will refer to this approach as "social justice anti-racism" rather than "radical anti-racism," as educational discourse has embraced the former rather than the latter label since the turn of the twenty-first century. While a multicultural approach to anti-racism work focuses on individuals learning about others and about their own biases, social justice pedagogies focus on teaching students to examine the social, political, and economic structures in which they live. In particular, it draws upon the framework of oppression, "a hierarchical relationship in which dominant or privileged groups benefit, often in unconscious ways, from the disempowerment of subordinated or targeted groups."[20] Or, in other words, social justice anti-racism assumes that racism lies not only in prejudiced individuals but also in the institutions that grant privileges and power to certain racial groups in a society, and restrict other racial groups from the same. Such a belief leads social justice anti-racism to demand that students question, deconstruct, and challenge those institutional structures that contribute to, or actively foster, racism.[21] Studying the redlining of Black neighborhoods; changing the name of "Columbus Day" to "Rethinking Columbus Day" on the school calendar; teaching how legal punishments for white drug users are often less severe than those for drug users of color—all are examples of social justice anti-racism pedagogy. Learning to recognize power and privilege in her own culture, rather than learning to appreciate the cultures of others, proves the key task for the student trained in social justice anti-racism.[22]

While both multiculturalism and social justice work would seem to align more closely with a relativist rather than a universalist approach, Bonnett suggests that such an assumption can be deceiving in the case of multiculturalism. "Multiculturalism affirms difference, but for universalist ends," he suggests. As evidence for this claim, he notes how often "rhetorics of 'world togetherness' and 'one world' are collided and conflated with those of 'cultural diversity' and 'cultural affirmation' throughout a great deal of multicultural discourse."[23]

Because of the inherent tensions between universalist and relativist approaches to anti-racism work, it is perhaps unsurprising that the practical approaches to anti-racism that stem from them would find much to criticize in each other. Multicultural anti-racists, who focus on working within existing social, political, and economic structures, often criticize social justice educators and activists for "hi-jacking anti-racism for its own [radical] political ends."[24] In turn, social justice advocates often view multicultural approaches, with their focus on the individual, as naïve, or even as conservative, working to distract students from the institutional (i.e., true) causes of racism.[25]

What approach to anti-racism education does J. K. Rowling draw upon in order to teach her anti-racism lessons? Intriguingly, readers can find evidence of both a multicultural *and* a social justice approach, as well as the tensions between them, in the seven novels that depict the coming of age of the teenage wizard. To demonstrate this, I would now like to turn to the novels, narrowing my focus to two of the main "races" depicted in Rowling's stories: the house-elves and the goblins. Most of the following discussion will draw upon *Harry Potter and the Deathly Hallows* to show how Rowling deploys these two approaches, exploring the benefits and limitations of each. We can see the multicultural approach in Rowling's depiction of the house-elves, while a social justice lens brings the more difficult race of the goblins into focus.

Rowling creates many different sentient races in the course of her *Harry Potter* novels. Such races can be grouped by how each interacts with the wizarding race. Some races, in traditional high-fantasy fashion, are purely evil. Wizards interact with races associated with the Dark Arts only as enemies. Giants form a subgroup of this type, racial others hunted to the point of extinction by Aurors or other wizards. A second group are racial others who may be at odds with, or dangers to, wizards in *some* circumstances, but in others work for them: for example, in book 1, the troll who invades the school is bad, but in book 3, the trolls who guard the Fat Lady's portrait serve wizarding interests. Leprechauns and Veelas seem to be in similar circumstances, at least as witnessed by their actions during the World Cup match at the opening of book 4. A third group consists of those races that choose to separate themselves entirely from the world of the wizards, such as the centaurs, who deem teaching wizards to be treason against their race.

This chapter is most interested in the final two groups, who interact more closely with wizards than any of the other races depicted in the novels: the house-elves and the goblins. House-elves willingly serve wizards as servants or slaves, accepting their subservient role in a racial hierarchy. In contrast, goblins interact with wizards in many ways as equals, a power relationship that causes much tension between the two groups.[26]

Several critics have discussed Rowling's depiction of house-elves in books 1–4. As Farah Mendlesohn, Elaine Ostry, and Brycchan Carey all point out, Rowling's depiction of Dobby and his fellow elves contains uncomfortable echoes of many of the stereotypes held by whites of enslaved African Americans.[27] Simple, loyal, and childlike, happy to serve their betters, Rowling's house-elves speak in a patois closer to 1930s and 1940s Hollywood misconceptions of "darky" dialect than to any actual African American speech pattern. Even the house-elf Dobby, who desires and gains freedom, proves more an object of humor (as were many Black characters in nineteenth- and twentieth-century popular culture) than a model of what a free elf can accomplish. Harry, and through him the reader, is invited to laugh at Dobby's mismatched clothing, his bargaining over wages with Dumbledore (he wants lower, rather than higher, wages than the headmaster offers), and his assertion of his "free will": "Dobby is a free house-elf and he can obey anyone he likes and Dobby will do whatever Harry Potter wants him to do!" (*Harry Potter and the Order of the Phoenix*, 421). The critics disagree, however, about Rowling's reasons for connecting Dobby in particular, and the house-elves in general, with negative stereotypes of enslaved African Americans. Ostry suggests that Rowling "means to help young readers understand the stereotypes about slaves when (or if) they learn about them in school,"[28] while Carey argues that Rowling intends for her readers to follow Hermione's lead into overt political anti-racist action once they have "grasped the truth" of bigotry and discrimination and have learned "how that truth has been applied or abused in the historical world."[29] Westman is more circumspect, arguing that the "*possibility* for change" lies within Rowling's portrayal of the characters' "increasing awareness of the culture's recurring prejudices based on supposedly 'natural' differences."[30] Mendlesohn, although she admits the possibility that the house-elves might eventually be freed by the end of the series, believes that Rowling's use of stereotypes points to her lack of imagination rather than to a deliberate political agenda, and suggests that such a lack of imagination is ultimately damaging to the young reader: "However much the house-elves may turn out to be happy that they are freed, it will never take away the impression of 'happy darky' that is created by the character of Winky."[31] Mendlesohn also points out that the humorous method by which house-elves can be set free—by a master giving them clothes—keeps all of the power in the hands of the oppressor rather than allowing agency to the oppressed.[32] Although Rowling's overt ideology is anti-racist, her implicit ideology, suggests Mendlesohn, is markedly at odds with her anti-racist intent.

Rowling's depiction of the house-elves, and how Harry learns to interact with them, can be understood as anti-racist when it is placed in the context of the universalist, multicultural approach to anti-racism work. The most important way to fight racism, Harry learns, is to be kind to the elves, to treat each individual elf as an equal. Or, to put it in Dumbledore's words, Harry must learn to see elves as "being[s] with feelings as acute as a human's" (*HP and the OP*, 832), a multicultural emphasis on universal emotional identity. In books 2–4, Harry begins to learn this lesson through his interactions with Dobby. But to bring the lesson into greater prominence, Rowling introduces a third major elf character in the series' last four volumes: Kreacher, the "distinctly unlovable" house-elf loyal to the Voldemort-sympathizing Black family (*HP and the DH*, 191).

Kreacher proves far less appealing an elf than does the comic Dobby. Old, almost naked, baggy-skinned, with bloodshot eyes and a snout-like nose, Kreacher continually whispers insults about Sirius and the other members of the Order of the Phoenix after the Order takes up residence in the Black family's London house in book 5. Mrs. Weasley is disgusted by Kreacher's lax housework, while Ron and his brothers find him a "nutter" for his devotion to pure-blood wizards and his life's ambition to "have his head cut off and stuck up on a plaque" (*HP and the OP*, 76). Sirius, although he advocates humane treatment of house-elves in general, has less tolerance for Kreacher; when no one has seen the elf for a while, Sirius speculates: "I expect I'll find him upstairs crying his eyes out over my mother's old bloomers or something. . . . Of course, he might have crawled into the airing cupboard and died. . . . But I mustn't get my hopes up" (*HP and the OP*, 505).

Hermione is the only one who defends Kreacher to the others. Despite his aspersions on her "Mudblood" lineage, she protests that Kreacher "isn't in his right mind" and that not only she, but also Dumbledore, "says we should be kind to Kreacher" (*HP and the OP*, 108, 76). Harry, like the Weasleys, finds Kreacher hard to like. But over the course of the last three novels, Harry must learn the lesson that Hermione and Dumbledore teach: he must learn to be as kind to the decrepit house-elf as he is to Dobby. When Harry grows angry at Kreacher's betrayal of the Order at the end of book 5, Dumbledore spells out the lesson directly:

> I warned Sirius when we adopted twelve Grimmauld Place as our headquarters that Kreacher must be treated with kindness and respect. I also told him that Kreacher could be dangerous to us. I do not think that Sirius took me very seriously, or that he ever saw Kreacher as a being with feelings as acute as a human's. . . . Sirius did not hate Kreacher. . . . He regarded him as a servant unworthy of much interest or notice. Indifference and neglect often do much more damage than outright dislike. (*HP and the OP*, 832–33)

Dumbledore's words prove more than an abstract idea when, at the start of book 6, Harry inherits not only the Sirius's family estate and household goods but also the Black family house-elf—the "distinctly unlovable" Kreacher. Although Harry does not make Kreacher an object of fun, as did Sirius and the Weasley boys, neither does he treat him with any semblance of kindness or even respect. On Dumbledore's advice, he sends the elf to work in the Hogwarts kitchens, only remembering him when he needs someone to spy on Draco Malfoy.

Although Harry is beginning to see how the work of the school is done quietly and unobtrusively by the house-elves (Harry assumes that the Christmas presents "must . . . have been delivered by house-elves in the night" [*Harry Potter and the Half-Blood Prince*, 389]), this realization doesn't yet allow him to challenge others when they mistreat elves. For example, when Professor Slughorn tells him he's tested his wine for poison by having a house-elf taste every bottle, Harry thinks to himself that the professor's actions amount to "abuse of house-elves." But Harry's thoughts turn not to what it must have been like to be one of those elves, but instead to Hermione and what she might think if she ever heard of the professor's actions. Rather than speaking up in the face of elf oppression, Harry remains quiet; he says nothing to Slughorn and even decides not to tell Hermione about it (presumably because he wants to avoid having to listen to Hermione's outrage) (*HP and the HBP*, 485). While Harry is beginning to see that wizarding culture relies on the labor of the elves, he is not yet ready to talk openly about it or to make elf liberation a cause worth fighting for. A social justice approach to anti-racism is not one that Rowling suggests her protagonist need pursue.

Instead, Harry, initially through Dumbledore and later on his own, learns to fight his unconsciously racist attitudes toward elves on a *personal* level, by learning to recognize that elves have feelings. Once he is able to recognize that elves, like humans, feel emotions, Harry can then learn to identify with, and have sympathy for, the plight of individual elves. Cultivating this ability to identify begins in earnest in book 6, when Dumbledore relates the story of the elf Hokey, whom Voldemort framed for murder. Actually, Dumbledore does not just *relate* Hokey's story; he takes Harry back through the Pensieve in order to witness scenes, allowing Harry to "meet" Hokey himself. Dumbledore leads Harry to recognize the way that Ministry prejudice against house-elves aided Voldemort's plan: "[T]he Ministry was predisposed to suspect Hokey—" he says, leading Harry to interrupt "—because she was a house-elf." Interestingly, Harry's recognition of the institutional prejudice makes him think of political rather than personal solutions: "He had rarely felt more in sympathy with the society Hermione had set up" (the Society for the Promotion of Elfish Welfare, or S.P.E.W.) (*HP and the HBP*, 439).

Yet Harry's feelings do not lead him to embrace Hermione's way of fighting social inequities. Instead, he continues to fight on a personal level, employing a multicultural approach, as witnessed by his changing behavior toward Kreacher in book 7. This change in Harry's behavior occurs, significantly, after he hears the story of how Kreacher was used and left for dead by Voldemort, and then had to witness the self-sacrificing death of his beloved master, Regulus Black. At first, Harry resists feeling sympathy for the elf, with Kreacher's betrayal of Sirius blinding him to all else. But when Hermione (of course!) points out that house-elves are loyal to those "who are kind to [them]," Harry remembers Dumbledore's words—"*I do not think Sirius ever saw Kreacher as a being with feelings as acute as a human's*"—and starts to realize that both he and Kreacher are mourning for dead Black brothers (*HP and the DH*, 199). Only after he recognizes this similarity between his and Kreacher's losses, and the feelings that stem from them, does Harry begin to take Dumbledore's lesson to heart. Harry still gives Kreacher orders, but does so kindly, with a marked change in tone. He says "please," asks "Do you think you could do that for us?" and even gives the elf a present (*HP and the DH*, 199). By the end of the series, Harry (and through him, the reader) has learned the central lesson of multicultural anti-racism: to treat others with kindness, respect, and sympathy.[33]

Multicultural anti-racism, unlike social justice ideology, focuses its response to racism on personal rather than political change. Thus, although Harry has "sympathy" for Hermione's overtly political efforts to liberate the house-elves through her creation of the Society for the Promotion of Elfish Welfare, he does not follow Hermione's lead, preferring personal to political solutions, a multicultural rather than a social justice approach. Several critics, basing their claims on only the earlier books in the series, suggested that Rowling's books do not completely eschew a social justice agenda. Westman argued that Rowling's humorous depiction of Hermione's liberation efforts through the ludicrously named S.P.E.W. is intended to satirize "numerous left-wing fringe movements more prominent in British than American culture and . . . the nineteenth-century tradition of well-to-do liberals speaking for the lower classes whom they have never met"; such satire can coexist, she suggested, with "Rowling's investigation of how cultural beliefs are naturalized as truth,"[34] a stance more in line with the critical thinking aspect of social justice pedagogy.[35] In his first essay on the topic, Carey was even more hopeful, declaring that Hermione's political actions reflect Rowling's explicit intention to promote "political participation for young people,"[36] an overt social justice goal. Do such interpretations hold up when we take the final books into consideration? Does Rowling both satirize *and* embrace the tenets of social justice anti-racism pedagogy? Looking at Hermione's anti-racism education in terms of both multicultural and social justice pedagogy can help us to better understand the ambiguity with which Rowling's novels treat her campaign for elf rights.

Hermione's introduction to the racism of the wizarding world is very different from Harry's. Rather than responding to an elf on a personal level, as does Harry toward Dobby, Hokey, and Kreacher, Hermione's awakening begins with a recognition of institutional racism. Her campaign on behalf of elf rights starts not when she witnesses an individual elf suffering or being mistreated, as did Harry, but rather when she recognizes how her own privileges as a student at Hogwarts are supported by the labor of others:

> "But they get *paid*?" she said. "They get *holidays*, don't they? And—and sick leave, and pensions, and everything?"
>
>   Nearly Headless Nick chortled so much that his ruff slipped and his head flopped off, dangling on the inch or so of ghostly skin and muscle that still attached it to his neck.

"Sick leave and pensions?" he said, pushing his head back onto his shoulders and securing it once more with his ruff. "House-elves don't want sick leave and pensions!"

Hermione looked down at her hardly touched plate of food, then put her knife and fork down upon it and pushed it away from her.

"Oh, c'mon, 'Er-my-knee," said Ron. . . . "You won't get them sick leave by starving yourself!"

"Slave labor," said Hermione, breathing hard through her nose. "That's what made this dinner. Slave *labor.*"

And she refused to eat another bite. (*Harry Potter and the Goblet of Fire*, 182)

Social justice anti-racism asks students to examine institution-wide structures of power, rather than looking only at the individual and his or her feelings/beliefs about race. In particular, it asks students to identify how such institutions place certain groups in dominant and other groups in subordinate positions, and calls for those in positions of power to examine their own privileges, recognizing how institutional practices that work to their advantage may rely on the *disadvantaging* of other groups.[37]

Hermione's recognition of institutional racism leads her not to individual acts but to the creation of an institution of her own, the abovementioned S.P.E.W., a group focused on political action. As she tells Ron and Harry, her organization will focus not on personal consciousness-raising but on agitating for institutional change:

I've been researching it thoroughly in the library. Elf enslavement goes back centuries. I can't believe no one's done anything about it before now. . . . Our short-term aims . . . are to secure house-elves fair wages and working conditions. Our long-term aims include changing the law about non-wand use, and trying to get an elf into the Department for the Regulation and Control of Magical Creatures, because they're shockingly underrepresented. (*HP and the GF*, 224–25)

In the early volumes of Rowling's series, as signaled by the humor-provoking acronym S.P.E.W., such an institutionally focused approach to anti-racism work is more an object of laughter for the reader than an example of how a reader should act against oppression. When Hermione tries to get other students to join her organization, no one gets as agitated about institutional racism as she does: "Some people, like Neville, had paid up just to stop Hermione from glowering at them. A few seemed mildly interested in what she had to say, but were reluctant to take a more active role in campaigning. Many regarded the whole thing as a joke" (*HP and the GF*, 328–29). When she fails to interest students, she thinks that perhaps "it's time for more direct action" and considers trying to contact the elves who work in Hogwarts kitchens to get the oppressed themselves to agitate for institutional rather than personal change: "decent wages and working conditions!" (*HP and the GF*, 320). But the text, like the Hogwarts students themselves, seems to regard Hermione's politically based anti-racism work as a joke.

In her denigration of Hermione's activism, Rowling may be creating a critique of the social justice approach to anti-racism work, similar to the accusations of multicultural anti-racists who accuse social justice anti-racists of hijacking their issues for their own political ends. A more nuanced reading suggests that Rowling may be attempting to critique a social justice approach that fails to first embrace a personal, multicultural approach. Such an interpretation seems to follow from Hermione's actions in the cause of elf liberation in books 5–7; such actions gradually become focused less on political agitation and more on personal acts. For example, the idea she has to help her fellow students better understand the oppression of the elves, a "sponsored scrub of Gryffindor common room, all proceeds to S.P.E.W." (*HP and the OP*, 159), is never pursued; instead, Hermione starts knitting hats and leaving them around for house-elves to pick up by accident, trying to trick them into setting themselves free (*HP and the OP*, 255). That Dobby collects all the hats himself shows not only Rowling's deft hand with humor but also her distrust of a social justice anti-racism pedagogy empty of the more personal approach embraced by multicultural anti-racism.

Rowling's depiction of the elves as a race that loves being enslaved may also be an attempt at humor. Yet this depiction places her in a difficult double bind as the series progressively sharpens its focus on anti-racist themes—how can you argue on one hand that Mudbloods should be granted the same rights as pure-blood wizards, but suggest on the other that another sentient race is, by nature, servile to another? Rowling may have begun to realize the corner she had backed herself into, as the references to S.P.E.W. grow sparser in book 5 and then disappear completely from the series' final two volumes.[38] Having pointed to the institutional as well as the personal roots of the racism of the wizarding world, Rowling seems to want to back away from Hermione's institutionally based solutions, replacing an ideology that suggests that institutions themselves may be inherently racist with one that points to the flaws of the people who *run* the institutions as the true culprits. The craven Fudge, and later the authoritarian Scrimgeour, are the real problem, not the way wizarding laws and culture create a system in which one group is granted greater rights and privileges at the expense of others. Get rid of racists who run the institutions (as well as the racists like Voldemort who want to take them over), and racism will be eradicated, the texts seem to suggest.

But if Hermione backs away from her politically based solutions to the racism she sees in wizarding society in the final volumes in the series, she does not stop talking about the institutionally based racism that she has begun to recognize. And it seems significant that it is not only the students who fail to respond to Hermione's calls for political action; throughout the final books in the series, whenever Hermione brings up the issue of elf rights with adults, her conversations are consistently interrupted, either by the narrator or by adult characters. For example, in book 4, when Percy and Hermione begin to argue about Winky, Mrs. Weasley breaks up the argument by insisting that the children go and finish packing (*HP and the GF*, 154), while Mr. Weasley tells Hermione that, although he agrees that Mr. Crouch treated Winky horribly, "now is not the time to discuss elf rights" (*HP and the GF*, 138–39). In book 5, Hermione tries to engage Lupin in a discussion of elf rights: "I mean, it's the same kind of nonsense as werewolf segregation, isn't it? It all stems from this horrible thing wizards have of thinking they're superior to other creatures" (*HP and the OP*, 170–71). But Rowling doesn't allow us to hear Lupin's reply, making us unsure about whether he agrees or not. While it is easy for these adult characters to see the racism of Voldemort's anti-Mudblood campaign, it seems less easy for them to engage in a discussion that might point out the ways in which their own culture is supported by the oppression of other races, especially that of the elves.[39]

In fact, Rowling's later texts demonstrate the ways in which many of the adults in the wizarding world collude with the racism that is articulated on a more overt level by those whom they are purportedly fighting against. For example, Mrs. Weasley wishes that she had a house-elf to do her housework, while Sirius (as Mendlesohn notes), although he advocates kindly treatment of the enslaved, never questions the institution of slavery itself ("If you want to know what a man's like, take a good look at how he treats his inferiors, not his equals" [*HP and the GF*, 525]). Even Fred, George, and Hagrid all agree with Ron that that the elves do not want to be freed. Westman argues that Rowling shows the reader that what wizarding culture holds forth as "natural" and thus not subject to change—house-elves are just "natural" slaves—is actually a cultural formation, one that the adults themselves play a role in maintaining.[40] Such ideology, though less explicitly stated than the overt racism of Voldemort and his followers, is, at heart, the same as Voldemort's prejudice against Mudbloods, which the trio must fight just as they fight against Voldemort. Such a fight may in fact be more difficult, because the ideology claiming that house-elves *want* to be enslaved is held not only by the overt icon of evil but also by almost every adult the teens respect—explicitly by Fred and George and Hagrid; implicitly by the Weasley parents, who silence Hermione's questions; and even by Dumbledore, who, though sympathetic to Dobby, does little as the leader of the institution of Hogwarts to change its reliance on uncompensated elf labor. When Ron ridicules S.P.E.W. in book 5, Hermione responds: "It's not 'spew' . . . It's the Society for the Promotion of Elfish Welfare, and it's not just me, Dumbledore says we should be kind to Kreacher too—" (*HP and the OP*, 76). While Hermione argues that Dumbledore is on the side of institutionally based change, the evidence she summons to link him to her cause—"Dumbledore says we should be kind to Kreacher too"—places him firmly within the multicultural rather than the social justice anti-racism camp.

Is Rowling intentionally demonstrating how adults, in the guise of protecting children, teach them through example to ignore the racism that underlies their own privilege? Or is she complicit in the silencing of Hermione? I would like to begin to answer this question by examining a racial "other" of the Potterverse few literary critics have explored—the race of the goblins—and comparing their depiction to Rowling's depiction of the house-elves.[41] First introduced in book 1 but not featured in any meaningful way until book 7, the goblin Griphook returns to play a vital role in the retrieval of one of the hidden Horcruxes. But Griphook proves more than a simple plot device; his return signals Rowling's attempt to rethink her earlier satirical dismissal of the social justice approach to anti-racism. With book 7's depiction of the goblins, Rowling uses racial difference less as comic relief, as in the case of the house-elves, and more as overt social critique. In particular, Rowling begins to take more seriously the idea that racism can be defined not simply as individual, personal acts of prejudice but also as cultural and institutional structures and policies that create advantages for dominant group members and disadvantage for people (or creatures) from subordinated groups. By examining the relationship between Griphook and Harry and, on a larger scale, between the goblin and wizard races, Rowling begins to demonstrate the ways that institutional and cultural racism can lead dominant group members to oppress racial others even when they do not intend to, even when they are explicitly trying *not* to be racist. Harry's interactions with the actual goblin Griphook and, perhaps more importantly, with the wizarding culture's assumptions about "goblins" point to the difficulties in fighting racial oppression when anti-racism work relies solely on a multicultural approach, one in which racism is defined only as a personal, rather than a social, ill.

Evil other; dangerous but used other; enslaved other; and separatist other—these are the four types of racial other that Rowling depicts during the course of the first six *Harry Potter* books. Goblins, however, do not seem to fall into any of these four groups. Unlike the centaurs, they interact with the wizarding world on a daily basis through the wizarding bank, Gringotts. They are clearly not slaves, as are the house-elves; nor are they unabatedly evil, or else why would wizards trust them with their money? They might perhaps be placed in the "dangerous but able to be used" category, yet their intelligence and power seem far greater than that of the trolls or the leprechauns. They don't simply "work for" Gringotts, a bank owned by humans; they "run" it (*Harry Potter and the Sorcerer's Stone*, 63). In fact, the goblin bank employs humans such as Bill Weasley; one possible path advertised in career pamphlets at Hogwarts proclaims that the bank employs human wizard "Curse-Breakers" looking for "thrilling opportunities abroad" (*HP and the OP*, 657). As Gornuk, another goblin, reveals when he explains why he left the bank in book 7, the Gringotts goblins do not work under the supervision of humans; once the Voldemort-controlled Ministry takes over the bank, humans try to make him perform "duties ill-befitting the dignity of [his] race," requests that he rejects, stating: "I am not a house-elf" (*HP and the DH*, 296). Griphook leaves the bank when it becomes clear that goblin autonomy and power is being undermined: "Gringotts is no longer under sole control of my race. I recognize no Wizarding master" (*HP and the DH*, 296). Goblins, then, clearly have more power than any of the other nonhuman species depicted in Rowling's novels.

Yet the goblins are clearly subordinated in some way to wizarding government control. In book 4, we hear that goblins are expected to interact with the "Department for the Regulation and Control of Magical Creatures" (*HP and the GF*, 449). The department includes a subdepartment: the "Goblin Liaison office," which suggests that wizards and goblins are of separate but fairly equal status. But house-elf Winky's fears that the rebellious Dobby will be "up in front of the Department for the Regulation and Control of Magical Creatures, like some common goblin," points more toward a subordinate, rather than equal, relationship (*HP and the OP*, 130; *HP and the GF*, 98).

Why would goblins, entrusted with the riches of the wizarding world, need to be "regulated" and "controlled" by wizarding government institutions? Although Ron and Harry, poor scholars of the history of magic, may not understand, those readers who, like Hermione, pay attention to Professor Binns's lessons could tell you that goblins, unlike house-elves, have not taken kindly to the assumption that wizards are by nature at the top of the hierarchy of sentient magical creatures. In book 3, Hermione's reading of *Sites of Historical Sorcery* informs her that the inn in Hogsmeade was "the headquarters of the 1612 goblin rebellion" (*Harry Potter and the Prisoner of Azkaban*, 77), while in book 4, we hear that early in the term, "Professor Binns, the ghost who taught History of Magic, had them writing weekly essays on the goblin rebellions of the eighteenth century" (*HP and the GF*, 234). That Binns is still lecturing on goblin rebellions and riots at Christmastime of the same term suggests that goblin resistance was not merely a single event but a way of life (*HP and the GF*, 392). Hermione makes it clear that goblins weren't rebelling against their own leaders but against wizards when she tells Ron that "Goblins don't need protection. . . . [T]hey're quite capable of dealing with wizards. . . . They're very clever. They're not like house-elves, who never stick up for themselves" (*HP and the GF*, 449). Just how goblins "stick up for themselves" is never discussed directly, yet the narrator's aside that Professor Binns "could make even bloody and vicious goblin riots sound as boring as Percy's cauldron-bottom report" suggests that the goblins fought with violence against the wizarding world (*HP and the GF*, 392). Such a violent response is a far cry from the obsequious self-abasement of the house-elves. In contrast, such a response calls to mind actual historical and current-day political movements against racial and social class oppression in Great Britain—the Scottish insurgencies of the eighteenth century, the Chartist riots of the nineteenth, and the uprisings of the Irish in the eighteenth and twentieth centuries.

What, precisely, were the goblins fighting for? Again, Rowling provides little specific information. Yet a careful reader, particularly one schooled in a social justice approach to anti-racism, can piece together an explanation: the wizarding world excluded, and continues to exclude, goblins from the privileges it accorded, and continues to accord, itself. In answering the exam question "*Describe the circumstances that led to the Formation of the International Confederation of Wizards and explain why the warlocks of Liechtenstein refused to join*" (*HP and the OP*, 725), Harry remembers: "The confederation had met for the first time in France. . . . Goblins had tried to attend and been ousted" (*HP and the OP*, 726). Not only have the wizards excluded goblins from their meetings; they have also denied them the privilege of carrying a wand by "Clause three of the Code of Wand Use" (*HP and the GF*, 132). That this restriction has been in place for many centuries can be inferred from the questions on the O.W.L. History of Magic exam, which asks: "*In your opinion, did wand legislation contribute to, or lead to better control of, goblin riots of the eighteenth century?*" (*HP and the OP*, 725).

Significantly, Harry skips this last question completely while taking his O.W.L. exams. Ron, too, has difficulties remembering goblin history; when his mother asks how he did on his History of Magic exam at the end of the fourth year, he cheerfully reports, "Oh . . . okay. . . . Couldn't remember all the goblin rebels' names, so I invented a few. It's all right . . . they're all called stuff like Bodrod the Bearded and Urg the Unclean; it wasn't hard" (*HP and the GF*, 618). Unsurprisingly, both Ron and Harry fail their History of Magic O.W.L.'s. Remembering the details of the lives of those who actively resist the naturalized norm of a social hierarchy that places human wizards on top seems of little concern to Rowling's male heroes, at least in the first six books of the series.

In place of historical information on the goblins, then, is the "idea" of the goblin in circulation within wizarding culture. Physically, the goblins are described in terms that link them with the villains of traditional British fantasy and adventure novels: "The goblin was about a head shorter than Harry. He had a swarthy, clever face, a pointed beard and, Harry noticed, very long fingers and feet. He bowed as they walked inside" (*HP and the SS*, 72). Their skin color, as well as their "dark, slanting eyes" (*HP and the GF*, 446), mark them as physically other, while their most visible work—lending money to wizards—suggests they are morally suspect, a modern-day embodiment of the stereotype of a Jewish moneylender or perhaps even an

Italian mafioso. Wizards who associate with goblins are immediately suspect; after seeing Ludo Bagman in the company of goblins in a Hogsmeade pub, both Hermione and Rita Skeeter question whether he is up to no good (*HP and the GF*, 450), while the *Daily Prophet* newspaper uses an "alleged link to subversive goblin groups" to discredit a witch who resigned her post in the Wizengamot in support of Dumbledore (*HP and the OP*, 308). That goblins are held in low regard by the wizarding world in general can be seen by the narrator's casual linkage between goblins and a creature Professor Lupin teaches his students to fight in his Defense against the Dark Arts class: "After boggarts, they studied Red Caps, nasty little goblin-like creatures that lurked wherever there had been bloodshed: in the dungeons of castles and the potholes of deserted battlefields, waiting to bludgeon those who had gotten lost" (*HP and the PA*, 141). Fred and George view the goblins as "play[ing] dirty" when they refuse to pay Ludo Bagman, who bet on Harry to win the Triwizard Tournament (*HP and the GF*, 732). Insisting that Harry didn't win outright but tied with Cedric seems to be a cheat to the Weasley twins, a mere technicality, one that portrays the goblins as poor keepers of their word, as is Ludo Bagman, who refuses to pay George and Fred after losing a bet on the Wizard World Cup.

Having planted clues both about the history of the goblins and about the general wizarding assumptions of this racial "other" throughout her first six books, Rowling forces her protagonist to confront the gap between history and stereotype by reintroducing in book 7 a character first mentioned way back in book 1: Griphook, the goblin who guided Harry to his parents' treasure vault at Gringotts. Although Griphook's behavior conforms to many of the stereotypes that the wizarding culture holds about goblins, it also calls such stereotypes into question in several important ways. It also begins to draw Harry's, and the reader's, attention away from defining racism in merely personal terms and toward seeing racism as a structural, institutional, and political system.

Griphook, along with Harry and his friends, is captured by Death Eaters and taken to Malfoy Manor. The sight of Gryffindor's sword in their possession sends Bellatrix Lestrange into a panic; to save Hermione from Bellatrix's wrath, Harry begs Griphook to lie to the witch: "Griphook . . . you must tell them that sword's a fake, they mustn't know it's the real one, Griphook, please—" (*HP and the DH*, 467). Despite the goblins' traditional enmity for humans, despite even being tortured himself, Griphook decides not to betray

Harry's trust (*HP and the DH*, 471). In return, Harry rescues the goblin, an act that surprises Griphook. He is also surprised when he sees Harry digging a grave himself for the dead house-elf, Dobby: "Goblins and elves are not used to the protection or the respect that you have shown this night. Not from wand-carriers" (*HP and the DH*, 488). Given the history of human interactions with goblins and house-elves, Griphook seems right to be surprised; kind, even loving, treatment of elves seems a rarity in the wizarding world.

Rowling seems to suggest that the first step in mending the breach between racial others lies in individual, personal acts of kindness, acts that force one to look beyond racial stereotypes and recognize the value in each individual. Yet as the relationship between Harry and Griphook unfolds, the larger social and institutional racism embedded in each's culture continually points to how difficult such rapprochement can be without an understanding of how power has been distributed between races and cultures in a society. The yawning gap between their societies is embodied in each culture's beliefs about Gryffindor's sword. Ron, like all wizards trained at Hogwarts, believes without doubt that the sword was made for Godric Gryffindor. But the goblins tell another story about its provenance:

> "No!" cried the goblin, bristling with anger as he pointed a long finger at Ron. "Wizarding arrogance again! That sword was Ragnuk the First's, taken from him by Godric Gryffindor! It is a lost treasure, a masterpiece of goblinwork! It belongs with the goblins!" (*HP and the DH*, 505–6)

Ron, drawing on cultural stereotypes, believes that Griphook's motives stem from greed and suggests that the goblin pick another reward instead of asking for Gryffindor's sword as a prize for helping Harry and his friends break into a Gringott's vault. Griphook bristles in anger at the assumptions behind Ron's statement: "I am not a thief, boy! I am not trying to procure treasures to which I have no right!" (*HP and the DH*, 506).

Throughout the novels, racial groups oppressed by the wizarding community have rarely had the chance to speak for themselves, to give direct witness to the damaging effects of wizarding acts and beliefs. Dumbledore and others are praised for their support of "Muggle Rights," but no Muggles speak of their oppression, oblivious as they are of it. Lupin does not speak out for werewolf rights; instead, he leaves Hogwarts when his true identity is revealed. Hagrid remains but hides his half-giant heritage in shame, and then hides his giant brother, whom he has rescued from abuse. Rita Skeeter makes fun of Elphias Doge for championing Merpeople rights (*HP and the DH*, 24). And, with the exception of Dobby, the house-elves are only too happy to accept their position subordinated to human wizards.

It seems significant, then, that Griphook here gives voice to the institutional and cultural oppression inherent not only in Voldemort's rule but within normal, everyday wizarding culture itself. In book 7, the goblins are the first racial other to speak directly to and in protest against the social hierarchy imposed upon them by the wizards. Griphook makes it clear that the oppression they experience is not just personal, but institutionalized:

> "The right to carry a wand," said the goblin quietly, "has long been contested between wizards and goblins."
>
> "Well, goblins can do magic without wands," said Ron.
>
> "That is immaterial! Wizards refuse to share the secrets of wandlore with other magical beings, they deny us the possibility of extending our powers!" (*HP and the DH*, 488)

When Ron and Griphook begin to fight about who's right and who's wrong, Harry attempts to diffuse the argument, protesting: "It doesn't matter. . . . This isn't about wizards versus goblins or any other sort of magical creature—" Griphook, however, won't allow Harry to compartmentalize the fight against Voldemort from the historical enmity between the goblins and the wizards: "But it is, it is about precisely that! As the Dark Lord becomes ever more powerful, your race is set still more firmly above mine! Gringotts falls under Wizarding rule, house-elves are slaughtered, and who amongst the wand-carriers protests?" (*HP and the DH*, 488–89).

Harry, brought up believing in a clear division between Voldemort and Dumbledore, between absolute evil and absolute good, wants to impose the same strict binary on wizards and goblins. But establishing such a binary proves difficult. When Harry asks Hermione if what Griphook has said about Gryffindor's sword is true, she replies, "I don't know. . . . Wizarding history often skates over what the wizards have done to other magical races, but there's no account that I know of that says Gryffindor stole the sword" (*HP and the DH*, 506). Bill muddies the moral waters even further when he urges Harry to be careful of working with Griphook, not because goblins are evil but because they have such different cultural norms:

"To a goblin, the rightful and true master of any object is the maker, not the purchaser. All goblin-made objects are, in goblin eyes, rightfully theirs."

"But if it was bought—"

"—then they would consider it rented by the one who had paid the money. They have, however, great difficulty with the idea of goblin-made objects passing from wizard to wizard. . . . They consider our habit of keeping goblin-made objects, passing them from wizard to wizard without further payment, little more than theft." (*HP and the DH*, 517)

While the Electronic Frontier Foundation has used the goblin concept of property rights as a symbolic representation of current-day arguments against the concept of perpetual copyright,[42] Rowling's depiction of the goblins and their quest to reclaim lost cultural artifacts such as Gryffindor's sword (or the goblin-made tiara offered by Mrs. Weasley to Fleur) echoes uncomfortably for this American reader with Native American struggles to reclaim artifacts taken by white anthropologists and collectors for study. British readers may be reminded of the claims of those who support the return of the Elgin Marbles and other antiquities "vandalized" by imperialist cultures to their nations of origin. Readers familiar with such real-life cultural protests may find it difficult to dismiss Griphook's version of Gryffindor's sword, as Ron does, deeming it just another "one of those goblin stories . . . about how the wizards are always trying to get one over on them" (*HP and the DH*, 506). Ron, as he does throughout the series, embodies the naturalized beliefs of the wizarding culture, beliefs that dismiss any claims of institutional oppression as mere "complaining" and "lying."

Bill assumes that Harry understands the history of human/goblin relations—"Dealings between wizards and goblins have been fraught for centuries—but you'll know all that from History of Magic" (*HP and the DH*, 517)—yet readers know that Harry's grasp of Professor Binns's subject is sketchy at best. And so, because Harry cannot reconcile his need for a clear line between good and evil with the situation at hand (and because he cannot learn to "like" the goblin), he comes to a decision that rejects the tentative rapprochement between goblin and wizard that Rowling holds out as a tantalizing possibility. Standing on the same type of technicality that George and Fred described as "play[ing] dirty" when the goblins did it to Ludo Bagman back in book 4, Harry decides: "We'll tell him he can have the sword after he's helped us get into that vault—but we'll be careful to avoid telling him exactly *when* he can have it" (*HP and the GF*, 732; *HP and the DH*, 508). Harry is uncomfortable with his decision, recognizing that his "ends justify the means" approach as disturbingly similar to that of the oppressive wizard Grindewald—"FOR THE GREATER GOOD." But he "pushed the idea away. What choice did they have?" (*HP and the DH*, 508). Throughout the novels, Rowling, through Dumbledore, has insisted that choice, rather than talent, is what decides a person's character. Thus, Harry's refusal to acknowledge that deceiving Griphook is a choice he made, rather than the only course open to him, seems particularly significant, a sign that the "shame" that Harry feels after making his decision is more than warranted.

But Rowling, unable to allow Harry, her hero, the same moral ambiguity that she later grants Dumbledore, backs away from the implications of Harry's shame. She does this by continuing to invoke the racial stereotypes of goblins established earlier in the series, in particular by pointing to how goblins, as a race, care little for the pain of others. She also allows Harry off the hook for deceiving Griphook by making Griphook betray Harry first. But there is a small sign that Harry may be growing more aware of his own participation in the construction of racist ideology; while Ron calls Griphook "that double-crossing little scab" for running away with Gryffindor's sword and leaving them to fight the goblins and Death Eaters alone (*HP and the DH*, 547), Harry, intriguingly, thinks about Griphook's actions not in terms of goblin treachery but in terms of wizarding perfidy: "[I]n that instant Harry knew that the goblin had never expected them to keep their word" (*HP and the DH*, 540).

In book 5, Harry recognizes that a wizard-made statue in the lobby of the Ministry of Magic depicting a noble wizard and witch surrounded by a fawning house-elf, centaur, and goblin is less a depiction of truth and more a fantasy intended to instill the belief in its viewers that the hierarchical relations between humans and racial others is natural and proper. Such a fantasy, Harry recognizes, does not reflect reality but rather *constructs* a racial hierarchy with wizards at the apex. It seems significant, then, that while both house-elves and centaurs join Harry in the final battle against Voldemort that concludes the series, the goblins are notably absent. Crafting a new vision of cooperation between the magical creatures of the Potterverse may be possible when racism is defined as personal, individual acts—be kinder to house-elves, and the problem is solved—but far less likely when a broader definition, one that calls attention to institutionalized as well as individual racism, enters the fantasy realm.

However, despite the series' inability to embrace a social justice anti-racism pedagogy, the ending of the final volume cannot help but show the problems inherent in cleaving solely to a multicultural approach (although I would suggest that these problems surface on the level of implicit rather than explicit ideology). Multicultural anti-racism has worked for Harry, for Harry now treats Kreacher with kindness, having learned the lesson that elves have feelings just as wizards do. Yet while multicultural anti-racism has changed the way Harry, a member of the privileged class, responds to the elves, what does it offer the elves themselves? The final volume of the series demonstrates an all-too-likely outcome of multicultural anti-racism—making the privileged feel better about themselves without doing much to change the oppression of the other. To begin with, the feelings that Harry witnesses and comes to understand in Kreacher and the falsely imprisoned Hokey are related to their roles as servants to wizards. Kreacher's despair stems from his witnessing the death of his master, Regulus Black, while Hokey's stems from being falsely accused of the murder of her mistress. Elves, it seems, are allowed to have feelings, as long as those feelings relate to the humans they serve. Elves are also allowed, in the best Rudyard Kipling/Gunga Din fashion, to die in order to save their human masters, as the fate of Dobby demonstrates. Finally, elves are allowed to remain servants, albeit happy ones. After Harry begins to recognize Kreacher's feelings, Kreacher changes his ways, becoming more pleasant—he calls Harry "Master Harry," he does what Harry asks willingly, he cleans up both himself and his house, and he even becomes an object of humor in his loyalty to his new owner:

> There was the sound of pattering feet, a blaze of shining copper, an echoing clang, and a shriek of agony: Kreacher had taken a run at Mundungus and hit him over the head with a saucepan.
>
> "Call 'im off, call 'im off, 'e should be locked up!" screamed Mundungus, cowering as Kreacher raised the heavy-bottomed pan again.
>
> "Kreacher, no!" shouted Harry.
>
> Kreacher's thin arms trembled with the weight of the pan, still held aloft.
>
> "Perhaps just one more, Master Harry, for luck?"
>
> Ron laughed.
>
> "We need him conscious, Kreacher, but if he needs persuading you can do the honors," said Harry.
>
> "Thank you very much, Master," said Kreacher with a bow. (*HP and the DH*, 221)

But while the elves participate in the final battle against Voldemort, Rowling offers no sign that the defeat of the Dark Lord will free the elves from their centuries of bondage to human wizards. In fact, in the very last line of the penultimate chapter, Harry wonders "whether Kreacher might bring him a sandwich" as he imagines resting in his bed in Gryffindor Tower after the end of the battle (*HP and the DH*, 749). While Harry's last thought—"I've had enough trouble for a lifetime"—explicitly refers to the troubles keeping the Elder Wand might bring, on the level of implicit ideology, it also seems to suggest that disturbing the "natural" order of the wizard/elf hierarchy is trouble that Harry would like to avoid. Although Voldemort's overt racial oppression of Mudbloods has been overturned, the parallel oppression of the elves and goblins that underlies wizarding power must once again be repressed, be forgotten, even by the series' self-sacrificing champion of anti-racism.

In her June 2008 commencement speech at Harvard University, "The Fringe Benefits of Failure, and the Importance of Imagination," J. K. Rowling links imagination directly to a multicultural anti-racist pedagogy. For Rowling, imagination is "not only the uniquely human capacity to envision that which is not, and therefore the fount of all invention and innovation. In its arguably most transformative and revelatory capacity, it is the power that enables us to empathise with humans whose experiences we have never shared."[43] Through the imagination, she argues, "Humans . . . can think themselves into other people's minds, imagine themselves into other people's places."[44] After defining imagination in this broad way, Rowling links it directly with anti-racism efforts by describing her time working in the research department of Amnesty International in London. In multicultural anti-racism fashion, she describes the *personal* effect witnessing the sufferings of oppressed others had on her. Such examples are immediate and compelling, and build in intensity as she describes them: "I saw photographs of those who had disappeared without a trace. . . . I read testimony of torture victims. . . . I opened handwritten, eye-witness accounts of summary trials and executions, of kidnappings and rapes."[45] Rowling, as she has demonstrated throughout her series, is a fervent believer that experiencing the situation of others through the imaginative power of story will lead the listener to a greater awareness of the oppression in the world.

Intriguingly, though, after relating her Amnesty experiences, Rowling goes on to point to the pitfall inherent in a solely multicultural approach to anti-oppression work: "[T]hose who choose not to empathise enable real monsters. For without ever committing an act of outright evil ourselves, we collude with it, through our own apathy."[46] Her choice of the collective pronoun "we" points to the idea that few are completely free of the wish not to empathize with the oppressed, not to act in the face of pain, not to see the pain that empathy shows us. The solution, then, Rowling suggests, lies not solely in empathy, in a multicultural anti-racism approach, but rather in an empathy that *gives rise* to acts of social justice: "Amnesty mobilizes thousands of people who have never been tortured or imprisoned for their beliefs to act on behalf of those who have. The power of human empathy, *leading to collective action*, saves lives, and frees prisoners."[47]

Rowling's speech does little to show what such collective action might look like, however, choosing instead to focus on stories of her personal responses to the reality of oppression. And though her novels show moments of collective action in the fight against Voldemort, at heart they are about the emotional growth of a boy rather than a depiction of the rise of a collective political movement. Many would say this focus is appropriate, given that this novel is intended for younger readers, who, according to Rowling's anti-racist pedagogy, need first to learn empathy, and only later to learn the ways of collective action. Child development theory might concur, urging that the intended readers of the *Potter* books aren't old enough for the more abstract concepts of social justice; instead, they must first work on envisioning anti-racism on a personal level. Yet, as recent work by social psychologists such as Andrew Scott Baron and Mahzarin R. Banaji, and Debra Van Ausdale and Joe Feagin, has begun to demonstrate, children as young as three understand and deploy abstract racial and ethnic concepts, in both positive and negative ways.[48] If children so young can learn and use such abstract concepts, might they also be capable of understanding collective action? Teachers such as Valerie Ooka Pang suggest that it is not only possible, but necessary, to combine a multicultural and a social justice approach in the K–12 classroom, teaching students to become both "self-directed *and* community oriented."[49] Asking students to see that "caring" and "justice" are integrally interrelated, and to explore how caring can lead to action, might be a better goal for anti-racist pedagogues to embrace, rather than espousing one approach at the expense of the other.[50]

As Rowling demonstrates in *Harry Potter and the Deathly Hallows*, it is easy to imagine collective action when the enemy is clearly defined, and is clearly evil, as is Voldemort and his power-hungry followers. But it is much more difficult to imagine what collective action might look like when deployed against one's own social institutions, and especially against one's own naturalized beliefs.[51]

I concluded the 2010 version of this essay by wondering: "Will Rowling create a new series, one in which Harry, Hermione, and Ron's children struggle with the more difficult task of recognizing the claims of the goblins and the elves, and work collectively with these marginalized groups to change the power structures of their society?"[52] In the years since, Rowling has shown little interest in such a project. In fact, as Amelia Tait's 2018 article in the *New Statesman* suggests, many millennials who learned about social justice and liberal values from Rowling's books are beginning to become frustrated with the limits of Rowling's own views.[53] Rowling fans have been upset by her refusal to push filmmakers to depict the young Dumbledore in the *Fantastic Beasts and How to Find Them* film franchise as gay (a sexual identity Rowling "revealed" in 2007, only a few weeks after the publication of *Harry Potter and the Deathly Hallows*); by her championing of the casting of Johnny Depp, who had been accused of abuse by his wife, in the *Fantastic Beasts* films; and especially by her less than straightforward embrace of diversity. As Stitch of Stich's Media Mix website argues:

> My big issue with all of this "after the fact diversity" that we're seeing around JR [*sic*] Rowling and the Harry Potter series is that she's getting so much credit for doing basically nothing with regard to representation. There's no reissuing covers where more characters are of color. There aren't any additional chapters showing Albus Dumbledore as gay in any capacity. JKR still *wrote* 99% of the Harry Potter cast as white and straight. . . . Almost all of her diversity comes after the fact, and I don't think she should be getting so much credit for it.[54]

It seems only fitting that Rowling, who "taught a generation liberal values," is now finding that generation "using [those liberal values] against her."[55]

And it seems more and more likely that we will have to look to a writer from that generation, rather than to Rowling herself, to create a new fantasy world in which social justice anti-racism will not just be hinted at, but will flourish.

Notes

1. Mendlesohn, "Crowning the King," 159.

2. Westman "Specters of Thatcherism," 328; and Carey, "Hermione and the House-Elves" (2003), 104.

3. Mendlesohn, "Crowning the King," 177.

4. Blake, *The Irresistible Rise of Harry Potter*; Anatol, "The Fallen Empire"; and Ostry, "Accepting Mudbloods."

5. In the wake of the publication of *Harry Potter and the Deathly Hallows*, several of the abovementioned critics revisited their original opinions. Carey acknowledged that, in hindsight, his claim that "the Harry Potter novels are among the most politically engaged novels to have been written for children in recent years" was "overassertive," yet he still emphasized the truth of his original essay's other claim, that "a significant aspect of Rowling's project is the promotion of political participation for young people" ("Hermione and the House-Elves Revisited"). Anatol continues to "push a reading of Rowling's narratives as harkening back to much earlier children's books," books with clear colonialist ideologies, a harkening that "undermines the antiracist message of the series" (introduction to *Reading Harry Potter Again*, xiii–xiv). And Westman builds upon her previous analysis in her chapter in this volume. In the years since I originally wrote this chapter, other critics have also weighed in on whether or not the *Harry Potter* books promote anti-racism: See Maza, "Deconstructing the Grand Narrative in *Harry Potter*"; Kellner, "J. K. Rowling's Ambivalence towards Feminism"; Rana, "The less you lot have ter do with these foreigners"; Saxena, *The Subversive Harry Potter*; Vezzali et al., "The Greatest Magic of Harry Potter"; and Wolosky, "Harry Potter's Ethical Paradigms."

6. Bonnett, *Anti-Racism*, 4.

7. Bonnett, *Anti-Racism*, 10.

8. Bonnett, *Anti-Racism*, 4.

9. Bonnett, *Anti-Racism*, 19.

10. Bonnett, *Anti-Racism*, 13.

11. The universalist approach can also assume the distorting spectacles of "color-blindness," the assumption that race doesn't exist, or that we are being anti-racist if we assume it does not. See Sarah Park Dahlen and Kallie Schell's chapter in this collection for a discussion of the problems of colorblindness in Rowling's writing.

12. Bonnett, *Anti-Racism*, 17.

13. Bonnett, *Anti-Racism*, 114.

14. The other four ways of "doing" anti-racism as described by Bonnett are as follows. "Everyday anti-racism" consists of the actions of individuals unaligned with government or political parties; it is most evident in "cultural production (especially music), youth cultures, media, and religion" (*Anti-Racism*, 89). "Psychological anti-racism" focuses on training in racism awareness and in developing positive racial images of previously oppressed groups. "Anti-Nazi and Anti-Fascist Anti-Racism" narrows its focus to fighting Nazi and neo-Nazi threats. Finally, "Representative Organization Anti-Racism" focuses on secondary education and the workplace, with the understanding that members of oppressed groups need help from those in power to overcome their disadvantage. This approach "rel[ies] on the notion that creating multiracial organizations changes the culture of these organizations and

enables them to become more sustainable and efficient in a multiracial market place and the local and wider community" (111–12). Affirmative action programs would be one example of this type of anti-racism.

15. For a longer discussion of the rise of multiculturalism in American education, see Jeynes, *American Educational History*, chap. 13; and Spring, *The Intersection of Cultures*, 442–46.

16. Bonnett, *Anti-Racism*, 94–95.

17. Bonnett, *Anti-Racism*, 97.

18. For examples of texts for teachers that model a multicultural approach to classroom pedagogy, see Kendall, *Diversity in the Classroom*; and Siccone, *Celebrating Diversity*.

19. Bonnett, *Anti-Racism*, 104–6. Bonnett suggests that in the United States during the 1980s, "multiculturalism" was often associated with a "radical, almost insurgent, meaning . . . a challenge to the status quo" (90). The *Oxford English Dictionary* listing for "multiculturalism," however, does not include the radical definition Bonnett mentions in passing, and today, the common knowledge meaning of "multicultural" aligns closely with the more general definition Bonnett discusses, "the celebration of cultural diversity, and not as a necessarily subversive programme" (90).

20. Adams, Bell, and Griffin, *Teaching for Diversity*, 5

21. Adams, Bell, and Griffin, *Teaching for Diversity*, 104.

22. Paulo Freire's *Pedagogy of the Oppressed* is a touchstone text for social justice pedagogues. See also Ayres, Hunt, and Quinn, *Teaching for Social Justice*; and Adams, Bell, and Griffin, *Teaching for Diversity*.

23. Bonnett, *Anti-Racism*, 95.

24. Bonnett, *Anti-Racism*, 115.

25. Bonnett, *Anti-Racism*, 107, 114–15. As example of a critique of multicultural anti-racism pedagogy from the left, see Godfrey Brandt's *The Realization of Anti-Racist Teaching*. Of course, there are those who criticize multiculturalism from the right, as well; for the neoconservative point of view, see, for example, the work of Dinesh D'Souza. Arun Kundnani ("Multiculturalism and Its Discontents") describes the ways in which the conservative racism that was dominant in 1980s critiques of multiculturalism has been revamped and reshaped in the twenty-first century, using the language of "values" rather than ethnicity.

26. I focus here on nonhumans only, recognizing that power relations among humans (wizards, Muggles, and Mudbloods) might also be productively examined. Mike Cadden helpfully suggests that Mudbloods might be thought of in terms of disability (personal communication, June 2008), another identity category critics are currently theorizing, as the rise of disability studies suggests.

27. Mendlesohn, "Crowning the King"; Ostry, "Accepting Mudbloods"; and Carey, "Hermione and the House-Elves" (2003). Rowling herself has confirmed the parallel between her elves and slavery in general: "The house elves [*sic*] is really for slavery, isn't it, the house elves are slaves, so that is an issue that I think we probably all feel strongly about enough in this room already" (Accio Quote, "Edinburgh 'Cub Reporter' Press Conference"). For British readers, Rowling's depiction of the elves may also evoke class-based stereotypes and discrimination, particularly involving Cockney identities.

28. Ostry, "Accepting Mudbloods," 96.

29. Carey, "Hermione and the House-Elves" (2003), 114.

30. Westman, "Specters of Thatcherism," 327; emphasis added.

31. Mendlesohn, "Crowning the King," 181.

32. Mendlesohn, "Crowning the King," 181.

33. In his 2009 reassessment of his arguments in his first (2003) essay on the house-elves, Bryccan Carey acknowledges that Rowling's depiction of Kreacher echoes the "grateful slave" stereotype and that the emotional connection forged between Harry, Hermione, and even Ron and Kreacher after Kreacher reveals his traumatic backstory "uses language almost identical to much abolitionist writing, which was frequently grounded in the eighteenth-century literature of sensibility, and which foregrounded the tears of suffering slaves as well as the tears of those who sympathized with them" ("Hermione and the House-Elves Revisited," 168).

34. Westman, "Specters of Thatcherism," 325.

35. It goes without saying that choosing Hermione as the character through which to satirize such liberal do-gooding is more than a bit sexist. Choosing to make fun of one of the only prominent young women in the series, and to alter her character so much to make her satirical point, shows that Rowling's depiction of the elves is problematic on multiple levels.

36. Carey, "Hermione and the House-Elves" (2003), 106.

37. This concept, articulated in terms of white privilege in the United States, dates from Peggy McIntosh's article "White Privilege: Unpacking the Invisible Knapsack." Since the publication of McIntosh's seminal article in 1988, several books and many articles have been published that explore the concept of race privilege in more detail; see Cassidy and Mikulich, *Interrupting White Privilege*; DiAngelo, *White Fragility*; Jensen, *The Heart of Whiteness*; Rothenberg, *White Privilege*; Sullivan, *Good White People*; Sullivan, *Revealing Whiteness*; and Williams, *The Constraint of Race*. While the concept of privilege has been linked primarily to whiteness, social justice pedagogy makes it clear that the concept of dominant and subordinate power structures, and the privileges and disadvantage they create for different groups, can be applied to multiple identities (racial, sexual orientation, religious, etc.), not just to whiteness. See the essays in Carol Vincent's collection *Nancy Fraser, Social Justice and Education* for essays on social justice as applied to class, sexual orientation, gender, ethnicity, and ability. See Schmidt, "More Than Men in White Sheets"; and Adams, Bell, and Griffin, *Teaching for Diversity*, for theory and practice.

38. Carey, "Hermione and the House-Elves Revisited," offers an explanation, if not an excuse, for Rowling's "decision to subordinate the role of S.P.E.W. in the later novels." Once Voldemort returns and the democratic government of the wizarding world falls, a pressure organization such as S.P.E.W. is no longer effective or even viable: "Hermione's campaign effectively ends at the point that the normal political processes of the wizarding world are curtailed."

39. When I presented an abbreviated version of this chapter at a conference, several audience members protested that Hermione's S.P.E.W. efforts were meant to show the problems that result when those who work for social justice do not listen to those for whom they are organizing. "What if the elves really *want* to be slaves?" these audience members protested. Such protests can seem valid when we remember the objections made by many Third World feminists against the assumptions made by feminists in the West, protests against the ways that Western feminists read their own assumptions about liberation from patriarchy onto Eastern women without taking into consideration differences in culture, geography, and history. One example would be to assume that wearing the hijab is inherently sexist and degrading without asking Muslim women themselves why they

wear the hijab or recognizing the role it played and continues to play in protesting Western colonization (Armstrong, *The Battle for God*, 295). Yet, I would argue, there is a significant difference between foisting one's own version of feminism onto another and insisting that another wants to be a slave for you and your kind. While Western women may benefit indirectly from Muslim women refusing the veil, Harry and his fellow wizards benefit *directly* from the idea that elves want to be their slaves. For Rowling to create another sentient race that truly desires enslavement is dangerous and irresponsible, I would argue; such a creation is far too likely to play into wish-fulfillment fantasies only too common in our own world that other races or nationalities desire to serve our needs.

40. Westman, "Specters of Thatcherism," 326–27.

41. Giselle Liza Anatol's "The Replication of Victorian Racial Ideology in Harry Potter," on echoes of imperialism in the *Harry Potter* books, includes a section on "Other Racial Allegories: Giants, Centaurs, and Goblins," which argues that Rowling's portrayal of the goblins draws on Orientalist ideology. Although we use different critical lenses, Anatol and I have both observed many of the same contradictions in Rowling's anti-racist messaging in her depiction of the goblin Griphook. Although Anatol's essay was published in 2009 and mine ("Harry and the Other: Answering the Race Question in J. K. Rowling's *Harry Potter*") in 2010, I did not have access to her work when I was drafting the original version of this essay.

42. Plummer, "Music Firm 'Goblins'"; and Pulsinelli, "Harry Potter and the (Re)Order of the Artists."

43. Rowling, "The Fringe Benefits of Failure."

44. Rowling, "The Fringe Benefits of Failure."

45. Rowling, "The Fringe Benefits of Failure."

46. Rowling, "The Fringe Benefits of Failure."

47. Rowling, "The Fringe Benefits of Failure"; emphasis added.

48. Banaji is one of the creators of the Implicit Association Test, which measures associations that we are not conscious of, including race-based association. In an interview, Banaji said: "We created a child version of the Implicit Association Test, so that kids as young as age 5 and 6 can take the test. It's all based on sound and pictures. We were expecting to see that children that age would show no bias. That's not at all what we found. And that surprised the hell out of us. Bias is shown early and at the same magnitude as it is in adults. We did a test with 3-year-olds. To our great surprise again, the bias is not only there, it's the same level as it is in adults. We think it has to do with cultural privileging" (Fogg, "Thinking in Black and White"). For more information on the test (or to try a version out yourself), go to https://implicit.harvard.edu/implicit/. Van Ausdale and Feagin's work focuses on classroom observations of preschoolers and describes the many ways that very young children can and do deploy abstract concepts of race ("Using Racial and Ethnic Concepts"; and *The First R*).

49. Pang, *Multicultural Education*, 77.

50. One can see how multicultural and anti-racist pedagogies are gradually becoming integrated by examining changes made in subsequent editions of a key teacher-training textbook, *Multicultural Education: Issues and Perspectives* by James A. Banks and Cherry A. McGee Banks. In the first edition of the book, published in 1989, the Bankses describe two of the goals of multicultural education in universalist terms: first, "to transform the school so that male and female students, exceptional students, as well as students from diverse cultural, social-class, racial, and ethnic groups will experience an equal opportunity to

learn in school"; and second, to develop more positive attitudes toward "others" (19–20). By the second edition (1993), the Bankses have become frustrated with the way multicultural education has become overly focused on changing the content of classroom teaching only; they argue that changes in content should only be one goal of multicultural pedagogy. Two others goals are calling attention to the "knowledge construction process" and embracing an "equity pedagogy," ideas taken from social justice approaches (20–21). By the fourth edition (2001), two additional goals have been added—"prejudice reduction" and the creation of "empowering school cultures" (20)—as has a new chapter, "The Colorblind Perspective in Schools: Causes and Consequences." Another key essay undergoes a title change; Geneva Gay's "Ethnic Minorities and Educational Equality" becomes "Educational Equality for Students of Color," while the section in which it appears changes from "Ethnicity and Language" to "Race, Ethnicity, and Language." Finally, in the sixth edition (2007), Gay's essay, which had focused on *children*, is dropped, replaced by Gloria Ladson-Billings's "Culturally Responsive Teaching: Theory and Practice," which shifts the focus to the need for teachers to change their explicit and implicit ideological assumptions in order to create culturally empowering classrooms for students from oppressed groups. Since I first wrote this essay, seventh, eighth, ninth, and tenth editions of this textbook have also been published, and additional changes have likely been made.

51. As Rowling's transphobic comments in 2020 so painfully illustrate.

52. Horne, "Harry and the Other," 99. Some might argue that the conventions of the high-fantasy genre, with its dependence on a good-versus-evil binary, are inherently unable to depict the more nuanced anti-racist agenda advocated here. Yet, as Karin E. Westman has argued, such an anti-oppression agenda is not unheard of in children's fiction, at least as far as class dynamics are concerned, as readers of Jonathan Stroud's *Bartimaeus* trilogy are well aware (Westman, "Power to the [Normal] People?").

53. Tait, "JK Rowling's Books Taught Millennials."

54. Stitch, "On J. K. Rowling's Thing about After the Fact Diversity."

55. Tait, "JK Rowling's Books Taught Millennials."

Bibliography

Accio Quote. "Edinburgh 'Cub Reporter' Press Conference." July 16, 2005. http://www.accio-quote.org/articles/2005/0705-edinburgh-ITVcubreporters.htm.

Adams, Maurianne, Lee Anne Bell, and Pat Griffin, eds. *Teaching for Diversity and Social Justice: A Sourcebook*. 3rd ed. New York: Routledge, 2016.

Anatol, Giselle Liza. "The Fallen Empire: Exploring Ethnic Otherness in the World of Harry Potter." In *Reading Harry Potter: Critical Essays*, edited by Giselle Liza Anatol, 163–78. Westport, CT: Praeger, 2003.

Anatol, Giselle Liza. Introduction to *Reading Harry Potter Again: New Critical Essays*, edited by Giselle Liza Anatol, ix–xv. Santa Barbara, CA: Praeger, 2009.

Anatol, Giselle Liza. "The Replication of Victorian Racial Ideology in Harry Potter." In *Reading Harry Potter Again: New Critical Essays*, edited by Giselle Liza Anatol, 109–26. Santa Barbara, CA: Praeger, 2009.

Anderson, Sonya L., Polly F. Attwood, and Lionel C. Howard, eds. *Facing Racism in Education*. Cambridge, MA: Harvard Educational Publishing Group, 2004.

Armstrong, Karen. *The Battle for God: Fundamentalism in Judaism, Christianity and Islam.* New York: HarperCollins, 2001.

Ayres, William, Jean Ann Hunt, and Therese Quinn, eds. *Teaching for Social Justice: A Democracy and Education Reader.* New York: New Press; Teachers College Press, 1998.

Banks, James A., and Cherry A. McGee Banks. *Multicultural Education: Issues and Perspectives.* 1st, 2nd, 4th, 6th eds. Boston: Allyn and Bacon, 1989, 1993; Hoboken, NJ: John Wiley, 2001, 2007.

Baron, Andrew Scott, and Mahzarin R. Banaji. "The Development of Implicit Attitudes: Evidence of Race Evaluations from Ages 6 and 10 and Adulthood." *Psychological Science* 17, no. 1 (January 2006): 53–58.

Blake, Andrew. *The Irresistible Rise of Harry Potter.* New York: Verso, 2002.

Bonnett, Alastair. *Anti-Racism: Key Ideas.* London: Routledge, 2000.

Brandt, Godfrey L. *The Realization of Anti-Racist Teaching.* London: Falmer Press, 1986.

Carey, Brycchan. "Hermione and the House-Elves: The Literary and Historical Contexts of J. K. Rowling's Antislavery Campaign." In *Reading Harry Potter: Critical Essays*, edited by Giselle Liza Anatol, 103–16. Westport, CT: Praeger, 2003.

Carey, Brycchan. "Hermione and the House-Elves Revisited: J. K. Rowling, Antislavery Campaigning, and the Politics of Potter." In *Reading Harry Potter Again: New Critical Essays*, edited by Giselle Liza Anatol, 159–74. Santa Barbara, CA: Praeger, 2009.

Cassidy, Laurie M. and Alex Mikulich, eds. *Interrupting White Privilege: Catholic Theologians Break the Silence.* Maryknoll, NY: Orbis Books, 2007.

DiAngelo, Robin. *White Fragility: Why It's So Hard for White People to Talk about Racism.* Boston: Beacon Press, 2018.

D'Souza, Dinesh. *Illiberal Education: The Politics of Race and Sex on Campus.* New York: Free Press, 1991.

Fogg, Piper. "Thinking in Black and White." *Chronicle of Higher Education*, July 25, 2008. https://www.chronicle.com/article/thinking-in-black-and-white/.

Freire, Paulo. *Pedagogy of the Oppressed.* Translated by Myra Bergman Ramos. New York: Continuum, 2000.

Horne, Jackie C. "Harry and the Other: Answering the Race Question in J. K. Rowling's *Harry Potter.*" *The Lion and the Unicorn* 34, no. 1 (January 2010): 76–104. doi:10.1353/uni.0.0488.

Jensen, Robert. *The Heart of Whiteness: Confronting Race, Racism, and White Privilege.* San Francisco: City Lights, 2005.

Jeynes, William H. *American Educational History: School, Society, and the Common Good.* Thousand Oaks, CA: Sage Publications, 2007.

Kellner, Rivka. "J. K. Rowling's Ambivalence towards Feminism: House Elves—Women in Disguise—in the 'Harry Potter' Books." *Midwest Quarterly* 51, no. 4 (2010): 367–85.

Kendall, Frances E. *Diversity in the Classroom: New Approaches to the Education of Young Children.* New York: Teachers College Press, 1996.

Kendall, Frances E. *Understanding White Privilege: Creating Pathways to Authentic Relationships across Race.* New York: Routledge, 2006.

Kundnani, Arun. "Multiculturalism and Its Discontents: Left, Right and Liberal." *European Journal of Cultural Studies* 15, no. 2 (2012): 155–66.

Maza, Luisa Grijalva. "Deconstructing the Grand Narrative in *Harry Potter*: Inclusion/Exclusion and Discriminatory Policies in Fiction and Practice." *Politics and Policy* 40, no. 3 (June 2012): 424–43.

McIntosh, Peggy. "White Privilege: Unpacking the Invisible Knapsack." In *Race, Class, and Gender in the United States: An Integrated Study*, 7th ed., edited by Paula S. Rothenberg, 177–81. New York: Worth Publishers, 2007.

Mendlesohn, Farah. "Crowning the King: Harry Potter and the Construction of Authority." In *The Ivory Tower and Harry Potter: Perspectives on a Literary Phenomenon*, edited by Lana A. Whited, 159–81. Columbia: University of Missouri Press, 2002.

Oluo, Ijeoma. *So You Want to Talk about Race*. New York: Seal Press, 2018.

Ostry, Elaine. "Accepting Mudbloods: The Ambivalent Social Vision of J. K. Rowling's Fairy Tales." In *Reading Harry Potter: Critical Essays*, edited by Giselle Liza Anatol, 89–102. Westport, CT: Praeger, 2003.

Pang, Valerie Ooka. *Multicultural Education: A Caring-Centered, Reflective Approach*. New York: McGraw-Hill, 2001.

Plummer, Robert. "Music Firm 'Goblins' in Copyright War." BBC News, June 3, 2008. http://news.bbc.co.uk/2/hi/business/7412671.stm.

Pulsinelli, Gary. "Harry Potter and the (Re)Order of the Artists: Are We Muggles or Goblins?" University of Tennessee Legal Studies Research Paper no. 18, October 17, 2007; rev. March 25, 2008. http://ssrn.com/abstract=1022214.

Rana, Marion. "'The less you lot have ter do with these foreigners, the happier yeh'll be': Cultural and National Otherness in J. K. Rowling's *Harry Potter* series." *International Research in Children's Literature* 4, no. 1 (July 2011): 45–58.

Rothenberg, Paula S., ed. *White Privilege: Essential Readings on the Other Side of Racism*. New York: Worth Publishers, 2002.

Rowling, J. K. "The Fringe Benefits of Failure, and the Importance of Imagination." *Harvard Magazine*, June 5, 2008. http://harvardmagazine.com/go/jkrowling.html.

Rowling, J. K. *Harry Potter and the Chamber of Secrets*. New York: Scholastic, 1999.

Rowling, J. K. *Harry Potter and the Deathly Hallows*. New York: Scholastic, 2007.

Rowling, J. K. *Harry Potter and the Goblet of Fire*. New York: Scholastic, 2000.

Rowling, J. K. *Harry Potter and the Half-Blood Prince*. New York: Scholastic, 2005.

Rowling, J. K. *Harry Potter and the Order of the Phoenix*. New York: Scholastic, 2003.

Rowling, J. K. *Harry Potter and the Prisoner of Azkaban*. New York: Scholastic, 1999.

Rowling, J. K. *Harry Potter and the Sorcerer's Stone*. New York: Scholastic, 1998. Originally published as *Harry Potter and the Philosopher's Stone*, London: Bloomsbury, 1997.

Saxena, Vandana. *The Subversive Harry Potter: Adolescent Rebellion and Containment in the J. K. Rowling Novels*. Jefferson, NC: McFarland, 2012.

Schmidt, Sheri Lyn. "More Than Men in White Sheets: Seven Concepts Critical to the Teaching of Racism as Systemic Inequality." *Equity and Excellence in Education* 38, no. 2 (2005): 110–22.

Siccone, Frank. *Celebrating Diversity: Building Self-Esteem in Today's Multicultural Classrooms*. Boston: Allyn and Bacon, 1995.

Spring, Joel. *The Intersection of Cultures: Multicultural Education in the United States and the Global Economy*. New York: Lawrence Erlbaum Associates, 2017.

Stitch. "On J. K. Rowling's Thing about After the Fact Diversity." Stitch's Media Mix, December 22, 2015. stitchmediamix.com/2015/12/22/on-jk-rowlings-thing-about-after-the-fact-diversity/.

Stroud, Jonathan. *The Amulet of Samarkand: The Bartimaeus Trilogy, Book 1*. New York: Hyperion, 2003.

Stroud, Jonathan. *The Golem's Eye: The Bartimaeus Trilogy, Book 2*. New York: Hyperion, 2004.

Stroud, Jonathan. *Ptolemy's Gate: The Bartimaeus Trilogy, Book 3*. New York: Hyperion, 2005.

Sullivan, Shannon. *Good White People: The Problem with Middle-Class White Anti-Racism*. Albany: State University of New York Press, 2014.

Sullivan, Shannon. *Revealing Whiteness: The Unconscious Habits of Racial Privilege*. Bloomington: Indiana University Press, 2006.

Tait, Amelia. "JK Rowling's Books Taught Millennials about Liberal Values. Now They Are Turning Against Her." *New Statesman*, February 10, 2018. Updated as "JK Rowling Created an Army of Liberals—Now They Are Turning Against Her," June 24, 2021, https://www.newstatesman.com/politics/2018/02/jk-rowling-created-army-liberals -now-they-are-turning-against-her.

Van Ausdale, Debra, and Joe R. Feagin. *The First R: How Children Learn Race and Racism*. Lanham, MD: Rowman and Littlefield, 2001.

Van Ausdale, Debra, and Joe R. Feagin. "Using Racial and Ethnic Concepts: The Critical Case of Very Young Children." *American Sociological Review* 61, no. 5 (October 1996): 779–93.

Vezzali, Loris, Sofia Stathi, Dino Giovannini, Dora Capozza, and Elena Trifiletti. "The Greatest Magic of Harry Potter: Reducing Prejudice." *Journal of Applied Social Psychology* 45, no. 2 (February 2015): 105–21.

Vincent, Carol, ed. *Nancy Fraser, Social Justice and Education*. Abingdon, Oxon., England: Routledge, 2019.

Westman, Karin E. "Power to the (Normal) People? Muggles, Commoners, and Magical Power in Rowling's *Harry Potter* and Stroud's *Bartimaeus* Trilogy." Paper presented at the Children's Literature Association conference, Normal, Illinois, June 2008.

Westman, Karin E. "Specters of Thatcherism: Contemporary British Culture in J. K. Rowling's Harry Potter Series." In *The Ivory Tower and Harry Potter: Perspectives on a Literary Phenomenon*, edited by Lana A. Whited, 305–28. Columbia: University of Missouri Press, 2002.

Williams, Linda Faye. *The Constraint of Race: Legacies of White Skin Privilege in America*. University Park: Pennsylvania State University Press, 2003.

Wolosky, Shira. "Harry Potter's Ethical Paradigms: Augustine, Kant, and Feminist Moral Theory." *Children's Literature* 40, no. 1 (January 2012): 191–217.

Wolosky, Shira. *The Riddles of Harry Potter: Secret Passages and Interpretive Quests*. New York: Palgrave Macmillan, 2010.

Realism and Race

The Narrative Politics of Harry Potter

Karin E. Westman

> Her novels, for all of their "magical" trappings, are
> prefigured in mundane reality, relying too wholly on the
> real from which she simultaneously wishes to escape. [. . .]
> [The series] is not true to its genre or mode.[1]

In order to talk about race in Rowling's *Harry Potter* series, we must talk about realism. In order to talk about realism in Harry Potter, we must first talk about fantasy. We must start, then, with a discussion of genre and the expectations that readers bring to Rowling's best-selling and award-winning series. Genre provides us with a way to understand the relationship between form and content, between readers' expectations for Rowling's imagined world and the limitations of Rowling's art.

If genre is best understood at a "set of expectations"[2] rather than fixed categories, as a performance contingent upon an audience's expectations as much as the text's form and content,[3] then many readers of Harry Potter have experienced Rowling's series as a performance of realism. Fantasy and the other genres contained in Rowling's intergeneric narrative recede from view relative to Rowling's attention to elements of literary realism: domestic subjects, social issues, close detail of setting, and the relationship of characters to each other within a given set of social circumstances and of a character to his or her own consciousness. The series' generic performance, then, would show Rowling to be a realist at heart: her series is "true to its genre or mode," to use John Pennington's words quoted in the epigraph above, but just not the "genre or mode" that he and some others expect.[4]

This expectation of realism is particularly evident in readers' responses to two additions to the Potterverse: Rowling's fictional history "History of Magic in North America," first published on her website Pottermore,[5] and the play *Harry Potter and the Cursed Child*, written by playwright Jack Thorne and director John Tiffany from a story by J. K. Rowling. Rowling's addition of these two genres—history and drama—into the series' hybrid narrative creates a divergent effect. On the one hand, these two additional genres intensify the forms and themes of the series, foregrounding its realism and focusing our attention even more on the materiality of the wizarding world, the relationship between parents and children and between individuals and social institutions, and the *Bildung* of the self. On the other hand, in doing so, these two additional genres also highlight significant narrative concerns for new and returning readers: the limitations of Rowling's imagined world in terms of race.

In pointing readers to everyday experience and our place in history, the realism underpinning Rowling's fantasy encourages readers to expect resonances between the world of Harry Potter and their own world. However, when readers' lives and Rowling's art fail to resonate, the fantasy wobbles, its realism undermined; experiences no longer align, and the realism no longer sustains the fantasy. This gap between representation and reader experience has consequences—not only in terms of genre but also for readers' opportunity to see themselves in Rowling's art.

We can find two moments of this narrative dynamic in action during the year 2016: the year when Rowling added new material to the website Pottermore and when *Harry Potter and the Cursed Child* made its debut on the London stage. While we can locate evidence of this narrative dynamic in the series itself, given how readers and scholars have responded to representations of race in the world of Harry Potter,[6] these two examples from 2016 demonstrate the degree to which elements of realism set the terms of readers' engagement with and critique of Rowling's representations of race.

The Fantastic Realism of Rowling's Harry Potter

In order to explore readerly expectations about race in "History of Magic in North America" and *Cursed Child*, it will be helpful to explain how Rowling's narrative choices create the expectation of realism for a series identified as fantasy. Contemporary theories of genre can assist us in this goal.

As I have explored elsewhere,[7] since the twentieth century, critical interest has turned from genre as an objective, stable set of categories to which one can assign a text according to formal characteristics or content, to the one who applies the taxonomy.[8] For contemporary theorists like Jonathan Frow, genre is "a set of conventional and highly organized constraints on the production and interpretation of meaning."[9] Those constraints might be formal, thematic, or material—or, most likely, a combination of those three in relative proportions, according to the expectations of an audience within a particular historical moment. This more recent view, developing from the work of Tzvetan Todorov, considers genre as discourse, as a speech act. For Todorov, "[t]he literary genres, indeed, are nothing but such choices among discursive possibilities, choices that a given society has made conventional."[10] For Todorov, as for other contemporary theorists of genre, a text's formal characteristics and content serve as the starting point for discussions of ideology, so we can explore how form and content reflect perception, convention, and belief.

Genre thus becomes a "set of expectations," in the words of Paul Cobley,[11] which readers bring to the text based on past experiences and current conditions. This rhetorical situation is precisely the one that Amy Devitt asks us to consider in the study *Writing Genres*: "Defining genre as a kind of text," Devitt explains, "becomes circular, since what we call a kind of text depends on what we think a genre is."[12] Instead, Devitt suggests, genres are better viewed as "shorthand terms for situations." Michael Goldman, theorizing genre as drama, echoes Devitt's approach: "Clearly," Goldman reminds us, "the first function of genre is that it be recognized."[13] Yet, like Devitt, what interests Goldman is the drama of generic recognition, this moment of audience expectations in action.[14] Like a performance, a text's generic classification is site specific, contingent upon an audience's expectations and response as much as the text's form and content. The audiences for a text—audiences past, present, and future—establish, maintain, or change generic expectations, which emerge from a negotiation between convention and innovation.

As a result, some genres are more worthy than others—at least, for certain audiences at certain times—and a genre's relative value and definition can shift over time. In the eighteenth century, for instance, the novel was the new kid on the block relative to the established genre of poetry. Now, the novel is part of the old guard. Further, what readers *expect* genre to be—in terms of size, shape, content, and audience—emerges from the tension between past rhetorical "situations," to use Devitt's term, and present ones. Such renegotiation, particularly in terms of fantasy, emerged with the success of Rowling's *Harry Potter* series (1997–2007).

Rowling's series defied late 1990s conventions for readers, authors, and publishers of children's literature in terms of its physical size and its intergeneric narrative. Imagining her series as "one big book,"[15] Rowling offers a seven-volume study of one character's development—a Bildungsroman of Harry's life from age eleven to seventeen. The novel of formation, however, is only one of many genres represented across the pages of the series, and this generic hybridity illustrates the significance of the series in terms of literary form as well as critical response. Individual genres are invoked, stretched, and transformed, creating new iterations and relations of literary forms that defy easy classification. Rowling's intergeneric narrative incorporates traditions of psychological realism, the Bildungsroman, the mystery, the gothic, the school story, the family story, satire, and—most obviously, given those wizards and their wands—fantasy. This blend of genres challenges and complicates the series' generic affiliation, especially with fantasy.

As Peter Hunt observes, fantasy is always "reactive": it is a "text which portrays some obvious deviance from 'consensus reality,' whatever that could possibly be—usually a change in physical laws."[16] This textual reaction can appear in several different forms, as Hunt enumerates: "the 'other world' fantasy," "future fantasies," "books in which magic intrudes into the contemporary world," "dreams," "excursions into parallel worlds," and "animal fantasies." While this running list implies discrete categories—"other world" fantasy versus "dreams"—Rowling's series illustrates how several of these "reactions" can occur within the same "reactive" text. Thus, if the reader of *Philosopher's Stone* and *Chamber of Secrets* recognizes an "other world" fantasy in the vein of J. R. R. Tolkien and Philip Pullman (to use Hunt's examples), given that the wizarding world appears to function as a separate fantastical space, that reader might need to readjust initial generic expectations by *Prisoner of Azkaban* and *Goblet of Fire*, where the categories of "excursions into parallel worlds" and then "books in which magic intrudes into the contemporary world" seem more appropriate. By *Order of the Phoenix*, our reader might need to add the category of "dreams," too, given the dominance of Harry's sleeping life over his waking reality.

Rowling's series may be typical rather than atypical in its multiple affiliations within the taxonomies of fantasy and its integration of more than one "reactive" approach. However, through reviews and scholarly articles, we can map a certain category of response to the series, particularly from adult readers who encounter a gap between their expectations and the narrative's generic hybridity: they are . . . disappointed readers whose generic expectations have not been met. Here, we can think back to this chapter's opening pronouncement, or denunciation, by John Pennington. Pennington hoped, expected, presumed that Rowling's series would offer a certain type of "reaction" and then expressed frustration at its failure to do so. For this audience, Rowling's series has failed to launch an alternative reality, failed to perform fantasy. What Pennington and others deem failure might, however, be described as another kind of performance of fantasy—what Hunt briefly notes in passing as the "[d]istinctions [. . .] made between 'high fantasy' [. . .] and 'domestic fantasy.'"[17] While Hunt does not elaborate on the distinction, it helps us understand the generic criticism of Rowling's series leveled by readers like Pennington. It also points us toward a way to recognize Rowling's dominant aesthetic: realism.

While all fantasy depends upon realism to build the narrative setting and characters of its world, different performances of fantasy depend on different combinations and tones of realistic elements. "High fantasy" (also called "epic fantasy") offers "complex worlds [. . .] [that draw from legend and myth] for their scope and serious tone,"[18] worlds that are often indebted to Arthurian legend or European mythology. Epic fantasy provides fully developed secondary worlds, featuring fully developed geographies, languages, and mythologies. Here in these stories, as Sheila Egoff succinctly explains, "[t]here are worlds to be won or lost, and the protagonists engage in a deeply personal and almost religious battle for the common good."[19] Like the epic poem, its generic namesake, the epic fantasy offers "an expansive setting, [in which] a hero, often with supernatural or magical assistance, struggles and saves a people or a way of life."[20] Given these qualities, high fantasy is a mode of "reactive" literature particularly well-suited to twentieth- and twenty-first-century British authors and readers who grapple with British cultural legacies of class privilege, entitlement, the rise (and fall) of empires, wars fought for good against evil, and how history informs identity. This fantasy's best-known practitioners include Tolkien, C. S. Lewis, Susan Cooper, Philip Pullman . . . and not Rowling.

Rowling, by contrast, excels at "domestic (low) fantasy." Here, the emphasis falls not on the epic qualities found, for instance, in the works of Tolkien, Lewis, and Cooper, or on the myth-based narratives found in the works of Alan Garner and Diana Wynne Jones. Instead, Rowling's artistic goals align her primarily with the domestic (or low) fantasy of E. Nesbit, Paul Gallico, and Elizabeth Goudge—all acknowledged by Rowling as personal favorites. Her artistic goals also align her with contemporary authors, like Jonathan Stroud, who use fantasy to explore the intersection of the personal with the political. The resulting narrative of Harry Potter, in this generic view, emphasizes how fantasy provides perspective on everyday experience, on the individual's place within the world of the human, the quotidian, and the bourgeois home. Rowling's series is thus a seven-volume Bildungsroman— a study of individual character—that begins in the petit bourgeois mind of Vernon Dursley, introduces its hero by way of a household cupboard under the stairs, and concludes with the desire for a sandwich (first ending) and parents sending children away to school (second ending).

Rowling's attention to material domestic experiences and social circumstances—food, physical sensation, quotidian objects—is therefore not at odds with her attention to fantasy, as Pennington and others claim. The everyday domestic and the fantastic coexist and mutually constitute our experience of the real, and the fantastic is in service to the psychologically real.

Rowling's use of fantasy thus returns us to an early meaning of the word that aligns the projects of realism and fantasy. As Deirdre Baker notes in her entry on "Fantasy" for *Keywords for Children's Literature*, "fantasy" refers to the "faculty of the mind" "necessary to reason and to our apprehension of reality."[21] Rowling's generic affiliation with the domestic fantasies of Nesbit, Goudge, Gallico, and others reminds us that her series' emphasis on domestic subjects, social issues, close detail of setting, and the psychology and relationships of characters combine to perform realism as much as fantasy.

The theorist Harry Shaw, in his study *Narrating Reality*, describes realism as "the attempt to come to grips with the fact that we live in a historical world": it is an attempt "to place us in history."[22] To "place us in history," to perform realism, Rowling incorporates fantasy. For some readers, the narrative result is failed fantasy because the fantasy world appears too realistic—as Harold Bloom laments, invoking classicist stereotypes of close-minded philistines, "[t]he sorcerers indeed seem as middle-class as the Muggles,"[23] and, as Pennington complains, her novels "are prefigured in mundane reality."[24] For other readers who embrace the generic hybridity of Rowling's series, the result is a new horizon of generic expectations for the performance of fantasy in twenty-first-century children's and young adult literature—a fantastic realism.

Within this narrative space of fantastic realism, elements of fantasy can work in the service of realism to offer a critique of the contemporary historical moment, a critique of a politics of absolute power based on self-interest, secrecy, and difference to value instead a more democratic power structure based on trust, altruism, and shared knowledge. However, that critique falters if elements of everyday realism slip or trip or fail to make an appearance on the narrative stage in ways that allow readers to have that moment of "realistic" recognition, that moment of being placed in their own history. Rowling's "History of Magic in North America" and the play script for *Harry Potter and the Cursed Child* are, for a number of readers, two such failed performances.

Fictional Histories: "History of Magic in North America"

Rowling's "History of Magic in North America" debuted on Pottermore in early March 2016 in advance of the film release of the Potterverse prequel *Fantastic Beasts and Where to Find Them*, teased with an online trailer and then released across several days. Since its arrival, this fictional history of the wizarding world in North America has prompted readers' concerns about Rowling's success at performing realism—the realism of race beyond Great Britain. The immediate conversations on Twitter, Facebook, blogs, and other online venues demonstrate the expectations that Rowling and her readers have about the relationship between life and art, between history and story: how art can and should represent life as well as the authority of the artist to make art from life.

Readers and scholars including Adrienne Keene, Debbie Reese, Paula Young Lee, and Loralee Sepsey have mapped Rowling's appropriations and misappropriations of Native American cultures, exploring in detail the political, cultural, and affective consequences of "History of Magic in North

America" for its readers as well as the authorial position from which Rowling writes this fictional history. The responses by Keene, Reese, Lee, Sepsey, and others provide significant and important cultural critique. Their responses make visible the extent to which the world of Rowling's series depends on and offers itself as realism—and why the fantasy of "History of Magic in North America" consequently fails for a number of readers.

Presented as a history of Rowling's fictional world, "History of Magic in North America" announces itself as one of the many genres within Rowling's intergeneric narrative. Offering a fictional "history," it invokes reading practices that tap into expectations associated with realism, but with additional ideological import, since it is separated from the narrative frame of fiction that surrounds the *Harry Potter* books. "History of Magic in North America"[25] initiates a set of narrative and ethical reading practices more akin to history than fantasy, with realism as the link between the two. Like *Hogwarts, A History*, the title "History of Magic in North America" signals art in the guise of historiography; unlike *Hogwarts, A History*, "History of Magic in North America" exists outside the text of Rowling's novels or other fictional narratives of the Potterverse. "History of Magic in North America" therefore has greater textual autonomy than other freestanding fictional histories of the wizarding world, such as *Quidditch through the Ages*, which assigns authorship to the fictional character Kennilworthy Whisp, a character whose book readers encounter first in the narrative of *Philosopher's Stone* before experiencing the volume on its own as a separate published text. Further, Kennilworthy Whisp's name appears on the title page of the printed version of *Quidditch through the Ages* that readers can hold in their hands. By contrast, Rowling's name appears as author for this new "History of Magic in North America," her name listed as a byline on the web page just below the title: "By J. K. Rowling." With this byline, Rowling and her website team remove a level of rhetorical mediation between Rowling as implied author and Rowling as author, diminishing the ironic distance between the two author functions.[26] In addition to collapsing this distinction, the attribution "By J. K. Rowling" also confers legitimacy and veracity to the information presented in "History of Magic in North America" in two ways: by asserting that the narrative's details are not only "true" to the canon of the Potterverse (they have been authored by Rowling herself) but also that they should be read as if "true" history rather than fictional story. The result: Rowling appears as historian rather than novelist, with all of the cultural expectations of bearing witness to the past that the role "historian" invokes.

Within the histories themselves, Rowling's narrative shows attention to the stylistic and narrative conventions of twentieth- and twenty-first-century historiography, mixing subjectivity with objectivity and selecting details of everyday experience to build the wizarding world of North America. The section on "1920s Wizarding America," for instance, includes a parenthetical aside typical within academic writing, which makes visible the historian's point of view and demonstrates the historian's knowledge: "After the Great Sasquatch Rebellion of 1892 (for full details, see Oritz O'Flaherty's highly-acclaimed book Big Foot's Last Stand), . . . " This same history's description of the Ilvermorny School of Witchcraft and Wizardry also offers an unapologetic and unqualified endorsement, naming it as "widely considered to be one of the greatest magical education establishments in the world." More generally, families and personal relationships serve as an organizing principle for this fictional history, whether in the aggregate for the section on "Fourteenth Century–Seventeenth Century" ("Certain families were clearly magical") or a specific family, the Rappaports, in the section on "Rappaport's Law" (we learn that this eighteenth-century national wizarding law emerges as the result of the romantic "indiscretions" of Dorcus Twelvetree and the nonmagical Bartholomew Barebone). The history's description of Dorcus, following a year's imprisonment for her being "totally oblivious to the danger" of sharing information out of love for Bartholomew, emphasizes personal, emotional, and quotidian factors over the political, rational, and extraordinary: "Thoroughly disgraced, utterly shellshocked, she emerged into a very different wizarding community and ended her days in seclusion, a mirror and her parrot her dearest companions."[27] As a result of these narrative choices, readers of "History of Magic in North America" experience a fairly seamless performance of history toward the goal of fictional world-building, a history crafted from details of the personal more than the political. Thus, even as readers fit "History of Magic in North America" into the canon of Rowling's fictional world, the content and bibliographic codes signal a performance of "history" as much as "story" in order to make real the fantasy.

Through its style, tone, and bibliographic codes, then, "History of Magic in North America" diminishes the implicit metafiction that underwrites the series and creates instead a relatively unironic historiography.[28] This historiography may be attentive to the ways that literary techniques inform the practice of history, as outlined by theorists Hayden White and Dominick LaCapra, but the resulting fictional history does not, like Rowling's novels, foster awareness for its readers about the politics of storytelling. In the original novels of the *Harry Potter* series, the narrative encourages through Harry's character a metafictive awareness on the part of the reader. Along with Harry, we become attuned to what Linda Hutcheon describes as "the processes by which we represent our selves and our world to ourselves," and how "storytelling [. . .] is a historical and a political act."[29] Think of Harry's indignant rebuff of Rufus Scrimgeour in *Deathly Hallows*, when that Minister for Magic asks Harry to foster a false perception of support for the Ministry, following Voldemort's return: Harry refuses to create a false narrative for the wizarding public, a decision the novel's narrative encourages us to support. Or, think of our growing awareness as readers—sometimes before Harry— that the narrative of Harry's life has been shaped, sometimes beyond his control, by the decisions of Voldemort, Snape, and Dumbledore. This metafictive awareness is absent from the writings collected as "History of Magic in North America." The history published there preserves what Hutcheon calls "the seamless quality of the history/fiction (or world/art) join implied by realist narrative."[30] The narrative of "History of Magic in North America" does not create for readers the possibility of alternative histories within the one it tells or the possibility of an ironic frame from which to gain purchase on that singular narrative.

Given the narrative form of "History of Magic in North America," it's not surprising that readerly expectations for its performance of realism are even higher, then, than for the bound stories of the wizarding world. When this fictional history fails to meet those expectations for readers through misappropriation or misrepresentation of Native American cultures, "History of Magic in North America" creates a sizeable gap between Rowling's efforts at narrative realism through a fictional historiography and readers' lived experience of the past and the present. These readers challenge Rowling's artistic prerogative of selection, omission, and transformation, a prerogative captured in a thread in Rowling's Twitter feed. In response to a reader's question on the release day for "History of Magic in North America" about the relationship between Native American skinwalkers and Animagi, Rowling replied, "In my wizarding world, there were no skin-walkers."[31] The initial questioner, @Weasley_dad, defends Rowling's craft decisions in the subsequent thread, seeing in her appropriation of Native American culture a performance of fantasy that draws from the realism of Native American culture while creating something new that feels real: "yes, no skin-walkers 'in her wizarding world.' But she doesn't [say] anything about 'the real world.'"[32] Other readers, of course, experience Native American cultures as part of their real world, their lived experience. Rowling's misuse of those details in a narrative that performs historiography diminishes even further the realism of "History of Magic in North America," serving as an echo of her misuse of Asian naming conventions and her inclusion of Orientalist tropes within the original series, as outlined by Sarah Park Dahlen and Kallie Schell in their chapter in this volume. In both cases, the decision denies the complex lived realities of her readers. In "History of Magic in North America," the narrative result of Rowling's realism is a compromised fantasy, a failed performance of fantastic realism—indeed, for many readers, a failed object of art.

Embodying Realism: *Harry Potter and the Cursed Child*

If "History of Magic in North America" uses historiography to build Rowling's fantastic realism, *Harry Potter and the Cursed Child* uses the drama of characters' relationships on the stage to extend the fantastic realism of the wizarding world into the future. Beginning in medias res of the epilogue to *Harry Potter and the Deathly Hallows* (2007), the play leaps forward from 2017 into multiple versions of 2020, Albus's fourth year at Hogwarts, each alternative future offering an increasingly grim world. Building this dystopian vision is psychological realism. Through its narrative structure, dialogue, and emotional conflict, the play reminds us of how Rowling's realism communicates many of the series' themes. However, in performance with Black British actress Noma Dumezweni in the role of Hermione, the script also highlights what is not included in the text of the play: the realism of embodied racial identity.

Harry Potter and the Cursed Child opens at King's Cross as the grown children of the *Harry Potter* series enact, "Nineteen Years Later," the epilogue's ritual departure of their own children for Hogwarts.[33] This opening scene, like many others that follow, weaves dialogue and plot points from the novels into the script, stitching the play's characters to the past while expanding their narratives into multiple futures. Along the way, we not only receive canonical confirmation that *Goblet of Fire* takes place in the years 1994 and 1995; we do so courtesy of a rogue Time-Turner, a heretofore unknown descendant of Voldemort, and characters' misguided attempts to prevent the death of Cedric Diggory. Each alternative future offers an increasingly grim world—worlds where Hermione follows the pedagogical methods of Snape, Dolores Umbridge remains in the post of Headmistress, students celebrate Voldemort Day, and Neville Longbottom and Harry Potter have died during the Battle of Hogwarts. The "cursed child" of the play's title may be Voldemort's heir, but many characters are eligible for that honorific, given the burdens they carry into their multiple futures.

Counterbalancing these dystopian plot points are the familiar generic elements on which the *Harry Potter* books thrive and at which Rowling excels: mystery, comedy, social satire, and—most notably, for *Cursed Child*—psychological realism. The play brings this generic preference into relief through the characters' dialogue and their relationships with each other, as the formal qualities of realist drama build the narrative's emotional power. We hear Harry and Draco struggle to talk with, and not just to, their respective sons; we observe these fathers interact as fellow Hogwarts parents rather than rivals; and we listen to the humor and care threaded through exchanges between Albus and his good friend and fellow Slytherin Scorpius Malfoy, son of Draco Malfoy. These inter- and intragenerational relationships link the twenty-first-century characters to their twentieth-century counterparts, echoing the narrative dynamics of the original series, in which the experiences of Harry and his friends parallel the experiences of his father James and his friends. In *Cursed Child*, time may turn, but the themes of the *Harry Potter* series remain constant, manifest through personal relationships between families and friends: "the complicated equation between destiny and free will, the pull between duty and love, [. . .] the role that loneliness and anger can play in fueling hate," and the array of "the forces of light (kindness, empathy, inclusion) [. . .] against the forces of darkness (fear, rage and authoritarian will to power)."[34] We watch, too, the contemporary concerns of middle- and upper-class parents as they balance obligations of work and family and as they find ways to maintain their own relationships alongside their children's wants and needs. We also watch the *Bildung* of Albus and Scorpius as they learn to balance high-risk bravery with warranted caution, self-imposed isolation with companionship. In weaving together these varied threads, the play's realism is of a piece with the world of Rowling's series, and it might sustain the narrative's fantasy.

However, if the play reminds us of Rowling's realist preferences through its dialogue and emotional conflict, the published script also highlights what's missing when Rowling provides narrative inspiration for, rather than authorship of, a text: ironic distance. Presented with a dystopian setting bereft of Rowling's usual "consuming sensory texture,"[35] readers of *Cursed Child* must take the bare bones of drama—dialogue and conflict—and animate them with details from the novels and their own imaginations.

Rowling's talent for world-building paradoxically disappears from the pages of a genre that asks bodies and objects to be present in space and time. The "Special Rehearsal Edition Script," as stated on the printed edition's dust jacket, is no Samuel French edition for working actors, directors, costumers, props managers, and set designers. Italicized scene descriptions assert a change of reality (act 1, scene 4: "*And now we enter a never-ending world of time change. And this scene is* all *about magic.*") or evoke abstract ideas (act 1, scene 13: "*This is chaos. This is magic.*"), while directions for shifts in time turn to anthropomorphism: "*There is a giant whoosh of light and smash of noise. And time stops. And then it turns over, thinks a bit, and begins spooling backwards*" (act 2, scene 19).[36] Such stage directions force the reader to fall back all the more on the characters' emotional experiences while ferrying to the imaginary stage the set designs of Rowling's novels or, in the case of Voldemort, the production values of the film adaptations, since the "*words said with an unmistakable voice*" presumably channel the intonations of Ralph Fiennes: "*Haaarry Pottttter.*" We are bereft of Rowling's narrative voice serving as a Tennessee Williams-esque playwright who dresses the stage and directs readers and actors in elaborate, italicized detail. As a result, we lose the possibility of an ironic frame consistent with the one provided by the series' narrator who announces, at the opening of the first book, how "Mr and Mrs Dursley, of number four, Privet Drive were proud to say that they were perfectly normal, thank you very much."[37] On the page, the drama reads as unironic, all the time. The script's singularity in tone, quite different from the novel's narrative play with perspective and voice and its implicit metafiction, keeps readers close to the play's characters and their emotional lives at the expense of critical distance and the possibility for alternative realities, alternative identities.

Given the loss of an ironic frame, when we consider the realism of the play and of the novels side by side, it's tempting to turn to a question often posed between fans after the publication of book 7: Does the epilogue provide the right ending for the series? If your answer is "Yes," you may be more favorably disposed to *Cursed Child* and how its realism extends the Harry Potter canon, given the play's focus on personal relationships, the next generation, and the dynamics between parents and children. If the epilogue offers an unsatisfactory conclusion to a seven-volume series that explored, through metaphor and analogy, a number of contemporary cultural and political concerns . . . well, you might then find the play failing to live up to its potential and extending the limitations that some readers found in the original series, especially in terms of race.

If the script's dialogue and emotional conflict remind us of Rowling's realist preferences and the series' themes that dominate the epilogue, then, in performance, the play highlights even further what is not part of its realism: an exploration of race beyond the casting of Black British actresses in the roles of Hermione and Rose Granger-Weasley. The announcement that Noma Dumezweni would play Hermione created a stir on social media that drew a quick response from Rowling.[38] For some readers, Hermione has existed on the page and on screen as only a white character, while for others her character has always held the potential for being Brown or Black.[39] Rowling's authorial intervention following the casting announcement—"Canon: brown eyes, frizzy hair and very clever. White skin was never specified. Rowling loves black Hermione,"[40] she tweeted in December 2015—further established Rowling as an ally of diverse representations of identity. In this context, Rowling's statement of support only serves as a reminder that the fictional world she has created lacks the very diversity she advocates within our contemporary world. Her tweet also offers further proof for what Sarah Park Dahlen and Kallie Schell in this volume identify as Rowling's "preference for color blindness" and concomitant failure to "critically engage with how race impacts the lived experiences of young people." *Cursed Child* thus offers absence of realist representation of race, while "History of Magic in North America" offers a realist misappropriation of race. In both cases, the resulting realism undermines the works' fantasy for readers whose everyday realities elude Rowling's realism.

If the realities of race remain absent from the play's script, missing, too, are representations of diverse gender identities and sexual orientations. While experiencing the world of *The Cursed Child*, readers have questioned why the relationship between Albus and Scorpius must toe a heteronormative line by the play's end. In a twenty-first-century wizarding world—and in our twenty-first-century world, where Rowling has announced that Dumbledore is gay[41] and that gay students attend Hogwarts[42]—couldn't the emotional and physical connections between Albus and Scorpius offer the possibility of same-sex love? Some readers fill the realist gap on Rowling's behalf, since Rowling's series provides the means, as Laurie Penny notes, to craft what the author has not: "to shift stories handed down with authority into a co-created continuity, a world that can update and adapt."[43] These readers are performing what Ebony Elizabeth Thomas and Amy Stornaiuolo call "restorying,"[44] finding ways to create revised narratives for themselves and the world. In our contemporary moment, choosing not to realize these alternatives feels like a failure of imagination—and the imagination is one of our most valuable assets, according to Rowling. As she describes in her 2008 commencement address for Harvard University, "The Fringe Benefits of Failure, and the Importance of Imagination," imagination is "the power that enables us to empathise with humans whose experiences we have never shared." While this power is "morally neutral," the imagination can be marshaled to ethical purposes. "We have," as Rowling tells members of the Class of 2008 and their family and friends, "the power to imagine better."[45]

Rowling's first novel following the *Harry Potter* series, *The Casual Vacancy* (2012), shows the condition of contemporary England to be rife with racial and ethnic prejudice, and she demonstrates, through its characters' stories, how we have an obligation to challenge the personal and cultural patterns that prevent empathy and change.[46] In *Casual Vacancy*, Rowling charges us to "imagine better." *Casual Vacancy* advances a solution, as Jackie C. Horne explains in her chapter for this volume, that "lies not solely in empathy, in a multicultural anti-racism approach, but rather in an empathy that *gives rise* to acts of social justice." "History of Magic in North America" and *Cursed Child* fall short of offering this same call to imagination and action in terms of race, consequently faltering in their realism and their fantasy.

Whether returning to the series as adults following its initial publication twenty years earlier or encountering the series now for the first time, younger and older readers engage with Rowling's series and subsequent narratives in the same way that Harry Shaw describes realism: as "the attempt to come to grips with the fact that we live in a historical world." Rowling's series and related Potterverse texts, read as and for realism, are for many contemporary readers an attempt "to place us in history"[47] for a better understanding of and for action within the current political moment. For a growing number of readers, "Magic in North America" and *Cursed Child* mark a dystopian future for the Potterverse: the cultural juggernaut that is the Harry Potter phenomenon should provide, through realism and fantasy, a collective opportunity "to imagine better." It is an opportunity that we can take up, separate from or with Rowling, as we create, through a fantastic realism, our own ethically imagined alternative worlds for our future.

Notes

1. Pennington, "From Elfland to Hogwarts," 78–97.

2. "Genre," in Cobley, "Glossary."

3. Goldman, *On Drama*.

4. See, for instance, Bloom, "Can 35 Million Book Buyers Be Wrong?"; Hensher, "Harry Potter, Give Me a Break"; Byatt, "Harry Potter and the Childish Adult," 13; and Levy and Mendlesohn, *Children's Fantasy Literature*.

5. "History of Magic in North America," a collection of original writings authored by Rowling, first appeared on the website Pottermore. These materials have since been republished in full at Rowling's newer site, Wizarding World, at http://www.wizardingworld.com, but without the overarching title "History of Magic in North America." Given this chapter's focus on their appearance in 2016, I will use the original web page title "History of Magic in North America" and refer to Pottermore as the site of publication. To view the content as it initially appeared at Pottermore, visit the Internet Archive's screen capture at https://web.archive.org/web/20160319063741/https://www.pottermore.com/collection-episodic/history-of-magic-in-north-america-en.

6. See, for instance, Horne, "Harry and the Other," 76–104, and Horne's updated chapter in this volume, "Harry and the Other: Multicultural and Social Justice Anti-Racism in J. K. Rowling's *Harry Potter* Series"; Whited, "1492, 1942, 1992: The Theme of Race"; Green, "Revealing Discrimination"; Velazquez, "The Occasional Ethnicities of Lavender Brown"; and Penny, "Harry Potter and the Conscience of a Liberal."

7. See Westman, "Beyond Periodization," 464–69; and Westman, "Genre," 85–88. Selected portions of those essays appear here in whole or in modified form.

8. Abrams, "Genre," 75–78.

9. Frow, *Genre*.

10. Todorov, *Genres in Discourse*, 10.

11. "Genre," in Cobley, "Glossary."

12. Devitt, *Writing Genres*, 7.

13. Goldman, *On Drama*, 8.

14. Goldman, *On Drama*, 4–5.

15. Anelli and Spartz, "The Leaky Cauldron and Mugglenet Interview."

16. Hunt, *Children's Literature*, 271.

17. Hunt, *Children's Literature*, 271.

18. Zipes et al., *The Norton Anthology of Children's Literature*, 555.

19. Egoff, *Worlds Within*, 6.

20. Zipes et al., *The Norton Anthology of Children's Literature*, 555.

21. Baker, "Fantasy," 77.

22. Shaw, *Narrating Reality*, 16, 36.

23. Bloom, "Can 35 Million Book Buyers Be Wrong?"

24. Pennington, "From Elfland to Hogwarts."

25. Rowling, "History of Magic in North America."

26. See Booth, *The Rhetoric of Fiction*, for a discussion of the implied author.

27. Booth, *The Rhetoric of Fiction*.

28. In her 1985 essay "Varieties of Children's Metafiction," Anita Moss describes metafictions as "works in which the imagined process by which the story is created becomes a central focus of the book" (79): "stories within stories interlace to form an overarching structure," and "characters function as both tellers and listeners" (80), in order to explore concerns about the relationship between art and life. "This metafictional quality," Moss continues, can be either "implicit" or "explicit" (80). Implicit metafictions will locate their "critical concerns about the nature of narrative in the dramatic and emotional conflicts of their characters" (91). By contrast, explicit metafictions "concentrate upon the process of their own making" (88), "self-consciously exploring" those critical concerns through "fictional authors" (91). Rowling's *Harry Potter* series, I believe, is best categorized as an implicit metafiction: for all of its references to characters' experiences with books, the series draws attention to story-making through the characters' interactions with each other and their attempts to shape their own history. Rowling's expansion of the Potterverse in "History of Magic in North America" is not.

29. Hutcheon, *The Politics of Postmodernism*, 53, 51.

30. Hutcheon, *The Politics of Postmodernism*, 53.

31. Rowling, "In my wizarding world."

32. Weasley, "Yes, no skin-walkers." On the same day, @weasleydad offers a similar statement in another post in a separate thread: "Ok, but she's only saying that, in her world, the skin-walkers didn't exist . . . in 'her' fictional world. It's fiction."

33. Rowling, Tiffany, and Thorne, *Harry Potter and the Cursed Child*.

34. Kakutani, "Review: 'Harry Potter and the Cursed Child.'"

35. Tolentino, "Finally, A New Harry Potter Story Worth Reading."

36. Rowling, Tiffany, and Thorne, *Harry Potter and the Cursed Child*, 19, 60, 153.

37. Rowling, *Harry Potter and the Philosopher's Stone*, 9.

38. See Tan, "Noma Dumezweni Cast as Hermione"; and Khomami, "JK Rowling 'Loves Black Hermione.'"

39. See, for instance, Bennett, "What a 'Racebent' Hermione Granger Really Represents"; and Ramaswamy, "Can Hermione Be Black?"

40. Rowling, "Canon: brown eyes."

41. Edward TLC, "J. K. Rowling at Carnegie Hall."

42. Rowling, "But of course."

43. Penny, "Harry Potter and the Conscience of a Liberal."

44. Thomas and Stornaiuolo, "Restorying the Self."

45. Rowling, "The Fringe Benefits of Failure."

46. Rowling, *The Casual Vacancy*.

47. Shaw, *Narrating Reality*, 6, 36.

Bibliography

Abrams, M. H. "Genre." In *A Glossary of Literary Terms*, 75–78. 6th ed. New York: Harcourt Brace Jovanovich, 1993.

Anelli, Melissa, and Emerson Spartz. "The Leaky Cauldron and Mugglenet Interview with Joanne Kathleen Rowling." The Leaky Cauldron, July 16, 2005. http://www.the-leaky -cauldron.org/2007/09/10/jkr1/.

Baker, Deirdre. "Fantasy." In *Keywords for Children's Literature*, edited by Philip Nel, Lissa Paul, and Nina Christensen, 77. New York: New York University Press, 2021.

Bennett, Alanna. "What a 'Racebent' Hermione Granger Really Represents." BuzzFeed, February 1, 2015. https://www.buzzfeed.com/alannabennett/what-a-racebent-hermione -granger-really-represen-d2yp?utm_term=.dcq92wRKv#.ntRXBn9Kz.

Bloom, Harold. "Can 35 Million Book Buyers Be Wrong? Yes." *Wall Street Journal*, July 11, 2000.

Booth, Wayne C. *The Rhetoric of Fiction*. Chicago: University of Chicago Press, 1963.

Byatt, A. S. "Harry Potter and the Childish Adult." *New York Times*, July 7, 2003.

Cobley, Paul. "Glossary." In *Narrative*, 243–61. London: Routledge, 2001.

Devitt, Amy J. *Writing Genres*. Carbondale: Southern Illinois University Press, 2004.

Edward TLC, "J. K. Rowling at Carnegie Hall Reveals Dumbledore Is Gay; Neville Marries Hannah Abbott, and Much More." The Leaky Cauldron, October 20, 2007. http://www .the-leaky-cauldron.org/2007/10/20/j-k-rowling-at-carnegie-hall-reveals-dumbledore -is-gay-neville-marries-hannah-abbott-and-scores-more/.

Egoff, Sheila A. *Worlds Within: Children's Fantasy from the Middle Ages to Today*. Chicago: American Library Association, 1988.

Frow, Jonathan. *Genre*. Abingdon, Oxon., England: Routledge, 2005.

Goldman, Michael. *On Drama: Boundaries of Genre, Borders of Self*. Ann Arbor: University of Michigan Press, 2000.

Green, Amy M. "Revealing Discrimination: Social Hierarchy and the Exclusion/ Enslavement of the Other in the Harry Potter Novels." *Looking Glass* 13, no. 3 (2009). https://ojs.latrobe.edu.au/ojs/index.php/tlg/article/view/162.

Hensher, Philip. "Harry Potter, Give Me a Break." *Guardian*, January 25, 2000.

Horne, Jackie C. "Harry and the Other: Answering the Race Question in J. K. Rowling's *Harry Potter*." *The Lion and the Unicorn* 34, no.1 (January 2010): 76–104.

Hunt, Peter. *Children's Literature*. Oxford: Blackwell, 2001.

Hutcheon, Linda. *The Politics of Postmodernism*. London: Routledge, 1989.

Kakutani, Michiko. "Review: 'Harry Potter and the Cursed Child' Explores the Power of Time." *New York Times*, August 1, 2016. http://www.nytimes.com/2016/08/02/books /harry-potter-and-the-cursed-child-review.html?_r=0.

Keene, Adrienne. "Dear JK Rowling, I'm Concerned about the American Wizarding School." *Native Appropriations* (blog), June 9, 2015. http://nativeappropriations.com/2015/06 /dear-jk-rowling-im-concerned-about-the-american-wizarding-school.html.

Keene, Adrienne. "Magic in North America Part 1: Ugh." *Native Appropriations* (blog), March 8, 2016. http://nativeappropriations.com/2016/03/magic-in-north-america-part -1-ugh.html.

Keene, Adrienne. "'Magic in North America': The Harry Potter Franchise Veers Too Close to Home." *Native Appropriations* (blog), March 7, 2016. http://nativeappropriations.com/2016 /03/magic-in-north-america-the-harry-potter-franchise-veers-too-close-to-home.html.

Khomami, Nadia. "JK Rowling 'Loves Black Hermione' Casting of Noma Dumezweni." *Guardian*, December 21, 2015. https://www.theguardian.com/books/2015/dec/21/jk -rowling-loves-black-hermione-casting-noma-dumezweni.

LaCapra, Dominick. *History, Politics, and the Novel*. Ithaca, NY: Cornell University Press, 1987.

Lee, Paula Young. "Pottermore Problems: Scholars and Writers Call Foul on J. K. Rowling's North American Magic." *Salon*, July 1, 2016. http://www.salon.com/2016/07/01/pottermore _problems_scholars_and_writers_call_foul_on_j_k_rowlings_north_american_magic/.

Levy, Michael, and Farah Mendlesohn. *Children's Fantasy Literature: An Introduction*. Cambridge: Cambridge University Press, 2016.

Moss, Anita. "Varieties of Children's Metafiction." *Studies in the Literary Imagination* 18, no. 2 (Fall 1985): 79–92.

Pennington, John. "From Elfland to Hogwarts; or, The Aesthetic Trouble with Harry Potter." *The Lion and the Unicorn* 26, no. 1 (January 2002): 78–97.

Penny, Laurie. "Harry Potter and the Conscience of a Liberal." *The Baffler*, September 2, 2016. https://thebaffler.com/blog/harry-potter-laurie-penny.

Ramaswamy, Chitra. "Can Hermione Be Black? What a Stupid Question." *Guardian*, December 21, 2015. https://www.theguardian.com/books/shortcuts/2015/dec/21 /hermione-granger-black-noma-dumezwani-harry-potter-cursed-child.

Reese, Debbie. "Native People Respond to Rowling." *American Indians in Children's Literature* (blog), March 10, 2016. https://americanindiansinchildrensliterature.blogspot .com/2016/03/native-people-respond-to-rowling.html.

Rowling, J. K. *The Casual Vacancy*. London: Little, Brown, 2012.

Rowling, J. K. "The Fringe Benefits of Failure, and the Importance of Imagination." *Harvard Gazette*, June 5, 2008. http://news.harvard.edu/gazette/story/2008/06/text-of-j-k -rowling-speech/.

Rowling, J. K. *Harry Potter and the Philosopher's Stone*. London: Bloomsbury, 1997.

Rowling, J. K. "History of Magic in North America." Pottermore, March 8, 2016. https:// www.pottermore.com/collection-episodic/history-of-magic-in-north-america-en. Archived at https://web.archive.org/web/2016031906374l/https://www.pottermore.com /collection-episodic/history-of-magic-in-north-america-en.

Rowling, J. K. (@jk_rowling). "But of course." Twitter, December 16, 2014. https://twitter.com /jk_rowling/status/544998416414412801.

Rowling, J. K. (@jk_rowling). "Canon: brown eyes, frizzy hair and very clever." Twitter, December 21, 2015. https://twitter.com/jk_rowling/status/678888094339366914?lang=en.

Rowling, J. K. (@jk_rowling). "In my wizarding world." Twitter, March 8, 2016. https:// twitter.com/jk_rowling/status/707219455621857280?lang=en.

Rowling, J. K., John Tiffany, and Jack Thorne. *Harry Potter and the Cursed Child*. New York: Scholastic, 2016.

Sepsey, Loralee. "Dear JK Rowling: We're Still Here." *Natives in America*, July 1, 2016. http:// nativesinamerica.com/2016/07/dear-jk-rowling-were-still-here/.

Shaw, Harry E. *Narrating Reality: Austen, Scott, Eliot*. Ithaca, NY: Cornell University Press, 1999.

Tan, Monica. "Noma Dumezweni Cast as Hermione in New Harry Potter Stage Play." *Guardian*, December 21, 2015. https://www.theguardian.com/film/2015/dec/21/noma -dumezweni-cast-as-hermione-in-new-harry-potter-stage-play.

Thomas, Ebony Elizabeth, and Amy Stornaiuolo. "Restorying the Self: Bending toward Textual Justice." *Harvard Educational Review* 86, no. 3 (Fall 2016): 313–38.

Todorov, Tzvetan. *Genres in Discourse*. Translated by Catherine Porter. Cambridge: Cambridge University Press, 1990.

Tolentino, Jia. "Finally, A New Harry Potter Story Worth Reading." *New Yorker*, August 8, 2016. http://www.newyorker.com/books/page-turner/finally-a-new-harry-potter-story -worth-reading.

Weasley, Arthur (@Weasley_dad). "Ok, but she's only saying." Twitter, March 8, 2016. https:// twitter.com/Weasley_dad/status/707333356002918400.

Weasley, Arthur (@Weasley_dad). "Yes, no skin-walkers." Twitter, March 8, 2016. https:// twitter.com/Weasley_dad/status/707361774752890880.4.

Westman, Karin E. "Beyond Periodization: Children's Literature, Genre, and Remediating Literary History." *Children's Literature Association Quarterly* 38, no. 4 (Winter 2013): 464–69.

Westman, Karin E. "Genre." In *Keywords for Children's Literature*, edited by Philip Nel, Lissa Paul, and Nina Christensen, 85–88. New York: New York University Press, 2021.

White, Hayden. *The Content of the Form: Narrative Discourse and Historical Representation*. Baltimore: Johns Hopkins University Press, 1987.

Whited, Lana. "1492, 1942, 1992: The Theme of Race in the Harry Potter Series." *Looking Glass* 10, no. 1 (2006). https://ojs.latrobe.edu.au/ojs/index.php/tlg/article/view/97.

Velazquez, Maria. "The Occasional Ethnicities of Lavender Brown: Race as a Boundary Object in Harry Potter." In *Critical Insights: Contemporary Speculative Fiction*, edited by M. Keith Booker, 100–114. Ipswich, MA: Salem Press, 2013.

Zipes, Jack, Lissa Paul, Lynne Vallone, Peter Hunt, and Gillian Avery, eds. *The Norton Anthology of Children's Literature: The Traditions in English*. New York: W. W. Norton, 2005.

The Magical (Racial) Contract

Understanding the Wizarding World
of Harry Potter through Whiteness

Christina M. Chica

Race is fashioned through racialization/racial formation—a fluid and dynamic social and historical process that involves creating institutions that produce racial subjects.[1] Race is foundational to J. K. Rowling's *Harry Potter* series and is best illuminated by examining the structural context of magical beings. Previous scholarship has demonstrated the utility of analyzing marginalized magical others through the lens of race[2] even if one could think of magical others as creatures warranting an interspecies analysis.[3] Racialization has historically rendered non-White others synonymous with different species.[4] If racially othered human beings can be made subhuman via fabricated but consequential biological distinctions, then one's personhood is not contingent on being human. Magical others are marginalized differently with different consequences.

In this chapter, I tie together examples of structural racism and racial formation in the Wizarding world discussed by other scholars through an analysis of White supremacy, which I understand to be mutually constitutive with capitalism and colonialism. Some understand this relationship through the term "racial capitalism," which Jasmine Wade expands upon in this volume. I argue that we can understand the structural context of race in our world and the Wizarding world philosophically by drawing on Charles Mills's *The Racial Contract* (1997) to illuminate what I call the "Magical Contract." I do not center the British colonial middle-class perspective that is Rowling's personal frame of reference[5] as the basis of the magical racial context, both because I am more familiar with US examples and because these power structures were/are internationally constructed and globally consequential.

I use Mills's philosophical scaffolding to demonstrate the logic behind a magical racial order in which Wizards—like White people—sit atop a racial hierarchy with other magical beings—like non-White people—positioned below them.[6] I deploy additional scholarship to argue that (1) human mixing across blood status (pure, half, Muggle) approximates the historical and sociological process of immigrant assimilation into Whiteness rather than interracial acceptance, and that (2) true miscegenation—reproduction between humans and nonhumans—is exceptional and largely repudiated.

To be clear, I am not making claims about Rowling's intellectual or political intentions about race, multiculturalism, or antiracism in this chapter; there is a wealth of scholarship that does just that—including other chapters in this volume.[7] Rather, I am interpreting this magical world as it has been constructed by exploring imperfect similarities between it and the social and historical facts within our "nonmagical" embodied reality. I provide a heuristic aided by concepts developed through real-world empirical examples of hierarchy and stratification across disciplines (legal studies, sociology of migration, political science, history) to be used to understand the Wizarding world.

The Magical (Racial) Contract Is Useful

Wizardness (Whiteness) is maintained by property and power over others. In a 1993 article, "Whiteness as Property," law professor Cheryl Harris historically and legally explores how Whiteness as a form of identity evolved into a form of property.[14] Property, in this case, means access to privileges and rights in addition to material goods. As Harris argues: "The possessors of whiteness were granted the legal right to exclude others from the privileges inhering in whiteness; whiteness became an exclusive club whose membership was closely and grudgingly guarded."[15] The pivotal case *Plessy v. Ferguson* is one example Harris uses to demonstrate a vested property interest in Whiteness and how the court system denying someone's Whiteness results in lost privileges, capital, and property.

Harris's concept of Whiteness as property is useful for understanding Wizardness as an exclusive group with privileges and property interests. Being a Wizard is synonymous with access to a particular piece of property— a wand. Rather than through phenotype, visual recognition of Wizardness happens through wand possession. Membership in the category of Wizard is not determined by magical ability but rather by permission to possess a wand. Insofar as property matters for power, denying property is the denial of power. Wand possession is symbolically powerful because it signals parity, and it is materially powerful because a wand is a well-protected magical tool.

As Harris has demonstrated with US courts protecting the exclusivity of Whiteness, Wizarding courts are integral to formally drawing boundaries between those who are real Wizards and those who are not. Wand possession is racial; other magical creatures are not allowed to possess wands[16] or the secrets of wand-making—as the Goblin Griphook reveals in *Harry Potter and the Deathly Hallows* (488). Wands are for Wizards, Muggles who become Wizards, and exceptional interracial others like Rubeus Hagrid (half Giant and half Wizard; *Harry Potter and the Goblet of Fire*, 428) and Fleur Delacour (a witch with Veela heritage; *HP and the GF*, 308). In *Deathly Hallows*, Ministry courts begin questioning employees' blood status and legitimate possession of their wands on the grounds that those born to Muggles cannot legitimately be Wizards. While Muggle-born Wizards can be compared to assimilated White people, pure-blood racial extremists—like White supremacists with regard to Jewish people—continue to see them as racial others without legitimate claims to Wizardness.

Radical pure-bloods and mainstream Wizards do not question the exclusivity of their Wizarding club, only where to draw the boundaries of membership. Radical pure-bloods might hate anyone who is not like them, but "liberal" Wizards make the distinction between Muggle-born Wizards and magical others, because Wizards with Muggle heritage are virtually indistinguishable from other Wizards over time through the process of assimilation. Just like European immigrants to the United States have shed their ethnic traits over time, so have Wizards with Muggle heritage. Yet, Muggle-born Wizards are not safe from radical pure-bloods. In *Deathly Hallows*, we see how Muggle-borns are rounded up, placed on a registry, and stripped of their claim to Wizardness (Whiteness) through confiscation of their wand (property) (*HP and the DH*, 209). For radical pure-blood Wizards, Muggle-born assimilation is not valid or even possible.

Institutional power goes beyond arbitrating claims to Wizardness. The Ministry of Magic is a governmental body run by Wizards that is responsible for regulating much of the activity of magical others.[17] Like Whiteness in its mutually constituting relationships with colonialism and capitalism, Wizardness involves dispossession. Rubeus Hagrid alludes to dispossession during a conversation with Harry and Hermione in the Forbidden Forest in which he predicts a Centaur revolt if the Ministry continues to limit the Centaurs' territory.[18] In contrast, Giants—who are seen as barbaric and self-destructive—are dispelled to mountain regions far away (*Harry Potter and the Order of the Phoenix*, 426–30).

Informal attitudes of Wizard superiority and magical strength also perpetuate Wizarding rule. In this way, the Magical Contract is both moral and epistemic, as I describe later in this chapter. Within Wizard-run institutions like the Ministry of Magic and Hogwarts School, political power rests on these informal (one might say cultural) understandings of superiority among Wizards. Lucius Malfoy (a sort of lobbyist who leverages powerful relationships at the Ministry) and Albus Dumbledore (the headmaster of Hogwarts) exemplify how status shaped by wealth and blood-purity in the first case and by exceptional magical achievement in the second facilitate institutional power.

Like for Whiteness, advantages in material accumulation are weighed in favor of those with the greatest claim to Wizardness through racial purity. If Wizards sit atop the racial hierarchy in the magical world, then pure-bloods traditionally sit atop the Wizarding hierarchy. These old Wizarding families typically have an economic privilege that corresponds to their racial privilege. As hinted in several *Harry Potter* books and confirmed in *Deathly Hallows*, they have come to possess over many generations the oldest, largest, and most protected vaults in the Goblin-run Gringotts Bank (*HP and the DH*, 509). This class standing is so taken for granted that the relative poverty of the Weasley family is the sticking point of ridicule that the Malfoys levy upon them, in addition to their unacceptable "love" of Muggles.

The Magical (Racial) Contract Is Real

In *The Racial Contract*, Charles Mills—in the spirit of classical Western philosophers who have used "contract" as a useful term to imagine what a just society should look like—proposes the "Racial Contract."[8] Mills uses this tradition beyond imagining a moral ideal to explain our historically and sociologically observable reality. This reality is one of White racial domination through a sometimes tacit and sometimes explicit agreement among White people to rule over non-White others. This agreement or "contract" is multidimensional as it is simultaneously "political, moral, and epistemological. . . . [A]nd economically, in determining who gets what, the Racial Contract is an exploitation contract."[9] The creation and reproduction of this agreement mutually facilitates and is facilitated by colonialism and capitalism. While we cannot neatly compare the historical structures of capitalism, colonialism, and White supremacy to possibly analogous structures in the Wizarding world, we can tease out similarities in the overall structure by comparing aspects of the Racial Contract to those of the Magical Contract.

The Racial Contract is not about race as much as it is about Whiteness; likewise, the Magical Contract is not about magic as much as it is about Wizardness. Mills tells us that "[a]ll whites are *beneficiaries* of the Contract, though some whites are not *signatories*."[10] In other words, White people are structurally privileged in this agreement over non-White people even if they do not agree with it or have the power to shape it. Wizards benefit from maintaining the magical racial order even if they see the position of other magical beings and creatures as unjust. The Weasleys, even in their relative poverty and low-status position,[11] can access the distinction and recognition of being pure-bloods and the protection that entails. In fact, although the Weasleys suffer from their low status relative to some of their pure-blood peers, Ron Weasley often promotes the status quo by playing devil's advocate during Hermione Granger's efforts to free house-elves—the enslaved servant class.[12] Sirius Black may have deviated from his family's political agenda by rejecting pure-blood ideology, but he nevertheless benefits from the services of his house-elf, Kreacher, whom he treats with disdain and whom Harry Potter continues to use as a bound servant even after having earlier disrupted the racial order by freeing Dobby—the Malfoy family's house-elf.[13]

The Magical (Racial) Contract Is Political

While magical others are marginalized as a group, a select few—either through their relationships with politically powerful people or their inter-racial claims to Wizardness—can live among Wizards and influence their ways of knowing. Political scientist Cathy Cohen describes this process of a select few people having access to dominant institutions and space as "integrative marginalization." Cohen "examines the political processes of black communities"[19] and conceptualizes different forms of marginalization to understand how Black people resist and function inside White society.

For Cohen, integrative marginalization refers to the limited mobility open to a select few marginal group members—typically Black elites inside White institutions. In the Wizarding world, selection for special status is based on racial proximity and/or personal relationships that result in proximity to power. Racial proximity for magical others is achieved through miscegenation. Rubeus Hagrid is half Giant and half Wizard; Professor Flitwick is rumored to have some Goblin ancestry due to his short stature;[20] Madame Olympe Maxime surely carries Giant heritage but knows to refrain from acknowledging it due to stigma (*HP and the GF*, 428–29);[21] and Fleur Delacour is part Veela.

Mixed-race Wizards are part of the select few included racial others because of their claim to Wizardness through a Wizard parent. As we learn in the series, this privilege is ultimately taken away from Hagrid when his wand is broken (*Harry Potter and the Sorcerer's Stone*, 83). These select few can integrate into Wizarding society and may play significant roles as intermediaries for those in power, like non-White elites in our society. We see this in Hagrid and Olympe's mission to recruit Giants for the fight against Voldemort despite their mistreatment by Wizards (*HP and the OP*, 424–33). Of course, while those from non-Wizard races are othered, the treatment that individuals from different social locations receive is disparate. Someone like Fleur, who is magically skilled and whose mixed parentage heightens her beauty—a sort of "model minority"—is treated better than Hagrid. Apart from her individual talent, Fleur may fare better due to the sexual exoticization of Veelas discussed by Amy Green; Hannah Lamb applies Edward Said's concept of Orientalism to Veelas.[22]

These select few incorporated into important social positions are not exclusively mixed-race individuals. Non-Wizard others, like non-White others, are incorporated due to their relational proximity to power, or their usefulness. Firenze is a Centaur who befriends and aids Wizards—activities Centaurs forbid, which results in his exile (*HP and the OP*, 602). His relationship with Albus Dumbledore, paired with his extraordinary ability to read stars and his mystical insight, facilitate both his hiring as a professor of divination at Hogwarts and his protection from those who wish to harm him for his perceived betrayal (*HP and the OP*, 599–603). This opportunity to teach and live among Wizards, however, is not a pathway to becoming a Wizard. That privilege is not open to Firenze. Nevertheless, his presence provides the opportunity for young Wizards to glimpse other ways of knowing and thinking, which I discuss at greater length below.

The Magical (Racial) Contract Is Moral

At the foundation of Wizard morality is respect for the autonomy, dignity, and safety of other Wizards. Wizards are not all equal in power, status, or magical skill, so there are many ways to endanger others. At a minimum, there is a basic regard for Wizard life that is expressed through a categorical ban on the Imperius (controlling) curse, the Cruciatus (torturing) curse, and the killing curse. These Unforgiveable Curses are heavily punished and used mostly by "dark Wizards." Mad-Eye Moody confirms that these curses are the most heavily punished and alludes to higher moral regard for Muggles over magical others by stating: "The use of any one of them on a fellow human being is enough to earn a life sentence in Azkaban" (*HP and the GF*, 217). A categorical ban on the use of these curses—even across axes of authority and power within the Wizard category—suggests that Wizards see each other as standing atop the same moral plane; Wizards are all people. What is more, Muggles—with their potential to birth Wizards—are also people. Meanwhile, non-Wizard magical beings, like non-Whites, are often shown to be not worthy of the same respect for autonomy, dignity, and safety.

Historically, non-Whites were "relegated to a lower rung on the moral ladder (the Great Chain of Being)" to distinguish between people and "racial subpersons," in other words, distinguishing who was and was not entitled to equal rights based on personhood.[23] This lower designation would likewise morally justify slavery, genocide, and extraction economies around the world for European benefit. This categorization of non-Whites normalized the exploitation of racialized others. Moving into the magical world, the logic goes that house-elf enslavement is justifiable because house-elves naturally want to serve. George Weasley, for example, justifies house-elf slavery to Hermione by claiming: "They're happy" (*HP and the GF*, 239). In fact, freeing them could have dire psychological consequences, like in the case of

Winky—the house-elf dismissed from the powerful Crouch family who would drink herself into a stupor in the Hogwarts School's kitchen because she saw "freedom" as a terrible fate (*HP and the OP*, 385–87). We also normalize exploitation through language. Dolores Umbridge from the Ministry of Magic refers to Centaurs as "half-breeds" and "creatures of near-human intelligence" when she encounters them in the Forbidden Forest (*HP and the OP*, 754–55). She makes clear that their place is below Wizards and, as such, feels justified to use near-fatal force when they are defiant.

Wizards normalize the oppression of racially distant magical others but are benevolent toward racially close nonmagical others, or Muggles. Radical pure-bloods like Lord Voldemort treat Muggles as subhuman or as another species, but the mainstream Wizarding population respects Muggle independence and protects them from harm. The magical potential of some Muggles, which leads to a process of immigration into the Wizarding world and assimilation into Wizardness, solidifies Wizarding interests in protecting Muggles. There are not enough pure-blood Wizards, so it is Muggles who can sustain the Wizard population even if pure-blood racists see them as no better than other marginalized magical races.[24]

A somewhat similar scenario unfolded in the late nineteenth and early twentieth centuries when large swaths of European immigrants entered the United States looking for work.[25] These immigrant waves largely consisted of uneducated laborers first from Ireland and later Italy and eastern Europe. While the Anglo-American population discriminated against them, over a couple generations, these waves of immigrants were encouraged to fully assimilate into US Whiteness and adopt a pan-ethnic White identity while protecting the boundaries of Whiteness from racial others.[26] Drawing these parallels might be confusing at first, because we know that Wizards are not all White. Yet what matters here is less the phenotype of light skin color, which has not always been constructed as White, and more the temporal and spatial process of moving individuals who have historically been discriminated against—like the Irish—into Whiteness. In this way, I am describing Wizardness as the foundation for the Wizarding world of magic in the way Whiteness has been constructed as a foundation of power in our global world over the past few hundred years.

Just as most non-White people are considered perpetual racial others who are barred from full assimilation, so are magical others barred from assimilation into Wizardness. The Muggle-born are not Wizards because of their ability to do magic—other magical races can do magic. Muggle-borns must first learn about and then be allowed to immigrate into the Wizarding world. Wizard gatekeepers choose to incorporate Muggle-borns like US Whites incorporated European immigrants first into the country as ostracized others, and then into Whiteness as more distant racialized others grew in number. In the Wizarding world, gatekeepers are necessary because the International Confederation of Warlocks' Statute of Secrecy keeps Muggles ignorant of the magical world (*Harry Potter and the Chamber of Secrets*, 21). Hogwarts school officials must invite students, and they are the first to acculturate students from the Muggle world; Albus Dumbledore visits and tells the half-blood Tom Riddle that "[a]ll new Wizards must accept that, in entering our world, they abide by our laws" (*Harry Potter and the Half-Blood Prince*, 273).

Ironically, the same people who are incorporated—Muggle-born Wizards or Wizards with some Muggle parentage—are charged with policing Wizarding boundaries and upholding the Magical Contract. This is not unlike the role played by the Irish in America, who taught newly arrived eastern Europeans how to be racist toward and reinforce boundaries against Black people in the United States.[27] Many Wizards with Muggle parentage deny that parentage, and some are enlisted in the oppression of Muggles and Muggle-born Wizards alike. Voldemort and Severus Snape are the most prominent examples of half-bloods who often pass for pure-bloods and engage in this kind of boundary keeping. Without pure-blood pedigree, being in the club requires both assimilation and reifying the boundaries between Wizards and everyone else.

Lord Voldemort may be enacting a personal vendetta against Muggles, but he is successful at accumulating followers by explicitly invoking the Magical Contract that lies at the foundation of Wizarding society. It is mainstream Wizards who perpetuate the Wizarding racial order by upholding the status quo—tacitly agreeing to the Magical Contract. As Jenn Sims demonstrates in her essay "Wanagoballwitme? Inter 'Racial' Dating at Hogwarts," Wizards can reject expressions of supremacy without rejecting or even interrogating the Wizard supremacist structure in which they live.[28] Hermione and Harry are both immigrants to the Wizarding world by virtue of their upbringing. However, only Harry is bestowed with the privileges associated with having a pure-blood father from an old Wizarding family, like inheriting an invisibility cloak and other riches (*Harry Potter and the Sorcerer's Stone*, 75, 202). Although Hermione and Harry are both taken aback by the marginalization of magical others, Harry is largely ambivalent about Hermione's efforts to fight for systemic change, including the abolition of house-elf slavery (*HP and the GF*, 224–25). Indeed, at the end of the series in a powerful nod to the status quo, Harry wonders if Kreacher would be up for fixing him something to eat upon his return (*HP and the DH*, 749).

The Magical (Racial) Contract Is Epistemic

Beyond coercion and the moral systems that justify coercion, oppression is perpetuated at the level of constituting legitimate knowledge. Mills concedes that we do not often think about contractual philosophy as epistemic, but that inherent in participating in a contractual agreement is a system of determining what is objectively true. What counts as the correct way of interpreting the world? The Racial Contract is epistemic both in establishing Whiteness as the arbiter of legitimate knowledge so that non-White perspectives and contributions are downplayed or ignored, and in prescribing a misunderstanding of the world so "that whites will in general be unable to understand the world they themselves have made."[29] This "misunderstanding, misrepresentation, evasion, and self-deception on matters related to race are among the most pervasive mental phenomena of the past few hundred years, a cognitive and moral economy psychically required for conquest, colonization, and enslavement."[30] In other words, a persistent mental gymnastics that includes collective forgetting, historical obfuscation, and general disassociation from past and present violence has been necessary for White people to sleep at night. Though, of course, some White people have worked and continue to work toward illuminating historical erasures and changing the status quo.

Likewise, Wizards largely take for granted the power structure that they have created; Wizards often overlook the contributions of magical others including their forms of magic, social organization, and understandings of the past. Wizards misunderstand the magical order they have created to morally digest wrongdoing. House-elf magic is powerful; house-elves can apparate and disapparate wherever they please, disarm Wizards of their wands, perform enchantments, and easily locate people.[31] However, their magical ability and power are taken for granted as unthreatening because they form the enslaved servant class of the Wizarding world. Somehow,

Wizards enslaved house-elves, retained sole responsibility for their freedom, and inflicted centuries of psychological damage so that freedom is undesirable and can potentially collapse house-elves' sense of self—like in the case of Winky. Within this reality, Dobby is the exception.

Centaurs and Giants—like others in the magical world—are not only oppressed by Wizards but also culturally misunderstood.[32] This misunderstanding coupled with structural oppression fuels the perspective that magical others are morally or epistemically inferior. Centaurs, who are separatist as a rule, are largely uninterested in the Wizarding world and perhaps do not care to be understood by Wizards. This does not mean, however, that they do not have to contend with the consequences of being viewed as morally or epistemically inferior. Wizard power and authority can affect their quality of life, access to land, resources, peace, and so on.

Goblins are curious magical others in their ability to monopolize metallurgy and banking, securing a more favorable position in the magical hierarchy. Wizards need their services in accumulating, protecting, and creating material wealth. In framing Goblins as categorically astute, mean, and tricky, Wizards acknowledge Goblin racial superiority over enslaved or banished magical others but frame them as morally inferior to Wizards (*HP and the DH*, 506, 516–17).[33] This inferiority is epistemic in that it extends to Goblins' understanding of history and social organization.

The origin story of Godric Gryffindor's sword is an example of competing understandings of history. The story goes that the powerful sword of Hogwarts cofounder Godric Gryffindor was made especially for him by a Goblin. In *Deathly Hallows*, Griphook tells Harry and his friends that the sword belonged to a Goblin king and that Gryffindor had stolen it (*HP and the DH*, 505–6). This is particularly interesting when we learn that Goblins connect ownership to a thing's maker, not to the person who purchased it (*HP and the DH*, 516–17). Purchasing is like leasing; ownership of Goblin-made things is collectively Goblin, and when a Wizard owner of such a property dies, Goblins believe that the property should be returned. Of course, property is not returned in such a matter but rather kept in Wizard hands because this definition of ownership is not legitimate to Wizards. Gryffindor may not have stolen the sword, but whether the sword was made for or purchased by Gryffindor matters. Either way, Wizards maintain their favorable origin stories and hold fast to acquired property rather than engage in a wider search for truth.

Conclusion

The term "Magical Contract" is shorthand for the political, moral, and epistemic foundation of Wizard supremacy in the *Harry Potter* series. The Magical Contract exists to protect and perpetuate Wizarding interests and control over magical others. Access to wands is exclusive to Wizards and necessary for accessing Wizardness. Through the process of integrative marginalization, a select few racialized magical others are included in Wizarding society due to their exceptionality, interracial claims, or special relationships with powerful Wizards. Intermarriage or reproduction between Wizards and Muggles approximates intermarriage or reproduction between US Whites and assimilating European immigrants to the United States. Muggles are incorporated into the Wizarding world by Wizard gatekeepers who determine the boundaries of Wizardness. Magical others in the magical world are not incorporated into Wizardness because they are seen as perpetually unassimilable racial others who can threaten Wizarding control of the magical world, their property (wand; land; house-elves), and their corresponding privileges (political power; freedom of movement).

There are limitations in comparing a fictional world and its social structures to extant social structures—especially the ever-expanding Harry Potter universe that now includes movie adaptations, additional story lines, a huge consumer market, a rich fandom, and post-series author commentary and revisions. Even so, it is worth examining how this extraordinarily influential cultural product with admirable intentions to promote decency, justice, and agency manages to produce racial logics similar to the ones that structure our world. There are moments of justice, underdog triumph, and respect for the other in the interactions Harry Potter and his friends have with other characters. Yet, the larger structure of oppression based in Wizard supremacy is left intact. J. K. Rowling's books condemn a particular brand of radical pure-blood extremism without condemning the tacitly Wizard supremacist foundation of the magical world she has constructed.

To tear up the Magical Contract would require disinvesting from Wizardness. To be clear, disinvesting from Wizardness is not about hiding or downplaying that one is a Wizard but rather about working to make the magical world, through relationships and institutions, one where Wizards are beings among many. This means negotiating power, resources, knowledge, and place as beings among many and not through a conjured superiority imposed on magical lived reality.

Notes

1. Omi and Winant, *Racial Formation in the United States*.

2. Some of this work includes Green, "Revealing Discrimination"; Horne, "Harry and the Other"; and Anatol, "The Replication of Victorian Racial Ideology."

3. Batty, "Harry Potter and the (Post)Human Animal Body."

4. Kendi, *Stamped from the Beginning*.

5. For more on this, see Lamb, "The Wizard, the Muggle, and the Other"; Baker, "You Have Your Mother's Eyes"; Anatol, "The Replication of Victorian Racial Ideology"; Rangwala, "A Marxist Inquiry"; and Park, "Class and Socioeconomic Identity."

6. We can understand Wizards as White while Goblins, house-elves, Giants, Centaurs, and so on are racialized others with varying degrees of power.

7. See Jasmine Wade's "Harry Potter and Black Liberation Movements: Addressing the Imagination Gap with History" and Jackie C. Horne's "Harry and the Other: Multicultural and Social Justice Anti-Racism in J. K. Rowling's *Harry Potter* Series" in this volume.

8. Mills, *The Racial Contract*.

9. Mills, *The Racial Contract*, 9.

10. Mills, *The Racial Contract*, 11.

11. The Weasley family's poverty is mentioned often in the series; one of the first instances is in *Harry Potter and the Sorcerer's Stone*, 86–87. Their debased position also derives from the low prestige associated with working on Muggle affairs, as discussed by Elizabeth Heilman and Anne Gregory ("Images of the Privileged Insider and Outcast Outsider"); and Alison Baker ("You Have Your Mother's Eyes").

12. Ron is one of several characters who patronize Hermione's antislavery efforts and/ or uphold the house-elf status quo. This is discussed in greater depth by Brycchan Carey ("Hermione and the House-Elves"); and Amy Green ("Revealing Discrimination").

13. We learn more about Black's family history and his relationship to Kreacher in *Harry Potter and the Order of the Phoenix*. Harry frees Dobby in *Harry Potter and the Chamber of Secrets*, 337–38.

14. Harris, "Whiteness as Property," 1707.

15. Harris, "Whiteness as Property," 1736.

16. The Code of Wand Use states that "*no non-human creature is permitted to carry or use a wand*" (*HP and the GF*, 132).

17. Hannah Lamb discusses regulation and control of magical others' activity including reproduction, and the colonial implications thereof, in greater depth in "The Wizard, the Muggle, and the Other."

18. While this scene occurs in the movie version of *Harry Potter and the Order of the Phoenix*, territorial conflicts are alluded to several times in the book series, such as during an altercation between Centaurs and Hagrid (*HP and the OP*, 698–99) and between Centaurs and Dolores Umbridge (*HP and the OP*, 754–55).

19. Cohen, *The Boundaries of Blackness*, 9.

20. While my intention is to rely on the written series as my primary source rather than venture into the larger Harry Potter universe, this information is taken from J. K. Rowling's official website: http://web.archive.org/web/20070724184245/http://www.jkrowling.com /textonly/en/faq_view.cfm?id=95.

21. See Heilman and Gregory, "Images of the Privileged Insider and Outcast Outsider," for a discussion of Wizard disdain for magical mixing.

22. Green, "Revealing Discrimination"; and Lamb, "The Wizard, the Muggle, and the Other."

23. Mills, *The Racial Contract*, 16.

24. Ron Weasley notes that Wizards would have died out if not for marrying Muggles (*HP and the CS*, 116).

25. Bodnar, *The Transplanted*.

26. The following scholarly sources are relevant here: Bodnar, *The Transplanted*; Roediger and Barrett, "Making New Immigrants 'Inbetween'"; and Kasinitz, "Race, Assimilation, and 'Second Generations.'"

27. Roediger and Barrett, "Making New Immigrants 'Inbetween.'"

28. Sims, "Wanagoballwitme?," 167.

29. Mills, *The Racial Contract*, 18.

30. Mills, *The Racial Contract*, 19.

31. Some examples include Kreacher disapparating from the place Voldemort hides his Horcrux locket while his Wizard master could not (*HP and the DH*, 195–96); Kreacher finding Mundungus Fletcher when he did not want to be found (*HP and the DH*, 220); and Dobby taking Narcissa Malfoy's wand using magic (*HP and the DH*, 474).

32. An example of Wizard ignorance of Centaurs can be found in *Order of the Phoenix*, 601–3; and of Giants in chapter 20 of the same book.

33. Horne ("Harry and the Other") and Anatol ("The Replication of Victorian Racial Ideology") both argue that Goblins represent a more structurally powerful racial other who are allowed through Griphook to denounce Wizard power.

Bibliography

Anatol, Giselle Liza. "The Replication of Victorian Racial Ideology in Harry Potter." In *Reading Harry Potter Again: New Critical Essays*, edited by Giselle Liza Anatol, 109–26. Santa Barbara, CA: Praeger, 2009.

Baker, Alison. "You Have Your Mother's Eyes: Inheritance and Social Class." In *Inside the World of Harry Potter: Critical Essays on the Books and Films*, edited by Christopher E. Bell, 103–15. Jefferson, NC: McFarland, 2018.

Batty, Holly. "Harry Potter and the (Post)Human Animal Body." *Bookbird* 53, no. 1 (February 2015): 24–37. doi:10.1353/bkb.2015.0020.

Bodnar, John. *The Transplanted: A History of Immigrants in Urban America*. Bloomington: Indiana University Press, 1987.

Carey, Brycchan. "Hermione and the House-Elves: The Literary and Historical Contexts of J. K. Rowling's Antislavery Campaign." In *Reading Harry Potter: Critical Essays*, edited by Giselle Liza Anatol, 103–16. Westport, CT: Praeger, 2003.

Cohen, Cathy J. *The Boundaries of Blackness: AIDS and the Breakdown of Black Politics*. Chicago: University of Chicago Press, 1999.

Green, Amy M. "Revealing Discrimination: Social Hierarchy and the Exclusion/ Enslavement of the Other in the Harry Potter Novels." *Looking Glass* 13, no. 3 (2009). http://www.lib.latrobe.edu.au/ojs/index.php/tlg/article/view/162.

Harris, Cheryl I. "Whiteness as Property." *Harvard Law Review* 106, no. 8 (June 1993): 1707–91.

Heilman, Elizabeth E., and Anne E. Gregory. "Images of the Privileged Insider and Outcast Outsider." In *Harry Potter's World: Multidisciplinary Critical Perspectives*, edited by Elizabeth E. Heilman. New York: RoutledgeFalmer, 2003.

Horne, Jackie C. "Harry and the Other: Answering the Race Question in J. K. Rowling's *Harry Potter*." *The Lion and the Unicorn* 34, no. 1 (January 2010): 76–104. doi:10.1353/uni.0.0488.

Kasinitz, Philip. "Race, Assimilation, and 'Second Generations,' Past and Present." In *Not Just Black and White: Historical and Contemporary Perspectives on Immigration, Race, and Ethnicity in the United States*, edited by Nancy Foner and George M. Fredrickson, 278–300. New York: Russell Sage Foundation, 2004.

Kendi, Ibram X. *Stamped from the Beginning: The Definitive History of Racist Ideas in America*. New York: Nation Books, 2016.

Lamb, Hannah. "The Wizard, the Muggle, and the Other: (Post) Colonialism in Harry Potter." In *A Wizard of Their Age: Critical Essays from the Harry Potter Generation*, edited by Cecilia Konchar Farr, 57–72. Albany: State University of New York Press, 2015.

Mills, Charles W. *The Racial Contract*. Ithaca, NY: Cornell University Press, 1997.

Omi, Michael, and Howard Winant. *Racial Formation in the United States: From the 1960s to the 1990s*. New York: Routledge, 1994.

Park, Julia. "Class and Socioeconomic Identity in Harry Potter's England." In *Reading Harry Potter: Critical Essays*, edited by Giselle Liza Anatol, 179–90. Westport, CT: Praeger, 2003.

Rangwala, Shama. "A Marxist Inquiry into J. K. Rowling's Harry Potter Series." In *Reading Harry Potter Again: New Critical Essays*, edited by Giselle Liza Anatol, 127–42. Santa Barbara, CA: Praeger, 2009.

Roediger, David, and James Barrett. "Making New Immigrants 'Inbetween': Irish Hosts and White Panethnicity, 1890 to 1930." In *Not Just Black and White: Historical and Contemporary Perspectives on Immigration, Race, and Ethnicity in the United States*, edited by Nancy Foner and George M. Fredrickson, 167–96. New York: Russell Sage Foundation, 2004.

Rowling, J. K. *Harry Potter and the Chamber of Secrets*. New York: Scholastic, 1999.

Rowling, J. K. *Harry Potter and the Deathly Hallows*. New York: Scholastic, 2007.

Rowling, J. K. *Harry Potter and the Goblet of Fire*. New York: Scholastic, 2000.

Rowling, J. K. *Harry Potter and the Half-Blood Prince*. New York: Scholastic, 2005.

Rowling, J. K. *Harry Potter and the Order of the Phoenix*. New York: Scholastic, 2003.

Rowling, J. K. *Harry Potter and the Prisoner of Azkaban*. New York: Scholastic, 1999.

Rowling, J. K. *Harry Potter and the Sorcerer's Stone*. New York: Scholastic, 1998.

Sims, Jenn. "Wanagoballwitme? Inter 'Racial' Dating at Hogwarts." In *The Sociology of Harry Potter: 22 Enchanting Essays on the Wizarding World*, edited by Jenn Sims, 164–71. Hamden, CT: Zossima Press, 2012.

"Cho Chang Is Trending"

What It Means to Be Asian in the Wizarding World

Sarah Park Dahlen and Kallie Schell

In June 2020, Phil Yu, *Angry Asian Man* blogger, tweeted, "Cho Chang is trending. Over 20 years after she was introduced in Harry Potter and the Prisoner of Azkaban, people are expressing irritation that JK Rowling lazily named her only East Asian character Cho Fucking Chang. Yes, we've been holding on to this one for a long time."[1] "Cho Chang" was trending as part of a catalog of grievances about the Harry Potter phenomenon in response to author J. K. Rowling's transphobic tweets. On June 6, 2020, Rowling infuriated Potter fans when she criticized the use of the word "people" instead "women" in a tweet about menstruation,[2] followed up with transphobic remarks,[3] and then, on June 10, doubled down on these comments in a blog post defending her statements.[4] As part of the pushback to her transphobia, people on Twitter pointed out that Rowling has been deeply problematic for more than twenty years, in both her writings and her attempts to control her fans' reception of the world she had created.

These accusations of transphobia and racism are interesting in light of the research by Loris Vezzali and colleagues, in which they claim that reading the *Harry Potter* series reduces prejudice in young people.[5] To be sure, the *Harry Potter* series addresses themes of injustice and attempts to call out prejudices through discussions regarding magical species and blood status hierarchies. However, Rowling seems to be less concerned about gender or sexual identity and ambivalent about race and racism. Specifically, analyzing the character of Cho Chang is a useful exercise in illuminating how Rowling's treatment of race points to a preference for color blindness and therefore fails to critically engage with how race impacts the lived experiences of young people.

Scholars of the *Harry Potter* series ask a variety of questions to better understand and explain the stories. For example, some address topics such as the role of the library in the wizarding world,[6] Christian interpretations of the story,[7] and whether or not the *Harry Potter* series is as original as many readers believe.[8] There are also scholarship and trade articles focusing on Rowling's emphasis on social justice themes[9] and how race functions in the *Harry Potter* series.[10] These analyses mostly attend to how the hierarchies of "pure-bloods," "Mudbloods," and "Muggles" and the unequal power relationships among wizards, house-elves, and other magical creatures impact each character's experience in the texts. As Philip Nel writes, real-life racial differences and racial discrimination are virtually absent in the books: "Apart from this metaphoric engagement, the books otherwise erase race from the lived experiences of minority characters; skin color and ethnicity are merely descriptors for non-white characters, not salient features of their identities."[11]

Hierarchy and Racialization in the Wizarding World

The inclusion of one-dimensional racialized characters fills a superficial diversity quota, engaging in what Karen Manners Smith calls the "cultural modernization of the school story genre" in which students are "clearly Irish, Indian, West Indian, and Chinese."[12] Characters in the series who appear to be nonwhite—as indicated by their non-British or nonwhite names—are the Patil sisters (Padma and Parvati) and Cho Chang. Padma and Parvati are (South Asian) Indian, and Cho can be either Chinese or Korean. Dean Thomas, Lee Jordan, and Angelina Johnson's names are not tied to Blackness in the same way, but the characters are described as Black and/or having brown skin. These racial minorities are secondary characters, and their nonwhite identities have little bearing on the plot or their character development; Rowling does not share any information about their heritage, families, or backgrounds as they pertain to race or culture.

Giselle Liza Anatol points out that "the novels portray not integration and acceptance, but the complete assimilation of Dean, Lee, Angelina, Parvati, Padma, and Cho into the all-white landscape of Hogwarts students and teachers."[13] Given how thoughtful Rowling is with naming her characters,[14] it is problematic and stereotypical for her to choose names with racial indicators and then not develop them in any meaningful way to integrate their cultural backgrounds into the social structure of Hogwarts. In reality, the lived experiences of racial Others in majority white communities are very much impacted by their perceived Otherness. Indeed, on *The Hooded Utilitarian* blog, Sarah Shoker asks, "If these books are 'very British' and the quintessential 'others' in British society are racialized minorities, then why has race been rendered invisible?"[15]

Race has also been rendered invisible through the ubiquity of whiteness. The trio—Harry, Ron, and Hermione, as well as nearly every wizard in a position of authority—is presented and/or read as white; this racial saturation underscores the white supremacist culture of the wizarding universe. The whiteness of the trio serves as a foil to the characters of color, all of whom are secondary characters. Ebony Elizabeth Thomas writes that she "had trouble imagining the origin stories for Harry Potter's characters of color—most of whom were relegated to the background,"[16] and Anatol points out that readers are regularly given indications of the whiteness of the major characters; Rowling shares extensive background information about their family history and physical characteristics.[17] For example, the Weasley boys are first described as having "flaming red hair" (*Harry Potter and the Sorcerer's Stone*, 92), and Ron is specifically described as "tall, thin, and gangling, with freckles and big hands and feet, and a long nose" (93). The series repeatedly brings up the red hair and freckles that characterize the Weasley family, and readers spend a lot of time with the Weasleys, both in their home and in other spaces, thus offering a "site of grounding for the reader."[18] Harry is also reinforced in whiteness with the repeated emphasis on his green eyes, which connects him to his mother; obviously, Harry's parents play a huge role throughout the series. Even though descriptions of Hermione are more ambiguous, with her first being described as having "lots of bushy brown hair, and rather large front teeth" (*HP and the SS*, 105), through the first couple of books there is no clear reason to believe she was anything but white. It is not until book 3, *Prisoner of Azkaban*, that Rowling describes Hermione explicitly as white: "Hermione's white face was sticking out from behind a tree" (401). In *The Dark Fantastic*, Thomas writes: "I never imagined Hermione Granger as Black. . . . [I]t never occurred to me to unmake my reality to read Hermione as anything other than White."[19] Moreover, illustrator Mary GrandPré's rendering of Hermione on the cover of *Prisoner of Azkaban* shows Harry and a white girl riding on a hippogriff, a scene that takes place in the book. Furthermore, the casting of Daniel Radcliffe, Rupert Grint, and Emma Watson in the movies concretizes the whiteness of the trio in the popular imagination. Therefore, both the texts and films reinforce the whiteness of the wizarding world.

The demographics of both the books and the films communicate a racial hierarchy in which white students are centered, while the more overt hierarchies apply to the blood status and speciesism of magical creatures. First, the categorization of Muggle, half-blood, pure-blood, and Squib is similar to racial categorizations and hierarchies in the real world, and these categories have parallel implications for the way people are treated in the series; characters without pure-blood status face injustice in the wizarding world. In terms of pure-blood wizards, Sirius Black tells Harry that "there are hardly any of us left" (*Harry Potter and the Order of the Phoenix*, 113), and some pure-blood wizards look down on families of half-blood status because they dilute their pure bloodlines. The distinction between half-bloods and pure-bloods is subtle; half-bloods are rarely demonized except by the most extreme pure-bloods, not unlike how white supremacists terrorize people of color. Muggles are more blatantly regarded as Other because they do not have one drop of magical blood. Racial identity dovetails with the symbolic racism in the magical world's blood status hierarchy. The blood status parallel to multiculturalism indicates that Rowling's inclusion of racialized characters—which is not fraught in the same way as blood status hierarchy—is filtered through a colorblind lens. This colorblind lens implies that the wizarding world is postracial, whereas in the real world race permeates every aspect of society.[20] The series substitutes blood status for race by hyperfocusing on blood status, as evidenced by the treatment of Muggles and half-bloods.

Second, as analyzed by Jackie C. Horne (in her chapter in this volume), the relationships between house-elves, goblins, and wizards illustrate Rowling's critique of social hierarchies. Rowling envisions a society that is marred by an obsession with blood status and different types of beings such as house-elves and goblins in an assumingly harmonious, postracial world. However, Horne observes that, "[although] Voldemort's overt racial oppression of Mudbloods has been overturned, the parallel oppression of the elves and goblins that underlines wizarding power must, once again, be repressed, be forgotten, even by the series' self-sacrificing champion of anti-racism."[21] Similarly, Christina M. Chica invokes Charles Mills's "Racial Contract" to explore the idea of what she calls a "Magical (Racial) Contract." In her chapter in this volume, Chica writes: "The Racial Contract is not about race as much as it is about Whiteness; likewise, the Magical Contract is not about magic as much as it is about Wizardness." In her earlier work, "Inter 'Racial' Dating at Hogwarts," Jenn Sims writes that "magic in the wizarding world is *racialized*."[22] She observes that Hogwarts students make no comment about interracial dating, which has a long, contentious history in the actual world, while many comment on romantic relationships between students from different blood status backgrounds in the wizarding world.

The Hogwarts community globalizes in *Harry Potter and the Goblet of Fire* (book 4), in which the students are introduced to the Quidditch World Cup, communicating for the first time to readers that wizarding communities exist in other parts of the world: "It was only just dawning on Harry how many witches and wizards there must be in the world; he had never really thought much about those in other countries" (*HP and the GF*, 81). Although Harry briefly acknowledges this fact, a more distinct introduction to wizards and witches outside of Britain is provided later when the students return to school for their fourth year and are told that they will be hosting a delegation of students from two of the "three largest European schools of wizardry" for the Triwizard Tournament (187). The Beauxbatons and Durmstrang schools are presented as French and "East German–Slavic–Russian,"[23] respectively. Similar to how Rowling never explicitly says that the Patil sisters are Indian or Chang is East Asian, she does not explicitly say that Beauxbatons students are French and Durmstrang students eastern European. That said, earlier in *Goblet of Fire*, Fred says, "Bulgaria has got Viktor Krum" (63),[24] and some scholars have made strong connections between Bulgaria and Durmstrang.[25] Again, Rowling expects readers to deduce their identities primarily based on their dialect, disposition, and/or appearance. Despite the Triwizard Tournament being a friendly competition between wizards and witches of different nationalities, "Rowling's novels do little to alter the Western notion that 'outlying regions of the world have no life, history, or culture to speak of, no independence or integrity worth representing without the West.'"[26]

Cho Chang

It is against this supposedly colorblind backdrop that readers are introduced to Cho Chang in *Harry Potter and the Prisoner of Azkaban*. Gryffindor Quidditch captain Oliver Wood tells Harry, "I've just found out who Ravenclaw is playing as Seeker. It's Cho Chang. She's a fourth year, and she's pretty good" (*HP and the PA*, 254). The first time Harry sees Cho, the text says that she "was shorter than Harry by about a head" and that he "couldn't help noticing, nervous as he was, that she was extremely pretty" (259). Immediately, readers get the following clues about Cho: because she's in Ravenclaw, she is smart; she is one year ahead of Harry but a head shorter; and she is pretty. Karen Manners Smith observes that "Rowling has established Harry's heterosexuality through his attraction to the pretty Cho Chang (coincidentally, also establishing Harry's freedom from race prejudice),"[27] but the first two characteristics—being smart and short—are Asian stereotypes, and the third, being pretty, makes her the object of Harry's white male gaze.[28]

While Rowling choosing to place Cho in Ravenclaw is a clear allusion to the model minority stereotype (a contention that Nadia Adelia also argues[29]), there was no other option: for example, Slytherin would have been a racist overdetermination of the villainous Asian stereotype while Gryffindor would have made her more present, engaged, and involved as a fellow house member. Also, her character is made more complex by other factors, such as how she is a star athlete and proactive in the resistance against Voldemort. For example, she suggests that Harry could see what a diadem looks like by examining the Rowena Ravenclaw statue in their common room (*Harry Potter and the Deathly Hallows*, 584). This, however, could also be read as a secondary character (a girl of color) helping the main character (a white male) achieve his goal, thus relegating her to a supporting role. Louise Derman-Sparks recognizes this dynamic as problematic, asking: "Are whites or male characters the central figures with people of color or female characters in essentially supporting roles?"[30] Cho Chang and all female characters and characters of color are essentially in supporting roles.[31]

One must also consider Cho's relationship to other female characters, especially when in competition for Harry's attention. For example, when Cho volunteers to take Harry to the common room herself, Ginny cuts in "rather fiercely" to suggest that Luna take him instead (*HP and the DH*, 585). Cho had been assertive throughout the meeting until this moment, when she "sat down again, looking disappointed" (*HP and the DH*, 585). Therefore, while readers are introduced to Cho as a star athlete, it's not her primary identifier, especially as her relationship with Harry evolves and in comparison with Ginny (as will be discussed in more detail below). The Asian stereotypes—her name and intelligence—are most visible and memorable to readers.

Throughout *Order of the Phoenix*, Cho Chang continues to be of great interest to Harry, with him repeating how pretty she is, but Rowling does not develop her backstory, rendering her flat in comparison with some of the other emerging characters such as Luna Lovegood and Neville Longbottom. The absence of Cho's backstory—or any character of color's backstory—suggests that race and cultural background do not exist substantially or matter within the world of Harry Potter, or the broader reality of England itself.[32] The absence of a more meaningful backstory or cultural framework for the characters of color also further reifies the notion of white privilege in that readers who are white may not notice or feel the need to understand the experiences of characters of other races; the story wants to be read through a colorblind lens as if race doesn't impact the characters, when in fact only the characters who are white play a substantial role, while characters of color are relegated to the background or act only when they are being used by one of the white characters (such as when Harry and Ron ask Cho and the Patil sisters to the Yule Ball, or when Lee Jordan serves as a commentator at the Quidditch games). This relegation is both subtle and obvious, as those who pay attention to race immediately notice the secondary status of the characters of color.

Cho Chang is the only East Asian–presenting character in the series, but it is not clear whether she is Chinese or Korean, and this ambiguity matters because Korean and Chinese people have distinct experiences due to their patterns of immigration and socialization. This distinction also matters because of the social propensity to collapse all East Asians together, or to assume that anything or anyone Asian is automatically Chinese.[33] Interestingly, some scholars read Cho as likely to be Chinese: Anatol says that "Cho Chang's name suggests that she is Chinese,"[34] and Elaine Ostry states that Cho is "presumably" Chinese.[35] The name "Cho Chang" is one of her most defining characteristics, and yet at the same time it means almost nothing in the text. Rowling's decision not to develop any of the characters of color is lazy and further renders them relatively insignificant in children's literature more broadly.

While the text does not specify whether Chang is Chinese or Korean, costume designers in the fourth movie, *Harry Potter and the Goblet of Fire*, dress Cho in "silver, Chinese-style robes" with geisha-like sleeves[36] for the Yule Ball, as pointed out by Olivia Favreau.[37] Fans have also created artwork depicting Cho Chang as East Asian.[38] Scholars, filmmakers, and fans have decided that Cho does not just "happen to be" Asian; for the most part, they render her as a specific Asian, that is, as Chinese.

Orientalism

Cho Chang's name is an egregious example of Orientalism, defined as "a style of thought based upon an ontological and epistemological distinction made between 'the Orient' and (most of the time) 'the Occident.'"[39] Orientalism is a study of and perspective on the Other, as defined by the center. This application of Orientalism must be understood in light of discussions of microaggressions—the "brief and commonplace daily verbal, behavioral, or environmental indignities, whether intentional or unintentional, that communicate hostile, derogatory, or negative racial slights and insults to people of color."[40] Racial microaggressions are Orientalist when directed at people of Asian descent.

Orientalist perspectives, comments, and behaviors—Orientalist microaggressions—build up over time to racial battle fatigue, which is defined by William Smith, Walter Allen, and Lynette Danley as "the physiological and psychological strain exacted on racially marginalized groups and the amount of energy lost dedicated to coping with racial microaggressions and racism."[41] Smith, Allen, and Danley examine the experiences of Black males in Historically White Institutions, revealing the ways in which these students are stereotyped and hypersurveilled in a variety of campus spaces. For Asians, racial microaggressions include being asked where one is from or how one has learned to speak such good English; these questions presume that Asians are foreigners rather than native to the United States or the United Kingdom. Implied in the questions is, "You're not from here." This racism is covert.

On the other hand, overt racism is intentionally hurtful, hostile, and derogatory. "Ching chong" is an example of an overt racist epithet; according to Wikipedia, "Ching chong or ching chang chong is a pejorative term sometimes employed by speakers of English to mock or play on the Chinese language, people of Chinese ancestry, or other East Asians who may be mistaken for Chinese that resided in Western countries."[42] It is unequivocally a verbal insult and a racial slur. "Ching chong" name-calling is an unfortunate staple of the bullying that Asian Americans face during childhood and young adulthood. Naturally, if one has not experienced a particular microaggression, it is possible to not recognize it. By definition, insiders are privy to certain experiences and knowledge that outsiders are not.

Using "ching chong" in racialized bullying can go viral in the age of social media. This includes Alexandra Wallace's YouTube rant, "Asians in the Library";[43] restaurant tickets on which the cashier wrote "Ching" and "Chong" instead of customers' names; and a similar instance when a cashier wrote "Lee, Ching Chong" rather than the customer's real name (Hyun Lee) on a CVS receipt.[44] The name "Cho Chang" therefore recalls these upsetting familiar racial taunts that many Asian Americans experience; it too closely echoes these racist slurs, and therefore is a microaggression. An Asian American who has been on the receiving end of a "ching chong chang" slur may have been uncomfortable reading the name "Cho Chang" in this series.

As discussed earlier, "Chang" could be either a Korean or Chinese surname. Suman Gupta and Cheng Xiao write:

> To the Chinese [and Korean] reader, "Cho Chang" poses a problem: it doesn't recall clearly any common Chinese name. The nearest sound equivalents to Cho have disagreeable meanings, unsuitable for names. . . . Cho vaguely reveals the quintessential Oriental woman, the Japanese Cho-Cho-San in Madam Butterfly. Both Cho and Chang could be Korean family names rendered in English, but are unlikely first names. At any rate, the name presents a vague East Asian connection but a very tenuous Chinese one.[45]

Gupta and Xiao are not the only scholars to criticize Rowling's use of the name "Cho Chang." Sarah Park makes the same contention, that Cho Chang's name is problematic: "'Cho' and 'Chang' could be either Chinese or Korean, and *both* are surnames."[46] Therefore, says Nel, "using the last name 'Cho' as a first name suggests a lack of cultural knowledge on Rowling's part."[47] Rowling is not the only white author who is out of touch with Asian naming conventions; in *Eleanor and Park* by Rainbow Rowell, one of the two protagonists is named Park, but one critic writes: "His name, Park, is a Korean surname, not an actual first name."[48] Chantal Cheung agrees: "The first issue that stood out to me is that 'Park' is a common Korean last name."[49] Cheung also makes the connection between Park's name and Cho Chang's name: "It is a similar case to J. K. Rowling's Cho Chang; a quick Google search reveals that the so-called first name of an Asian character is actually a common last name."[50]

Nel also observes that the film adaptation of *Harry Potter and the Order of the Phoenix*

> compounds the problematic representation of ethnicity by collapsing Marietta Edgecombe and Cho Chang into the same character. Although this move helps streamline the plot and solidifies Harry's break with Cho, it also means that the only [East] Asian character in the films falls into the stereotype of the "treacherous Asian," suggesting, as Edward Said puts it, that "the Orient at bottom is something either to be feared . . . or controlled."[51]

Chang being described as "pretty," "short," and the object of Harry's white male gaze marks her as what Kent Ono and Vincent Pham describe as a "Lotus Blossom of Madame Butterfly" because she is "sexually attractive and alluring and demure, passive, obedient, physically non-imposing, self-sacrificial, and supplicant (especially to white male suitors)."[52] However, the film transforms her into a Dragon Lady, "a sinister and surreptitious . . . feminized version of yellow peril,"[53] when she betrays Dumbledore's Army. Therefore, the cinematic adjustments made to Cho's character cement her Asianness in stereotypical and harmful ways.

Rachel Rostad's Letter to J. K. Rowling

Similar to how scholars, filmmakers, and fans have read Cho Chang as Chinese, then–college student Rachel Rostad posted a YouTube video of her monologue, "To JK Rowling, from Cho Chang,"[54] in which she also claimed that Cho Chang was Chinese, but given a first and last name that are both Korean last names. Rostad says,

> Ms. Rowling. Let's talk about my name. Cho. Chang.
> Cho and Chang are both last names.
> They are both Korean last names.
> I am supposed to be Chinese.
> Me being named "Cho Chang" is like a Frenchman being named "Garcia Sanchez."

Rostad's criticisms echo Sarah Park's, and Suman Gupta and Cheng Xiao's, observations that Cho Chang's name is racially problematic. She continues, "When you put me in your books, millions of Asian girls across America rejoiced! Finally, a potential Halloween costume that wasn't a geisha or Mulan!," pointing to the fact that Asian girls have limited reflections in popular culture, and consequently, that potential Asian Halloween costumes are limited to the problematic representations of geishas or Disney's Mulan.[55] Echoing Rostad, in the documentary *The Claudia Kishi Club*,[56] young adult writer Sarah Kuhn says: "[U]sually the Asian character or woman of color character is the one you feel like you *have* to be, right? So if you're playing Harry Potter, you have to be Cho Chang."[57] This is confirmed by Lara Jean, the mixed Korean protagonist of the *New York Times* best-selling young adult novel *To All the Boys I've Loved Before*, when she says, "There are very limited options for Asian girls on Halloween. . . . This year I'm going as Cho Chang from *Harry Potter*."[58]

Diana Lee, who at the time was a student in Henry Jenkins's Public Intellectuals seminar at the University of Southern California, wrote on his blog that Rostad "makes the case that when we don't see other representations of characters with depth and breadth that look and sound and think and love like real people, then the limited portrayals can impact not only the possibilities we can imagine for ourselves, but also what others see as possible for or with us."[59] Lee also claims that "JK Rowling intentionally set up Cho as weak to make Ginny, Harry's eventual love interest and a White woman, look stronger."[60] These assertions are supported by Rowling's handwritten notes displayed at *A History of Magic*,[61] an exhibit originally hosted by the British Library in 2017; these notes are also reproduced in the book *Harry Potter: A History of Magic*, a companion to the exhibit.[62] Six pages of handwritten notes include a column titled "Cho/Ginny," indicating that, indeed, Rowling set them up as foils for one another. For example, some notes include these details as Rowling plots out the love triangle: "Cho + Harry back on (ish)"; "miserable Valentine date – row"; "Ginny great [?] Cho wants back – Harry can't take"; "Harry back with Cho at meeting." She also uses Cho and Ginny as foils for one another when she characterizes Cho as "morbid" for being "attracted" to Harry's scar, while Ginny is "practical."[63] This comparison is disingenuous, given that when Ginny first meets Harry Potter at King's Cross Station, she is obsessed with him, and also because everyone is fascinated by Harry's famous scar.

Letters from the Editor

On April 17, 2013, Sarah Park Dahlen sent an email with a link to Rostad's performance to the Child_lit listserv (now shut down).[64] Focusing on Cho Chang's name as a stereotype, Sarah asked, "I'm wondering if you (or anyone else) had thoughts about the (to me) still apparent orientalism in her name? When I read 'Cho Chang,' I hear echoes of the 'ching chong' that is used to mock Asians and Asian Americans; it's a trigger for many of us because of the bullying we experienced and continue to experience."[65] Cheryl Klein, then editor at Arthur A. Levine Books (Scholastic), which publishes the *Harry Potter* books in the United States, responded, "I certainly can't speak for Ms. Rowling here, as I have no idea what her intent was or what kinds of conversations went on around the character's first appearance. But based upon my experience of similar situations with other authors, there are a couple of different possibilities."[66] Klein offered some rationales, beginning with: "She didn't make the 'ching chong' connection that you do," and that it was possible that "[e]ven if it occurred to her that someone might take offense, she really liked the name and wanted to keep it," or that "[s]he actually has a friend named Cho Chang." In a follow-up email, Klein admitted: "Most editors back in 1999 (me included) simply wouldn't have known to question 'Cho Chang' as a name."[67] Regarding the fact that "Cho Chang" sounds similar to "ching chong," she pointed out that the use of "ching chong" as a racist insult is likely more specific to the United States, whereas the series was originally published in the United Kingdom; by the time it was published in the United States, the name would have been established in the UK publication. Regardless, it remains that her name is an Orientalist stereotype, and her character lacks the cultural specificity necessary to make her more three-dimensional. Contacted in 2021, Klein noted that her feelings had changed significantly since 2013 and that she regretted her earlier words.[68]

Conclusion

In *The Dark Fantastic*, Thomas echoes what multiple scholars observed and what we argue in this chapter: "J. K. Rowling's treatment of race in the Harry Potter series almost seems like an afterthought."[69] Readers of Harry Potter—including Asian American readers—learn that Asian girls at Hogwarts are not central characters; that they can be used as a foil for the white girl who eventually marries the hero; that they have stereotypical names like Cho Chang. Young Asian girls know that they are represented in these stories only because Rowling gave a character a stereotypical Asian name.

It's also disappointing that Rowling does not present racial minority characters with any sense of depth or complexity;[70] furthermore, hardly any of the scenes with people of color reflect what might be their actual lived experiences in still racialized societies: "[R]ace and ethnicity *are* not important for those who experience life from this position—hardly true of late twentieth/ early twenty-first century Britain, Canada, the United States, or much of the rest of the world."[71] Britain is a diverse country, but no country is postracial. The *Harry Potter* series could have been a productive site through which to reflect and critique the social realities of the diverse and racially stratified world in which we live. When a character's race is implied through name, national allegiance, and/or racial markers, the question of why these diverse characters exist should have some bearing on the story.

As Rostad points out, the inclusion of an Asian character is meaningful, and it is significant to a lot of people, specifically readers who are people of color; however, it still deserves critique. Phil Yu posted Rostad's video to his blog, *Angry Asian Man*, and thousands of people shared the video across social media platforms. Seven years later, in the aftermath of Rowling's transphobic comments on Twitter, the issue of Asian stereotyping erupted again, as fans reminded the public once again of Cho Chang and also of the fact that Nagini was played by a Korean actress (Claudia Kim) in *Fantastic Beasts: The Crimes of Grindelwald*, a film based on Rowling's screenplay.[72]

The popularity of Harry Potter continues to grow as books are rereleased, with the establishment of Pottermore, the Wizarding World amusement parks, and the Warner Bros. Studio Tour in London. As the wizarding world expands, so too do critical discussions on the series and its related media. Especially, and not only as Rowling shares more information about the series, an increasingly socially conscious fanbase is pushing back and asking questions about who exactly is a valued member of the wizarding world. It is clear that, as Rowling reifies the secondary status of characters of color while simultaneously amplifying the prominent white characters, the wizarding world continues the tradition of the "all-white world of children's literature."[73]

Notes

1. Yu, "Cho Chang is trending."
2. Rowling, "People who menstruate."
3. Rowling, "If sex isn't real."
4. Rowling, "J. K. Rowling Writes about Her Reasons."
5. Vezzali et al., "The Greatest Magic of Harry Potter."
6. Pierce, "What's Harry Potter Doing in the Library?"
7. Ciaccio, "Harry Potter and Christian Theology"; and Hamako, "Harry Potter and the Mistaken Myth."
8. Zipes, "The Phenomenon of Harry Potter."
9. Schulzke, "Wizard's Justice and Elf Liberation"; and Yandoli, "13 Lessons about Social Justice."
10. Horne, "Harry and the Other" (updated in Horne's chapter in this volume, "Harry and the Other: Multicultural and Social Justice Anti-Racism in J. K. Rowling's *Harry Potter* Series"); Kozlowska, "Can 'Harry Potter' Change the World?"; and Sims, "Wanagoballwitme?"
11. Nel, "Lost in Translation," 285.
12. Smith, "Harry Potter's Schooldays," 83.
13. Anatol, "The Fallen Empire," 174.
14. Nel, "Harry Potter, Seriously."
15. Shoker, "Harry Potter, Race, and British Multiculturalism."
16. Thomas, "Hermione Is Black," 145.
17. Anatol, "The Fallen Empire," 173.
18. Anatol, "The Fallen Empire," 174.
19. Thomas, "Hermione Is Black," 153.
20. Delgado and Stefancic, *Critical Race Theory*; and Omi and Winant, *Racial Formation in the United States.*
21. Horne, "Harry and the Other," 97. See also Jackie C. Horne's chapter in this volume, "Harry and the Other: Multicultural and Social Justice Anti-Racism in J. K. Rowling's *Harry Potter* Series."
22. Sims, "Wanagoballwitme?," 165.
23. Anatol, "The Fallen Empire," 172.
24. Wikipedia's "List of *Harry Potter* Characters" also claims that Viktor Krum is Bulgarian; he is the only character mentioned to have a national background. See https://en.wikipedia.org/wiki/List_of_Harry_Potter_characters.
25. Katsarska, "The Bulgarian Connection in Harry Potter"; and Cheshmedzhieva-Stoycheva, "Igor Karkaroff: A Key Bulgarian Figure."
26. Anatol, "The Fallen Empire," 172, citing Edward Said's *Culture and Imperialism.*
27. Smith, "Harry Potter's Schooldays," 75.
28. Pham, "Respect, Cho Chang, and Asian Representation."
29. Adelia, "Stereotyping and Othering of Non-White Characters."
30. Derman-Sparks, "Guide for Selecting Anti-Bias Children's Books."
31. Adelia, "Stereotyping and Othering of Non-White Characters," 14.
32. See Christina M. Chica's chapter in this volume, "The Magical (Racial) Contract: Understanding the Wizarding World of Harry Potter through Whiteness."
33. Lowe, *Immigrant Acts*, 67, 71; and Kim, *Asian American Literature*, xii, 4.
34. Anatol, "The Fallen Empire," 172.

35. Ostry, "Accepting Mudbloods," 94.

36. Harry Potter Wiki, "Cho Chang's Dress Robes."

37. Favreau, "Minor Inconveniences"; see also Adelia, "Stereotyping and Othering of Non-White Characters."

38. See the fanart in "Cho Chang: A Look at Racial Stereotypes in Harry Potter."

39. Said, *Orientalism*, 2.

40. Sue et al., "Racial Microaggressions in Everyday Life," 271.

41. Smith, Allen, and Danley, "Assume the Position . . . You Fit the Description," 555.

42. See Wikipedia's entry for "ching chong," http://en.wikipedia.org/wiki/Ching_chong.

43. *Huffington Post*, "Alexandra Wallace, UCLA Student."

44. *Huffington Post*, "'Ching Chong' CVS Receipt."

45. Gupta and Xiao, "Harry Potter Goes to China," 199–200.

46. Nel, "Lost in Translation," 285.

47. Nel, "Lost in Translation," 285.

48. Jung, "A Korean-American's Thoughts."

49. Cheung, "The Problem with Eleanor & Park."

50. Cheung, "The Problem with Eleanor & Park."

51. Nel, "Lost in Translation," 285.

52. Ono and Pham, *Asian Americans and the Media*, 66.

53. Ono and Pham, *Asian Americans and the Media*, 66.

54. At this time of writing, the YouTube video is not available online. Rostad's Tumblr is public: https://rachelrostad.tumblr.com. At the time of writing, the full text of the poem could be found here: https://lyrics.lol/artist/46221-rachel-rostad/lyrics/140472-to-jk-rowling-from-cho-chang.

55. Ironically, one fan interpreted Cho Chang as a geisha, rendering her with white skin, red lips, and an elaborate updo, all characteristics of geishas.

56. Ding, *The Claudia Kishi Club*.

57. Chon, "Thanks to Netflix's *The Baby-Sitter's Club* Reboot."

58. Han, *To All the Boys I've Loved Before*, 225.

59. Lee, "To JK Rowling, from Cho Chang."

60. Lee, "To JK Rowling, from Cho Chang."

61. Special thanks to Cecilia Konchar Farr, who saw the original exhibition at the British Library and alerted Sarah Park Dahlen about these notes. Sarah then visited the exhibition on January 10, 2019, when it was hosted by the New York Historical Society. Photographs were not allowed, so the quotations are based on Sarah's notes.

62. British Library, *Harry Potter: A History of Magic*.

63. British Library, *Harry Potter: A History of Magic*, 240–41.

64. Sarah Park Dahlen, email to Child_lit, April 16, 2013.

65. Sarah Park Dahlen, email to Child_lit, April 17, 2013.

66. Cheryl Klein, email to Child_lit, April 17, 2013.

67. Cheryl Klein, email to Sarah Park Dahlen, September 6, 2013.

68. Cheryl Klein, email to Sarah Park Dahlen, July 1, 2021. At the time of writing, Cheryl Klein is editorial director at Lee and Low Books, the largest multicultural publishing company in the country currently known as the United States. She has edited award-winning books such as *When Aidan Became a Brother*, written by Kyle Lukoff and illustrated by Kaylani Juanita.

69. Thomas, "Hermione Is Black," 145.

70. Adelia, "Stereotyping and Othering of Non-White Characters," 14.

71. Anatol, "The Fallen Empire," 174; emphasis in original.

72. See Jennifer Patrice Sims's chapter in this volume, "When the Subaltern Speak Parseltongue: Orientalism, Racial Re-Presentation, and Claudia Kim as Nagini." Also, see the tweet by Ellen Oh, cofounder, president, and CEO of We Need Diverse Books: "As long as we are talking about Cho Chang, can we remember that she also made a Korean actress play Nagini, the pet snake of an evil white man? That shit is still horrifying to me" (Oh, "As long as we are talking about Cho Chang").

73. Larrick, "The All-White World of Children's Books."

Bibliography

Adelia, Nadia. "Stereotyping and Othering of Non-White Characters in 'Harry Potter' Movies." *Kata Kita* 7, no. 1 (January 2019): 14–21.

Anatol, Giselle Liza. "The Fallen Empire: Exploring Ethnic Otherness in the World of Harry Potter." In *Reading Harry Potter: Critical Essays*, edited by Giselle Liza Anatol, 163–78. Westport, CT: Praeger, 2003.

British Library. *Harry Potter: A History of Magic*. London: Bloomsbury, 2017.

Cheshmedzhieva-Stoycheva, Desislava. "Igor Karkaroff: A Key Bulgarian Figure in J. K. Rowling's Harry Potter and the Goblet of Fire." Conference paper, Plovdiv, Bulgaria, May 20, 2004. https://www.researchgate.net/publication/315770718_igor_karkaroff_-_a_key_bulgarian_figure_in_j_k_rowling's_harry_potter_and_the_goblet_of_fire.

Cheung, Chantal. "The Problem with Eleanor & Park." *Northeastern University Political Review*, October 31, 2018. https://www.nupoliticalreview.com/2018/10/31/the-problem-with-eleanor-park/.

"Cho Chang: A Look at Racial Stereotypes in Harry Potter." *Fantasy Lit 2014* (blog), April 13, 2014. http://fantasylit2014.blogspot.com/2014/04/cho-chang-look-at-racial-stereotypes-in.html.

Chon, Monica. "Thanks to Netflix's *The Baby-Sitter's Club* Reboot, Everybody Wants To Be Claudia Kishi." *Oprah Daily*, July 16, 2020. https://www.oprahmag.com/entertainment/tv-movies/a33309985/the-baby-sitters-club-claudia-kishi-representation/.

Ciaccio, Peter. "Harry Potter and Christian Theology." In *Critical Perspectives on Harry Potter*, edited by Elizabeth E. Heilman, 33–46. New York: Routledge, 2009.

Delgado, Richard, and Jean Stefancic. *Critical Race Theory: An Introduction*. 3rd ed. New York: New York University Press, 2017.

Derman-Sparks, Louise. "Guide for Selecting Anti-Bias Children's Books." Social Justice Books. https://socialjusticebooks.org/guide-for-selecting-anti-bias-childrens-books/.

Ding, Sue, dir. *The Claudia Kishi Club*. Netflix, 2020. https://www.netflix.com/title/81284581.

Favreau, Olivia. "Minor Inconveniences: Cho Chang Lacked Depth, and I Can Prove It." *Haida Gwaii Observer* (Haida Gwaii, BC), August 11, 2017.

Gupta, Suman, and Cheng Xiao. "Harry Potter Goes to China." In *Children's Literature: Approaches and Territories*, edited by Janet Maybin and Nicola J. Watson, 338–51. Basingstoke, Hants., England: Palgrave Macmillan, 2009.

Hamako, Eric. "Harry Potter and the Mistaken Myth of the Mixed-Race Messiah." Paper presented at the Critical Mixed Race Studies conference, Chicago, November 2012.

Han, Jenny. *To All the Boys I've Loved Before*. New York: Simon and Schuster, 2014.

Harry Potter Wiki. "Cho Chang's Dress Robes." https://harrypotter.fandom.com/wiki/Cho _Chang%27s_dress_robes#cite_note-GOFF-0.

Horne, Jackie C. "Harry and the Other: Answering the Race Question in J. K. Rowling's *Harry Potter.*" *The Lion and the Unicorn* 34, no. 1 (January 2010): 76–104. doi:10.1353/ uni.0.0488.

Huffington Post. "Alexandra Wallace, UCLA Student, Films Racist Rant." March 14, 2011; updated December 6, 2017. https://www.huffpost.com/entry/alexandra-wallace-racist -video_n_835505?

Huffington Post. "'Ching Chong' CVS Receipt Leads to Million Dollar Lawsuit from Enraged New Jersey Customer (PHOTO)." April 18, 2013; updated December 6, 2017. https:// www.huffpost.com/entry/cvs-receipt-ching-chong-lawsuit-new-jersey_n_3112410.

Jung, Lynn D. "A Korean-American's Thoughts on Eleanor & Park." *Lynn D. Jung* (blog), July 15, 2020. https://lynndjung.wordpress.com/2020/07/15/a-korean-americans-thoughts-on -eleanor-park/.

Katsarska, Milena. "The Bulgarian Connection in *Harry Potter.*" In *Re-Reading Harry Potter*, edited by Suman Gupta, 183–97. 2nd ed. Basingstoke, Hants., England: Palgrave Macmillan, 2009.

Kim, Elaine H. *Asian American Literature: An Introduction to the Writings and Their Social Context*. Philadelphia: Temple University Press, 1982.

Kozlowska, Hanna. "Can 'Harry Potter' Change the World?" *Op-Talk* (blog). *New York Times*, September 17, 2014. https://op-talk.blogs.nytimes.com/2014/09/17/can-harry -potter-change-the-world/?_php=true&_type=blogs&smprod=opinion-ios&smid =opinion-ios-share&_r=0.

Larrick, Nancy. "The All-White World of Children's Books." *Saturday Review*, September 11, 1965, 63–65, 84–85.

Lee, Diana. "'To JK Rowling, from Cho Chang': Responding to Asian Stereotyping in Popular Culture." *Henry Jenkins* (blog), October 9, 2013. http://henryjenkins.org/2013/10 /to-jk-rowling-from-cho-chang-responding-to-asian-american-stereotyping-in-popular -culture.html.

Lowe, Lisa. *Immigrant Acts: On Asian American Cultural Politics*. Durham, NC: Duke University Press, 1996.

Nel, Philip. "Harry Potter, Seriously." *Nine Kinds of Pie* (blog), May 30, 2012. https://philnel .com/2012/05/30/potterstudies/.

Nel, Philip. "Lost in Translation: Harry Potter, from Page to Screen." In *Critical Perspectives on Harry Potter*, edited by Elizabeth E. Heilman, 275–90. New York: Routledge, 2009.

Oh, Ellen (@ElloEllenOh). "As long as we are talking about Cho Chang." Twitter, June 7, 2020. https://twitter.com/elloellenoh/status/1269517256297455618.

Omi, Michael, and Howard Winant. *Racial Formation in the United States: From the 1960s to the 1990s*. New York: Routledge, 1994.

Ono, Kent A., and Vincent N. Pham. *Asian Americans and the Media*. Cambridge: Polity Press, 2009.

Ostry, Elaine. "Accepting Mudbloods: The Ambivalent Social Vision of J. K. Rowling's Fairy Tales." In *Reading Harry Potter: Critical Essays*, edited by Giselle Liza Anatol, 89–102. Westport, CT: Praeger, 2003.

Pham, Kaitlin. "Respect, Cho Chang, and Asian Representation: A Critical Analysis of the White Gaze in Harry Potter." Senior project, California Polytechnic State University, 2014.

Pierce, Jennifer Burek. "What's Harry Potter Doing in the Library? Depictions of Young Adult Information Seeking Behavior in Contemporary Fantasy Fiction." Paper presented at the International Association of School Librarianship conference, Dublin, June 2004. https://ir.uiowa.edu/cgi/viewcontent.cgi?referer=https://www.google.com/& httpsredir=1&article=1003&context=slis_pubs.

Rowling, J. K. *Harry Potter and the Deathly Hallows.* New York: Scholastic, 2007.

Rowling, J. K. *Harry Potter and the Goblet of Fire.* New York: Scholastic, 2000.

Rowling, J. K. *Harry Potter and the Order of the Phoenix.* New York: Scholastic, 2003.

Rowling, J. K. *Harry Potter and the Prisoner of Azkaban.* New York: Scholastic, 1999.

Rowling, J. K. *Harry Potter and the Sorcerer's Stone.* New York: Scholastic, 1998.

Rowling, J. K. "J. K. Rowling Writes about Her Reasons for Speaking Out on Sex and Gender Issues." *J. K. Rowling* (blog), June 10, 2020. https://www.jkrowling.com/opinions/j-k -rowling-writes-about-her-reasons-for-speaking-out-on-sex-and-gender-issues/.

Rowling, J. K. "Pottermore: The Digital Heart of the Wizarding World." *J. K. Rowling* (blog), September 22, 2015. https://www.jkrowling.com/pottermore-digital-heart-wizarding -world/.

Rowling, J. K. (@jk_rowling). "If sex isn't real, there's no same-sex attraction." Twitter, June 6, 2020. https://twitter.com/jk_rowling/status/1269389298664701952?s=20.

Rowling, J. K. (@jk_rowling). "'People who menstruate.' I'm sure there used to be a word for those people." Twitter, June 6, 2020. https://twitter.com/jk_rowling/status/126938251836 2509313?s=20.

Said, Edward W. *Orientalism.* New York: Vintage Books, 1979.

Schulzke, Marcus. "Wizard's Justice and Elf Liberation: Politics and Political Activism in *Harry Potter.*" In *JK Rowling: Harry Potter,* edited by Cynthia J. Hallett and Peggy J. Huey, 111–21. Basingstoke, Hants., England: Palgrave Macmillan, 2012.

Shoker, Sarah. "Harry Potter, Race, and British Multiculturalism." *The Hooded Utilitarian* (blog), April 2, 2013. http://www.hoodedutilitarian.com/2013/04/harry-potter-race-and -british-multiculturalism/.

Sims, Jenn. "'Wanagoballwitme?' Inter 'Racial' Dating at Hogwarts." In *The Sociology of Harry Potter: 22 Enchanting Essays of the Wizarding World,* edited by Jenn Sims, 164–71. Hamden, CT: Zossima Press, 2012.

Smith, Karen Manners. "Harry Potter's Schooldays: J. K. Rowling and the British Boarding School Novel." In *Reading Harry Potter: Critical Essays,* edited by Giselle Liza Anatol, 69–88. Westport, CT: Praeger, 2003.

Smith, William A., Walter R. Allen, and Lynette L. Danley. "'Assume the Position . . . You Fit the Description': Psychosocial Experiences and Racial Battle Fatigue among African American Male College Students." *American Behavioral Scientist* 51, no. 4 (December 2007): 551–78. doi:10.1177/0002764207307742.

Sue, Derald W., Christina M. Capodilupo, Gina C. Torino, Jennifer M. Bucceri, Aisha M. B. Holder, Kevin L. Nadal, and Marta Esquilin. "Racial Microaggressions in Everyday Life: Implications for Clinical Practice." *American Psychologist* 62, no. 4 (2007): 271–86. doi:10.1037/0003-066X.62.4.271.

Thomas, Ebony Elizabeth. "Hermione Is Black: A Postscript to Harry Potter and the Crisis of Infinite Dark Fantastic Worlds." In *The Dark Fantastic: Race and Imagination from Harry Potter to the Hunger Games,* 143–70. New York: New York University Press, 2019.

Vezzali, Loris, Sofia Stathi, Dino Giovannini, Dora Capozza, and Elena Trifiletti. "The Greatest Magic of Harry Potter: Reducing Prejudice." *Journal of Applied Social Psychology* 45, no. 2 (February 2015): 105–21. doi:10.1111/jasp.12279.

Yandoli, Krystie Lee. "13 Lessons about Social Justice from 'Harry Potter.'" BuzzFeed, August 14, 2013. https://www.buzzfeed.com/krystieyandoli/essons-about-social-justice-from -harry-potter?utm_term=.quPjejlPRY#.ipRz1zjqwL.

Yu, Phil. "'A Letter to JK Rowling from Cho Chang' by Rachel Rostad." *Angry Asian Man* (blog), April 15, 2013. http://blog.angryasianman.com/2013/04/a-letter-to-jk-rowling -from-cho-chang.html.

Yu, Phil (@angryasianman). "Cho Chang is trending." Twitter, June 6, 2020. https://twitter. com/angryasianman/status/1269478248376762368?s=20.

Zipes, Jack. "The Phenomenon of Harry Potter, or Why All the Talk?" In *Sticks and Stones: The Troublesome Success of Children's Literature from Slovenly Peter to Harry Potter*, 170–89. New York: Routledge, 2002.

When the Subaltern Speak Parseltongue

Orientalism, Racial Re-Presentation, and Claudia Kim as Nagini

Jennifer Patrice Sims

As the heir of Salazar "serpent-tongue" Slytherin, it is appropriate that Lord Voldemort, too, would have an affinity for snakes. His pet snake, Nagini, is introduced as her master finalizes his plans to use Harry Potter to regain his body (*Harry Potter and the Goblet of Fire*). Nagini is described as a "gigantic snake, at least 12 feet long" (*HP and the GF*, 12). Readers learn that Peter Pettigrew milked her to provide food to sustain Voldemort's feeble and partial physical form prior to his return to full power (*HP and the GF*), and that once he was back, she was frequently by his side or on his shoulder (*Harry Potter and the Deathly Hallows*). Throughout the series, Nagini does Voldemort's bidding, including attempted murder (*Harry Potter and the Order of the Phoenix*), completed murder (*HP and the DH*), animating dead bodies (*HP and the DH*), and disposing of dead bodies (*HP and the DH*). Her connection with Voldemort goes even deeper than mere pet-servant, though. When Harry witnesses Nagini's attack on Mr. Weasley from her vantage point, many suspected it was because Voldemort was possessing her at the time (*HP and the OP*). However, it is later revealed that Nagini is her master's final Horcrux; in other words, like Harry, she shares a bit of Voldemort's soul and thus has a mental connection with him (*HP and the DH*). Nagini meets her end during the Battle of Hogwarts at the hands of Neville Longbottom wielding the Sword of Gryffindor (*HP and the DH*).

A decade after readers witnessed Neville's heroic defeat of Nagini, the trailer for the spin-off movie, *Fantastic Beast: The Crimes of Grindelwald*, revealed that Voldemort's pet-servant, companion, nursemaid, and last surviving vessel of his soul was originally an Asian woman. Played by South Korean model-turned-actress Claudia Kim, Nagini, as fans learned, is a Maledictus—a person born with a blood curse that allows them to transform into a snake at will, but that will ultimately turn them into a snake permanently later in life.[1] Many Harry Potter fans called the news "an incredible insult,"[2] and J. K. Rowling[3] was instantly criticized over the revelation. Although there was ambiguity as to whether the new information was an attempt at "diversifying via revisionism" or simply the public disclosure of an author's twenty-year-old secret, critics were in consensus that making an Asian woman the pet snake of a white man was blatantly racist.[4]

For example, author Jen Moulton (in a now deleted or restricted tweet) commented that "suddenly making Nagini into a Korean woman is garbage" because "[r]epresentation as an afterthought for more woke points is not good representation."[5] Rowling responded to her by explaining:

> The Naga are snake-like mythical creatures of Indonesian mythology, hence the name "Nagini." They are sometimes depicted as winged, sometimes as half-human, half-snake. Indonesia comprises a few hundred ethnic groups, including Javanese, Chinese and Betawi. Have a lovely day [snake emoji].[6]

Rather than quelling the criticism against her, this response set off a new angle of critique, since, as numerous fans and journalists were quick to correct, the Naga mythology actually originated in India. Rowling's casual conflation of South Koreans, Indonesians, Indians, and "a few hundred ethnic groups" revealed her arrogant homogenization of the cultures of Asia and exposed her as the quintessential white Westerner who sees heterogeneous non-Europeans as "an undifferentiated type called Oriental."[7]

Concurrently with the backlash, other fans opined that we should "be celebrating diversity instead of dissecting it with visceral reactions."[8] Indeed, in her book *Reel Inequality*, sociologist Nancy Wang Yuen cites sobering statistics on Asian women's underrepresentation in Hollywood. Calculations of the race of women characters in the one hundred top-grossing US films of 2013 reveal that only 3 percent were Asian; and since "otherworldly" characters were also 3 percent, Yuen quipped that US moviegoers are "as likely to see an alien woman as an Asian woman."[9] Even though Asian women's representation rose to 6 percent by 2020, nonetheless when Asian women are on screen, research shows that it is for a fraction of the time of characters of other races, and they have fewer speaking roles.[10] Looking forward to the movie, one fan wrote on MuggleNet that she had "complete confidence that Rowling will deliver a dynamic character in Nagini."[11] Likewise, in a prerelease interview, Claudia Kim herself said that she was looking forward to "the controversy fading away once the film premieres."[12]

Unfortunately, upon watching *The Crimes of Grindelwald* it becomes clear that Nagini was designed, as one *Harvard Crimson* writer suspected, by "dumping several Hollywood-produced Orientalist stereotypes into a cauldron and stirring them with a pinch of magic."[13] Drawing on Orientalism and other postcolonial perspectives, this chapter examines Claudia Kim as Nagini. It also explains what the ensuing controversy demonstrates about the strength of biased perceptions of women of color, and it reveals that the inability to comprehend critiques thereof is frustratingly common.

Orientalism, Racial Re-Presentation, and Claudia Kim as Nagini

Orientalism, as set forth by postcolonial studies scholar Edward Said in his book of that name, is a general "style of thought based upon an ontological and epistemological distinction made between 'the Orient' and (most of the time) 'the Occident.'"[14] The places, mainly in Asia and the Middle East, that were "Europe's greatest and richest and oldest colonies" constitute the Orient, while the Occident, or "the West," is represented principally by imperial France and Britain and the post–World War II United States.[15] Said explains that while not "merely" imaginative, both locations are nonetheless discursive; that is, their *real* geography, people, culture, and history often bear little resemblance to how they are *portrayed* in Western scholarship, literature, and cinema.

One consistent (mis)representation, according to Said, is the West's positioning of itself as superior. While Said notes that many terms have been used to express this imagined relationship, a few common ones are that "[t]he Oriental is irrational, depraved (fallen), childlike, 'different'; thus the

European is rational, virtuous, mature, 'normal.'"[16] This is especially visible when the gendered nature of depictions is considered. Regarding women, in the Western imagination Asian women are submissive and hypersexual.[17] Whether in nineteenth-century novels like *Madame Chrysanthéme* and *Madame Butterfly* or on contemporary television shows, Asian women are exoticized as the objects of (non-Asian, typically white) men's desire.[18]

Critical analysis of Cho Chang, the only East Asian character in the *Harry Potter* novels and movies, has already demonstrated the franchise's panache for Orientalism (see Sarah Park Dahlen and Kallie Schell's chapter in this volume). Cho is described in the books via stereotypes of Asian women students: short, pretty, and smart (Ravenclaw) (*Harry Potter and the Prisoner of Azkaban*; *Harry Potter and the Goblet of Fire*). Analysis of Katie Leung's portrayal of Cho in the films reveals even more othering since, as literary scholar Ebony Elizabeth Thomas has observed, "when the fantastic is transmediated from page to screen, conventions become that much more amplified."[19] For example, in a movie scene that is not in the books, Cho's lines are overly polite compared to white characters' lines; and throughout the movies, her hair and clothes are styled as more childlike than same-age white characters.[20] Moreover, in the movie *Harry Potter and the Goblet of Fire*, Cho and the Patil twins are dressed in Yule Ball gowns that reflect their respective Asian ethnic heritages, even though their robes are not described as such in the book. Compared to the undifferentiated attire of actual cultural outsiders like white French student Fleur Delacour, Cho's and the twins' gowns function to amplify and reify the importance of racialized otherness.[21]

Whether book or movie, though, Cho's main role in the plot is also Orientalist, as it centers on her being attractive to and having romantic relationships with multiple white boys.[22] In other words, Cho serves "the sole purpose of showing [Harry] the melodramatic trials of teenage love,"[23] thereby providing him with experience as he develops sexual maturity.[24] Moreover, while audiences repeatedly witness Harry's thoughts and feelings on their relationship, we rarely see Cho articulate hers.[25] It is a white character, Hermione Granger, who voices Cho's thoughts and feelings, which is right in line with Thomas's observation that "the Dark Other is always focalized through a White protagonist's eyes."[26] Finally, Rowling's admittedly purposeful juxtaposing of Cho and Ginny Weasley throughout the series—in Quidditch, in naming Dumbledore's Army, in personality traits like a tendency to cry versus not, and more—and always setting Ginny as the victor, is thus deeper than the literary tropes of character foils and triangulated desire as discussed by English literature scholars.[27] It is also Orientalist thinking in that it imagines "the Westerner in a whole series of possible relationships with the Orient without ever losing him the relative upper hand."[28]

Rowling's Orientalist portrayal of Asian women continues with Nagini. She is first seen in *The Crimes of Grindelwald* as a member of a traveling magical circus in Paris, France, in the 1920s. Dressed in a tight, low-necklined dark blue dress, she is apparently participating against her will, as evidenced by her initial inaction when the Circus Master calls for her to transform into a snake for the audience. Nagini and Credence (the orphaned Obscurial from the first film in the series, *Fantastic Beasts and Where to Find Them*, played by white American actor Ezra Miller) soon escape and embark on his mission to learn about his past.[29] Kim explained in an interview that Nagini is Credence's "only friend," and she sentimentalized: "It's amazing these two broken souls [she a Maledictus and he an Obscurial] are able to form some kind of friendship."[30] Unfortunately, though, the audience is not shown evidence of a mutually beneficial or reciprocal friendship. Throughout the movie, Nagini is simply accompanying Credence. Her only role is to provide unidirectional emotional support. For example, at the home of the woman listed on Credence's birth certificate, Nagini holds onto his arm as the woman begins to reveal chilling information about his tragic origins. At the end of the movie, by contrast, when Nagini is scared during a magical fight scene, Credence unceremoniously leaves her with strangers (Eddie Redmayne's Newt Scamander and others) to join Grindelwald and depart with him to Nurmengard.

Claudia Kim as Nagini is thus not laudable diversity as suggested by Rowling's apologists. She is the embodiment of Orientalist ideas of the sexy, agentic Asian woman who silently supports Western men's pursuit of knowledge and power, at least until they discard her—quite literally treating her as the used then forgotten "other"[31]—once her services are no longer needed. Keeping in the mind the murders she will commit for Voldemort later in her life as a snake, she also embodies the "Yellow Peril" trope that typecasts Asian characters as criminals, gang members, and other "morally corrupt physical or cultural threats to the fabric of [Euro-]American society."[32] In sum, just like Cho before her, Nagini's character is "plainly one dimensional and half-baked."[33] Rather than the much-needed nuanced representation of Asian women as real and active subjects and citizens, Nagini is nothing more than a "re-presentation" of a centuries-old Orientalist construct.

The negative results of depicting women from Asian countries as a discursive construct is explained by postcolonial feminist theorist Chandra Mohanty in her article "Under Western Eyes."[34] Critiquing much of the feminist writing produced in Western cultures, she writes that such scholarship "discursively colonize[s] the material and historical heterogeneities of the lives of women in the third world, thereby producing/re-presenting a composite, singular 'Third World Woman.'"[35] Mohanty explains that, in Eurocentric Western thinking:

> This average third world woman leads an essentially truncated life based on her feminine gender (read: sexually constrained) and being "third world" (read: ignorant, poor, uneducated, tradition-bound, domestic, family-oriented, victimized, etc.). This, I suggest, is in contrast to the (implicit) self-representation of Western women as educated, modern, as having control over their own bodies and sexualities, and the freedom to make their own decisions.[36]

Evidence of Mohanty's points can be seen in Nagini's lack of character development in *The Crimes of Grindelwald*. As with Rowling's previous Asian women characters, the audience is given absolutely no background information about her. The only thing audiences know about Nagini is her name, which Western men call her instead of she herself speaking, and what can be seen of her—that she is a somewhat provocatively dressed East Asian woman who can turn into a snake and who spends her time in service to men who use her to accomplish their aims. In failing to provide any information at all on Nagini's life before the circus or on her thoughts or feelings regarding the events in the movie, *Crimes* suppresses the lived experience of real Asian women and instead re-presents the one-dimensional colonial fantasy of the "Asian Woman."

Mohanty points out that, although this imagined view of Third World women operates at the level of the discursive, it has dangerous material consequences. Third World women being seen as "a homogeneous 'powerless' group,"[37] for example, has led well-meaning Western feminists and others to support or implement outside interventionist policies that are unhelpful at best and harmful at worst because they do not take into account actual culture or context. Asian women in particular being seen as monolithically tradition bound, domestic, yet also exotic, sexy, and available and desirous to serve Western men has been the ideological basis for various types of institutional and individual abuses. Historically, it is this style of thought that contributed to the "U.S. military's long, uncomfortable history with prostitution."[38] From the post–World War II occupation of Japan through subsequent wars in Asian countries like Korea and Vietnam, multiple generations of Western men, "500 or 600 soldiers"[39] at a time, have stood in line to be sexually "serviced" by coerced Asian women.[40] Contemporaneously, Orientalist perspectives of Asian women contribute to sex tourism in the Global South,[41] the vulgar messages Asian women receive from men on dating apps,[42] and even assault and murder by white men like Brock Turner and Robert Long.[43] While movies' limited and stereotypical portrayal of Asian characters is of course not solely responsible for anti-Asian sentiment and violence, nonetheless when movies perpetuate Orientalist caricatures of Asian women, they contribute to the "dangerous real life repercussions"[44] of that ideology.

When the Subaltern Speak Parseltongue

Despite Orientalism being the hegemonic—the dominant yet typically unnamed—discourse, research shows that some viewers are nonetheless highly critical of it. Recent interview research with Chinese students, for example, reveals that they have concerns that Hollywood's "grossly biased impression of China" influences Westerners' views.[45] One interviewee shared that US Americans ask them ignorant and insulting questions because "[f] oreigners have a lot of misunderstandings about China."[46] "This is something I don't like about Hollywood," another interviewee confessed.[47]

Chinese students are not the only ones exasperated at Orientalism in movies. If The Crimes of Grindelwald is yet another "heterogeneous project to constitute the colonial subject as Other,"[48] then the backlash against casting an Asian woman as Nagini is proof that many Harry Potter fans have counterhegemonic views. Postcolonial studies scholar Gayatri Spivak explains that the subaltern do not only perceive the world and themselves solely through the dominating group's hegemonic lens.[49] In Du Boisian terms, they have a "double consciousness" that allows them to perceive the world through both hegemonic and counterhegemonic frameworks.[50] However, because the West's Orientalism is hegemonic, when the subaltern speak outside of, challenge, or reject Orientalism, their perspective is often unintelligible to others.

To illustrate this phenomenon, Spivak recounts the suicide of an Indian liberation activist in her now classic essay "Can the Subaltern Speak?"[51] In an attempt to prevent her death from being erroneously attributed to "illicit pregnancy," as was the dominant understanding of young women's suicide, she waited until she was menstruating (i.e., very clearly not pregnant) to hang herself. Despite the activist's attempt to "speak by turning her body into a text," her death was nonetheless attributed to "illicit love," and Spivak was "so unnerved by this failure of communication" that she initially lamented that "the subaltern cannot speak!"[52] In later formulations of her thesis, however, she revised her position to clarify that "the subaltern as female cannot be heard or read" despite the fact that they clearly do speak.[53]

Although less extreme than a political activist's suicide, the Harry Potter fans who critiqued rather than celebrated the news that Voldemort's snake was to be portrayed as an Asian woman were nonetheless offering a counterhegemonic view on the racialization of characters. And this is not the first time fans have done so. As Kathryn Coto explains in her chapter in this volume, Harry Potter fanart often "racebends" characters by rejecting the hegemonic "default to white when no race is specified,"[54] instead depicting characters whose race is not specified in the text as people of color. Thus, racebent fanart reveals that part of the typical "imagination gap"[55] in literature stems from authors' failure to envision counterhegemonic characters.

Nevertheless, like the community drawing the standard "illicit love" conclusion despite the Indian activist's strategically timed suicide, there are many people in the Harry Potter world who are so marred in Orientalist logics that they cannot comprehend a counterhegemonic perspective. Rowling's and her supporters' response to the controversy over Nagini demonstrates this clearly. Rowling responded to criticism over making a South Korean woman a white man's pet snake by passive aggressively whitesplaining the *non*-Korean myth of the Naga. Her supporters responded to the criticism by claiming that Asians on screen should be celebrated regardless of quality,[56] by asserting that Rowling conducted "research and [had] good intentions,"[57] and by bleating that authors have "every right to write how [they] want to write."[58] This all reveals that both Rowling and her supporters literally cannot comprehend that homogenizing Asian cultures is problematic, that subjugating a colonial caricature of an Asian woman to a white man is racist, and that a white Westerner's shoddy "research," "intentions," and "right" to write what she wants are not what is most important. Additionally, Kim herself, finding the backlash against her character "unexpected" and in response offering her "support of the casting decision,"[59] demonstrates, as Spivak despaired, that subalterns' counterhegemonic attempts at speaking often fail even among their "own family."[60] In short, whether magical or Muggle, when the subaltern speak, many people cannot hear them because counterhegemonic perspectives are frequently as unintelligible as Parseltongue.

Fantastic Future Movies and Where to Find Them

Edward Said explains that what is "thought, said, or even done about the Orient follows (perhaps occurs within) certain distinct and intellectually knowable lines."[61] White Westerners from the Middle Ages to today draw on these imagined lines in their writing and produce images of Asians that are neither real nor benign. Thus, while increasing the representation of Asian women in TV and movies is a worthy pursuit, if the characters presented are Orientalist, then they simply reify white Western male dominance. Voldemort's pet snake Nagini being an Asian woman who previously served a white man Obscurial is problematic because it perpetuates the colonial fantasy about a dominant masculine Occident and a submissive exotic Orient. In bringing the wizarding world of the 1920s to the silver screen, *Fantastic Beasts* has thus far followed in the *Harry Potter* series' footsteps to disappointingly re-present the only East Asian character as a clichéd colonial stereotype, despite the fact that such images "skew real-life perceptions" and affect the treatment of real people.[62]

Both the casting of Kim and the dismissal of the resulting backlash are clear expressions of Orientalism. The rush to defend white writers when they perpetuate dangerous narratives about people of color affirms that many people continue to assume that the Western viewpoint, no matter how wrong or harmful, should be unquestioningly accepted and celebrated. Said explains that "the hegemony of European ideas about the Orient," in particular the idea of "European superiority over Oriental backwardness," can completely override "the possibility that a more independent, or more skeptical, thinking might have had different views on the matter."[63] In other words, as demonstrated by Rowling and her supporters during the Nagini controversy, Western thought is so steeped in the illusion of its own superiority that on the whole it lacks the capacity to comprehend reality or any future alternative.

Luckily, *The Crimes of Grindelwald* is only the second in a slated five-movie series. Kim has revealed that her character is "a wonderful and vulnerable woman who wants to live" and who "has powers that are yet to be explored."[64] This provides a bit of optimism that subsequent movies will portray Nagini multidimensionally. Additionally, although Credence left her at the end of *Crimes*, Kim's statement that "Credence is special to [Nagini] because he encourages her to use her power"[65] can perhaps be interpreted as a hint that, like Ron during the Horcrux Hunt (*HP and the DH*), Credence will remorsefully return to his friend later in the story.

As Nancy Wang Yuen reminds us, "the idea that white writers can never write authentic stories about people of color is problematic" because it "gives primacy to race" over other axes of difference, and it "assumes immutable differences between racial groups."[66] Though it would require introspection, humility, actual research, and consultation with minority communities, J. K. Rowling and the others at the helm of the *Fantastic Beasts* franchise can—*if they choose*—move beyond their default Orientalist thinking and bring to life a Nagini who is portrayed in the same nuanced, holistically human way as other characters. Over the next three movies, therefore, fans will be watching to see if Nagini's character will be developed to be more than simply a magical re-presentation of Orientalist fantasies.

Notes

1. Pottermore, "Everything You Need to Know about Nagini."
2. Clark, "Why Casting Nagini As an Asian Woman."
3. The criticism over Kim's casting as Nagini appears to have been directed solely at J. K. Rowling. This is in stark contrast to Nancy Wang Yuen's finding that while the limited number of available nonstereotyped roles means that "most actors of color do not have the luxury of avoiding stereotyped roles," they nonetheless "get the brunt of the criticism, even if they are not responsible for the content" (*Reel Inequality*, 78) Perhaps because *Fantastic Beasts* is an outgrowth of Rowling's Harry Potter franchise, or perhaps because Nagini is simply the latest in a growing number of examples of racist typecasting and cultural appropriation in Rowling's magical world, there appears to have been little to no blame levied against Kim for accepting the role. In fact, some commenters (e.g., Miranda, "How and Why J. K. Rowling's 'Nagini' Character Reveal") have specifically clarified that the fault lies with Rowling, and they "don't blame Claudia Kim for being cast as Nagini, or being excited about her role." Given Yuen's explanations of how "critiques from the community often add to the emotional burden [actors of color] bear when portraying stereotyped roles," it is a sign of progress that Harry Potter fans are "placing the onus of change on executives and creators instead of actors of color" as Yuen recommends (*Reel Inequality*, 79).

4. Clark, "Why Casting Nagini As an Asian Woman"; Chow, "What the Hell Happened"; Cao, "Why Casting an Asian Woman as Nagini"; and Miranda, "How and Why J. K. Rowling's 'Nagini' Character Reveal."

5. Moulton, "Listen Joanne, we get it."

6. Rowling, "The Naga are snake-like mythical creatures."

7. Said, *Orientalism*, 252.

8. Martin, "The Nagini Controversy."

9. Yuen, *Reel Inequality*, 28; and Lauzen, "It's a Man's (Celluloid) World: On-Screen Representations of Female Characters in the Top 100 Films of 2013."

10. DuCros et al., "Asian Americans and Pacific Islanders on TV"; and Lauzen, "It's a Man's (Celluloid) World: Portrayals of Female Characters in the Top Grossing U.S. Films of 2020."

11. Martin, "The Nagini Controversy."

12. Bhat, "'Fantastic Beasts' Star Claudia Kim."

13. Chow, "What the Hell Happened."

14. Said, *Orientalism*, 10.

15. Said, *Orientalism*, 9–23.

16. Said, *Orientalism*, 40.

17. Collins, *Black Feminist Thought*; and Chou, *Asian American Sexual Politics*.

18. DuCros et al., "Asian Americans and Pacific Islanders on TV."

19. Thomas, *The Dark Fantastic*.

20. Adelia, "Stereotyping and Othering of Non-White Characters."

21. Adelia, "Stereotyping and Othering of Non-White Characters."

22. Adelia, "Stereotyping and Othering of Non-White Characters."

23. Pham, "Respect, Cho Chang, and Asian Representation," 23.

24. Limbach, "Ginny Weasley, Girl Next-Doormat?"

25. Pham, "Respect, Cho Chang, and Asian Representation."

26. Pham, "Respect, Cho Chang, and Asian Representation"; and Thomas, *The Dark Fantastic*, 59.

27. Limbach, "Ginny Weasley, Girl Next-Doormat?"

28. Said, *Orientalism*, 15.

29. Although Ezra Miller is nonbinary, stating in interviews: "I don't identify as a man. I don't identify as a woman" (Bollinger, "Actor Ezra Miller Says He Doesn't Identify As a Man or a Woman"), the character of Credence is portrayed as a man by Western cultural standards such as attire and pronouns. In this analysis, it is Credence's gender vis-à-vis Nagini's gender (portrayed in accordance with Western cultural standards of femininity) that is discussed, since that is what is contained on screen. It is beyond the scope of this chapter to also analyze the potentially subversive aspect of a nonbinary actor portraying a Western man; however, it is my expectation that such analysis will be forthcoming from critical queer theorists as Credence's character and plot arc are developed in the coming movies.

30. Hibberd, "*Fantastic Beasts* Actress Claudia Kim."

31. hooks, "Eating the Other," 39.

32. DuCros et al., "Asian Americans and Pacific Islanders on TV," 16.

33. Pham, "Respect, Cho Chang, and Asian Representation," 23.

34. Mohanty, "Under Western Eyes," 334.

35. Mohanty, "Under Western Eyes," 334.

36. Mohanty, "Under Western Eyes," 337.

37. Mohanty, "Under Western Eyes," 338.

38. Lamothe, "The U.S. Military's Long, Uncomfortable History."

39. Associated Press, "U.S. Troops Used Japanese Brothels."

40. Lamothe, "The U.S. Military's Long, Uncomfortable History"; Associated Press, "U.S. Troops Used Japanese Brothels"; Tanaka, *Japan's Comfort Women*; and Lie, "The State as Pimp," 3.

41. Oppermann, "Sex Tourism"; and Vidal-Ortiz, Robinson, and Khan, *Race and Sexuality*.

42. Nigatu, "10 Ridiculously Offensive Things People Tell Asian Women."

43. Jeong, "The Deep American Roots of the Atlanta Shootings."

44. Cao, "Why Casting an Asian Woman as Nagini."

45. Gao and Wayt, "Through the Looking-Glass."

46. Gao and Wayt, "Through the Looking-Glass."

47. Gao and Wayt, "Through the Looking-Glass."

48. Spivak, "Can the Subaltern Speak?," 31. For this 2006 anthology, Spivak abbreviated her essay from its original 1988 publication.

49. The "subaltern" is Antonio Gramsci's theoretical term for groups who are structurally excluded from society. See Gramsci, *Selections from the Prison Notebooks*.

50. Du Bois, *The Souls of Black Folk*.

51. Spivak, "Can the Subaltern Speak?"

52. Spivak, "Can the Subaltern Speak?," 35.

53. Spivak, "Can the Subaltern Speak?," 35.

54. Sims, "The Reality of Imaginary Whiteness."

55. Thomas, *The Dark Fantastic*.

56. Martin, "The Nagini Controversy."

57. Martin, "The Nagini Controversy."

58. Wijanarko, "Never ever change @jk_rowling."

59. Bhat, "'Fantastic Beasts' Star Claudia Kim."

60. Spivak, "Can the Subaltern Speak?," 35.

61. Said, *Orientalism*, 13.

62. Yuen, *Reel Inequality*, 20.

63. Said, *Orientalism*, 15.

64. Hibberd, "*Fantastic Beasts* Actress Claudia Kim."

65. Hibberd, "*Fantastic Beasts* Actress Claudia Kim."

66. Yuen, *Reel Inequality*, 58.

Bibliography

Adelia, Nadia. "Stereotyping and Othering of Non-White Characters in 'Harry Potter' Movies." *Kata Kita* 7, no. 1 (January 2019): 14–21. doi:10.9744/katakita.7.1.14–21.

Associated Press. "U.S. Troops Used Japanese Brothels after WWII." NBC News, April 27, 2007. https://www.nbcnews.com/id/wbna18355292.

Bhat, Anjali. "'Fantastic Beasts' Star Claudia Kim Defended Her Casting: The Controversy Was 'Unexpected.'" *Teen Vogue*, October 25, 2018. https://www.teenvogue.com/story/fantastic-beasts-crimes-of-grindelwald-criticism-casting-asian-actor-claudia-kim-nagini.

Bollinger, Alex. "Actor Ezra Miller Says He Doesn't Identify as a Man or a Woman." *LGBTQ Nation*, November 8, 2018. https://www.lgbtqnation.com/2018/11/actor-ezra-miller-says-doesnt-identify-man-woman.

Cao, Linh. "Why Casting an Asian Woman as Nagini Is Yet Another Mistake for J. K. Rowling." *Wear Your Voice*, October 1, 2018. https://wearyourvoicemag.com/culture/casting-asian-woman-nagini-yet-another-mistake-j-k-rowling.

Chou, Rosalind S. *Asian American Sexual Politics: The Construction of Race, Gender, and Sexuality*. Lanham, MD: Rowman and Littlefield, 2012.

Chow, Liana E. "What the Hell Happened: Voldemort's Snake Is Actually an Asian Woman." *Harvard Crimson*, October 2, 2018. https://www.thecrimson.com/article/2018/10/2/nagini-asian-woman/.

Clark, Nicole. "Why Casting Nagini As an Asian Woman in 'Fantastic Beasts' Is So Offensive." *Vice*, September 26, 2018. https://www.vice.com/en_us/article/d3jybm/why-the-casting-of-nagini-as-an-asian-woman-in-fantastic-beasts-is-so-offensive.

Collins, Patricia Hill. *Black Feminist Thought: Knowledge, Consciousness, and the Politics of Empowerment*. 2nd ed. New York: Routledge, 2000.

Du Bois, W. E. B. *The Souls of Black Folk: Essays and Sketches*. Chicago: A. C. McClurg, 1903.

DuCros, Faustina M., Christina B. Chin, Jenny Jong-Hwa Lee, Nancy Wang Yuen, Meera E. Deo, and Noriko Milman. "Asian Americans and Pacific Islanders on TV." *Contexts* 17, no. 4 (November 2018): 12–17. doi:10.1177/1536504218812863.

Gao, Yang, and Virginia Wayt. "Through the Looking-Glass: Reception of Chinese Elements in Hollywood Movies among Chinese College Students." Paper presented at the Southern Sociological Society conference, virtual meeting, April 7–10, 2021.

Gramsci, Antonio. *Selections from the Prison Notebooks*. Translated and edited by Quintin Hoare and Geoffrey Nowell Smith. New York: International Publishers, 1971.

Hibberd, James. "*Fantastic Beasts* Actress Claudia Kim Breaks Silence on Playing Nagini." *Entertainment Weekly*, September 25, 2018. https://ew.com/movies/2018/09/25/fantastic-beasts-claudia-kim-nagini/.

hooks, bell, "Eating the Other: Desire and Resistance." In *Black Looks: Race and Representation*, 21–39. Boston: South End Press, 1992.

Jeong, May. "The Deep American Roots of the Atlanta Shootings." *New York Times*, March 19, 2021. https://www.nytimes.com/2021/03/19/opinion/atlanta-shooting-massage-sex-work.html.

Lamothe, Dan "The U.S. Military's Long, Uncomfortable History with Prostitution Gets New Attention." *Washington Post*, October 31, 2014. https://www.washingtonpost.com/news/checkpoint/wp/2014/10/31/the-u-s-militarys-long-uncomfortable-history-with-prostitution-gets-new-attention/.

Lauzen, Martha M. "It's a Man's (Celluloid) World: On-Screen Representations of Female Characters in the Top 100 Films of 2013." Center for the Study of Women in Television and Film, San Diego State University, 2014.

Lauzen, Martha M. "It's a Man's (Celluloid) World: Portrayals of Female Characters in the Top Grossing U.S. Films of 2020." Center for the Study of Women in Television and Film, San Diego State University, 2021. https://womenintvfilm.sdsu.edu/wp-content/uploads/2021/04/2020_Its_a_Mans_World_Report_v2.pdf.

Lie, John. "The State as Pimp: Prostitution and the Patriarchal State in Japan in the 1940s." *Sociological Quarterly* 38, no. 2 (Spring 1997): 251–63.

Limbach, Gwendolyn. "Ginny Weasley, Girl Next-Doormat?" In *Hog's Head Conversations: Essays on Harry Potter*, edited by Travis Prinzi, 168–87. Allentown, PA: Zossima Press, 2009.

Martin, Mikaela. "The Nagini Controversy: Optimism Is Underrated." MuggleNet, October 27, 2018. http://www.mugglenet.com/2018/10/the-nagini-controversy-optimism-is-underrated/.

Miranda, Desirée. "How and Why J. K. Rowling's 'Nagini' Character Reveal Is Touching on Racist Tropes about Asian Women." *Medium*, September 28, 2018. https://medium.com/@desireewrites/how-and-why-j-k-rowlings-nagini-character-reveal-is-touching-on-racist-tropes-about-asian-women-8a382f0f89fa.

Mohanty, Chandra Talpade. "Under Western Eyes: Feminist Scholarship and Colonial Discourses." *Boundary 2* 12, no. 3 (Spring–Autumn 1984): 333–58. doi:10.2307/302821.

Moulton, Jen. "Listen Joanne, we get it, you didn't include enough representation when you wrote the books." Twitter, September 26, 2018. https://twitter.com/j_a_moulton/status/1044898830444105728?lang=en.

Nigatu, Heben. "10 Ridiculously Offensive Things People Tell Asian Women on OkCupid." BuzzFeed, April 8, 2013. https://www.buzzfeed.com/hnigatu/10-ridiculously-offensive-things-people-tell-asian-women-on.

Oppermann, Martin. "Sex Tourism." *Annals of Tourism Research* 26, no. 2 (April 1999): 251–66.

Pham, Kaitlin. "Respect, Cho Chang, and Asian Representation: A Critical Analysis of the White Gaze in Harry Potter." Senior project, California Polytechnic State University, 2014.

Pottermore. "Everything You Need to Know about Nagini." September 24, 2018. https://www.pottermore.com/features/everything-you-need-to-know-about-nagini.

Rowling, J. K. *Harry Potter and the Deathly Hallows*. New York: Scholastic, 2007.

Rowling, J. K. *Harry Potter and the Goblet of Fire*. New York: Scholastic, 2000.

Rowling, J. K. *Harry Potter and the Order of the Phoenix*. New York: Scholastic, 2003.

Rowling, J. K. *Harry Potter and the Prisoner of Azkaban*. New York: Scholastic, 1999.

Rowling, J. K. (@jk_rowling). "The Naga are snake-like mythical creatures of Indonesian mythology." Twitter, September 26, 2018. https://twitter.com/jk_rowling/status/1044907311058358273.

Said, Edward. *Orientalism*. New York: Random House, 1978.

Sims, Jennifer Patrice. "The Reality of Imaginary Whiteness." *Black Perspectives*, July 24, 2016. https://www.aaihs.org/the-reality-of-imaginary-whiteness/.

Spivak, Gayatri Chakravorty. "Can the Subaltern Speak?" In *The Post-Colonial Studies Reader*, edited by Bill Ashcroft, Gareth Griffiths, and Helen Tiffin, 28–36. Abingdon, Oxon., England: Routledge, 2006.

Tanaka, Yuki. *Japan's Comfort Women: Sexual Slavery and Prostitution during World War II and the US Occupation*. Abingdon, Oxon., England: Routledge, 2002.

Thomas, Ebony Elizabeth. *The Dark Fantastic: Race and the Imagination from Harry Potter to the Hunger Games*. New York: New York University Press, 2019.

Vidal-Ortiz, Salvador, Brandon Andrew Robinson, and Cristina Khan. *Race and Sexuality*. Cambridge: Polity Press, 2018.

Wijanarko, Harun (@HarunWijanarko). "Never ever change @jk_rowling. The universe that you've made is still the universe that we all love." Twitter, September 26, 2018. https://twitter.com/HarunWijanarko/status/1044913596881223681.

Yuen, Nancy Wang. *Reel Inequality: Hollywood Actors and Racism*. New Brunswick, NJ: Rutgers University Press, 2017.

Racebending Potter

How Fan Artists Are Recoloring the Wizarding World

Kathryn Coto

Racebending Harry Potter Fan Work
in Conversation with Canon and Academic Critique

Fan productions are fan-made creative and critical responses to original published media texts. Original texts are also referred to within fandom as canonical works or simply as canon. Fan creations are varied and include visual art (fanart) and stories (fanfiction); cosplay through which fans dress up as canonical characters and attend fan conventions or post their images on social media; fancasts or *re*casts through which fans imagine their ideal casts for television and film media texts or hypothetical adaptations of literary media texts; and blog and vlog posts offering critical commentary on canon. This chapter looks at a very specific type of resistant fan production—racebent fanart, which seeks to add diversity to canon by rewriting white characters as people of color—responding to J. K. Rowling's *Harry Potter* series to examine how memory and the cultural process of remembering together via social media affinity spaces are integral to a critical, antiracist project realized through collective fan artists' work.

Jessica Seymour identifies the three most common categories of fanart as homage, collaboration, and intervention: "Intervention fanart identifies a gap or perceived shortcoming in the original and works to fix it."[1] She suggests that one motivation behind intervention fanart is "a desire to promote activism."[2] While I discuss racebent fanart as revisionist, resistant, transformative, and corrective rather than interventionist, this chapter builds on Seymour's examination of fanart. I use fan, media, and cultural studies to theorize the production, viewing, and response to racebending Potter fanart as an act of collective activist remembering and reinvention. This collective conversation takes place as fans share their work through social media affinity spaces such as the blogging and microblogging platforms Tumblr, LiveJournal, Facebook, and Twitter and the photo- and video-sharing sites Instagram and YouTube. Using an organizational system of hashtags and code words, fans link their works together in an ever expanding, patchwork archive published across a variety of affinity spaces.[3] For instance, works tagged "slash" focus on queer romantic relationships and most often represent a queering of canonically heteronormative characters.

Grouped or archived together, racebent fan productions, for instance, represent a collective discussion or debate on a specific topic that is engaged with by different members of the fandom community at large, such as fans of racebending in general, fans of racebending who only participate in the discussion within the narrower context of the bending of a specific character(s) or within a specific fandom, detractors of racebending,[4] and so on. This collective yet diverse fan discussion reflects the complex relationship media consumers have with published texts, at once celebratory—representing a fannish love of canonical works—and critical or transformative, through which fan creators respond to, resist, and correct problematic elements of canon. I begin by placing the fannish discussion of racebent Potter fanart within the context of an academic critique of race in Rowling's novels and film adaptations, and eventually examine several fanart images that are drawings of imaginary photographs or photographic cosplay art and their metatexts—or hashtags and commentary—to emphasize fanart's sophisticated, multilayered intertextuality or metafictionality. My aim is to argue that despite its complexity as text, the visual medium gives racebent Potter fanart currency as an activist tool and deserves consideration as connecting to both a larger antiracist activist tradition and a contemporary activist movement.

To illustrate the complexity of fannish dialogue, I will look at one long, multiauthored conversation about the recasting of the minor character

Lavender Brown in the film adaptations of J. K. Rowling's *Harry Potter* series. For years, fans have been circulating via the blogging platform Tumblr different versions of a photographic assemblage of screen grabs and still shots exploring the recasting of Lavender Brown. These posts collect images of Lavender, first played by Black actress Kathleen Cauley in *Harry Potter and the Chamber of Secrets*, then by Black actress Jennifer Smith in *Harry Potter and the Prisoner of Azkaban*, and finally by white actress Jessie Cave in *Harry Potter and the Half-Blood Prince*, notably when Lavender becomes a more significant character because she starts dating main character Ron Weasley.[5] These fan works include commentary critiquing the recasting as a whitewashing of the character. One such post is accompanied by the ironic question, "did she get a haircut." To date, this particular post has 400,000 plus likes and reblogs,[6] and includes the addition of critical commentary by several Tumblr users.

One notable critical addition to this post was made by seriousbrat,[7] who lists from the American edition of the sixth book, *Half-Blood Prince*, the page numbers of every scene in which Lavender appears in order to prove that the filmmakers had no canonical evidence on which to base whitewashing her character, writing, "I just went through the entire book, and there was NOT A SINGLE PHYSICAL DESCRIPTION OF LAVENDER. Not hair, not eyes, not skin. Nothing." Maria Velazquez identifies these fan "debates over the casting of Lavender Brown [. . .] [as] an opportunity for antiracist fans to engage in an extended, ongoing critique of real-world racism(s) in both fandom and the series itself."[8] In one such critique, fan artist Ran, after encountering the above post about Lavender's recasting on her Tumblr dashboard—the digital news feed composed of the original and reblogged posts of the bloggers she follows—created a piece of fanart of a Black Lavender (fig. 6.1).[9] In addition to racebending the character, Ran also creates a femslash pairing, a fandom term to describe a romantic relationship between two female characters, of Lavender and her best friend, Parvati Patil. The combined racebending and queering of the character is interesting to note because it is evidence of the complex, intersectional conversations happening in fandom. Likewise, Ran's choice to pair Lavender and Parvati is significant because while racebending Lavender she also uses the opportunity to center her visual text on a minor *canonical* character of color.

As seriousbrat points out, there is no canonical textual evidence to prove that Lavender is white, but it is reasonable to read the sixth film as a

Figure 6.1. Fanart shared on Tumblr by Ran of Parvati Patil and racebent Lavender Brown (right).

Rowling-approved extension of the original novels that directs (and corrects) how the fan audience is intended to see her. The caption that accompanies Ran's art—"I didn't know the actress for Lavender was recast for [*Half-Blood Prince*], wow. So Lavender's design is based on the original actress"—reveals how other fan creators' work has evolved her relationship to and feelings about the source text. The years-long chain of discussion on Tumblr reveals the complicated relationship between fans and original texts as well as the incredibly complex intertextual relationship between multiauthored fan productions—in this case the reassemblage of film shots, the critical commentary, the collection of textual references to Lavender, and finally Ran's fanart—and original media texts. Velazquez points out that fans straddle "two knowledge worlds: that of the canonical texts of the Harry Potter series and that of the contemporary real world."[10] Here, any and all of these anti-racist Lavender Brown fan works, from the original poster's assemblage of film images, to seriousbrat's literary commentary, to Ran's fanart, not only engage with the "knowledge worlds" of the Potter films and novels and the Potter fandom but also participate in a discussion about the "contemporary real-world" politics of the lack of diversity and/or whitewashing in published media texts.

One argument that sometimes appears in fannish debate about racebent Potter fan works suggests that while it would be nice if Rowling gave greater space to marginalized subject positions in her Potterverse, as an artist she is under no obligation to do so.[11] I want to head off this debate by briefly placing antiracist racebending fan works within the conversation about race that began within the *Potter* novels and the academic critique of Rowling's handling of race narratives. Indeed, the *Potter* novels appropriate several latent race narratives, including the enslavement of house-elves, a race of magical creatures; the segregation and restriction of magic use for many magical creatures, including the prohibition of wand use by goblins; and Voldemort as blood supremacist who aims to cleanse the wizarding world of the Muggle-born (or "Mudbloods"), half-bloods, and pure-blood blood traitors. On the handling of Voldemort's racist agenda, Megan Justine Fowler writes:

> The magical politics of the series, in which a war breaks out over blood purity and purebloods seek to exterminate mudbloods, obviously parallels white supremacist rhetoric and the racism that people of color experience in the real world. However, because the victims of this prejudice in the text are largely presented as white, the series falls into the narrative trappings of what is colloquially known as fantastic racism, or the use of fictional forms of racism in fantasy and science fiction as a metaphor or parallel to real-world racism without centering this narrative around actual characters of color.[12]

In her excellent essay on race in the *Potter* series reprinted in this volume, Jackie C. Horne examines how discussions of race more often surround *not* Rowling's human characters, but magical creatures like house-elves and goblins. Rowling's focus on nonhuman characters places another degree of separation between her discussion of race narratives and her (minor) canonical characters of color, and as a result again alienates her real-world readers of color. For the purposes of this chapter, Horne's most important claim is her identification of two antiracist pedagogies present in the series: multicultural antiracism, which encourages empathy, so that "by learning about the culture of other races [. . .] students will learn to rid themselves of their prejudices," and social justice antiracism, which "asks students to examine institution-wide structures of power" in order to "question, deconstruct, and challenge those institutional structures that contribute to, or actively foster, racism."[13]

Horne suggests that the goblins' resistance to and defense against the prejudices enacted by wizarding law in the final book in the series, *Harry Potter and the Deathly Hallows* (as opposed to previous series installments in which Hermione speaks *for* and without the permission *of* enslaved house-elves), is the first opportunity for a "racial other to speak directly to and in protest against the [institutionalized] social hierarchy imposed upon them by the wizards." Although Horne recognizes this thread of social justice antiracist rhetoric in Rowling's texts, ultimately she concludes that no institutional change occurs for goblins (or house-elves, for that matter), and that "though [Rowling's] novels show moments of collective action in the fight against Voldemort, at the heart they are about the emotional growth of a boy rather than a depiction of the rise of a collective political movement." Horne points out that even the enslavement of the house-elves is a part of Harry's narrative of growth, so that through Dumbledore's multicultural antiracist rhetoric Harry learns to empathize with elves, but this engenders a personal rather than an institutional evolution.

If Rowling arguably drops the ball in appropriating race narratives to tell a coming of age story about a white boy, Fowler proposes that "[f]ans use racebent Harry Potter fan work to [. . .] recuperate the radical potential of the series to oppose white supremacist rhetoric."[14] She writes: "Racebending in the Harry Potter fandom reinscribes the subtextual racial implications of the pureblood-privileging wizarding society onto actual bodies of color, repairing the political potential of the metaphorical conflict in the series."[15] It is important to consider whether racebending fan work is an antiracist repairing of canon or an extension of work *begun* but not finished by Rowling. In the distinction lies a potential conclusion that Rowling's use of race narratives is a collaborative relay between her and her fans, or is in fact a racist appropriation that *needs* racebending fan work in order to make the *Potter* series relevant to a discussion of race and racism in our contemporary, real world.

In a Tumblr post, Potter fan Ayesha highlights the ways in which Rowling appropriates a race narrative, by pointing out how easy it is to map a contemporary race narrative onto Harry's character arc. Ayesha counters the critique that depicting Harry as Black "doesn't make sense" by adopting an ironic voice, writing: "[A] character who is forced into adult roles from a very early age, persecuted by the media, and subject to having their loved ones killed or imprisoned by a biased justice system? You're right, how could that narrative *ever* work with POC as main characters?"[16] As Ayesha rightly points out, Harry's narrative correlates to a recognizable narrative of institutional racism impacting contemporary people of color.

After Harry, bookworm Hermione Granger is the most popular character to racebend.[17] Just as Harry's status as a half-blood is a major point of contention within the wizarding world, Hermione's experience as an outsider/Other because she is a Muggle-born witch is a theme running throughout the series, especially when she becomes the target of hate speech. The slur "Mudblood" first appears in the second novel, *Harry Potter and the Chamber of Secrets*, when aimed at Hermione by Draco Malfoy, whom Velazquez identifies as an obvious stand-in for a real-world white supremacist because he is "blond, white, aristocratic [. . .] the face of Slytherin, the Hogwarts house most overtly associated with classism and anti-Muggle sentiment" (*HP and the CS*, 103). Although neither Harry nor Hermione have ever heard the word "Mudblood," Harry knows that it "must've been really bad, because everyone went wild," and Hermione can just tell that "it was really rude" (*HP and the CS*, 115), which arguably represents how readers might also instinctually recognize through discomfort Rowling's implicit appropriation of white supremacist rhetoric.

Figure 6.2 is walkingnorth's fanart of racebent Hermione, who wears a shirt that says "Mudblood Pride," overtly conflating the slur "Mudblood" with racist discourse and echoing the practice through which marginalized people resist hate speech by embracing the language that is intended to shame. Just in case the visual message communicated by her fanart is not clear enough, walkingnorth makes plain the connection between the term "Mudblood" and racist discourse by captioning the piece, "Hermione Jean Granger, fighting wizarding racism since 1991." Walkingnorth's racebent Hermione elucidates a race narrative contained *within* (not imposed by fans *upon*) the *Potter* novels, a narrative that is arguably undermined in canon by the lack of major characters of color. As Jennifer Patrice Sims points out in her chapter in this book, Rowling's intentions with regard to discussions of race in her texts are

Figure 6.2. "Hermione Jean Granger, fighting wizarding racism since 1991." Racebending fanart by walkingnorth. http://walkingnorth.tumblr.com/post/119120163771/walkingnorth-art-hermione-jean-granger#notes.

irrelevant. "Good intentions" do not prevent the end product from reinforcing homogenizing and controlling images.[18] Applying this argument to racebent Hermione fanart suggests that fan intervention is necessary in order to give Rowling's race narrative a context, so that Hermione becomes not an example of "fantastic racism" but a point of connection for real readers of color.

Theorizing Visual Fan Productions

The somewhat underground nature of fandom means that fan works remain ostensibly invisible to the wider population of media consumers. However, Marita Sturken and Lisa Cartwright suggest that "contemporary intertextuality operates on a level that is [. . .] ironic and complex. It often presumes a significant amount of media literacy and familiarity with many cultural products on the parts of viewers. It *interpellates* a media and visually literate viewer who is familiar with image conventions and genres."[19] Sturken and Cartwright's "media and visually literate viewer" is extremely important to a discussion of activist fanart, because—as evidenced by the long chain of engagement with media texts and fandom discussion that led to Ran's race-bent Lavender Brown—a person looking at a piece of racebending fanart must seemingly interpret *several* intertextual strands in order for the work to be effective as a critique of canon. The most basic requirement of the viewer of a racebending fan production is that they be familiar with at least part of the canonical Potter visual archive, such as the novels' covers or chapter header illustrations or the faces of the Potter film actors, in order to recognize that a character's race has been changed; a critical viewer would be familiar with the canonical text's descriptions of racialized bodies and narratives as well as fandom's discussion of these topics; and, finally, the most sophisticated viewer would understand how these images relate to activist movements happening across social media that do not always overtly intersect with the Potter fandom.

In order to read this fan-produced visual counternarrative as a text with political currency, I explore how casual viewers—and not just expert readers who are already a part of the fandom—are literate enough to interpret the intertextuality of these racebending image-texts. Critical work from visual and cultural studies offers some basis for suggesting that visual fan productions do not necessarily require the same extensive repertoire of knowledge for interpretation as fanfiction, which Catherine Tosenberger suggests is unpublishable without significant expository additions.[20]

Perry Nodelman argues that "[t]he simple text" of stories written for children "implies an unspoken and much more complex repertoire that amounts to a second, hidden text—what I will call a 'shadow text.'"[21] Nodelman suggests that one might interpret that "[t]he reason for the simplicity is the author's assumption about the limited abilities of the implied [young] audience,"[22] but that readers—including children—"can extrapolate more information" from this hidden text "by referring to a 'repertoire' of knowledge already possessed."[23] Tosenberger extends Nodelman's concept of the "shadow text" to fanfiction, suggesting that the reader of fanfiction holds in their mind a complex "shadow text" or repertoire of knowledge, including the canonical or "source text upon which the fandom is based" and "'fanon'—the history of fannish theorizing, interpretation, and previous fanfiction [. . .] that has become widely accepted, or at least recognized as such, within the fandom."[24]

Tosenberger's application of Nodelman's definition of the "shadow text" to fanfiction is also useful when considering whether fanart must always nostalgically carry a canonical text's "hidden assumptions" about identity, including oppressive figurations of gender, class, sexuality, and race. At least a part of the *Potter* novels' "shadow text" is the default assumption of whiteness, a legacy transmitted through the text's genre, the British school story, and the exclusion of people of color from this narrative. Lily Anne Welty Tamai and Paul Spickard, in their chapter in this volume, point to a contemporary, default colorblindness in Rowling's version of the British school story:

> All of the characters in Potter present as White. Even people who have Asian names, like Cho Chang and the Patil twins, Padma and Parvati, behave like White people. Where race exists in the Potter world is in the divisions between Muggle and wizard. [. . .] Rowling is doing racework, but it is done amid these racialized categories.[25]

Much of the fan conversation about racebending fanart questions and rejects the text's default "assumptions" that the students of Hogwarts must always be read as white, because in assuming her readers' subject position to be white, Rowling—likely unintentionally—offers up characters who have little to no canonical physical descriptions, like Harry Potter and Hermione Granger.

It is useful to connect Tosenberger's rendering of fanfiction as containing a complex shadow text with Roger I. Simon's discussion of the ways in which social media provides a space for resistant collective remembering in order to read visual fan productions as dialogically reconstructing and rewriting a repressive shadow text. According to Simon, contemporary "remembering together is construed as a practice through which a cluster of people" use social media to "collectively archive material that when subsequently retrieved might serve future purposes."[26] He argues that "social media participants are not only articulating personal encounters with the traces of a particular history but, as well, collectively redefining what might be understood as temporal and spatial parameters of a historical event. In this respect, a practice of 'remembering together' may be said to restructure historical consciousness, instituting a viscerally felt 'historical present.'"[27] Racebending fanart that seems to celebrate an exclusionist text like the *Potter* series, rather than white aping, represents a resistant collective archival remembering. These images, through the collective act of social media archiving, become a searchable visual counterhistory to the dominant cultural narrative that is a part of a reader's shadow text.

Sturken and Cartwright suggest that "Western culture has come to be dominated by visual rather than oral or textual media,"[28] and their scholarship and the work being done in contemporary visual and cultural studies by critics like Margaret Dikovitskaya and Winfried Nöth, who theorize our visual culture, is indebted to W. J. T. Mitchell's identification of a contemporary pictorial turn through which "pictures form a point of peculiar friction and discomfort across a broad range of intellectual inquiry."[29] We might take from this idea of *discomfort* the suggestion that a piece of racebending fanart *need only* produce a sense of "discomfort" or estrangement within the viewer as it rubs up against our default assumptions in order to trigger an awareness of an image's intertextuality, prompting a critical response.

According to Mitchell, this pictorial turn "is not a return to naïve mimesis, copy or correspondence theories of representation" but rather a "rediscovery of the picture as a complex interplay between visuality, apparatus, institutions, discourse, bodies, and figurality."[30] Dikovitskaya evolves Mitchell's pictorial turn into a cultural turn through which the "study of images [becomes] a reflection on the complex interrelationships between power and knowledge. Representation began to be studied as a structure and process of ideology that produces subject positions."[31] Racebending fan artists are intertextually participating in an interdisciplinary and intermedium conversation about how images rub up against systems of "power and knowledge," creating "friction" or "discomfort"—using social media archival tools to resist the way in which canonical *Potter* texts and images reproduce the ideological assumption that the default reader subject position is white.

To return to Ran's racebent Lavender: a viewer need not be cognizant of the entire critical conversation or the casting decisions to which she alludes in her caption to experience discomfort at the way her image and text interact with canon and to understand that there is a mistrust and resistance to the Potterverse's handling of representation of race. Dikovitskaya suggests that the visual is a construction of the social in that it is "a place for examining the social mechanisms of differentiation."[32] To extend this understanding of the visual to fanart, an image's readability as social critique requires the viewer to be able to identify how the art recognizes and *re*constructs the contemporary "social mechanisms of differentiation." Ran's fan production combines image with text in order to make explicit the "social mechanisms of differentiation" at work in the film—in this case the "recast[ing]" or whitewashing of Lavender—and to undo this process by celebrating the "original actress."

Part of what makes racebending fanart *decipherable* by a mass audience is that it is participating in and *borrowing visibility* from an archival *visual* (and literary) activist movement. The fannish practice of racebending extends from the civil rights era's "Black Is Beautiful" movement, which

> enabled the 1970s to become an era of cultural producers who were unapologetically Black, beautiful, and bold. Before the 70s, there was a goal for Black people to align with mainstream, white middle-class culture. But the 70s [. . .] was a time of embracing Blackness as a point of pride, where Black people could wear cornrows, Afros, and braids, and include African fabrics and design in their wardrobe. [. . .] With an emphasis on loving Blackness, these cultural producers infused a critical consciousness on the nation that still shapes the hearts, minds, and actions of the next generation of artists and activists.[33]

Elizabeth Gilliland suggests that racebending fan works are "a 21st-century, cyber-inspired descendent"[34] of literary Afrofuturism, which "might be viewed as any text that explores the future of people of African descent, as well as how that future reflects the reality of today and/or the realities of the past."[35] Afrofuturism, she argues, contains an activist project, "using these depictions of the future as a strong critique of the present, working to make the world we live in better now."[36] Although Gilliland sees fan work as a "result" of Afrofuturism, she is reluctant to go as far as to say "that racebending accomplishes the same work as Afro- and other ethno futurisms,"[37] because "plugging characters of color at random to add some flavor and diversity [. . .] can be just as problematic as the alternative."[38] Simply inserting a character of color (or a queer person, for that matter) into a media text without exploring how race affects that character produces a colorblind narrative that says nothing real about being a member of a marginalized group.[39] Racebent Potter fan works arguably participate in and continue the activist project of literary Afro- and ethno-futuristic texts, because they do not arbitrarily or (color) blindly insert characters of color into Rowling's narratives but, as previously discussed, recenter a metaphorical or fantastic race narrative on "actual characters of color."[40] Racebent Potter fanart also connects to contemporary instances of collective remembering happening across social media platforms right now. The most obvious contemporary example of photography as a radical reconstruction of Black identity and a pushing back against the assumption that the dominant subject position is white, is the social media activist #BlackoutDay movement. Using the hashtags #BlackoutDay or #Blackout, social media users who "identify as Black, either from Africa or from within the African Diaspora, mixed (or part) Black," can post selfies, "GIFs or Videos [. . .] [s]elf portrait artwork [. . .] [and] Original Characters" "for others to admire and reblog/retweet/report."[41] Started in March 2015, #BlackoutDay continues as "a quarterly call-to-action" to use social media as an archive to "(re)define Blackness."[42] Marissa Rei, T'von Green, and nukirk write: "[We] came together because we noticed that while we were living in an age of protests, movements, and demands for diversity, there was still a need for a positive, widespread celebration of every-day Black folks."[43] Writing in 1995, before the internet was widely accessible through handheld devices like phones and tablets, bell hooks describes the wall of photographs in "black homes as a critical intervention, a disruption of white control over black images."[44]

Further, hooks suggests that "it is essential that any theoretical discussion of the relationship of black life to the visual, to art making, make photography central. Access and mass appeal have historically made photography a powerful location for the construction of an oppositional black aesthetic."[45] The archiving and sharing of images such as selfies through social media is the twenty-first century's equivalent of hooks's wall of photography. The Facebook News Feed, where people share their lives through "status" updates and photo posts; the Tumblr dashboard, which collects the posts of the blog-gers an individual user follows in a single feed in real time; and the Instagram account, through which users create a (sometimes seemingly disparate) visual narrative, all serve as modern archival spaces. Apryl Williams and Beatriz Aldana Marquez suggest that, much like resistant fan productions, "selfies have become social artifacts that deliver social messages created or negotiated by the culture that produces them."[46] As hooks argues that photography is key to Black empowerment, Mehita Iqani and Jonathan E. Schroeder posit that "selfies may represent a moment of complete agency and self-expres-sion, which is almost certainly pleasurable and meaningful."[47] They write: "Although all selfies do not resemble snapshots, a *snapshot aesthetic* often informs posing for, taking, sharing, and viewing selfies. Snapshots help us narrate and make sense of our lives."[48] I would like to borrow Simon's and hooks's conception of cultural remembering to consider racebending visual fan productions as a fragment of the whole archive, a part of this oppositional visual aesthetic.

Although hooks and the #BlackoutDay creators are discussing collective remembering specifically as it relates to personal photography and its connection to the real, I find that fanart seems to be in conversation with this medium even though these works are *imagined* images reconstructing *fictional* media texts. Mitchell provides us with the term "metapicture"—"a picture about itself, a picture that refers to its own making"[49]—and racebending fanart is arguably an extension of this self-referential image genre in that it intertextually alludes to its creation as a product of resistant reading. These images are visual products of real readers' personal experiences with texts. Susan Sontag's theorizing on the photograph also gets close to what I think of as the project of racebending fanart. She suggests that "a photograph is not only like its subject, a homage to the subject. It is part of, an extension of that subject; and a potent means of acquiring it, of gaining control over it."[50] Racebending Potter fanart is certainly "like its subject," a celebratory reconstruction or "homage," but it is also a way to gain control over the *real*, which in this case is the representation of bodies in the source material.

Drawings of Photos

Artist refrigerator_art21,[51] who shares her fan productions through Tumblr, provides us with perhaps the most salient connection between the activist movement #BlackoutDay and racebending Potter fanart. She's created several racebent Potter images, archived on her blog with the hashtags #Blackout and #HogwartsBlackout (fig. 6.3), that depict Harry Potter and friends posing for selfies and "sharing" them across social media platforms. Not only does refrigerator_art21 tag her posts so as to draw the attention of "real" social media users interested in #BlackoutDay (who track the tag across platforms like Tumblr and Instagram) to her Potter art, but the images metafictionally reference the act of sharing photos in online archival spaces, because over the drawings of photographs are words that are meant to be read as the *characters'* (rather than the artist's) tags.

"Photography," hooks argues, connects us "to a recuperative, redemptive memory that enables us to construct radical identities, images of ourselves

Figure 6.3. "#HogwartsBlackout." Fan artist refrigerator_art21's racebent Hermione Granger and Harry Potter. https://www.instagram.com/p/BwYIIoBFDxd/.

that transcend the limits of the colonizing eye."[52] Refrigerator_art21 emphasizes the fact that racebending fan works are participating in a decolonization project, linking fan artists' reconstruction of Potter canon with the *remembering* and recuperation of more visible archival movements like #BlackoutDay, whereby the bank of white faces represented on the internet is overwritten or *decolonized*. Indeed, Fowler argues that "fans' racebending of Harry [. . .] offers postcolonial revisions of *Harry Potter*."[53] Significantly, by overlaying her Potter fanart set during Harry's early 1990s school years with text that anachronistically references a contemporary *online* activist movement, refrigerator_art21 remembers the novels through a modern critical lens.

Not only does refrigerator_art21's work emphasize minor canonical Black characters such as Lee Jordan and Blaise Zabini but she racebends Harry, Hermione, and Lavender Brown. Just as participants in #BlackoutDay seek to increase the visibility of Black social media users, refrigerator_art21 draws attention to the whiteness of Potter by making almost all of the characters in this *series* of images people of color. Whether or not a viewer is an insider participant in the fandom, they can't help but notice that something is different. Refrigerator_art21's overcrowded #BlackoutDay "selfie" of canonical characters of color—including Kingsley Shacklebolt, Lee Jordan, Blaise Zabini, and Dean Thomas, as well as racebent Lavender Brown, Hermione Granger, and Harry Potter—in which the characters are squeezed into and bursting from the imagined photograph's frame (fig. 6.4), seems to make a perhaps unconscious connection to activist Dylan Marron's Every Single Word Spoken project.[54]

Marron collects and assembles montages of every word spoken by a person of color in popular films, including the *Potter* series, and shares these productions through Tumblr and YouTube. His Potter montage reveals that out of almost twenty hours of film, the words spoken by persons of color only add up to six minutes and eighteen seconds. Whereas Marron's fan production emphasizes the lack of space for people of color in the Potterverse, refrigerator_art21's crowded selfie overwrites the visual representation of the films; in her drawing of a photograph, there are so many persons of color that they are overlapping, bursting at the seams of the image.

Refrigerator_art21's drawing of racebent Harry and Hermione (with Ron Weasley) (fig. 6.5) goes a step further in metafictionally creating a sense of discomfort in the viewer, because her Harry is wearing a shirt made out of his mugshot poster from the seventh novel—except her art makes absolutely

Figure 6.4. "Happy Anniversary #Blackout." Fanart by refrigerator_art21. Includes minor canonical characters of color Kingsley Shacklebolt, Lee Jordan, Blaise Zabini, and Dean Thomas, as well as racebent Lavender Brown, Hermione Granger, and Harry Potter. http://refrigerator-art.tumblr.com/post/140566638700/happy-anniversary-everyone-i-just-want-to-let.

Figure 6.5. Refrigerator_art21's "When the Whole Squad Glos Up," featuring Ron Weasley, Harry Potter, and Hermione Granger. http://refrigerator-art.tumblr.com/post/145526778550/when-the-whole-squad-glos-up-back-in-2014-i#notes.

clear her alteration of canon, because on his shirt is a real *photograph* of Daniel Radcliffe, the white actor who plays Harry in the films. Interestingly, refrigerator_art21 also connects Hermione's activism (she's wearing a S.P.E.W. badge) with criminality *and* the past—her shirt references the troublemaking Marauders, who belonged to the previous generation and included Harry's father. This piece reminds the viewer that racebending Harry and Hermione requires a re-remembering and revision of the past as contained in the novels and films, and pushes for critical thought because the institutional controls of government and school (alluded to on their shirts) still exist and must be challenged.

V Swain's fanart of James Potter and Lily Evans (fig. 6.6) and Harry Potter (fig. 6.7) in which their faces are framed by the white border of a photograph nicely connects the activist potential of racebending fanart to hooks's conception of private family photography as forming an "oppositional black aesthetic." The project of "remembering" is emphasized by the fact that the "photos" of his parents and Harry are dated 1976 and 1996, respectively. Swain captioned the racebent pieces by excerpting dialogue from the film version of *Harry Potter and the Prisoner of Azkaban* in which Professor Remus Lupin says to Harry, "[T]he very first time I saw you, Harry, I recognized you immediately. Not by your scar, by your eyes. They're your mother Lily's. Yes, oh yes, I knew her."[55] By borrowing a quotation from canon, Swain not only emphasizes this moment wherein Lupin remembers *for* Harry, but they make clear that they are *re*writing this episode of *positive* familial remembering within the context of a biracial family.

I have chosen these images that are pictures of imaginary photographs to emphasize fanart's intertextuality or metafictionality. Winfried Nöth suggests that "[e]*very* picture contains a self-referential pictorial metasign in the form of its *frame*, which is an indexical sign conveying a metamessage such as: 'I am a picture.'"[56] She suggests that a "frame in a metaphorical sense" is an "enunciative picture frame": it "refers to the circumstances which make pictorial information a message emitted by an addresser and addressed to an addressee."[57] Refrigerator_art21's and Swain's drawings of fictional photographs use the photographic frame to help enunciate their indexical counternarratives so that the reader is hyperaware of the images' metamessages: "I am a picture of a text," "I am a picture *about* a text, a picture *changing* a text." Within the context of Rowling's novels, part of what makes Harry Potter an effective symbol of political power is his visibility: everyone in the wizarding world knows him by his round glasses and lightning-shaped scar. Fan producers like refrigerator_art21 and Swain are capitalizing on Harry Potter's visibility or recognizability in our *real* world, combining his political currency within fandom with real-world activist movements to make their metamessages relevant and legible to a wider audience of social media users.

I want to close this chapter by looking at a visual collage or photoset of Potter cosplay (fig. 6.8), which brings together my discussion of fanart's relationship to photography. This piece of fanart, created by Tumblr user

Figures 6.6, 6.7. V Swain, "The Very First Time." Fanart of James Potter, Lilly Evans, and Harry Potter. http://vondellswain.tumblr.com/post/78697960953/the-very-first-time-i-saw-you-harry-i-recognised.

Figure 6.8. "The Harry and Hermione the World Deserves." Tumblr users Syena and literallyprince charming, racebending Potter cosplay. http://toddalquist.tumblr.com/post/112878612406/me-and -literallyprincecharming-are-the-harry-and.

Syena, mirrors aesthetic posts or fancasts, through which fan producers collect images that conjure up the *Potter* novels and pair them with the faces of models and actors, sometimes with the aim to "recast" the characters as nonwhite. In this fancast, however, Syena uses her own face along with photographs of Tumblr user literallyprincecharming to give her readers "the Harry and Hermione the world deserves." The use of the word "deserves" here emphasizes the fact that a major part of the Potterverse's audience feels underrepresented in and underserved by these texts—and that this is a wrong that needs to be corrected. Not only does Syena use the faces of "real" readers, suggesting that Potter fans literally want to *see* themselves in Rowling's books, but she tags her post #Blackout, likewise linking resistant reading fan practices with the contemporary social activist movement. Often, racebending art is created by white fans, but Syena's fancast uses photography to make undeniable the fact that "real" Black Potter fans are longing for representation.

In their discussion of racebending fan works, Ebony Elizabeth Thomas and Amy Stornaiuolo describe the process of "restorying" as a means for fan creators to "reimagin[e] stories from nondominant, marginalized, and silenced perspectives [. . .] that draws from and makes manifest [their] embodied, lived realities and identities."[58] Although the fanart that I have examined undoubtedly participates in this "restorying" process, the fan practice of racebending cosplay emphasizes the fan creator's embodiment, making explicit the fact that these are *real* POC fans reading themselves into Rowling's texts even as the process requires them to become resistant.

Notes

1. Seymour, "Homage, Collaboration, or Intervention," 100.

2. Seymour, "Homage, Collaboration, or Intervention."

3. Although not referred to in this chapter, it is useful to know that contemporary fandom's most popular website through which fan creators share fanfiction is Archive of Our Own or AO3, the name notable because it alludes to the archival nature of fandom and the communally assembled, multiauthored texts created when many diverse multimedia fan works are collected, preserved, and read together.

4. This chapter does not look at specific fan productions that argue against racebending, but it is important to know that fan works that might be labeled as "racist" do exist within the fan community, including fanart. I don't engage with anti-racebending fan works in this chapter because I believe that these discussions should take place within the fandom community, where a back-and-forth dialogue is possible.

5. The internet sleuthing of user seriousbrat reveals that Jennifer Smith plays not another reincarnation of Lavender but "a character made for the movies named Kellah."

6. Tumblr's format allows users to publish original blog posts as well as reblog, with or without their own additions, posts from other users. New commentary can come in the form of a reblog with information added below the words of the original poster or through the tags a reblogger uses to organize the post on their own blog.

7. I have not included a citation for this post in my bibliography, because it was originally made under a different Tumblr username that now belongs to another blogger. seriousbrat has given me permission to include her commentary and asked that I refer to her using her current Potter fandom Tumblr username. Likewise, many different versions of the reblogged post can be found easily through a Google search, but the original poster has since deactivated their account, so I do not provide a citation with a URL.

8. Velazquez, "The Occasional Ethnicities of Lavender Brown," 112.

9. While Ran has given me permission to include her art in this chapter, I do not provide a URL or bibliographic citation because she has since left the Potter fandom. Her art still exists within the Potter fandom through thousands of reblogs, but she has deleted her images from her own Tumblr account.

10. Velazquez, "The Occasional Ethnicities of Lavender Brown," 105.

11. While there are many social media posts made by detractors of racebending, including critical additions to the original post about Lavender Brown's recasting, they are not quoted here. It is not the goal of this chapter to call out or shame specific fan creators but rather to highlight and celebrate racebending fans' antiracist interventions in Rowling's series.

12. Fowler, "Rewriting the School Story," 4.1.

13. For quotations in this and the following paragraph, see Jackie C. Horne's chapter in this volume, "Harry and the Other: Multicultural and Social Justice Anti-Racism in J. K. Rowling's *Harry Potter* Series."

14. Fowler, "Rewriting the School Story," 4.3.

15. Fowler, "Rewriting the School Story," 3.7.

16. Ayesha, "It's almost hilarious."

17. Interestingly, a line from the third *Potter* film, *Harry Potter and the Prisoner of Azkaban*, in which Professor Lupin remarks that Hermione is "the brightest witch of her age," is used to title many racebent Hermione images. These fan artists are clearly making a point that people of color are believable as the brightest characters in a book.

18. See Jennifer Patrice Sims's chapter in this volume, "When the Subaltern Speak Parseltongue: Orientalism, Racial Re-Presentation, and Claudia Kim as Nagini."

19. Sturken and Cartwright, *Practices of Looking*, 265.

20. Tosenberger, "Mature Poets Steal."

21. Nodelman, *The Hidden Adult*, 8.

22. Nodelman, *The Hidden Adult*, 8.

23. Nodelman, *The Hidden Adult*, 9.

24. Tosenberger, "Mature Poets Steal," 10.

25. See Lily Anne Welty Tamai and Paul Spickard's chapter in this volume, "Half-Blood: Mixed-Race Tropes Old and New in Harry Potter's World."

26. Simon, "Remembering Together," 90.

27. Simon, "Remembering Together," 92–93.

28. Sturken and Cartwright, *Practices of Looking*, 1.

29. Mitchell, *Picture Theory*, 13.

30. Mitchell, *Picture Theory*, 16.

31. Dikovitskaya, *Visual Culture*, 48.

32. Dikovitskaya, *Visual Culture*, 58.
33. Jackson and Macklin, "Nice & Rough," 151–52.
34. Gilliland, "Racebending Fandoms and Digital Futurism," 3.9.
35. Gilliland, "Racebending Fandoms and Digital Futurism," 3.2.
36. Gilliland, "Racebending Fandoms and Digital Futurism," 3.3.
37. Gilliland, "Racebending Fandoms and Digital Futurism," 3.4.
38. Gilliland, "Racebending Fandoms and Digital Futurism," 3.4.
39. See Sarah Park Dahlen and Kallie Schell's chapter in this volume, "'Cho Chang Is Trending': What It Means to Be Asian in the Wizarding World."
40. Fowler, "Rewriting the School Story," 4.1.
41. Rei, nukirk, and Green, "What's Blackout Day."
42. Rei, nukirk, and Green, "What's Blackout Day."
43. nukirk, "So . . . What Is #BlackoutDay?" The original creators of #BlackoutDay are no longer actively involved in the movement and have purged the original website of most of its content. They have archived the history of the movement on Tumblr in a post called #TheBlackout Masterpost. See http://tumblr.theblackout.org/post/114966275331/official-blackoutday-masterpost-created-march.
44. hooks, "In Our Glory," 59.
45. hooks, "In Our Glory," 57.
46. Williams and Marquez, "The Lonely Selfie King," 1775.
47. Iqani and Schroeder, "#selfie: Digital Self-Portraits," 412.
48. Iqani and Schroeder, "#selfie: Digital Self-Portraits," 408.
49. Mitchell, *Picture Theory*, 42.
50. Sontag, *On Photography*, 121.
51. Refrigerator_art21 has asked me to include her Instagram username, @refrigerator_art21, as that is where she is most active on social media at time of publication.
52. hooks, "In Our Glory," 64.
53. Fowler, "Rewriting the School Story," 1.2.
54. Marron, "Every Single Word Spoken."
55. Cuarón, *Harry Potter and the Prisoner of Azkaban*, 45:50–46:60.
56. Nöth, "Metapictures and Self-Referential Pictures," 69.
57. Nöth, "Metapictures and Self-Referential Pictures," 69.
58. Thomas and Stornaiuolo, "Restorying the Self," 3.

Bibliography

Ayesha. "It's almost hilarious when people tell you off for interpreting your fave HP characters as POC." *Planting a Nuisance Tree* (blog), March 26, 2015. http://prongsmydeer.Tumblr.com/post/114687524511/its-almost-hilarious-when-people-tell-you-off-for.
Cuarón, Alfonso, dir. 2004. *Harry Potter and the Prisoner of Azkaban*. Warner Bros., 2004.
Dikovitskaya, Margaret. *Visual Culture: The Study of the Visual after the Cultural Turn*. Cambridge, MA: MIT Press, 2006.
Fowler, Megan Justine. "Rewriting the School Story through Racebending in the Harry Potter and Raven Cycle Fandoms." *Transformative Works and Cultures* 29 (March 2019). doi:10.3983/twc.2019.1492.

Gilliland, Elizabeth. "Racebending Fandoms and Digital Futurism." *Transformative Works and Cultures* 22 (2016). doi:10.3983/twc.2016.0702.

hooks, bell. "In Our Glory: Photography and Black Life." In *Art on My Mind: Visual Politics*, 54–64. New York: New Press, 1995.

Iqani, Mehita, and Jonathan E. Schroeder. "#selfie: Digital Self-Portraits as Commodity Form and Consumption Practice." *Consumption Markets and Culture* 19, no. 5 (2015): 405–15. doi:10.1080/10253866.2015.1116784.

Jackson, Sheila, and Angelica Macklin. "*Nice & Rough*: Unapologetically Black, Beautiful, and Bold; A Conversation with Sheila Jackson on Black Women's Participation in Cultural Production in the 1970s." *Women's Studies Quarterly* 43, nos. 3–4 (Fall–Winter 2015): 151–65. doi:10.1353/wsq.2015.0045.

Marron, Dylan. "Every Single Word Spoken by a Person of Color in the Entire 'Harry Potter' Film Series." YouTube, August 18, 2015. https://www.youtube.com/watch?v=x67OjOLj11g.

Mitchell, W. J. T. *Picture Theory: Essays on Verbal and Visual Representation*. Chicago: University of Chicago Press, 1995.

Nodelman, Perry. *The Hidden Adult: Defining Children's Literature*. Baltimore: Johns Hopkins University Press, 2008.

Nöth, Winfried. "Metapictures and Self-Referential Pictures." In *Self-Reference in the Media*, edited by Winfried Nöth and Nina Bishara, 61–78. Berlin: Mouton de Gruyter, 2007.

nukirk. "So . . . What Is #BlackoutDay?" YouTube, September 8, 2016. https://youtu.be/hIrnTCtMRQk.

Rei, Marissa, nukirk, and T'von Green. "What's Blackout Day." The Blackout, September 1, 2015. http://tumblr.theblackout.org/post/114966275331/official-blackoutday-master post-created-march.

Rowling, J. K. *Harry Potter and the Chamber of Secrets*. New York: Scholastic, 1999.

Seymour, Jessica. "Homage, Collaboration, or Intervention: How Framing Fanart Affects Its Interpretation." *Participations* 15, no. 2 (November 2018): 98–114.

Simon, Roger I. "Remembering Together: Social Media and the Formation of the Historical Present." In *Heritage and Social Media: Understanding Heritage in a Participatory Culture*, edited by Elisa Giaccardi, 89–106. Abingdon, Oxon., England: Routledge, 2012.

Sontag, Susan. *On Photography*. New York: RosettaBooks, 2005.

Sturken, Marita, and Lisa Cartwright. *Practices of Looking: An Introduction to Visual Culture*. New York: Oxford University Press, 2001.

Thomas, Ebony Elizabeth, and Amy Stornaiuolo. "Restorying the Self: Bending toward Textual Justice." *Harvard Educational Review* 86, no. 3 (Fall 2016): 313–38. doi:10.17763/1943-5045-86.3.313.

Tosenberger, Catherine. "Mature Poets Steal: Children's Literature and the Unpublishability of Fanfiction." *Children's Literature Association Quarterly* 39, no. 1 (Spring 2014): 4–27. doi:10.1353/chq.2014.0010.

Velazquez, Maria. "The Occasional Ethnicities of Lavender Brown: Race as a Boundary Object in *Harry Potter*." In *Critical Insights: Contemporary Speculative Fiction*, edited by M. Keith Booker, 100–114. Ipswich, MA: Salem Press, 2013.

Williams, Apryl A., and Beatriz Aldana Marquez. "The Lonely Selfie King: Selfies and the Conspicuous Prosumption of Gender and Race." *International Journal of Communications* 9, no. 1 (January 2015): 1775–87.

Half-Blood

Mixed-Race Tropes Old and New in Harry Potter's World

Lily Anne Welty Tamai and Paul Spickard[1]

The use of mixed race and blood purity in J. K. Rowling's *Harry Potter* series highlights mixed-race tropes both old and new. This chapter seeks to unpack those racial tropes by bringing together the insights of critical mixed-race studies and ethnic studies to explore Rowling's use of race, blood quantum, and mixed-blood characters. The trope of the tragic mulatto,[2] the unfortunate mixed-race individual whose blood is impure, has been at the crux of the hybrid-degeneracy versus hybrid-vigor discussion for at least a couple of centuries.[3] It appears repeatedly in the *Potter* books, as does the mixed-race hero archetype—Harry himself—whose mixedness dramatically raises the stakes of literary tension. Furthermore, in this chapter we compare how the language of race is used in the original English-language version of Potter with how it appears in versions translated into Hawaiian, Japanese, and Spanish. Our goal in that move is to spark a discussion of how the racialized language of blood purity varies in cultural significance when it appears in English, in a non-English European language, in an Indigenous language, and in an Asian language.

Race is not absent from Harry Potter.[4] All of the characters in Potter present as White. Even people who have Asian names, like Cho Chang and the Patil twins, Padma and Parvati, behave like White people. Where race exists in the Potter world is in the divisions between Muggle and wizard, and at a secondary level, giant and elf. That's where all the discussion of pure-blood, impure blood, and half-blood takes place. J. K. Rowling is doing racework, but it is done amid these racialized categories. Harry Potter is half-wizard and half-Muggle. Rubeus Hagrid is half-wizard and half-giant. Hermione Granger is pure Muggle, but she somehow has wizardly skills—perhaps there is some long-lost trace of recessive wizardly genes from many generations back that suddenly are expressing themselves in her.[5] Squibs are born into wizarding families but do not possess magical powers.

These groups are not exactly analogous to modern European and North American race categories, but certainly they operate in much the same way.[6] One cannot match up Rowling's blood groupings to particular races in our world. But there are some harmonic resemblances: the house-elves are slaves; the Gringotts goblins have a role in the wizarding world that resembles that of European Jews in our world; Cho Chang might well stand in as the Asian model minority; and Padma and Parvati Patil can be taken to stand for the remnants of the British colonial empire. It is within this setting that we will use a mixed-race lens to examine the racial tropes and racial rules within the *Harry Potter* series.[7]

Degeneracy and Vigor

The tragic mulatto was born with mixed genetic ancestry, from parents of two different races, typically one Black parent and one White parent.[8] This person is likable and is seen as a victim of their divided racial inheritance. Throughout much of modern history, people who are the products of interracial sex and marriage were thought to be genetically defective, mongrels, hybrids—even sterile—and they were assumed to possess a deep identity crisis.[9] They are in turmoil because of their race and can never escape. Their morals and loyalties are questionable, as is their intelligence. They may be assumed to be sexually abnormal or perverse. Sometimes the abnormality is so great that the only conceivable resolution is suicide. The problem is manifested within the mixed-race individual, yet they are merely the product; the origin is rooted in their parents' miscegenation. An enduring example is Giacomo Puccini's opera *Madama Butterfly*.[10] Furthermore, Madama Butterfly's Eurasian child symbolizes the catastrophe from the interracial relationship as a tragedy that bleeds into the lives, the souls, and the futures of mixed-race children. The mixed-race products of miscegenation are presented as so misfortunate that they are often marked as orphans or as unwanted children. The trope of the tragic mulatto embodies the problems of miscegenation and racial impurity. Harry Potter is an orphaned tragic mulatto.[11]

Yet Harry Potter's character differs from the old tragic mulatto stereotypes in literature in several ways. Harry is successful. He is the hero of the tale. Although his Muggle relatives have a problem with his mixedness, Harry is not burdened by it. He is mixed, but not troubled. His family environment is awful, as he is an orphan living with terrible relatives who are more than unkind. Harry is half-wizard, and he lived for the first part of his life as a regular boy who knew nothing of his background because his bloodlines were hidden from him. Upon discovering his background, he adjusts to his identity as a wizard in a household of monoracial Muggle relatives. Harry is the moral compass throughout the series, and his mixedness is not a source of misery for him. His abilities as a powerful wizard reflect his hybrid vigor. Some people, such as his Muggle family, are distressed by his mixedness. Others see him as a savior because of his mixedness.

Harry Potter fits squarely into the generations-old discussion over whether multiracial people embody hybrid degeneracy or hybrid vigor, the best of both worlds or the worst of both.[12] A mixed-race character can have either hybrid vigor, meaning their mixedness has a positive aspect, or hybrid degeneracy, whereby their mixed-race status is negative and complicated, leading to a perceived identity crisis. Often, the mixed-blood person's role is symbolic, because they threaten the existing structures of power by their very multiraciality and force a "re-evaluation of group identity."[13] The tragic mulatto is simultaneously feared and revered, detested and admired.

Despite the obvious reason why Harry Potter is an example of hybrid vigor, another tragic mulatto in the series with hybrid degeneracy is the half-wizard, half-giant Rubeus Hagrid. (His father was a wizard and his mother a giant.) When Hagrid was three years old, his mother decided to return to the giant colony, leaving her child to be raised by his father (*Harry Potter and the Goblet of Fire*, 427–48). Hagrid's body, which stands at eleven and a half feet tall and does not fit into the spaces of Muggles or wizards, is physical evidence of the grotesque crisis that some imagine is inevitable with miscegenation.

An example of how Rowling centers miscegenation is through the tragedy manifested in the bodies of half-giants like Hagrid and Madame Olympe

Maxime. Hagrid was raised among wizards, but he is large. At times, Hagrid's movements are clumsy due to his size. He is too big to fit comfortably among the wizards, and so he lives in a hut adjacent to Hogwarts near the Forbidden Forest. His body size does not fit into wizardly places with ease, and his background is the reason. During Hagrid's time at Hogwarts, his father died, and later he is expelled. His expulsion means that he can no longer practice magic. In addition to their degenerate ancestry, tragic mulattos in literature often lose their parents, severing the direct connection to genetic ancestry while also leaving them abandoned or orphaned.

The quintessential tragic mulatto in the *Harry Potter* series is Tom Marvolo Riddle. Lord Voldemort, or He-Who-Shall-Not-Be-Named, is the ultimate psychotic villain, and his mixedness is the source of his torment. His checkered racial past explains his villainy. His evil is rooted in his background. He is passing for a powerful pure-blood wizard and consciously chose to use his Muggle name during his time at Hogwarts.

I AM LORD VOLDEMORT

"You see?" he whispered. "[Tom Riddle] was a name I was already using at Hogwarts, to my most intimate friends only, of course. You think I was going to use my filthy Muggle father's name forever? I, in whose veins runs the blood of Salazar Slytherin himself, through my mother's side? I, keep the name of a foul, common Muggle, who abandoned me even before I was born, just because he found out his wife was a witch? No, Harry—I fashioned myself a new name, a name I knew wizards everywhere would one day fear to speak, when I had become the greatest sorcerer in the world!" (*Harry Potter and the Chamber of Secrets*, 314)

He is tormented by his mixed-race background, which legitimizes his wickedness and his desire for power over others. His life is tragic, and the reader can make sense of the logic behind his motives.[14] He loathes half-bloods and values pure-blood supremacy, although that purity of blood is the very thing he lacks. He can't help being evil, because evil cannot be separated from his half-blood being.

Some extreme White supremacists read miscegenation in Harry Potter as portending the genocide of White people. They consider this a very dangerous message for children. On the White supremacist website Stormfront, Niata wrote:

I truly fear the negative impact *Harry Potter* has probably had on our White children. Harry and his friends are the "good guys." They have no problem with race mixing and oppose that evil Voldemort who wants to kill everyone who isn't of pure blood. Harry is the hero, so if he is okay with race mixing, it must be all right. Evil Voldemort doesn't support miscegenation and the eradication of witches and wizards so White people who don't support miscegenation and the eradication of Whites are just as bad as Voldemort. [. . .] The message given by J. K. Rowling's body of work is that there is nothing wrong with miscegenation, and if you oppose it, you are evil.[15]

This interpretation of race mixing in Harry Potter reveals the thought process of some who are threatened by miscegenation. They worry that the discussion and presence of blood mixing in the *Potter* series may significantly influence children, who are the intended recipients of this young adult literature. For White supremacists, race mixing is not only tragic but also dangerous, because it may lead to diluting the perceived pure-blood gene pool, thereby leading to White genocide. Rowling is actually challenging White supremacy in the series by bringing examples of interracial relationships,[16] thereby using children's literature to confront the race-based hierarchy and hypocrisy behind blood purity.

The Literary Trope of Mixedness

The mixed-race character is a useful literary device. A racially flexible character gives the author and the reader more room to explore complicated loyalties. Such characters provide added tension about those loyalties. Authors who employ this strategy do not need to delve into the actual complexities of a mixed-race identity navigating monoracial spaces. The reader can automatically assume a constant crisis of identity. Will the person be outed? Will their secret be revealed? What will happen if their true identity is exposed? An example is the conversation between Rubeus Hagrid and Madame Olympe Maxime about his half-giant background, and hers. In an emotional tone, he shares his family's giant lineage. Madame Maxime listens with intent, until Hagrid begins asking her about her size.

"Eh?" said Hagrid blankly. "No, don' go! I've—I've never met another one before!"

"Anuzzer what, precisely?" said Madame Maxime, her tone icy.

Harry could have told Hagrid it was best not to answer; he stood there in the shadows gritting his teeth hoping against hope he wouldn't—but it was no good.

"Another half-giant, o'course!" said Hagrid.

"'Ow dare you!" shrieked Madame Maxime. Her voice exploded through the peaceful night air like a foghorn; behind him, Harry heard Fleur and Roger fall out of their rosebush. "I 'ave nevair been more insulted in my life! 'Alf-giant? *Moi*? I 'ave—I 'ave big bones!" (*HP and the GF*, 428–29)

Hagrid's questions are off-putting to Madame Maxime, and she storms out and leaves him behind. Their encounter as mixed people (although Madame Maxime never admits it) sets up further tension in Rowling's racial story.

Certainly, Harry's own discovery of his magical ability aids in creating tension in the text. Rowling makes this known in the first book, *Harry Potter and the Sorcerer's Stone*. A better example of the use of a mixed-race person to raise tension and mystery is when Severus Snape is outed as a mixed-blood double agent in book 6, *Harry Potter and the Half-Blood Prince*. Over the course of the first five books, Rowling builds the pressure of Snape's tense and tenuous relationship with Harry. Later, the reader finds out not only about Snape's racially complicated past but also about his loyalty to and love for Harry's mother, Lily Potter.

Snape's father, Tobias Snape, was a Muggle, and his mother, Eileen Prince, was a witch. It was from his parents that Snape took the nickname "the Half-Blood Prince." Snape works as double agent, as a spy for the Dark Lord, as a part of Albus Dumbledore's staff teaching Defense against the Dark Arts, and as a member of the Order of the Phoenix. In a conversation with Bellatrix Lestrange and Narcissa Malfoy, he admits his background as a spy:

By waiting two hours, just two hours, I ensured that I could remain at Hogwarts as a spy! By allowing Dumbledore to think that I was only returning to the Dark Lord's side because I was ordered to, I have been able to pass information on Dumbledore and the Order of the Phoenix ever since. [. . .] The Dark Lord's initial displeasure at my lateness vanished entirely, I assure you, when I explained that I remained faithful, although Dumbledore thought I was his man. Yes, the Dark Lord thought that I had left him forever, but he was wrong. (*HP and the HBP*, 28–29)

Snape's disclosure as a double agent allows Rowling time to build the climax, to complicate the narrative of his mixed background. Using a mixed-race character is a strategy for the author to create tension and explore access within the text. The mixed-race person's background gives that character permission not only to enter certain spaces but also to camouflage and cover, to create a racial veil to cover themself with ambiguity so that they can have a magical access pass that a monoracial person normally could not have. The mixed-race person is capable of shifting shapes—being now a member of the wizarding world, now a Muggle, now a devotee of the Dark Lord, and now a member of the Order of the Phoenix. Making characters multiracial gives an author enormous freedom and flexibility. Half-bloods can be trusted until their secret is revealed.

The multiracial character has always been a convenient trope for plot development. Mixed-race characters are useful and complicated; authors often depict them as conflicted with questionable loyalties because of their mixed identity.[17] They are token characters who are easy for readers to understand. In the *Harry Potter* series, we have two kinds of mixed-race characters: (1) Harry Potter, a product of hybrid vigor; and (2) the rest of the mixed-race characters, who are products of hybrid degeneracy, Voldemort being the most degenerate. All are conflicted, including Harry. Mixed-race characters in the series embody all of the classic tropes of the tragic mulatto and are positioned within that binary. The mixed-race character is a straightforward way for a writer to convey inner conflict and conflicting emotions and loyalties. But used this way, such a character is only a literary device. Actual mixed-race people do not experience their lives the way that such literature portrays them. Furthermore, the experiences readers have with race within the text may vary with the language of the text, and that language's cultural and historical relationship to English and the English-speaking world.

Pure-Bloods, Half-Bloods, and Mudbloods in Language

To try to get another angle of view on the meanings of mixed race in Harry Potter, we turned to the books' translations into a few other languages: for our purposes, Spanish, Hawaiian, and Japanese. We have chosen specifically to examine the terms "pure-blood," "half-blood," and "mixed blood" in Hawaiian, Japanese, and Spanish editions of the *Harry Potter* books (see table 1).

Scholars who work with children's literature in English are prone to interpret the issues only in a national standard English idiom. For analytical purposes, we would like to look at the mixed-race issues Rowling raises in the idioms of some other languages and put them in conversation with each other.

In Harry Potter, without question, blood purity is the default, and deviations from the norm are considered impure, socially and later legally when the Ministry of Magic changes the laws. The importance of blood purity is especially significant because it reinforces race and the hierarchy of perceived superiority and power within the wizarding world, while also harking back to colonial times and the colonization of language.

The following examples highlight several places where the text's meaning, translated from English, reflects not only the direct wording but also the cultural position of that wording in the target languages. In what appears to be a casual conversation about the password to gain entry to a common room, the use of the word *pure-blood* can be inferred as hegemonic pure-blood supremacy.

> "What's the new password again?" [Malfoy] said to Harry.
>
> "Er—" said Harry.
>
> "Oh, yeah—*pure-blood!*" said Malfoy, not listening, and a stone door in the concealed wall slid open. Malfoy marched through and Harry and Ron followed him. (*HP and the CS*, 221)

> 「新しい合言葉はなんだったかな？」マルフォイはハリーに聞いた。
>
> 「えーとーーー」
>
> 「あ、そうそうーー純血！」マルフォイは答えも聞かずに合言葉を言うた。壁にかくされた石の扉がするすると開いた。マルフォイがそこを通り、ハリーとロンがそれに続いた。[18]

> (*Atarashii aikotoba wa nandatta kana? Marufoi wa hari ni kiita. Eto—*
>
> *A sousou jyunketsu! Marufoi wa kotae mo kikazuni aikotoba wo iuta. Kabe ni kakusareta ishi no tobira ga surusuru to kiita. Marufoi ga soko wo toori, hari to ron ga sore ni tsuzuita.*)

In the original English, no one in the scene questions the "pure-blood" itself; it is simply part of the everyday conversation, unremarkable and mundane. When examining the same text in the Japanese translation, the term *jyunketsu*

(純血) can also mean "pure lineage" or "pure pedigree." In the Spanish-language edition, the term *sangre limpia*, or "clean blood," is the phrase of choice, reflecting blood purity.

Rowling's choice of the term "half-blood" is vivid and suggests a muscularity and threat. Using "half" also quantifies ancestry and builds into the language a hierarchy of racial categories. The pure-blood wizards have set themselves at the top of that hierarchy, and they do what they can to maintain it. They even go so far as to change the laws at the Ministry of Magic. When less than pure-blood wizards feel the need to put on airs, they try to pass as pure-blood. Blood quantum and purity are measured and evaluated for rank. This is true not only for the adults but also for the students at Hogwarts.

> "I'm **half-and-half**," said Seamus. "Me dad's a Muggle. Mom didn't tell him she was a witch 'til after they were married. Bit of a nasty shock for him." (*HP and the SS*, 125)

> 「私はハーフなんだ。私のパパはマグルで、ママは結婚するまで魔女だと言わなかったんだ。パパはずいぶんドッキリしたみたいだよ。」[19] (*Watashi wa **hafu** nanda. Watashi no papa wa maguru de, mama wa kekkon suru made majyo da to iuwanakattan da. Papa wa zuibun dokkiri shitamitai da yo.*)

> "He **hapa** wau," wahi a Seamus. "He Mākala koʻu pāpā. ʻAʻole I hōʻike aku koʻu māmā iā ia he uitiʻo ia ā paʻa lāua ika male. Ua ʻano pūʻiwa ʻino ʻo ia."[20]

> —Yo soy **mitad y mitad**—dijo Seamus—. Mi padre es muggle. Mamá no le dijo que era una bruja hasta que se casaron. Fue una sorpresa algo desagradable para él.[21]

Here, in the example of Seamus Finnigan's disclosure of his mixed-race background, his use of the phrase "half-and-half" is presented as *hafu* in Japanese, a borrowed word from the English word "half." However, in Japanese, the term is often used to describe a person of mixed parentage, someone who is mixed race, often a person with a foreign or non-Japanese parent. The meaning of foreignness and difference is that the person's mixedness evokes the meaning of impurity. *Hafu* was used in the Japanese edition to describe Finnigan's mixed background. Given the context, his phenotype would not warrant an explanation of foreignness, but rather one of mixedness. The meaning of the word *hafu* in this case is not the same as that of half, but a nuanced way to describe mixedness in Japanese.

In the Hawaiian translation, the term used to describe Seamus's mixedness is *hapa*, the Hawaiian transliteration of the English word "half." The word *hapa* came into the Hawaiian lexicon in the 1820s when White settlers and Hawaiians were discussing mathematics and fractions.[22] It was a borrowed word from the English word "half," but because Hawaiian does not have an *f* sound, *p* is the closest consonant, resulting in the word *hapa*. Later, Native Hawaiians used *hapa* to describe the mixed offspring of Hawaiians and White settlers. Much of the word's current usage derives from the Hawaiian phrase *hapa haole*, meaning "half-White." The term *hapa* eventually found its way to the continental United States, and it has since been co-opted by Asian and Pacific Islander Americans of mixed-race decent.[23] The word in modern-day speech in Hawai'i is quite common; translator R. Keao NeSmith describes it as "very pedestrian."[24] The term initially referred to mixed-race Hawaiians and later came to include mixed-race Asian Americans and Pacific Islanders in general. In the statement, "'He hapa wau,' wahi a Seamus," it is clear that Seamus is neither Hawaiian nor mixed-race, as the term *hapa* would suggest. *Hapa* was the word chosen to describe generic mixedness. The use of *hapa* in the text of Seamus's disclosure about his background is similar to the aforementioned example of *hafu*, illustrating how a borrowed word from English became Hawaiian, then boomeranged back into English with even more meaning.

When examining the Spanish phrase, the translator's choice of *mitad y mitad* is very much a literal translation of English, meaning equal parts of something. This phrasing lacks the cultural baggage of multiraciality that a word like *criollo* or *mestizo* would have: as words associated with foreign influence like *hafu* and *hapa*.[25] The word *mitad* originated from Latin and is not borrowed from English. Therefore, it did not go through the same succession of changes in meaning as did *hafu* and *hapa*. One place where the word "half-blood" is omitted is the title of book 6, *Harry Potter and the Half-Blood Prince*. In the Spanish-language edition, the title is *Harry Potter y el misterio del príncipe*, "Harry Potter and the Mysterious Prince." Here, the translator abandoned entirely the blood-quantum connotations of the English title and opted for a more generic theme: mystery. The same meaning is true for the Japanese-language edition, titled ハリー・ポッターと謎の プリンス (*Hari potta to nazo no purinsu*, "Harry Potter and the Mysterious

Prince"), in which the word *nazo* (謎, "mysterious") has an entirely different meaning than the English term, "half-blood." Other words describing race and their translations carry less benign meanings in the series.

Hermione Granger is a full Muggle who comes from nonmagical parentage with monoracial wizards, yet is living as a witch. Draco Malfoy refers to her as a Mudblood, or someone with dirty blood. This is recounted in the following scene:

> "It's about the most insulting thing he could think of," gasped Ron, coming back up. "Mudblood's a really foul name for someone who is Muggle born— you know, non-magic parents. There are some wizards—like Malfoy's family—who think they're better than everyone else because they're what people call pure-blood." (*HP and the CS*, 115–16)

> 「マルフォイがハーマイオニーのことをなんとかって呼んだんだ。ものすごくひどい悪口なんだと思う。だって、みんなかんかんだったもの」

> 「ほんとにひどい悪口さ。」

> テーブルの下からロンの汗だらけの青い顔がひょいっと現れ、しゃがれ声で言うった。

> 「マルフォイのやつ彼女のこと『穢れた血』って言ったんだよ、ハグリッドー」

> ロンの顔がまたひょいとテーブルの下に消えた。[26]

> (*Marufoi ga hamaioni no koto wo nantokatte yondan da. Monosugoku hidoi waruguchi nanda to omou. Datte, minna kankan datta mono. Hontoni hidoi waruguchi sa. Teburu no shita kara ron no asedarake no aoi kao ga hyoi to araware, shyagare goi de iutta. Marufoi no yatsu kanojyo no koto 『kegareta chi』 te iutandayo, haguriddo, ron no kao ga mata hyoi to teburu no shita ni kieta.*)

> –Es lo más insultante que se le podri ocurrir—dijo Ron, volviendo a incorporarse—*Sangre sucia* es un nombre realmente repugnante con el que llaman a los hijos de muggle, ya sabes, de padres que no son magos. Hay algunos magos, como la familia de Malfoy, que creen que son mejores que nadie porque tienen lo que ellos llaman *sangre limpia*.[27]

The term used for Mudblood in Japanese in this case is *kegareta chi* (穢れ
た血); *kegareta* can mean several things including polluted, unclean, cor-
rupted, dirty, evil, and wicked, while *chi* (血) means blood. The meaning of
kegareta chi is very close to the intended association of impure blood but
not the literal meaning of mud.

The terms for Mudblood and pure-blood in Spanish are *sangre sucia* and
sangre limpia, dirty blood and clean blood. The term *sucia*, or dirty, suggests
filth, mess, and dishonesty. The word *limpia* means cleanliness or neatness,
and it implies moral purity. Both *sucia* and *limpia* are less about lineage and
ancestry and more about the literal meaning of dirty and clean. Certainly
the context evokes the offensiveness of being called *sangre sucia*. Here is
another example in which the Spanish translation is closely aligned with
the context in English.

An example where the term in English does not change much in the
Japanese and Spanish translations is "half-giant" (*HP and the GF*, 428). In
the Japanese text, the word to describe Rubeus Hagrid is *hankyojin* (半巨人),
which means half (半) and giant (巨) person (人).[28] In the Spanish series,
the term used for "half-giant" is *semigigante*.[29] In other words, depending
on the cultural and historical context of the word, the meaning may or may
not change. This is important, because the translated terms for Mudblood
mean pure and impure (dirty). Whereas with *hapa*, *hafu*, and half-and-half,
the racial and colonial baggage associated with those terms is a part of the
translation and meaning within the text.

Conclusion

The *Harry Potter* series is a brilliant tale of how pre-Brexit Britain imagined
itself: a place where the empire had come home. The series chronicles a
co-ed boarding school (that's revolutionary enough) where White Brits live
alongside unmarked minorities like Cho Chang and the Patil sisters, all of
whom Rowling presents as uncomplicatedly British. It is not among the
racial groups of humans that race erupts in Harry Potter. It is in the matter
of Muggles and wizards that we encounter racialized conflicts in the stories.

Mixed-race characters are not people, but emblems of the tragic mulatto
in the series. Rowling's use of the tragic mulatto figure is convenient, but it
comes without the Blackness so often associated with the trope. Her choice

is safe: her half-bloods do not phenotypically reveal their difference to others visually. She does not need to deal with the complexity of tragic mulattos, adding actual Black-and-White mixed race to her wizard-and-Muggle mixed racedness. In using mixed-race characters in the series, Rowling deploys the tragic mulatto to build her story about a boarding school for wizards. In framing the series in a way that examines race in the wizarding world, what Rowling is actually doing is critiquing White supremacy. Products of miscegenation like Hagrid, Harry, Snape, and Voldemort all exhibit predictable tragic mulatto tropes like hybrid vigor and hybrid degeneracy, questionable loyalties, and suspicion. However, unlike in other books featuring an evil mixed-race central character, Harry Potter is the hero; his mixed background is not a curse, and it will not lead to his downfall, although his life is not exactly a cakewalk.

Lastly, it is important to consider White privilege, English language privilege, and Western hegemony in texts that are not necessarily being read by English speakers if we are to better understand the complexity and contingency of the language surrounding race. The young readers whose lives have been touched by the *Harry Potter* series are not all English speakers. Because of English language hegemony, English-speaking scholars pay less attention to how readers in other languages might interpret translations of text differently. We hope to begin a conversation on how words, especially those surrounding mixed race and blood purity, take on a new meaning when we look at them before they were borrowed from English and after they spent time taking on a nuanced meaning within another language. Authors and translators have a contemporary relationship with the languages they are using, yet the words they choose may have a markedly different interpretation depending on their cultural setting, their relationship with the English language and the English-speaking world, or even the development of a Western colonial relationship such as with Hawai'i or a neocolonial relationship as with Japan. Analyzing the language used to describe race in Harry Potter in different languages expands our understanding of the ways in which terms about race undergo a change similar to diaspora and homeland return, much like Harry's passage through Platform 9¾ and back to 4 Privet Drive.

Table 1: Pure-Bloods, Half-Bloods, and Mudbloods in Language

English	Spanish	Japanese	Hawaiian*
pure-blood	sangre limpia	純血 jyunketsu	
Mudblood	sangre sucia	穢れた血 kegareta chi	
half-blood	mestizo o sangre mestiza	混血 konketsu	
half-and-half	mitad y mitad	ハーフ hafu	hapa
half-giant	semigigante	半巨人 hankyojin	
Squib	squib	スクイブ sukuibu	
half-blood prince	misterio príncipe	謎のプリンス nazo no purinsu	

*As of this writing, only the first book of the *Harry Potter* series has been translated into 'Ōlelo Hawai'i (the Hawaiian language).

Notes

1. The authors would like to thank Cindy Nakashima for her helpful comments on an earlier version of this chapter, and for being one of the foremothers of mixed-race studies. We would like to thank the two reviewers, as well as editors Sarah Park Dahlen and Ebony Elizabeth Thomas, for their useful critiques. Lastly, we want to thank our students, many of whom are Harry Potter fans, for their excellent questions and comments.

2. The tragic mulatto is one of the hoariest tropes of American literature and film. See, e.g., William Wells Brown, *Clotel; or, The President's Daughter: A Narrative of Slave Life in the United States* (1853; Boston: Bedford/St. Martin's, 2000); Frank J. Webb, *The Garies and Their Friends* (1857; Baltimore: Johns Hopkins University Press, 1997); William Dean Howells, *An Imperative Duty* (New York: Harper and Brothers, 1891); Frances E. W. Harper, *Iola LeRoy; or, Shadows Uplifted* (Philadelphia: Garrigues Brothers, 1893); Mark Twain, *Pudd'nhead Wilson* (London: Chatto and Windus, 1894); Charles W. Chesnutt, *The House behind the Cedars* (Boston: Houghton Mifflin, 1900); Pauline Hopkins, *Hagar's Daughter: A Story of Southern Caste Prejudice*, in *The Magazine Novels of Pauline Hopkins* (1901–1902; New York: Oxford University Press, 1988), 1–284; Sutton E. Griggs, *The Hindered Hand; or, The Reign of the Repressionist* (Nashville: Orion, 1905); James Weldon Johnson, *The Autobiography of an Ex-Colored Man* (Boston: Sherman, French and Company, 1912); Edna Ferber, *Show Boat* (1926; New York: Random House, 2014); Walter White, *Flight* (New York: Alfred A. Knopf, 1926); Nella Larsen, *Quicksand* (New York: Alfred A. Knopf, 1928); Jessie Redmon Fauset, *Plum Bun* (New York: Frederick A. Stokes, 1929); Nella Larsen, *Passing* (New York: Alfred A. Knopf, 1929); George S. Schuyler, *Black No More* (New York: Macaulay, 1931); Fannie Hurst, *Imitation of Life* (New York: Harper and Brothers, 1933); Dorothy Lee Dickens, *Black on the Rainbow* (New York: Pageant Press, 1952); Reba Lee [Mary Hastings Bradley], *I Passed for White* (New York: Longmans, Green, 1955); John Howard Griffin, *Black Like Me* (Boston: Houghton Mifflin, 1961); Grace Halsell, *Soul Sister* (New York: World, 1969); Walter Mosley, *Devil in a Blue Dress* (New York: Norton, 1990); Dorothy West, *The Wedding* (New York: Doubleday, 1995); Danzy Senna, *Caucasia* (New York: Riverhead Books, 1998); Philip

Roth, *The Human Stain* (Boston: Houghton Mifflin, 2000); and Anita Reynolds, *American Cocktail: A "Colored Girl" in the World*, ed. George Hutchinson (Cambridge, MA: Harvard University Press, 2014).

For literary analysis, see, e.g., Elaine K. Ginsberg, ed., *Passing and the Fictions of Identity* (Durham, NC: Duke University Press, 1995); Werner Sollors, *Neither Black Nor White Yet Both: Thematic Explorations of Interracial Literature* (New York: Oxford University Press, 1997); Juda Bennett, *The Passing Figure: Racial Confusion in Modern Literature* (New York: Peter Lang, 1998); Gayle Wald, *Crossing the Line: Racial Passing in Twentieth-Century U.S. Literature and Culture* (Durham, NC: Duke University Press, 2000); M. Giulia Fabi, *Passing and the Rise of the African American Novel* (Urbana: University of Illinois Press, 2003); Mar Gallego, ed., *Passing Novels in the Harlem Renaissance: Identity Politics and Textual Strategies* (Münster, Germany: Lit Verlag, 2003); Steven J. Belluscio, *To Be Suddenly White: Literary Realism and Racial Passing* (Columbia: University of Missouri Press, 2006); Baz Dreisinger, *Near Black: White-to-Black Passing in American Culture* (Amherst: University of Massachusetts Press, 2008); Susan Prothro Wright and Ernestine Pickens Glass, eds., *Passing in the Works of Charles W. Chesnutt* (Jackson: University Press of Mississippi, 2010); Kathleen Pfeiffer, *Race Passing and American Individualism* (Amherst: University of Massachusetts Press, 2010); Teresa C. Zackodnik, *The Mulatta and the Politics of Race* (Jackson: University Press of Mississippi, 2010); Sinéad Moynihan, *Passing into the Present: Contemporary American Fiction of Racial and Gender Passing* (Manchester: Manchester University Press, 2011); Michele Elam, *The Souls of Mixed Folks: Race, Politics, and Aesthetics in the New Millennium* (Stanford, CA: Stanford University Press, 2011), 96–124; Sika A. Dagbovie-Mullins, *Crossing B(l)ack: Mixed-Race Identity in Modern American Fiction and Culture* (Knoxville: University of Tennessee Press, 2013); and Julie Cary Nerad, ed., *Passing Interest: Racial Passing in US Novels, Memoirs, Television, and Film, 1990–2010* (Albany: State University of New York Press, 2014).

Prominent performance pieces include *Show Boat* (Warner Bros., 1936), dir. James Whale, written by Edna Ferber and Oscar Hammerstein II, starring Irene Dunne, Allan Jones, Charles Winninger, and Paul Robeson; *Show Boat* (Metro-Goldwyn-Mayer, 1951), dir. George Sidney, written by Edna Ferber, Oscar Hammerstein II, Jerome Kern, and John Lee Mahin, starring Kathryn Grayson, Ava Gardner, Howard Keel, Marge Champion, and Gower Champion; *Imitation of Life* (Universal Pictures, 1934), dir. John M. Stahl, written by Fannie Hurst and William Hurlbut, starring Claudette Colbert, Louise Beavers, and Fredi Washington; *Imitation of Life* (Universal Pictures, 1959), dir. Douglas Sirk, written by Fannie Hurst, Eleanore Griffin, and Allan Scott, starring Lana Turner, John Gavin, Sandra Dee, and Juanita Moore; and *Pinky* (20th Century Fox, 1949), dir. Elia Kazan, written by Cid Ricketts Sumner, Philip Dunne, and Dudley Nichols, starring Jeanne Crain, Ethel Barrymore, and Ethel Waters.

Cinematic analyses include Leilani Nishime, "*The Matrix* Trilogy, Keanu Reeves, and Multiraciality at the End of Time," in *Mixed Race Hollywood*, ed. Mary Beltrán and Camilla Fojas, 290–310 (New York: New York University Press, 2008); Leilani Nishime, *Undercover Asian: Multiracial Asian Americans in Visual Culture* (Urbana: University of Illinois Press, 2014); Jane Park, "Virtual Race: The Racially Ambiguous Action Hero in *The Matrix* and *Pitch Black*," in *Mixed Race Hollywood*, 182–202; Annalee Newitz, "When Will White People Stop Making Movies Like *Avatar*?," *Gizmodo*, December 18, 2009, https://gizmodo.com /when-will-white-people-stop-making-movies-like-avatar-5422666; Mikhail Lyubansky,

"The Racial Politics of *Avatar*," *Psychology Today*, December 28, 2009; and David Brooks, "The Messiah Complex," *New York Times*, January 7, 2010.

3. Nakashima, "Servants of Culture"; and Nakashima, "An Invisible Monster."

4. A place to begin on race and the Potter world is Thomas, *The Dark Fantastic*. See also Anne, "J. K. Rowling, We All Know You Didn't Write Hermione As Black"; Tate, "The Evolving Role of Race"; Weekes, "The *Harry Potter* Series Makes a Mess"; Whited, "1492, 1942, 1992: The Theme of Race"; Goldstein, "Harry Potter and the Complicated Identity Politics"; Walters, "Not So Magical"; Nejad, "Literal and Metaphorical"; Carey, "Hermione and the House-Elves"; and Carey, "Hermione and the House-Elves Revisited."

5. Douthat, "The Muggle Problem"; and Berlatsky, "Harry Potter and Contradictions."

6. Anatol, "The Fallen Empire"; Anatol, "The Replication of Victorian Racial Ideology"; and Ostry, "Accepting Mudbloods."

7. Stockslager, "What It Means"; and Horne, "Harry and the Other."

8. Bogle, *Toms, Coons, Mulattoes*. "Tragic mulatto" refers to people who have mixed Black and White ancestry, with one Black parent and one White parent. According to the *New Oxford American Dictionary*, the word originates from the late sixteenth century, from the Spanish *mulato*, originally from the Arabic *muwallad*, "person of mixed race."

9. Reuter, *The Mulatto in the United States*; Reuter, *Race Mixture*; Day, *A Study of Some Negro-White Families*; Spickard, *Mixed Blood*; Williamson, *New People*; Spencer, *The New Colored People*; Sexton, *Amalgamation Schemes*; Beltrán and Fojas, *Mixed Race Hollywood*; McNeil, *Sex and Race in the Black Atlantic*; Elam, *The Souls of Mixed Folk*; Joseph, *Transcending Blackness*; and Hobbs, *A Chosen Exile*.

10. Giacomo Puccini's *Madama Butterfly* premiered in Milan in 1904. The three-act play is about a forbidden and tragic romance set during the nineteenth century in Nagasaki, Japan. Lieutenant B. F. Pinkerton is an American sailor on leave who meets the fifteen-year-old Cio-Cio San (Madame Butterfly), and they marry for convenience. He returns to the United States alone and later brings his American wife to Japan for a visit, because she has agreed to raise the mixed-race son he had with Cio-Cio, born only after he left Japan years earlier. Upon their arrival, Cio-Cio finds out about Pinkerton's wife and commits suicide. Madame Butterfly's themes are echoed in the 1957 film *Sayonara*, set during World War II, and later in the 1989 musical *Miss Saigon*, which chronicled a forbidden romance during the Vietnam War set in the early 1970s. Tragedies springing from interracial relationships bleed into the lives of the children: how people perceive the children, and how they should be treated. Puccini based his opera on John Luther Long's short story "Madame Butterfly" (1898); Long had taken the idea from Pierre Loti's 1887 novel *Madame Chrysanthème*. Van Rij, *Madame Butterfly*.

11. Barratt, "Purebloods and Mudbloods." Rena Heinrich opens up another angle on Puccini's depictions in "Half-Butterfly, Half-Caste," discussing the writing of Sadakichi Hartmann, who tells the story from the point of view of the rejected child.

12. Nakashima, "An Invisible Monster."

13. Nakashima, "Servants of Culture," 37.

14. Characters illustrating extreme hybrid degeneracy can be found elsewhere. In Khaled Hosseini's *The Kite Runner*, the sociopath Assef, who is half-Pashtun and half-German, is tormented by his mixedness and deathly afraid he might be found out to be less than full Pashtun. So he rapes and tortures everyone he encounters. In Marc Olden's novel *Oni*, Viktor Poltava is the consummate degenerate Eurasian with an alcoholic Russian father and a poor

Japanese mother; he is orphaned, then has a violent upbringing, in the end becoming a murderer.

15. Niata, "Why Harry Potter Is Poison for White Kids."

16. For a discussion on interracial dating in the *Harry Potter* series, see Sims, "Wanagoballwitme?"

17. Examples include Nguyen, *The Sympathizer*; Sidney, dir., *Show Boat*; Hurst, *Imitation of Life*; Stahl, dir., *Imitation of Life* (1934); Sirk, dir., *Imitation of Life* (1959); Kazan, dir., *Pinky*; Nishime, "The Matrix Trilogy, Keanu Reeves, and Multiraciality"; Nishime, *Undercover Asian*; Park, "Virtual Race"; Newitz, "When Will White People Stop Making Movies Like *Avatar*?"; Lyubansky, "The Racial Politics of *Avatar*"; and Brooks, "The Messiah Complex."

18. Rowling, *Harry Potter and the Chamber of Secrets*, Japanese edition, ハリーポッターと秘密の部屋 (*Hari Potta to himitsu no heya*), 328.

19. Rowling, *Harry Potter and the Philosopher's Stone*, Japanese edition, ハリーポッターと賢者の石 (*Hari Potta to kenjya no ishi*), 185–86.

20. Rowling, *Harry Potter and the Philosopher's Stone*, Hawaiian edition, *Harry Potter a me ka Pōhaku Akeakamai*, 128.

21. Rowling, *Harry Potter y la piedra filosofal*, 108.

22. NeSmith, "The Etymology of Hapa."

23. Spickard, afterword to *Part Asian, 100% Hapa*.

24. NeSmith, "Etymology of Hapa."

25. Katsew, *Casta Painting*.

26. Rowling, *Harry Potter and the Chamber of Secrets*, Japanese edition, ハリーポッターと秘密の部屋 (*Hari Potta to himitsu no heya*), 170.

27. Rowling, *Harry Potter y la cámara secreta*, 101.

28. Rowling, *Harry Potter and the Goblet of Fire*, Japanese edition, part 2, ハリーポッターと炎のゴブレット下 (*Hari Potta to honoo no goburetto*), 108.

29. Rowling, *Harry Potter y el cáliz de fuego*, 388.

Bibliography

Anatol, Giselle Liza. "The Fallen Empire: Exploring Ethnic Otherness in the World of Harry Potter." In *Reading Harry Potter: Critical Essays*, edited by Giselle Liza Anatol, 163–78. Westport, CT: Praeger, 2003.

Anatol, Giselle Liza. "The Replication of Victorian Racial Ideology in Harry Potter." In *Reading Harry Potter Again: New Critical Essays*, edited by Giselle Liza Anatol, 109–26. Santa Barbara, CA: Praeger, 2009.

Anne, Kayleigh. "J. K. Rowling, We All Know You Didn't Write Hermione As Black in the Harry Potter Books—but It Doesn't Matter." *Independent*, December 21, 2015.

Barratt, Bethany. "Purebloods and Mudbloods: Race, Species, and Power." In *The Politics of Harry Potter*, 59–84. New York: Palgrave Macmillan, 2012.

Beltrán, Mary, and Camilla Fojas, eds. *Mixed Race Hollywood*. New York: New York University Press, 2008.

Berlatsky, Noah. "Harry Potter and Contradictions about Racial Justice." *Guardian*, September 20, 2017.

Bogle, Donald. *Toms, Coons, Mulattoes, Mammies, and Bucks: An Interpretive History of Blacks in American Films*. New York: Continuum, 1998.

Carey, Brycchan. "Hermione and the House-Elves: The Literary and Historical Contexts of J. K. Rowling's Antislavery Campaign." In *Reading Harry Potter: Critical Essays*, edited by Giselle Liza Anatol, 103–15. Westport, CT: Praeger, 2003.

Carey, Brycchan. "Hermione and the House-Elves Revisited: J. K. Rowling, Antislavery Campaigning, and the Politics of Potter." In *Reading Harry Potter Again: New Critical Essays*, edited by Giselle Liza Anatol, 159–73. Santa Barbara, CA: Praeger, 2009.

Day, Caroline Bond. *A Study of Some Negro-White Families in the United States.* Cambridge, MA: Peabody Museum of Harvard University, 1932.

Douthat, Ross. "The Muggle Problem." *New York Times*, June 28, 2017.

Elam, Michele. *The Souls of Mixed Folk: Race, Politics, and Aesthetics in the New Millennium.* Stanford, CA: Stanford University Press, 2011.

Fulbeck, Kip. *Part Asian, 100% Hapa.* San Francisco: Chronicle Books, 2006.

Goldstein, Dana. "Harry Potter and the Complicated Identity Politics." *American Prospect*, July 24, 2007. https://prospect.org/article/harry-potter-complicated-identity-politics/.

Heinrich, Rena M. "Half-Butterfly, Half-Caste: Sadakichi Hartmann and the Mixed-Japanese Drama *Osadda's Revenge*." In *Shape Shifters: Journeys across Terrains of Race and Identity*, edited by Lily Anne Y. Welty Tamai, Ingrid Dineen-Wimberly, and Paul Spickard. Lincoln: University of Nebraska Press, 2019.

Hobbs, Allyson. *A Chosen Exile: A History of Racial Passing in American Life.* Cambridge, MA: Harvard University Press, 2014.

Horne, Jackie C. "Harry and the Other: Answering the Race Question in J. K. Rowling's *Harry Potter*." *The Lion and the Unicorn* 34, no. 1 (January 2010): 76–104.

Hosseini, Khaled. *The Kite Runner.* New York: Riverhead Books, 2004.

Joseph, Ralina L. *Transcending Blackness: From the New Millennium Mulatta to the Exceptional Multiracial.* Durham, NC: Duke University Press, 2012.

Katsew, Ilona. *Casta Painting: Images of Race in Eighteenth-Century Mexico.* New Haven, CT: Yale University Press, 2005.

Kim, Heidi. *Invisible Subjects: Asian America in Postwar Literature.* New York: Oxford University Press, 2016.

Mathison, Ymitri, ed. *Growing Up Asian American in Young Adult Fiction.* Jackson: University Press of Mississippi, 2017.

McNeil, Daniel. *Sex and Race in the Black Atlantic: Mulatto Devils and Multiracial Messiahs.* New York: Routledge, 2010.

Nakashima, Cynthia L. "An Invisible Monster: The Creation and Denial of Mixed-Race People in America." In *Racially Mixed People in America*, edited by Maria P. P. Root, 162–80. Newbury Park, CA: Sage Publications, 1992.

Nakashima, Cynthia L. "Servants of Culture: The Symbolic Role of Mixed-Race Asians in American Discourse." In *The Sum of Our Parts: Mixed-Heritage Asian Americans*, edited by Teresa Williams-León and Cynthia L. Nakashima, 35–48. Philadelphia: Temple University Press, 2001.

Nejad, Kayhan. "Literal and Metaphorical: Racial Themes in Harry Potter." *e.g.: A Journal of Exemplary Undergraduate Scholarship*, March 15, 2012. http://depts.washington.edu/egonline/2012/03/2010-11-winner-literal-and-metaphorical-racial-themes-in-harry-potter-by-kayhan-nejad/.

NeSmith, R. Keao. "The Etymology of Hapa." Japanese American National Museum, Los Angeles. YouTube, April 28, 2018. https://www.youtube.com/watch?v=ZZPa_yyoJc8.

Nguyen, Viet Thanh. *The Sympathizer.* New York: Grove Press, 2015.

Niata. "Why Harry Potter Is Poison for White Kids: It's Multiracial, Left Wing Propaganda." Stormfront, July 17, 2011. https://www.stormfront.org/forum/t760706-7/.

Olden, Marc. *Oni*. New York: Jove Books, 1988.

Ostry, Elaine. "Accepting Mudbloods: The Ambivalent Social Vision of J. K. Rowling's Fairy Tales." In *Reading Harry Potter: Critical Essays*, edited by Giselle Liza Anatol, 89–101. Westport, CT: Praeger, 2003.

Reuter, Edward Byron. *The Mulatto in the United States, Including a Study of the Rôle of Mixed-Blood Races throughout the World*. Boston: Richard G. Badger, 1918.

Reuter, Edward Byron. *Race Mixture: Studies in Intermarriage and Miscegenation*. New York: Whittlesey House, 1931.

Rowling, J. K. *Harry Potter and the Chamber of Secrets*. New York: Scholastic, 1999.

Rowling, J. K. *Harry Potter y la cámara secreta*. Translated by Adolfo Muñoz García and Nieves Martín Azofra. Barcelona: Ediciones Salamandra, 1998.

Rowling, J. K. *Harry Potter and the Chamber of Secrets*. ハリーポッターと秘密の部屋 (*Hari Potta to himitsu no heya*). Translated by Matsuoka Yuko. Tokyo: Say-zan-sha Publications, 2000.

Rowling, J. K. *Harry Potter and the Deathly Hallows*. New York: Scholastic, 2007.

Rowling, J. K. *Harry Potter and the Goblet of Fire*. New York: Scholastic, 2000.

Rowling, J. K. *Harry Potter y el cáliz de fuego*. Translated by Adolfo Muñoz García, Alicia Dellepiane Rawson, and Nieves Martín Azofra. Barcelona: Ediciones Salamandra, 2015.

Rowling, J. K. *Harry Potter and the Goblet of Fire*. ハリーポッターと炎のゴブレット上 (*Hari Potta to honoo no goburetto*). Translated by Matsuoka Yuko. Tokyo: Say-zan-sha Publications, 2002.

Rowling, J. K. *Harry Potter and the Goblet of Fire*. ハリーポッターと炎のゴブレット下 (*Hari Potta to honoo no goburetto*). Translated by Matsuoka Yuko. Tokyo: Say-zan-sha Publications, 2002.

Rowling, J. K. *Harry Potter and the Half-Blood Prince*. New York: Scholastic, 2005.

Rowling, J. K. *Harry Potter y el misterio del príncipe*. Translated by Gemma Rovira Ortega. Barcelona: Ediciones Salamandra, 2006.

Rowling, J. K. *Harry Potter and the Half-Blood Prince*. ハリー・ポッターと謎のプリンス 上 (*Hari potta to nazo no purinsu*). Translated by Matsuoka Yuko. Tokyo: Say-zan-sha Publications, 2006.

Rowling, J. K. *Harry Potter and the Half-Blood Prince*. ハリー・ポッターと謎のプリンス 下 (*Hari potta to nazo no purinsu*). Translated by Matsuoka Yuko. Tokyo: Say-zan-sha Publications, 2006.

Rowling, J. K. *Harry Potter and the Order of the Phoenix*. New York: Scholastic, 2003.

Rowling, J. K. *Harry Potter and the Sorcerer's Stone*. New York: Scholastic, 1998.

Rowling, J. K. *Harry Potter y la piedra filosofal*. Translated by Alicia Dellepiane Rawson. Barcelona: Ediciones Salamandra, 1999.

Rowling, J. K. *Harry Potter a me ka Pōhaku Akeakamai: Harry Potter and the Philosopher's Stone*. Translated by R. Keao NeSmith. Dundee, Scotland: Evertype, 2018.

Rowling, J. K. *Harry Potter and the Philosopher's Stone*. ハリーポッターと賢者の石 (*Hari Potta to kenjya no ishi*). Translated by Matsuoka Yuko. Tokyo: Say-zan-sha Publications, 1999.

Rowling, J. K. *Harry Potter and the Prisoner of Azkaban*. New York: Scholastic, 1999.

Sexton, Jared. *Amalgamation Schemes: Antiblackness and the Critique of Multiracialism*. Minneapolis: University of Minnesota Press, 2008.

Sims, Jenn. "Wanagoballwitme? Inter 'Racial' Dating at Hogwarts." In *The Sociology of Harry Potter: 22 Enchanting Essays on the Wizarding World*, edited by Jenn Sims, 164–71. Hamden, CT: Zossima Press, 2012.

Sohn, Stephen Hong. *Racial Asymmetries: Asian American Fictional Worlds*. New York: New York University Press, 2014.

Spencer, Jon Michael. *The New Colored People: The Mixed-Race Movement in America*. New York: New York University Press, 2000.

Spickard, Paul R. Afterword to *Part Asian, 100% Hapa*, by Kip Fulbeck, 258–62. San Francisco: Chronicle Books, 2006.

Spickard, Paul R. *Mixed Blood: Intermarriage and Ethnic Identity in Twentieth-Century America*. Madison: University of Wisconsin Press, 1989.

Stockslager, Tess. "What It Means to Be a Half-Blood: Integrity versus Fragmentation in Biracial Identity." In *J. K. Rowling: Harry Potter*, edited by Cynthia J. Hallett and Peggy J. Huey, 122–34. Basingstoke, Hants., England: Palgrave Macmillan, 2012.

Tate, Emily. "The Evolving Role of Race in Children's Lit, from 'Harry Potter' to 'The Hate U Give.'" EdSurge, March 5, 2019. https://www.edsurge.com/news/2019-03-05-the-evolving-role-of-race-in-children-s-lit-from-harry-potter-to-the-hate-u-give.

Thomas, Ebony Elizabeth. *The Dark Fantastic: Race and the Imagination from Harry Potter to the Hunger Games*. New York: New York University Press, 2019.

Van Rij, Jan. *Madame Butterfly: Japonisme, Puccini, and the Search for the Real Cho-Cho-San*. Berkeley, CA: Stone Bridge Press, 2001.

Walters, Tiffany L. "Not So Magical: Issues with Racism, Classism, and Ideology in *Harry Potter*." Master's thesis, Northern Michigan University, 2015.

Weekes, Princess. "The *Harry Potter* Series Makes a Mess of Its Commentary on Racism." The Mary Sue, August 8, 2018. https://www.themarysue.com/race-in-harry-potter-is-messy/.

Whited, Lana A. "1492, 1942, 1992: The Theme of Race in the Harry Potter Series." *Looking Glass* 10, no. 1 (2006). https://ojs.latrobe.edu.au/ojs/index.php/tlg/article/view/97.

Williamson, Joel. *New People: Miscegenation and Mulattoes in the United States*. Baton Rouge: Louisiana State University Press, 1995.

Chosen Names, Changed Appearances, and Unchallenged Binaries

Trans-Exclusionary Themes in Harry Potter

Tolonda Henderson

In *Harry Potter and the Half-Blood Prince*, Dumbledore asks Harry to join him for private lessons. These lessons involve diving into memories of various people to learn about Voldemort's origins and past. In one of Dumbledore's own memories, Harry watches as Voldemort enters Dumbledore's office and asks for a teaching job. Before that request is made, though, Voldemort objects to Dumbledore calling him Tom: "They do not call me 'Tom' anymore. . . . These days I am known as—" (*HP and the HBP*, 442).[1] Dumbledore interrupts him, explaining that he knows about the name "Voldemort" but that to Dumbledore, Voldemort "will always be Tom Riddle" (*HP and the HBP*, 442). When watching this scene unfold, "Harry felt the atmosphere in the room change subtly: Dumbledore's refusal to use Voldemort's chosen name was a refusal to allow Voldemort to dictate the terms of the meeting, and Harry could tell that Voldemort took it as such" (*HP and the HBP*, 442). This moment is significant in part because in any other instance, Dumbledore would insist on using the name "Voldemort" rather than You-Know-Who or He-Who-Must-Not-Be-Named as most of the wizarding community does. When face-to-face with the son of Merope Gaunt, however, he insists on using the name his mother gave him when he was born.

The text presents Dumbledore's use of an old name for Voldemort as a brilliant strategy, a way of claiming power that is celebrated because Dumbledore represents all that is good and Voldemort represents all that is evil. When reading this passage through a transgender lens, however, it is impossible to ignore parallels to the "many times when trans people are addressed by their birth name as a way to aggressively dismiss and reject their gender identity and new name."[2] When trans people socially transition, they may choose a new name that is more in line with their gender identity. Ignoring the chosen name in favor of the previous name is known as deadnaming.[3] Calling someone by their deadname is incredibly disrespectful and harms the person whose chosen name is ignored. While I want Dumbledore to triumph over Voldemort, it is unsettling that a key method of establishing power over Voldemort is to deadname him. Even though there are no characters in Harry Potter who identify with a gender other than the one they were assigned at birth, there are themes and issues related to trans experience throughout the series. These include the use and disrespect of chosen names, the ways in which the text confines long-term changes in appearance to an evil character, and the strict policing of a magic/nonmagic binary. In this chapter, I will show that the wizarding world demonstrates and is built on trans-exclusionary concepts.

The summer of 2020 was a hard time to be a trans Harry Potter scholar. There had been previous indications that She-Who-Must-Not-Be-Named was transphobic, most notably her December 2019 support of Maya Forstater's campaign to position the misgendering of trans people—for example, calling a trans woman a man or he or him—as protected speech rather than the hate speech the British courts upheld it to be. I stopped saying (or writing) You-Know-Who's name at that point in time, not because I thought it would hurt her but because doing so allowed me to protect myself from centering her in my life. Six months later, I had even more reason to remove her name from my vocabulary, as the *Harry Potter* author first mocked a gender-inclusive tweet about people who menstruate and then doubled down on her transphobia when called out on it. The screed she published to her website[4] was difficult to read but impossible to ignore. Many fans suggested that it was time to reject the author but keep the texts, but to me this was an overly simplistic solution.

There is a tension, then, at the heart of setting out to craft this essay. On the one side, I want to demonstrate that the seven *Harry Potter* novels do not contradict the rampant transphobia evident in that June 2020 essay. On another side, however, I do not want to drive another wedge between fans and the texts by pointing out their transphobic tendencies. On yet another side, I do not want to give You-Know-Who a pass. What do I mean by this? To begin with, the *Harry Potter* series has long had a reputation of being liberal and progressive. Studies have shown that students who read Harry Potter are more likely to empathize with stigmatized groups[5] and that older Harry Potter readers showed a profound dislike of then presidential candidate Donald Trump.[6] The series' author has encouraged this perception, in part by continuing to release details about the fictional universe that suggest diversity (Dumbledore was gay, Anthony Goldstein was Jewish, Hermione might have been Black) but that were not discussed in the texts themselves. It would be easy to assume, then, that the novels would not show any relationship to the June 2020 essay. That is, one might think that the trans-exclusionary rhetoric of the essay was a wholly new development in the thinking of the author. As this chapter will show, however, the text reveals otherwise.

That being said, it is never my intention as a Harry Potter scholar to suggest that a problematic aspect of the series means we should stop (re)reading the novels. When I wrote that the series promotes a thin-thinking perspective at the expense of fat characters,[7] my goal was to raise the awareness of the reader as they continued interacting with these books, not to discourage people from being a fan of Harry Potter. The same applies here: reading the series with a trans lens reveals certain problems but does not have to mean throwing out the baby with the bathwater.

At the same time, we should absolutely hold You-Know-Who responsible for her bigotry and the harm that she continues to cause. There is early evidence that people are buying fewer of her books since her 2020 essay was published, for example.[8] As I mentioned above, I do not say (or write) her name anymore—partly a symbolic gesture that will never harm her directly but mostly a way of maintaining my own dignity as a nonbinary person. Taking her name out of my vocabulary is a form of resistance that helps me to remember that I am not powerless in the face of her extremely large platform. In the end, it is up to each person how they want to navigate this tension; I hope that this essay will help people to make an informed decision.

As a nonbinary person whose community includes trans people who have medically and/or socially transitioned, I draw on direct and indirect personal experience to build a trans lens with which to read the text. Unlike scholarship that looks for and at transgender characters,[9] this essay will ask questions based in transgender experience that go beyond gender. Specifically, what do the *Harry Potter* novels have to say about people who choose their own name and/or permanently and deliberately change their physical appearance? Without reducing trans experience to these two changes, as many trans people do not have surgery or change their names, this question is important because many trans people do in fact seek these gender-affirming changes in their lives. What does it mean, then, that the only character to welcome long-term changes to his appearance and to choose an entirely new name (as opposed to a nickname) is Voldemort, the embodiment of pure evil?

Beyond the individual person of Voldemort, I am interested in the ways the magic/nonmagic binary—one that the books' author constructed for her fantasy world—structures the lives of everyone in the narrative. How is this binary constructed, challenged, and policed? What does it mean that from a wizarding perspective—the dominant perspective of the series—this binary is entirely static? In other words, how a character is born is who they are; there are no examples of individuals shifting within or existing outside the magic/nonmagic divide. If you are born with magic, you are part of the wizarding world, and if not, you are excluded from or devalued within it. This binary essentialism echoes the biological essentialism at the heart of She-Who-Must-Not-Be-Named's transphobia.

The Many Names of Merope Gaunt's Son

Throughout the seven books of the *Harry Potter* series, the Heir of Slytherin is referred to by many names and titles. Those who do not call him Voldemort have a variety of reasons for making that choice. Much of the wizarding community call him You-Know-Who and He-Who-Must-Not-Be-Named out of fear (*Harry Potter and the Sorcerer's Stone*, 298). They shudder, wince, and flinch at the sound of the name (*HP and the SS*, 54; *Harry Potter and the Goblet of Fire*, 565; *HP and the SS*, 11), presumably because it is associated with death and violence. Death Eaters also do not use the name Voldemort, preferring to call him the Dark Lord (*Harry Potter and the Order of the*

Phoenix, 593). They do not seem to be afraid of the name Voldemort but rather to use an honorific out of respect. When the Order of the Phoenix is forced to abandon the use of the name Voldemort so as not to risk being captured (*Harry Potter and the Deathly Hallows*, 389), they switch to calling him the Chief Death Eater (*HP and the DH*, 442). This title is a clever way to continue to name Voldemort's role in the wizarding world rather than adopt the fearful titles You-Know-Who and He-Who-Must-Not-Be-Named.

For the purposes of this essay, the most interesting name that Voldemort is called when he is not called Voldemort is the name his mother gave him at birth: Tom Riddle. This is the only name or title that we know Voldemort would rather not be called. Voldemort began to abandon the name Tom Riddle while he was a student at Hogwarts (*Harry Potter and the Chamber of Secrets*, 314) and rejected it entirely when he returned to the wizarding world after having immersed himself in the Dark Arts (*HP and the CS*, 329). Once he has established himself as Lord Voldemort, there are only two people who call him Tom Riddle: Albus Dumbledore and Harry Potter. As we have seen in the opening example, Dumbledore uses the name Tom when face-to-face with Merope Gaunt's son as a way of establishing power over the encounter and within the relationship. This also happens at the Ministry of Magic when Dumbledore battles Voldemort after the death of Sirius Black (*HP and the OP*, 813). The use of the name Tom weakens Voldemort's status as an adult, positioning him instead as the young boy Dumbledore first met in the orphanage in London. It also undermines Voldemort's right to choose his own name. The series is designed to approve of the dismissal of this particular choice of Voldemort because his other choices are evil, but this particular choice harms no one. Some might say that the name Voldemort harms the community because of the fear it inspires, but if he had remained Tom Riddle, no one would have said "Tom Riddle." It is disrespectful to disregard the name someone has chosen for themselves. There may have been other ways for Dumbledore to establish control over their interactions without reducing Voldemort to his "youthful beginnings" (*HP and the HBP*, 442). Just because Dumbledore knows the name that Voldemort was given at birth does not mean he has the right to use that name when it suits him.

Harry begins to think of the young Voldemort as Tom Riddle in *Deathly Hallows*. When the trio locates a Horcrux in the Lestrange vault in Gringotts, it is described as "the cup that had belonged to Helga Hufflepuff, which had passed into the possession of Hepzibah Smith, from whom it had been stolen by Tom Riddle" (*HP and the DH*, 538). Later, when Harry asks the Gray Lady—the ghost of Ravenclaw tower—for information on the diadem of Ravenclaw, he reflects that "Tom Riddle would certainly have understood Helena Ravenclaw's desire to possess fabulous objects to which she had little right" (*HP and the DH*, 617). On the surface, this use of the name Merope Gaunt's son was using at the time of the events being discussed makes sense. He wasn't Voldemort yet when he stole the cup or charmed the ghost of Helena Ravenclaw—or was he? The fact that he had already started using the name Voldemort among his friends while in school suggests that he identified as Voldemort even as he continued to use Tom Riddle in certain circumstances.

Beyond thinking of Voldemort as Tom Riddle, Harry calls him "Riddle" and "Tom Riddle" to his face (*HP and the DH*, 740–42, 738). This is in keeping with Dumbledore's strategy of calling him Tom in person. While using the last name or the full name instead of just the first seems to imply a modicum of respect—Harry Potter and Tom Riddle have never been formally introduced—the use of any part of the name he was given at birth is once again a power move. Harry wants Voldemort to know that he knows where Voldemort came from, that he has power in the final confrontation, that he is "Dumbledore's man, through and through" (*HP and the HBP*, 348). When Merope Gaunt's son is finally killed, the text does not seem to know how to refer to him. At first "Voldemort [falls] backward, arms splayed, the slit pupils of the scarlet eyes rolling upward" (*HP and the DH*, 744). Later we learn that "Voldemort [is] dead" (*HP and the DH*, 744). In between these two moments in the text, however, "Tom Riddle hit[s] the floor with a mundane finality" (*HP and the DH*, 744). Voldemort cannot escape his deadname, even in death.

No Need for Polyjuice Potion

In addition to being the only character with a chosen name unrelated to his given name, Voldemort is also unique in having a permanent and welcomed change to his physical appearance. To contain this type of physical change within the person who is described as "the most evil wizard of all time" (*HP and the OP*, 37) is not a neutral choice. In the context of the deadnaming discussed above and the strict policing of the magic/nonmagic binary discussed below, this containment implies that transgender people who seek out gender-affirming surgery are on the wrong side of justice and morality.

This is not because Voldemort is himself transgender but rather because all of the good and righteous characters in the series strive to maintain over the long term the appearance and anatomy they were born with. Because it is only an evil character who welcomes permanent change to his appearance, seeking out such changes is positioned as an evil choice.

When he was known as Tom Riddle, Voldemort was described as "handsome" (*HP and the CS*, 329; *HP and the HBP*, 269, 434, 441). After leaving Hogwarts, he "disappeared . . . traveled far and wide . . . sank so deeply into the Dark Arts, consorted with the very worst of [wizarding] kind, underwent so many dangerous, magical transformations, that when he resurfaced as Lord Voldemort, he was barely recognizable" (*HP and the CS*, 329). Harry sees the beginning of these changes in the Pensieve when visiting Dumbledore's memory of the night Voldemort asked for a job teaching at Hogwarts:

> His features were not those Harry had seen emerge from the great stone cauldron almost two years ago: They were not as snakelike, the eyes were not yet scarlet, the face not yet masklike, and yet he was no longer handsome Tom Riddle. It was as though his features had been burned and blurred; they were waxy and oddly distorted, and the whites of the eyes now had a permanently bloody look, though the pupils were not yet the slits that Harry knew they would become. (*HP and the HBP*, 441)

This physical transformation takes time, but it is not temporary. The first time Harry sees Voldemort's face, it is described as "the most terrible face Harry had ever seen. It was chalk white with glaring red eyes and slits for nostrils, like a snake" (*HP and the SS*, 293). Three years later, when a reembodied Voldemort emerges from the cauldron in the graveyard, "Harry stared back into a face that had haunted his nightmares for three years. Whiter than a skull, with wide, livid scarlet eyes and a nose that was flat as a snake's with slits for nostrils" (*HP and the GF*, 643). While in Voldemort's mind during his fifth year at Hogwarts, Harry looks into a mirror and sees "a face whiter than a skull . . . red eyes with slits for pupils" (*HP and the OP*, 586). At the beginning of *Deathly Hallows*, Voldemort's face "shone through the gloom, hairless, snakelike, with slits for nostrils and gleaming red eyes whose pupils were vertical" (*HP and the DH*, 3). When hit by his own rebounding curse in the last chapter of the series, Voldemort's "snakelike face [is] vacant and unknowing" (*HP and the DH*, 744). In other words, once it changes, Voldemort's face stays changed.

There are, of course, other characters whose appearances change over the course of the series. These characters tend to be on Harry's side, though, and the changes to their appearance are either temporary or imposed. As a metamorphmagus, Nymphadora Tonks can change her appearance at will—at least until she is so depressed over Remus Lupin's rejection of her that she loses her powers (*HP and the OP*, 52; *HP and the HBP*, 95). Barty Crouch Jr. disguises himself as Mad-Eye Moody for almost a year using Polyjuice Potion, but when he misses a dose on the day of the third Triwizard task, he reverts to his earlier form (*HP and the GF*, 682). Lupin's appearance changes every month, but that is both a temporary change and one that was imposed upon him (*Harry Potter and the Prisoner of Azkaban*, 352–53). The wounds to Bill's face and George's ear are permanent in that cursed wounds cannot be healed (*HP and the HBP*, 613; *HP and the DH*, 71), but again these are not changes that resulted from deliberate action on their part but rather things that happened to them. Peter Pettigrew's existence as Scabbers for twelve years stretches the definition of temporary, but when Lupin and Sirius Black get hold of him in the Shrieking Shack, they intend to "force him to show himself" (*HP and the PA*, 365). The animal form of an animagus, then, is not intended to be forever. Hermione transfigures Ron's face when they join Harry and Griphook to break into Gringotts (*HP and the DH*, 523), but this temporary disguise is undone by the Thief's Downfall (*HP and the DH*, 534).

Voldemort's physical transformation, however, is neither temporary nor imposed. He may not have set out to change his appearance, but he is never described as being disappointed with this likely side effect of his "many dangerous, magical transformations" (*HP and the CS*, 329). Indeed, as a young man, Merope Gaunt's son "was his handsome father in miniature" (*HP and the HBP*, 269), something he very likely wished to distance himself from just as he rejected his father's name. This is important because a long-term and sought-out change to one's physical appearance is a common identity marker for transgender people. Within the *Harry Potter* series, however, this type of change is something to be feared rather than valued or celebrated.

His Name Has Been Down for Hogwarts since Birth

As a nonbinary person, I exist outside of the gender binary, something that no character within Harry Potter does. Gender is not, however, the only binary in the series. While She-Who-Must-Not-Be-Named has imported the gender binary from the world in which she was raised, she has invented another binary—magic/nonmagic—which is central to the way the wizarding world works. A person is either born with magical talent or they are not. When Hagrid bursts into the hut on the rock in *Sorcerer's Stone*, he does not say, "Harry, you've become a wizard today." He says, "Harry, yer a wizard" (*HP and the SS*, 50). In other words, Harry has always been a wizard, as underscored by the fact that his "name's been down" for Hogwarts since birth (*HP and the SS*, 58). Very early in the series, then, we learn that magic is something you're born with. When Neville Longbottom tells the stories of his family being concerned that he might not be magical, there was no talk of remedies or treatment, only schemes to force him to show what they hoped he had been born with. This opens the door to learning about Squibs in *Chamber of Secrets* (145). Knowing that there are people who are born into magical families without any magical abilities underscores the idea that a person is either born with magic or not born with magic. There is nothing you can do to switch categories or exist outside that binary. This is reinforced by the fact that Ariana Dumbledore is not able to get rid of magic after she is attacked (*HP and the DH*, 564). When she's done with it, it stays with her.

Some might argue that the gender binary serves as an analogy to the magic/nonmagic binary in a way that is trans-inclusionary. One way to see the trajectory of a Muggle-born is that you have a child who is raised as a Muggle and who then learns that they are magical. The analogy does not hold, however, because most Muggles raising a magical child don't know they are Muggles, the exception being the Dursleys. They do not raise Harry as a magical child, however. He and other wand carriers raised by Muggles experience only one side of the binary, and they don't even know that there *is* a binary until they are eleven years old. So it's not the same as growing up in a society that constructs and polices a binary; it's not the same as being assigned to one of two options at birth and then realizing later that that assignment was wrong. The magic/nonmagic binary defines everything about who a person is in the wizarding world.

One way the magic/nonmagic binary is policed is that the wizarding community encourages Muggle-borns to integrate fully into the magical world while at the same time encouraging Squibs to integrate fully into Muggle society. The Ministry of Magic is so disinterested in the fate of Squibs that it does not keep track of where they live, for example (*HP and the OP*, 143).

Part of policing the binary is encouraging like to be with like: all people who don't have magical abilities should be together and all people who do have magical abilities should be together, and never the two shall meet. Muggle-born witches and wizards go home to their parents during school holidays, but the fact that Hermione increasingly spends those holidays with Ron and Harry (*HP and the OP*, 10, 498) indicates that even this connection is waning. Consider also that Ron's father is mentioned in the epilogue, but Hermione's parents are not (*HP and the DH*, 756). Argus Filch and Arabella Figg serve as exceptions to the complete expulsion of Squibs from wizarding life, but these exceptions prove the rule.

The construction, reinforcement, and policing of the magic/nonmagic binary is important because when pure-blood ideology takes over at the Ministry of Magic, those who are not pure-blood are at risk of persecution. Muggle-borns, or Mudbloods, are accused of having stolen magic even though there is no evidence that this is possible. This theft-of-magic rhetoric allows the Ministry under Voldemort to round up and punish a whole segment of wizarding society. It is not a matter of sending Muggle-borns away, exiling them from wizarding society, but rather of labeling Muggle-borns as deviant and therefore needing to be punished. The magic/nonmagic binary is not being questioned here, it is being policed. According to this logic, if you were born to Muggles, you are a Muggle. Being a Muggle means that you were not born with magic; the fact that you have magic now means that you have broken the rules by trying to switch teams—something that is not allowed. If how you were born is who you are, then transitioning from how you were understood by the wizarding world at birth to who you actually are is not something that is possible, and it is a lie to think that you can do it.

This form of policing the magic/nonmagic binary appears nonsensical to Ron, who points out that "if you could steal magic, there wouldn't be any Squibs" (*HP and the DH*, 209). The confusion comes from the fact that the Muggle-born Registry is based on a type of evidence that he has never accepted as the way to tell the difference between magic and nonmagic people: parentage. The Ministry does not ask Muggle-borns to perform magic to prove that they are a witch or a wizard; they give them a questionnaire and ask about their parents' professions. When Mary Cattermole tells Dolores Umbridge that her wand chose her in Ollivander's when she was eleven years old, Umbridge replies that this is a lie because wands "only choose witches or wizards and you are not a witch" (*HP and the DH*, 261). Umbridge's evidence

for this pronouncement is the fact that Cattermole's parents were "green gro-
cers" (*HP and the DH*, 261). This racist ideology that only pure-bloods are real
witches and wizards is not new information in *Deathly Hallows*; Harry hears
about it on his first trip to Diagon Alley when Draco Malfoy drawls that only
"the old families" should be allowed into Hogwarts and that "the other sort"
shouldn't be let in (*HP and the SS*, 78). The difference is that in the seventh
book, those with this belief are in a position of power. The persecution of
Muggle-borns is possible because of the extension of this discriminatory
ideology into Ministry policy.

The ideology of the Muggle-born Registration Commission is eerily
similar to the ideology of trans-exclusionary arguments in the here and
now because both disregard certain kinds of evidence to keep a population
and the space it inhabits pure. The Muggle-born Registration Commission
does not take personal testimony seriously as evidence in the policing of the
magic/nonmagic binary. They have very specific and immutable ideas about
how to tell who is and is not magical, and they refuse to hear anything to the
contrary. Similarly, for trans-exclusionary thinkers, if someone says, "This is
my gender," it is perfectly acceptable to contradict them based on what the
doctors said when that person was born. By this logic, trans men are actually
women who have been taught to hate their sex,[10] and trans women are men
attempting to steal womanhood in order to gain access to all-women spaces.
If you respect what people say about themselves, however, trans men are
men, trans women are women, and nonbinary and intersex people are valid.
You-Know-Who can disagree with this fundamental truth, but she is wrong.

What Is a Transgender Harry Potter Scholar to Do?

The binary essentialism evident in the *Harry Potter* series is dangerous, as
is the idea that permanent physical change and choosing a new name can
only happen in the embodiment of pure evil. When fans of Harry Potter
renounce the author because of her transphobia while maintaining a claim
on the fictional universe, trans-exclusionary ideology is part of the world
they are keeping. There is no easy answer for what to do. Many people have
said that the essay She-Who-Must-Not-Be-Named posted on her website
in June 2020 should not be a surprise, pointing out that her transphobia
has been on display for years.[11] For some that means rejecting the books

entirely. Melkorka Licea reports that some former fans are willing to spend hundreds of dollars to get Harry Potter tattoos removed.[12] For others, it is not that simple. Kacen Callender describes how the *Harry Potter* series saved their life, for example. They sit with the irony that She-Who-Must-Not-Be-Named inspired them and "so many other transgender and nonbinary people to become authors"[13] and await the day that the hateful speech of the series' author will be drowned out.

Personally, I first turned to Roland Barthes's theory of the Death of the Author in an attempt to separate the artist from the art. The idea is that once a text is finished, its meaning is not informed by careful study of the author's biography but rather by the interaction between the text and the reader. In order for the reader—or the fan—to be born, Barthes argues, the author must undergo a figurative death.[14] Unfortunately, while the Death of the Author divorces the author from the text,[15] it does not divorce the text from the text itself. Trans-exclusionary ideas do not solely exist in the person of the series' author, they run through the series. I will never again be able to listen to Jim Dale's audio rendition of *Harry Potter* without being reminded of the problematic aspects of the text that I have raised here. I will also be haunted by the anti-Semitic stereotypes embodied in the goblins, the racist portrayal of happily enslaved house-elves, and the shallow portrayal of the unfortunately named Cho Chang.[16] None of these things mean that I will never again be able to listen to the audiobooks, though. No text is perfect, and I have chosen to continue to interact with the *Harry Potter* series, warts and all. I refuse to allow the actions and speech of their author or the fact that there are problems in the text to interfere with my enjoyment of the narrative as a whole or with my growth as a scholar. Instead, I will maintain a critical eye—and ear—while interacting with the wizarding world and encourage others to do the same.

Notes

1. I am using the US (Scholastic) rather than UK (Bloomsbury) editions of the books.
2. Sinclair-Palm, "It's Non-Existent," 5.
3. Sinclair-Palm, "It's Non-Existent," 5.
4. [Redacted], "[Redacted] Writes about Her Reasons."
5. Vezzali et al., "The Greatest Magic of Harry Potter."
6. Mutz, "Harry Potter and the Deathly Donald."
7. Henderson, "I Don't Think You're a Waste of Space."
8. Vary, "[Redacted]'s Book Sales Lagging."

9. Carroll, *Transgender and the Literary Imagination*; and Eastwood, "How, Then, Might the Transsexual Read?"

10. Jacobs, "'Free Debate' Has Hidden Costs."

11. Fairchild, "[Redacted] Confirms Stance"; and Zacny, "[Redacted]'s Transphobia Wasn't Hard to Find."

12. Licea, "'Harry Potter' Fans Removing Tattoos."

13. Callender, "Harry Potter Saved My Life."

14. Barthes, "The Death of the Author," 1326.

15. Goodman, "Disappointing Fans"; and Donaldson, "[Redacted] Is the Exemplification."

16. See Sarah Park Dahlen and Kallie Schell's chapter in this volume, "'Cho Chang Is Trending': What It Means to Be Asian in the Wizarding World."

Bibliography

Barthes, Roland. "The Death of the Author." Translated by Stephen Heath. In *The Norton Anthology of Theory and Criticism*, edited by Vincent B. Leitch et al., 1322–26. New York: W. W. Norton, 2010.

Callender, Kacen. "Harry Potter Saved My Life. [Redacted] Is Now Endangering Trans People Like Me." them, June 8, 2020. https://www.them.us/story/kacen-callender-op -ed-jk-rowling.

Carroll, Rachel. *Transgender and the Literary Imagination: Changing Gender in Twentieth-Century Writing*. Edinburgh: Edinburgh University Press, 2018.

Donaldson, Kayleigh. "[Redacted] Is the Exemplification of Why We Need the Death of the Author." Pajiba, December 24, 2019. https://www.pajiba.com/miscellaneous/jk-rowling -is-the-exemplification-of-why-we-need-the-death-of-the-author.php.

Eastwood, Alexander. "How, Then, Might the Transsexual Read? Notes toward a Trans Literary History." *Transgender Studies Quarterly* 1, no. 4 (November 2014): 590–604. doi:10.1215/23289252-2815111.

Fairchild, Phaylen. "[Redacted] Confirms Stance against Transgender Women." *Medium*, June 24, 2019. https://medium.com/@Phaylen/jk-rowling-confirms-stance-against -transgender-women-9bd83f7ca623.

Goodman, Lesley. "Disappointing Fans: Fandom, Fictional Theory, and the Death of the Author." *Journal of Popular Culture* 48, no. 4 (August 2015): 662–76.

Henderson, Tolonda. "'I Don't Think You're a Waste of Space': Activity, Redemption, and the Social Construction of Fatness." In *Inside the World of Harry Potter: Critical Essays on the Books and Films*, edited by Christopher E. Bell, 33–43. Jefferson, NC: McFarland, 2018.

Jacobs, TD. "'Free Debate' Has Hidden Costs." *Researching Early Modern History* (blog), July 17, 2020. https://earlymodern.blog/2020/07/17/free-debate-has-hidden-costs-td -jacobs/?fbclid=IwAR3aPLe_4nL_RoY8xms52YJ4-kpPlDLLJVROPOODlYOwgM4C_ 2lNOtENLXU.

Licea, Melkorka. "'Harry Potter' Fans Removing Tattoos after [Redacted]'s Trans Comments." *New York Post*, June 12, 2020. https://nypost.com/2020/06/12/harry-potter -fans-removing-tattoos-after-j-k-rowling-trans-tweets/.

Mutz, Diana C. "Harry Potter and the Deathly Donald." *PS: Political Science and Politics* 49, no. 4 (October 2016): 722–29. doi:10.1017/S1049096516001633.

[Redacted]. "[Redacted] Writes about Her Reasons for Speaking Out on Sex and Gender Issues." June 10, 2020. https://www.jkrowling.com/opinions/j-k-rowling-writes-about -her-reasons-for-speaking-out-on-sex-and-gender-issues/.

Sinclair-Palm, Julia. "'It's Non-Existent': Haunting in Trans Youth Narratives about Naming." Bank Street Occasional Paper Series, no. 37, 2017. https://educate.bankstreet.edu/occasional -paper-series/vol2017/iss37/7.

Vary, Adam B. "[Redacted]'s Book Sales Lagging Despite Industry Boom in June." *Variety*, July 16, 2020. https://variety.com/2020/film/news/jk-rowling-book-sales-harry-potter -1234708777/.

Vezzali, Loris, Sofia Stathi, Dino Giovannini, Dora Capozza, and Elena Trifiletti. "The Greatest Magic of Harry Potter: Reducing Prejudice." *Journal of Applied Social Psychology* 45, no. 2 (February 2015): 105–21. doi:10.1111/jasp.12279.

Zacny, Rob. "[Redacted]'s Transphobia Wasn't Hard to Find, She Wrote a Book about It." *Vice*, December 20, 2019. https://www.vice.com/en_us/article/pkeynz/jk-rowlings -transphobia-wasnt-hard-to-find-she-wrote-a-book-about-it.

PART II.

#Black Hermione

Hermione Is Black

Harry Potter and the Crisis of Infinite Dark Fantastic Worlds

Ebony Elizabeth Thomas

> Words can't express how elated I am that it's common
> knowledge in 2015 that Hermione is Black. . . . This is so
> beautiful and idk what started it, if it was a text post, a
> racebent fancast, or ppl just collectively coming out and
> saying "hey, I thought that while reading the books, too"
> but I am forever grateful.
>
> **—Breianna Harvey,** "Hermione is Black," Tumblr post

My immersion in Harry Potter fandom now seems like it was a lifetime ago.[1] It has been more than twenty years since I opened my first *Harry Potter* novel, a hardcover copy of *Harry Potter and the Chamber of Secrets* that one of my fifth graders left in the classroom. After failing to uncover its original owner, I took the book home over the weekend and immediately fell in love with the wizarding world. I devoured everything about Harry Potter that I could find online, discovering Fanfiction.net later that spring. By the time the fourth novel in the series, *Harry Potter and the Goblet of Fire*, was released in the summer of 2000, I had discovered the Harry Potter for Grownups Yahoo! group (HP4GU for short). From July 2000 until August 2006, I was a highly visible member of Harry Potter fandom. Online and in person, I openly used my real-life professional name, Ebony Elizabeth Thomas, as well as the alias AngieJ (short for Angelina Johnson, a Black British witch in the novels).

Digital Pottermania in the early 2000s was an intimate online community that consisted of less than a thousand members and perhaps fewer than one hundred regular posters across several websites, forums, and listservs. Within that small community, I was the first—and during its earliest days, one of the most prominent—Black fans.[2] My fandom participation was a daily event, as I logged on eagerly after teaching and classes in the final few years before smartphones became ubiquitous. I volunteered for a number of Potter websites, including the Harry Potter for Grownups Yahoo! group, FictionAlley, and the now defunct PumpkinPie.org. I worked on the first Harry Potter fan-initiated conference—Nimbus 2003 in Orlando—cochairing one of two programming committees. And between 2000 and 2004, I wrote and posted a popular post-Hogwarts fanfiction duology, *Trouble in Paradise* and *Paradise Lost*, which had beta readers from Britain to Brazil and enjoyed a broad international readership.[3]

Written between December 2000 and August 2001, *Trouble in Paradise* is narrated from the first-person perspective of Angelina Johnson, a witch who is described in *Harry Potter and the Goblet of Fire* as "a tall black girl who played Chaser on the Gryffindor Quidditch team." Those twelve words introducing the only Black girl character in the story launched this dark fantastic journey of mine. Set ten years after the Battle of Hogwarts, but written before the last three books in the series were published, *Trouble in Paradise* was the beginning of my recognition of the dark fantastic cycle. Since this was many years before the emergence of Pottermore (and controversies like #MagicInNorthAmerica[4]), I wondered how wizards and witches of color like Angelina had ended up in the Western world, let alone England. At the time, Rowling hadn't left us much to go on. Wrapping my head around a magical theory for Black characters in high fantasy was something for which I had no precedent. I'd avidly read Octavia Butler, Tananarive Due, and Nalo Hopkinson in high school and college, but this was different.

In contrast to Black authors who wrote emancipatory Black fantastic and Afrofuturistic tales, centering Black characters in their narratives, race in the *Harry Potter* series almost seemed like an afterthought. I thought it odd that the Black witches and wizards had British surnames. I didn't understand how that could be possible. How could anyone subject a magical person in

Rowling's legendarium to chattel slavery? Wouldn't their magic prevent it? These echoes from the afterlife of slavery seemed inconsistent with the rules of the otherwise compelling wizarding world that J. K. Rowling had built. In a series featuring a boarding school where magical children and adolescents were learning how to defy the laws of physics, I had trouble imagining the origin stories for *Harry Potter*'s characters of color—most of whom were relegated to the background.

In order to come up with a good explanation for Angelina's magical ancestry, I revisited folklore of the African diaspora, just as fantasy writers of European descent revisit their own ancestral folkloric traditions. African and Caribbean folklore, while foundational for much contemporary Black speculative fiction, simply did not sufficiently account for why the character would be surnamed Johnson. In the process of this research, I rediscovered one of my favorite stories from childhood, Virginia Hamilton's "The People Could Fly," which is the final story in a book of Black American folktales of the same name. This was Hamilton's rendering of a classic Black folktale in African American English. I had heard it read aloud as a child, and I had read it aloud to younger family members and students. In the story, I wanted Angelina to do the same thing for her daughter. In a sense, I was inscribing myself into multiple beloved narratives at the same time.

In chapter 6 of *Trouble in Paradise*, I created a scene in which Angelina tells her daughter Malinda, a character original to my fanfiction, about the origins of magical people of African descent who were enslaved. For that origin story, I used long passages from "The People Could Fly," putting Hamilton's words into Angelina's mouth. The file on my computer is dated February 1, 2001. The disclaimer on the chapter reads as follows:

> I'm emphatically not JKR—she owns Harry and company, and the fact that I'm writing about them doesn't mean that I want to infringe her copyright, it simply means that I'm obsessed with the fictional world she has created. Certain elements of this chapter were inspired by Virginia Hamilton's award-winning folklore collection *The People Could Fly* and Zora Neale Hurston's *excellent* anthropological study of magic, superstition, and voodoo in the Caribbean, *Tell My Horse*.

But in reality, the passage was more than just "inspired." I had my fanfictional version of Angelina Johnson-Weasley treat *The People Could Fly* as if it were oral folklore, leaving it unclear where my words ended and Hamilton's began. Here's a brief excerpt from the long scene:

> "Tell me a story, will you?"
>
> I kissed her cheek impulsively. "All right, I will. This is a story that my father heard when he was a little boy growing up around Muggles."
>
> "Oh, good! I love Grandpa's Muggle stories!"
>
> "I know you do, darling. Which one do you want to hear?"
>
> Malinda whipped her head out of my hand to beam at me. "Tell me the one about the people who could fly!"
>
> She would choose *that* one. The only one that was real.
>
> They say the people could fly. Say that long ago in Africa, some of the people knew magic. And they would walk up on air like climbin' up on a gate. And they flew like blackbirds over the fields. Black, shiny wings flappin' against the blue up there.
>
> *Then, many of the Blackbird people were captured for slavery. The ones that could fly shed their wings. They couldn't take their wings across the water on the slave ships. Too crowded, don't you know.*
>
> *The folks were full of misery, then. Got sick with the up and down of the sea. So they nearly forgot about flyin' when they could no longer breathe the sweet scent of Africa.*
>
> *Say the people who could fly kept their power, although they shed their wings. They kept their secret magic in the lands of slavery. They looked the same as the other people from Africa who had been coming over, who had dark skin. Say you couldn't tell anymore one who could fly from one who couldn't.*
>
> My father told my mother this folktale long before they were married. Although she was full-blooded Society, she'd never heard of it before. She was astonished to learn that it is by far the most cherished and treasured tale in all of black Muggle lore. The story has several variations, but the main points of the narrative are universal amongst Muggle descendants of the black Diaspora. Mum was also stunned by how accurate the details were.[5]

The italicized portion of the excerpt is Hamilton's retelling of the African American folktale. They are her words, not mine. The part that I quoted was also italicized in the original posted chapter on Fanfiction.net. In the balance of that scene, I went on to have Angelina reflect at some length upon *The People Could Fly* in her own words, filling out more of the details and positioning it as an origin story for Black Atlantic peoples within Rowling's wizarding world—a legend within a legend. I ended the section with Angelina snapping out of her reflections, using another long quotation from Hamilton as she wrapped up the folktale for her daughter. In all, about one-seventh of the scene is from *The People Could Fly*, and the chapter itself is fifty-two pages long. (I was infamous for my long chapters back in those days.)

Five years after completing *Trouble in Paradise*, in August 2006, I was accused of plagiarism in a post on bad_penny, an anonymous LiveJournal dedicated to exposing bad fan behavior. In the post, passages from "The People Could Fly" were placed side-by-side with verbatim passages from chapter 6 of *Trouble in Paradise*. I had intentionally used Hamilton's story within that fanfiction, and the accusation of plagiarism surprised me. There's no question that I was naïve in thinking that it was okay to use Hamilton's writing without formal attribution, even in fanfiction, but during the time that I wrote the story—December 2000 to August 2001—there were few fandom conventions for digital citation. Fan authors regularly quoted phrases, sentences, and passages from the *Harry Potter* series with only vague attributions. For many of us, it was our first time in any kind of fandom, writing fanfiction. Fanfiction was seen as a place of freedom, where we could play, borrow and blend, and practice creative writing skills for our own original work. There was also the thrill of the forbidden and the taboo, of taking a popular work that was swiftly becoming part of the cultural landscape and appropriating it for our own purposes.

Hidden behind anonymous internet handles, people were quite nasty, saying that I was always so self-righteous, that a teacher should have known better than to *steal* a Black writer's story, and that I had deceived the fandom. My position as a prominent supporter of the Harry/Hermione ship also was noted, as *Trouble in Paradise* and *Paradise Lost* were written to support my preferred pairing.[6] Several prominent Potter fans stopped speaking to me altogether. There were other repercussions as well. Prior to the controversy, I had received an invitation to be a featured guest speaker at Phoenix Rising 2007, a Harry Potter fan conference in New Orleans, and to review proposals for the event, much as I had during Nimbus 2003. It was mutually agreed that I should excuse myself from the conference as well as any further involvement in Potter fandom, including my own HP_Paradise Yahoo! group and the FictionAlley website. After posting a message of apology to the LiveJournal community Blackfolk, which was discussing the scandal, I posted a good-bye message to my LiveJournal on August 16, 2006.[7] Within a week of my apology, I decided to pull *Trouble in Paradise* and *Paradise Lost* from all the websites where I could control access. Thus, my years in Harry Potter fandom came to an ignoble end.

In retrospect, the fandom provided many lasting benefits for me. It was at Nimbus 2003 that I met children's literature scholars Philip Nel and Karin E. Westman, who were among those who encouraged me to pursue a PhD. Later that fall, I joined the Child_Lit listserv, hosted by Rutgers University and moderated for more than two decades by Michael Joseph before coming to an end in September 2017. These experiences put me on the path to becoming a professor of education specializing in children's and young adult literature. Many of the ideas in this book germinated during my time in Harry Potter fandom and in the years immediately afterward, when I tried (and failed) to publish my original fantasy novel series featuring Black characters. (I gave up in 2007, when I had to choose between revising my novel manuscript or completing my doctoral exams.)

But in the wake of the plagiarism accusation and my ensuing self-imposed exile, I began to recognize a not-so-idyllic side of Harry Potter fandom that I largely ignored while I was in it, a side that led me to seek LiveJournal communities like Blackfolk to converse with geeks of color before the dawn of the social media age. I had only glimpsed that side before, but it was always there. It was there in the way that I was taunted in an otherwise fun AOL chat when I code-switched into African American English. It was in the argument I had over Dean Thomas's name signaling his Welshness, one in which I retorted that *my* last name is Thomas, and I've never been to Wales. It was in being unaware that my special status within the early fandom as *the* Black fan was a form of tokenization as much as my chosen name in fandom—Ebony AKA AngieJ—signaled the presence of the only named Black girl character. It was in my inability to see that I was hypervisible while inside Harry Potter fandom but still marginalized in ways that surfaced only after I withdrew from the community that defined my twenties.

For many of us, fandom is as much about the source material as it is about the community and the friendships one makes. After the plagiarism scandal, few of my friends in Potter fandom reached out to me. Heidi Tandy, Flourish Klink, Clare Worley, and Josh Aronovitch were notable exceptions to that rule, as were most of the regulars on the Harry Potter for Grownups Yahoo! group who'd been around during the genesis of *Trouble in Paradise*.

In recent years, I have been asked to sit on the Harry Potter fandom panel at San Diego Comic-Con International as an academic and fandom old-timer. However, the scandal ended some of my newer friendships and distanced me from others I thought would be there through thick and thin. Some of the people in question I'd invited to my home, traveled with, attended Potter movie premieres with, and thought would be there for a lifetime. In short, the fandom scandal marked the start of my exile from a digital community that I'd loved.

When I saw others who had been involved in similar plagiarism exposés defended vigorously by the community, and then reconciled and restored to fandom, while I remained at the margins, I couldn't help but wonder what happened. I was far from innocent, but the fact that I remained ostracized while others remained in the fold bothered me greatly. The exile—*social death*—that I suffered initially both hurt and puzzled me. Was it because I was still seen by some as a shameless plagiarist, although my intentions for including a slice of my own childhood—and solving the dark fantastic dilemma at the heart of the *Potter* series—were noble? Was it because I was associated with the Big Name Fan clique in early Harry Potter fandom, and thus a mean girl? Was it because I was open about being religious at times?

Or was my race ever a factor?

Was any of it because I was Black?

In the Wake: What Does It Mean to Defend the Dead?

In her introduction to *In the Wake: On Blackness and Being*, Christina Sharpe asks a poignant question, which she then answers:

> What does it mean to defend the dead? To tend to the Black dead and dying, to tend to the Black person, to Black people, always living in the push toward our death. It means work. It is work: hard emotional, physical, and intellectual work that demands vigilant attendance to the needs of the dying, to each their way, and also to the needs of the living.[8]

This question is not limited to humans who have been labeled as Black in the past and present, both quick and dead, but extends to Black *characters*, and to the very idea of Blackness itself. As the title of Sharpe's book suggests, this is an ontological question that every Black child, woman, and man is confronted with throughout the course of a lifetime. It is a question that demands an answer.

The wake, according to Sharpe, is the path behind a ship, keeping watch with the dead, coming to consciousness, all at once. This applies to Black people in real life and to Black girl characters caught in the wake within the storied realms of the collective imagination. These girls-that-never-were, but who nonetheless remain with us due to their very fictionality, are dying and *not* dead, present and *not* present, inconsequential to speculative narratives yet vital to their functioning. Rue's impossible dark innocence in *The Hunger Games*, Gwen's impossible dark beauty in the BBC's *Merlin*, and Bonnie Bennett's impossible dark virtue in *The Vampire Diaries* are signs that Black girls in speculative fiction are the *real* "impossible girls" (with due respect to Doctor Who). Yet the conundrum is that these Black girl characters (like Black girls in the real world) are both impossible *and* necessary at the same time.

I am by no means the only one who has observed the myriad ways that the fantastic, the speculative, and the collective imagination have rendered Black presence impossible and Black nonexistence compulsory. Most Black fans and other fans of color have thought quite a bit about our precarious state even within realms of supposedly infinite possibilities. During a Twitter chat, an observer with the handle @relicUA noted: "I think poor non-white people are in a state of quantum super-position, such that they only exist when the narrative requires."[9] Indeed, young Black women and girls exist in a state of quantum superposition in the fantastic.[10] They cannot exist, and yet, they must: when it comes to the fantastic, Schrödinger's cat is a young Black girl.[11]

Due to the quantum problem created by the Door of No Return, a profound crisis is created for stories fantastic and real. This crisis is found in infinite fantastic worlds. As Michelle M. Wright observes in *Physics of Blackness*, when all of Blackness is refracted through the Middle Passage, dilemmas of space and time result. These dilemmas are resolved through both progress (calls toward greater diversity in the fantastic) and regress (doubling down on the violence and erasure of the Dark Other). To note but one example among many, in the same year pioneering Black women authors N. K. Jemisin and Nnedi Okorafor won the prestigious Hugo Award for their emancipatory fantastic stories, detective Abbie Mills (portrayed magnificently by actress Nicole Beharie) in the genre television show *Sleepy Hollow* was caught in the gears of the dark fantastic cycle and killed. Showrunners were unmoved by the pleas of Black fans and audiences about the trauma of losing a beloved Black woman lead in a horror show, perhaps unwittingly echoing painful long-ago words of Thomas Jefferson about people of African descent: "[T]heir griefs are transient."[12] Even as a growing number of Black authors, artists, screenwriters, and showrunners are producing extraordinarily creative work to endarken the popular imagination, the shadows of the past remain.

In the wake of these shadows and echoes, it seems vital to examine the ways that Black writers, fans, and audiences are narrating the self into existence in the face of narrative erasure—and have *always* had to read themselves into fantastic canons that excluded them. The traditional fantastic has historically assumed a White audience, and, in turn, those endarkened and Othered have had to read those stories to understand the cartographies of the imagination. In contrast to histories of fandom and audience that portray audiences for the speculative and the fantastic as predominantly White, new work from scholars like Rebecca Wanzo[13] and André Carrington[14] sheds light on the ways that Black fans and audiences have interpreted fantastic media that does not always imagine us as part of the audience—a view that I share. It is my hope that future scholars and researchers will extend Sharpe's call for wake work into the dark fantastic.

How Hermione Became Black: Black Girls' Emancipatory Readings

When I finished *Trouble in Paradise* in the summer of 2001, it was such a hit in the fandom that, like many fan writers, I penned a sequel. Posting the first chapter just before 9/11, I centered the second half of my Potter fanfiction duology on Hermione Granger, one of the "Golden Trio" of central characters in the series. But instead of taking the first-viewpoint perspective as I did with Angelina in *Trouble in Paradise*, I wrote my alternate universe Hermione's story in the third person:

> Hermione Granger sat bolt upright in bed. Her heart was pounding at a frenetic rate and her teeth clattered. Underneath the covers that she'd clutched with trembling fingers, her chest heaved with her quickened breathing. She felt rather as if she'd just finished flying at a fantastic 250 m.p.h. . . . but there, she wasn't supposed to be thinking about flying anymore, was she?[15]

While I loved Hermione Granger, perhaps too much for a young adult needing to leave childhood behind, she wasn't a mirror for my experiences. Because I did not look like her, I knew that I could never view the wizarding world through her eyes, but only peer over her shoulder. Even after writing half a million words about what I imagined Rowling's most beloved character might be like as a young adult, I never imagined Hermione Granger as Black. Reading the first few *Harry Potter* novels as a twenty-two-year-old school-teacher, it never occurred to me to unmake my reality to read Hermione as anything except White. That is why it never occurred to me to cosplay her, although in the early 2000s I owned everything from magic wands to figurines to editions of *Harry Potter* from multiple countries. Instead, as with *Anne of Green Gables* and *Alice in Wonderland*, I could only directly experience Hermione's inner world by donning my Invisibility Cloak.

Unlike my own and previous generations, today's young readers are choosing to read characters as mirrors of their own experiences. After a viral BuzzFeed article by Alanna Bennett, "What a 'Racebent' Hermione Granger Really Represents," was shared among Harry Potter fans online in early 2015, a new movement on social media formed insisting that Hermione's description in the popular novels meant she was really Black.[16] One young adult author of several "Hermione is Black" Tumblr posts, Breianna Harvey, talked with me about growing up with the *Harry Potter* book series as a child and reading the überpopular girl protagonist of the series as a mirror of the self:

> Prior to Tumblr, I had thought Hermione was like me and it was my first experience at being upset with deviations from the book, specifically casting. But like many other Black girls in my situation, I kept my mouth shut. It wasn't until Tumblr that I started to speak up about it. I saw drawings of Hermione . . . where the artists would subconsciously draw Hermione darker than everyone else. Then my friend started posting fancasts of [Welsh actress] Jessica Sula as Hermione and I really loved it. Then I started to see fanart where she was darker than Jessica and followers were engaging in conversation with me about how much a Black Hermione would make sense along with speculation of her origins.[17]

Breianna's reading of Hermione as a Black girl may seem radical, yet she is in good company. Posts in the "Hermione is Black" Tumblr tags have been shared thousands of times by Tumblr users. It is clear that some dark girls and women today are choosing to enter their reading experiences, to quote Audre Lorde, "Blackened and whole." Their interpretive agency brings to mind a reader of Chimamanda Ngozi Adichie's books, who loved one of the stories so much that she excitedly told Adichie how the story should continue.[18] In my work with digital literacies scholar Amy Stornaiuolo, I have examined how readers use digital literary affinity spaces, such as fan communities, to restory their worlds and subvert traditional expectations about relationships between readers, authors, and texts.[19] As readers and viewers begin to claim interpretive agency, they not only imagine themselves into stories but also *reimagine the very stories themselves.* This imaginative restorying work is often viewed as transgressive, as authors fight for the official word, cultural pundits trivialize readers' efforts, and the general public positions authors as "under attack" by wayward readers. But there are signs of change.

Shifting cultural attitudes toward texts—and the contemporary struggle for interpretive authority over them—characterize meaning-making. While theorists point out the historical nature of this struggle (and the longtime absence of the author), the question of reader-author relationships must be revisited in a digital age in which more people than ever before are writing for work and leisure, readers connect with one another in powerful networks, lines between readers and writers blur, definitions of what counts as text are negotiated and reconfigured in hybrid multimodal and multilingual constellations, and texts and people circulate across asymmetrical trajectories.

It should be noted that long before Rowling left Hermione's racial and ethnic identities up for reader interpretation in a tweet,[20] she'd established a propensity toward providing details for the vast wizarding world outside the official books and movies. Years earlier, she had revealed to fans that Dumbledore was gay. Catherine Tosenberger, in "Oh My God, the Fanfiction! Dumbledore's Outing and the Online Harry Potter Fandom," notes:

> Among participatory fans, one contingent was unsurprised when Rowling, during an appearance at Carnegie Hall, announced that Hogwarts headmaster Albus Dumbledore was gay: readers and writers of "slash" fanfiction. Slash— fanfiction that concerns a romantic and/or sexual relationship between characters of the same gender—is one of the most popular forms of Potter fanfiction. Slash fans are always on the lookout for hints of homoeroticism in the source text that can be spun into a story, and the description of the relationship between Dumbledore and his boyhood friend-turned-

enemy Gellert Grindelwald proved especially fruitful in this respect; fans
began creating stories, art, and critical essays concerning their relationship
immediately following the release of *Harry Potter and the Deathly Hallows*—
anticipating Rowling's announcement by three months. Immediately after
her revelation, Rowling laughed, "Oh my god, the *fanfiction*." Over the
years, Rowling has proven to be not simply aware, but actively supportive,
of fanfiction; her confirmation of Dumbledore's sexuality lends support to
Sara Gwenllian Jones's articulation of slash not as a perverse "resistance" to a
given text's presumed heteronormativity but rather "an actualization of latent
textual elements."[21]

More recently, Rowling expressed doubts about the way she tied up the main
characters' romances in the epilogue of the final book, *Harry Potter and the
Deathly Hallows*. Within twenty-four hours of the interview in which she
expressed these doubts, readers around the world who had grown up with
Harry and his friends responded with passion. Using social media, teens
and young adults wrote numerous articles, columns, essays, and fanfictions
responding to Rowling's revelation. Some defended the series epilogue, while
others preferred Rowling's statement about Harry and Hermione that "it
could have gone that way."[22] (As a one-time Harry and Hermione supporter,
I admit that her remarks vindicated our long-suffering ship!)[23]

What Rowling's statements and the ensuing backlash revealed was the
extent to which readers felt ownership over Potter's narrative landscape.
Some in Harry Potter fandom asserted that the reader's role was to imagine
possible futures for the story, a role threatened by Rowling's apparent efforts
to wrest control of the narrative from fans. Perhaps the best summary of
this reading rebellion belonged to popular young adult author John Green,
who wrote on Twitter at the height of the controversy: "Books belong to
their readers."[24] Green's statement, reposted by Twitter and Tumblr users
more than forty-five thousand times within six weeks of its initial posting,
demonstrated the role of contemporary audiences in determining narrative
meaning.[25] Today's readers are using the tools of social media to make meanings that are not just independent of authorial intent but can also deliberately
contradict it—in other words, meaning itself is in the process of becoming
crowdsourced and jointly imagined.

As I discussed in my earlier book *The Dark Fantastic*, constructing new
meanings in a speculative fiction landscape where the Dark Other remains

trapped within the narrative is potentially quite challenging. Most readers, viewers, and fans have not responded to Bonnie, Rue, or Gwen by moving them to the center of the narrative, leading me to search for meaning at the margins for those characters' lives. Yet from *Harry Potter* to *Hamilton*, there has been a new movement in which previously White cisgender heterosexual characters (and, in *Hamilton*, historical figures) are now being imagined as Others. The rising generation is not only inscribing themselves into the narrative but also demanding to be the center of all their worlds, literate, fannish, and otherwise. Thus, in a textual landscape where the author of *Harry Potter* has told us that Dumbledore is gay, Harry and Hermione *could have* ended up together, and Hermione's appearance is left up to the readers' imagination, we are left with the possibility of infinite storyworlds. Although this plurality of possible worlds might represent a crisis for some audiences, it may provide an answer for emancipating the imagination for readers and fans who have for too long inhabited the margins—real and imagined.

Reading and Restorying after Hermione: Reconciling the Dark Fantastic Crisis on Infinite Storyworlds

In the 1980s, the two major US comic houses, Marvel and DC, reconciled years of discontinuities and alterities in their canons with two series that are now legendary: DC's Crisis on Infinite Earths and Marvel's Secret Wars. In both cases, several decades of changes in the writing staff as well as changes in the audience meant that all the top superheroes were given different story arcs, many of which contradicted each other. For instance, in one series, Superman aged and became elderly, while in another, he was still young. Multiverse series like Crisis on Infinite Earths reconciled the question "which Superman is the real Superman?" by presenting the possibility of parallel worlds. But multiple storyworlds featuring different outcomes for the same character may be difficult to process, as comics scholar Karin Kukkonen notes:

> Cognitive-psychological research on mental models, that is, scenarios we mentally develop in order to reason, also stresses that situations triggering the creation of multiple mental models are difficult to process . . . and that we construct mental models in order to eliminate alternatives and create coherence. Thus, when reading fiction, interpreters construct a "three-

dimensional model akin to an actual model of the scene" in order to locate the characters, monitor the events, and project the narrative's progress.[26]

Given that multiple worlds are notably difficult for readers to process, encountering the racial Other within a narrative presents even more difficulty for some mainstream audiences. While Kukkonen rightly notes that readers and fans of contemporary superhero comics are far more comfortable with alterity than most because of canon discontinuities,[27] the comics readership is not notably better on race than others. While the production of transformative fan work and vigorous discussion show that fans are invested in alternate worlds, there is a vast gulf between the acceptance of slash celebrating gay relationships between White cisgender male characters, and the disdain for racial and ethnic diversity in many fan communities. This shows that not all alterities are created equal, producing a dilemma that must be reconciled.

This dilemma can be reconciled by accepting all storyworlds as possible. Comments from authors like Rowling stating that "it could have gone that way" and "never specified" open up narrative space for difference. Changing the mode of storytelling also opens up this narrative space. Potter fans noted many changes when the books were transmediated to the screen, and yet the eight-movie series was still wildly successful. The play makes further changes, not only to Hermione's race and ethnicity but also in time, for the Golden Trio of Harry, Ron, and Hermione are now middle-aged adults. Changes like these ask audience participants to reimagine the narrative. But some changes are more acceptable than others. It is certainly the case that differentiating a character's race seems to be more difficult than other kinds of changes.

How, then, can creators of stories and worlds assist audiences in opening up their imaginations to racial difference in the fantastic? Returning to Kukkonen, readers of superhero comics are able to accept multiple versions of the same characters because writers and artists provide two aids to help reconcile multiple storyworlds: iconography and reader/viewer/audience surrogates. Iconography such as costuming, shields, and logos "provide shortcuts into readers' knowledge structures, enabling them to keep different character versions distinct and connect them to their original storyworlds."[28] For example, Superman's iconic *S* logo has undergone multiple makeovers from his original appearance in 1938's *Action Comics #1* through his more recent appearances in movies such as *Man of Steel* and *Batman v Superman*. No matter what Superman's situation is in the comics, no matter what he looks like, as long as he has his logo, he is recognizable.[29] These icons exist beyond comics. Returning to Harry Potter, wands from Ollivanders, brooms from Quality Quidditch Supplies, and even Harry's scar are iconographic in nature and help orient readers within the wizarding world.

Audience surrogates, in contrast, provide secondary characters with whom the audience can identify as the narrative unfolds.[30] One of the best and most enduring examples of a surrogate comes not from books or comics but from television—Doctor Who's traveling companions are ordinary people whose purpose is to react to the time traveling, eponymous Gallifreyan alien as the audience might. Although the Doctor has regenerated (changed actors) more than a dozen times, no matter what he looks like, each generation of companions marvels in turn that the TARDIS, Doctor Who's flying police box phone booth of a spaceship, is "bigger on the inside" and "smaller on the outside."[31] Surrogates thus provide important narrative continuity. As surrogates provide explanations for in-universe phenomena, "readers acquire by proxy the mental model that the surrogates construct at the [narrative] level."[32] Within Harry Potter, Harry's best friends Ron Weasley and Hermione Granger provide perspectives on the wizarding world from both the inside (Ron, born to a wizarding family) and outside (Hermione, raised by non-magical parents). Characters of color, like Cho Chang, Viktor Krum, Fleur Delacour, Dean Thomas, and my own favorite, Angelina Johnson, provide tantalizing yet fleeting glimpses of diverse possibilities for fantastic worlds, providing even more surrogates for Harry.

The challenge comes when neither iconography nor reader surrogates suffice to diversify and decolonize the baseline world. How we make sense of reader response, audience, and transaction must be revisited in a global digital age in which diversity and social change are no longer at the margins of life but, increasingly, at the center.[33] In an era of struggle and contestation over narrative and meaning, young people today are, in the words of literacy scholar Vivian Vasquez, "reading and writing the self into existence,"[34] using fan communities and other digital infinity groups to *restory* the popular imagination by making it into their own image. Restorying describes the complex ways that contemporary young people narrate the word and the world, analyze their lived experiences, then synthesize and recontextualize a multiplicity of stories in order to form new narratives. In other words, as young readers imagine themselves into stories, they *reimagine the very stories themselves*. Now more than ever before, people of all ages are collectively

Figure 9.1. Forms of Restorying.

reimagining time, place, identity, perspective, mode, and metanarratives through retold stories (represented in fig. 9.1).

Restorying time and place. One of the most common forms of restorying involves readers changing the location of narratives to alternate times and places. In classrooms, this practice might include shifting canonical works into current settings, like actor, director, and playwright Ricardo Pitts-Wiley did with a group of incarcerated youth in Rhode Island as they restoried *Moby-Dick* for current times, with Ahab as a powerful drug dealer.[35] This act of taking characters and situations to new locations is prevalent in fiction and fanfiction (e.g., *Romeo and Juliet* and *West Side Story*). Similarly, the speculative fiction genre known as alternate history features stories that have an identifiable point of divergence from the history of our present reality, although some alternate histories also feature anachronism, magic, or advanced technology. Similarly, within fan communities, a phenomenon known as alternate universe (AU) fan work—fanart, fanfiction, fan videos, and fan "meta" essays—explores divergences from source texts. For instance, young fanfiction authors imagine the young adult lives of the characters from Harry Potter between the final chapter of *Harry Potter and the Deathly Hallows* and the epilogue, which takes place many years later, moving Rowling's narrative forward in time.[36] Some of this fanfiction imagines the wizarding world in other locations and during other periods of history. This is important work that disrupts predominant metanarratives and epistemologies that lock people into a single story.[37]

Restorying perspective. From *Wide Sargasso Sea* to *Grendel*, and the more recent *The Wind Done Gone*, telling stories from a nonprotagonist's point of view has long been the province of parallel novels and avant-garde Hollywood movies. Playing with perspective has also been a hallmark of storytelling in comics and graphic novels[38] as well as in popular television series like *The Wire* and *Game of Thrones*. But people from nondominant groups—people of color, women, religious and sexual minorities, and the disabled—have always had alternate stories to tell and have used many different means of telling them. As these examples make clear, young people in digital communities who sympathize with unsympathetic characters, like Draco Malfoy in the *Harry Potter* series,[39] or want to know more about characters in the margins, like Rue in *The Hunger Games*,[40] are participating in an age-old tradition of restorying from different points of view. Retelling the same story through a number of different perspectives has the power to build empathy and understanding. For, as postcolonial theorist Shaobo Xie notes, "to speak from an other's thought is to redefine and renarrativize the world."[41]

Restorying across modes. In addition to digital media, whenever young people retell stories through, for instance, hip-hop, the visual arts, dance, or slam poetry, they are engaging in yet another kind of narrative transformation. In 2013, Thomas Philip and Antero Garcia noted that "traditional texts can be transformed by ease of access as well as by their availability through new modalities. Students' experiences outside of the classroom, encapsulated by images, video, sound, notes, and GPS tags, can ever more easily become texts for study. New technologies have also multiplied the prospects for students to create and exchange multimodal texts."[42] While Philip and Garcia rightly note that it is ultimately the job of teachers to facilitate discussions about cultural relevance and power during multimodal lessons in the class-room so that multimodality is connected to academic literacies, we have observed youth and young adults engaged in multimodal restorying in out-of-school spaces as well. While a growing body of literature talks about the potential of out-of-school literacies to inform effective classroom practice, including the work of Ernest Morrell, Valerie Kinloch, and Maisha Winn, some of these spaces include virtual affinity communities online.

Restorying together. Today's teens and young adults are increasingly using new forms of communication to engage in textual and visual production that is collaborative, patched together with pastiche and allusions, and shared in what has been characterized as environments of digital intimacy.[43] Digitally intimate virtual communities have their own ever-evolving rules, norms, and assumptions about meaning-making processes, authorship, and com-posing. As young people participate with one another across these affinity spaces[44] and networked publics,[45] they engage in participatory cultures "in which everyday citizens have an expanded capacity to communicate and circulate their ideas . . . [and] networked communities can shape our col-lective agendas."[46] Some scholars have noted that the digital age is merely facilitating a return to a previous era before the advent of the printing press and the rise of the novel, when stories belonged not to individual authors but to the collective and evolved according to the needs of the times.[47] If, as literacy scholar Peter Smagorinsky observes, the reader's construction of new texts is truly the source of meaning in reading,[48] today's readers are using the tools of social media to collectively make meanings that are not just independent of authorial intent but that can deliberately *contradict* it—in other words, meaning itself is in the process of becoming crowdsourced and jointly imagined. Twitter campaigns such as #WeNeedDiverseBooks offer a compelling example of this restorying work, as people together challenge the predominantly White world of children's and young adult fiction by offering alternate readings of the "normal" families portrayed in most published books for youth. These collective forms of restorying can challenge metanarratives through collective action.

Restorying identity. One of the most compelling forms of reclaiming narrative is restorying identity, as young people change the identities of characters to more accurately reflect the diversity of the world, to play with identities to blur boundaries between traditional categories, or to create characters whose identities more closely mirror their own. In our work together and individually, Amy Stornaiuolo and I have found young readers' restorying of identity to be particularly visible in the fandom practice of bending characters to make them more diverse. In online spaces, racebending occurs when artists, fanfiction writers, video makers, and others create fan works about popular, usually White, characters but change their racial or ethnic makeup. Although there has been some significant backlash to racebending (and analogous forms of bending, such as genderbending and queerbending), it is clear that young people are not only writing themselves into existence[49] but also *reading* themselves into existence within what has been characterized as the "all-White world of children's literature" and youth media.[50] Transmediated racebending of characters from popular children's and young adult stories within fan communities has the potential to be culturally transformative.

Restorying the imagination itself. Today's literary and media landscapes, mediated by digital communication, increasingly require audiences to restory imagination itself. In the past, reading, viewing, and participating required people who were marginalized and minoritized to acquire the dominant reader position—a position that was all too often White, male, able-bodied, cisgender, and middle class or wealthy. In my field of literacy education, we often talk about culturally relevant, culturally responsive, and culturally sustaining pedagogy as a way to bridge these gaps for diverse students, families, and communities.[51] However, teaching *all* people to coexist with contradictions between their lived experiences and the lifeworlds of others while maintaining a core self that one can live with is an even greater challenge. Naïve attempts at resolving dilemmas of race and difference have thus far ended in atrocity, tragedy, and continued inequality. Literature, media, and the popular imagination continue to be weighted with dilemmas of race, ethnicity, and other aspects of identity for which there is little productive discourse. How, then, can readers and audiences of youth literature, media, and culture navigate the multiple worlds that one must exist in during this century?

Beyond restorying the fantastic, when iconography and surrogacy are ineffective in breaking the dark fantastic cycle, one solution seems to be to provide audiences little choice but to accept diversity and racial difference. *Hamilton*, the revolutionary Broadway musical by Lin-Manuel Miranda, is a case in point. In his staged adaptation of Ron Chernow's biography of US founding father Alexander Hamilton, Miranda chose to use nontraditional casting. The only visibly White actor with a speaking role is Jonathan Groff, who plays a comical yet ominous King George III. The rest of the characters, including Alexander Hamilton, Aaron Burr, George Washington, Thomas Jefferson, and the Schuyler sisters, are all magnificently played by actors of color.

When asked about the impact of *Hamilton* on society, Miranda said:

> What I can tell you is that works of art are the only silver bullet we have against racism and sexism and hatred. [Vice President] Joe Biden happened to see *Hamilton* on the same day James Burrows was here. James Burrows directed every episode of *Will & Grace*, and remember when Biden went on *Meet the Press* and essentially said, "Yeah, gay people should get married"? He very openly credited *Will & Grace* with changing the temperature on how we discuss gays and lesbians in this country. It was great to see Jim Burrows and Joe Biden talk about that, and Jim thanked Biden and Biden thanked Jim because that was a piece of art changing the temperature of how we talked about a divisive issue. It sounds silly. It's a sitcom, but that doesn't make it not true. Art engenders empathy in a way that politics doesn't, and in a way that nothing else really does. Art creates change in people's hearts. But it happens slowly.[52]

The reception to *Hamilton*, albeit contested, provides hope that change is coming faster than even Miranda might have imagined. The rising generation is moving toward a kind of collective restorying—what Chinua Achebe once suggested as a "balance of stories"[53]—to begin to address the crisis of infinite storyworlds. In our current landscape of persistent inequality, the efforts of marginalized people to author themselves in order to be heard, seen, and noticed—to assert that their lives matter—contribute to emancipating the imagination. If overcoming these inequities requires that, collectively, we must enter an exciting new Wonderland where we imagine seven impossible things, and words mean what we want them to mean, so be it. Today, when Alexander Hamilton can be portrayed by Puerto Rican actors, and the "smartest witch of her age," Hermione Granger, can be Black, there are infinite narrative possibilities.[54] As Alanna Bennett puts it:

> Hermione will always be an icon, no matter what color her skin. The least we can do is provide her with more room to be that icon. Maybe along the way more people will be able to see themselves reflected back at them.[55]

Notes

1. This chapter was adapted from chapter 6 of my book *The Dark Fantastic: Race and the Imagination from Harry Potter to the Hunger Games*. It is a truncated version of the original.

2. As of January 2022, I was listed on Fanlore.org, the Wiki for fandom history (https://fanlore.org/wiki/Ebony_Elizabeth_Thomas).

3. For more about my fanfiction *Trouble in Paradise* and the 2006 controversy described later in this chapter, refer to its Fanlore page: https://fanlore.org/wiki/Trouble_in_Paradise.

4. #MagicInNorthAmerica was a hashtag protest against J. K. Rowling's erasure of Native American culture, history, and contemporary peoples after the Pottermore feature of the same name was released in the spring of 2016. In her blog *Native Appropriations*, Cherokee scholar Adrienne Keene writes:

The problem . . . is that we as Indigenous peoples are constantly situated as fantasy creatures. Think about *Peter Pan*, where Neverland has mermaids, pirates . . . and Indians. Or on Halloween, children dress up as monsters, zombies, princesses, Disney characters . . . and Indians. Beyond the positioning as "not real," there is also a pervasive and problematic narrative wherein Native peoples are always "mystical" and "magical" and "spiritual"—able to talk to animals, conjure spirits, perform magic, heal with "medicine" and destroy with "curses." Think about Grandmother Willow in *Pocahontas*, or Tonto talking to his bird and horse in *The Long Ranger*, or the wolfpack in *Twilight* . . . or any other number of examples. (Keene, "Magic in North America")

Nambé Pueblo scholar and activist Debbie Reese of the blog *American Indians in Children's Literature* created a useful resource guide to the controversy (Reese, "Native People Respond to Rowling"). In solidarity with Native and Indigenous scholars and activists, I Storified my tweets about the matter: https://storify.com/Ebonyteach/the-trouble-with-magicinnorthamerica.

5. AngieJ, *Trouble in Paradise*, chapter 6; and Hamilton, *The People Could Fly*.

6. Between the publication of *Harry Potter and the Goblet of Fire* in 2000 and *Harry Potter and the Half-Blood Prince* in 2005 (which effectively settled the shipping question), advocates of the Harry and Hermione and Ron and Hermione pairings engaged in extensive textual and semiotic warfare over whose reading of the *Harry Potter* novels was most correct. As an advocate of the Harry and Hermione pairing, I participated with enthusiasm in these debates, controversies, and flame wars, engendering quite a bit of justified animosity.

7. AngieJ, "General Public Statement to the Latter-Day HP Fandom."

8. Sharpe, *In the Wake*.

9. Heavy D & Du Bois, "I think poor non-white people."

10. According to physicist and feminist theorist Karen Barad, "superpositions represent ontologically indeterminate states—states with no determinate fact of the matter concerning the property in question." She goes on to note that "superpositions embody quantum indeterminacy." Barad, *Meeting the Universe Halfway*, 265.

11. Margaret Rouse, a writer and director at WhatIs.com, provides a layperson's definition of the famous physics experiment known as the Schrödinger's cat paradox:

In 1935, Erwin Schrödinger proposed an analogy to show how superposition would operate in the everyday world: the somewhat cruel analogy of Schrödinger's cat. . . . We place a living cat into a steel chamber, along with a device containing a vial of hydrocyanic acid. There is, in the chamber, a very small amount of a radioactive substance. If even a single atom of the substance decays during the test period, a relay mechanism will trip a hammer, which will, in turn, break the vial and kill the cat. The observer cannot know whether or not an atom of the substance has decayed, and consequently, cannot know whether the vial has been broken, the hydrocyanic acid released, and the cat killed. Since we cannot know, the cat is both dead and alive according to quantum law, in a superposition of states. It is only when we break open the box and learn the condition of the cat that the superposition is lost, and the cat becomes one or the other (dead or alive). This situation is sometimes called *quantum indeterminacy* or *the observer's paradox*: the observation or measurement itself affects an outcome, so that the outcome as such does not exist unless the measurement is made. (That is, there is no single outcome unless it is observed.) (Rouse, "Superposition")

12. Jefferson, *Notes on the State of Virginia*.

13. Wanzo, "African American Acafandom and Other Strangers."

14. Carrington, *Speculative Blackness*.

15. AngieJ, *Paradise Lost*, chapter 1.

16. Bennett, "What a 'Racebent' Hermione Granger Really Represents."

17. Breianna Harvey, personal communication, November 12, 2015; originally cited in Thomas and Stornaiuolo, "Restorying the Self."

18. Adichie, "The Danger of a Single Story." The author condemns Adichie's transphobic statements.

19. Thomas and Stornaiuolo, "Restorying the Self."

20. Rowling tweets: "Canon: brown eyes, frizzy hair and very clever. White skin was never specified. Rowling loves black Hermione." Rowling, "Canon: brown eyes."

21. Tosenberger. "Oh My God, the Fanfiction!" Tosenberger quotes from Sara Gwenllian Jones, "The Sex Lives of Cult Television Characters," *Screen* 43, no. 1 (Spring 2002): 79–90.

22. Gonzalez, "J. K. Rowling Says Hermione Should Have Married Harry."

23. Incidentally, Rowling's revelation that she'd chosen the romances that ended her series for personal reasons is something that I'd predicted more than thirteen years earlier in a post on the Harry Potter for Grownups Yahoo! group. See ebonyink@hotmail.com, "Freudian/Lacanian Support for H/H (long)," Harry Potter for Grownups, December 19, 2000, http://groups.yahoo.com/neo/groups/HPforGrownups/conversations/messages/7284.

24. Green, "Books belong to their readers."

25. Smagorinsky, "If Meaning Is Constructed, What Is It Made From?"

26. Kukkonen, "Navigating Infinite Earths," 39–40.

27. Kukkonen, "Navigating Infinite Earths," 40.

28. Kukkonen, "Navigating Infinite Earths," 42.

29. "Superman Image Gallery," SupermanHomepage, last updated November 7, 2021, http://www.supermanhomepage.com/images.php.

30. Kukkonen, "Navigating Infinite Earths," 42.

31. The name of the Doctor's famous spacetime ship is the TARDIS, an acronym for Time and Relative Dimension in Space. For an explanation of what has become known as TARDIS transcendentalism, refer to Andrew Ireland, "This Planet Has Four Walls."

32. Kukkonen, "Navigating Infinite Earths," 43.

33. Thomas and Stornaiuolo, "Restorying the Self."

34. Vasquez, "Critical Ethnography and Pedagogy."

35. Jenkins, Ford, and Green, *Spreadable Media*.

36. Bond and Michelson, "Writing Harry's World."

37. Wright, *Physics of Blackness*.

38. Sousanis, *Unflattening*.

39. Sklar, "Narrative as Experience."

40. Garcia and Haddix, "The Revolution Starts with Rue."

41. Xie, "Rethinking the Identity of Cultural Otherness," 1.

42. Philip and Garcia, "The Importance of Still Teaching the iGeneration."

43. Thompson, "Brave New World of Digital Intimacy."

44. Gee and Hayes, *Language and Learning in the Digital Age*.

45. boyd, "Why Youth (Heart) Social Network Sites."

46. boyd, "Why Youth (Heart) Social Network Sites," 7.

47. Ong, *Orality and Literacy*; Pettit, "Before the Gutenberg Parenthesis"; and Sauerberg, "The Encyclopedia and the Gutenberg Parenthesis."

48. Smagorinsky, "If Meaning Is Constructed, What Is It Made From?"

49. The idea of "reading and/or writing the self into existence" was inspired by Vivian Vasquez's keynote address "Critical Ethnography and Pedagogy." The most popular search pulled up Michael Eric Dyson and Sohail Daulatzai's *Born to Use Mics: Reading Nas's "Illmatic."* However, the first citation of writing the self into existence that I could find was Noliwe Rooks's "Writing Themselves into Existence: The Intersection of History and Literature in Writings on Black Women."

50. Larrick, "The All-White World of Children's Books."

51. Gay, *Culturally Responsive Teaching*; Ladson-Billings and Tate, "Toward a Critical Race Theory of Education"; and Paris, "Culturally Sustaining Pedagogy."

52. Miranda and DiGiacomo, "'Hamilton's' Lin-Manuel Miranda on Finding Originality."

53. Bacon, "An African Voice."

54. Holmes, "Having Hermione Look Like Me Is Amazing."

55. Bennett, "What a 'Racebent' Hermione Granger Really Represents."

Bibliography

Adichie, Chimamanda Ngozi. "The Danger of a Single Story." TED Talks, July 2009. http://www.ted.com/talks/chimamanda_adichie_the_danger_of_a_single_story.

AngieJ. "General Public Statement to the Latter-Day HP Fandom." LiveJournal, August 16, 2006. http://angiej.livejournal.com/2006/08/16/.

AngieJ. *Paradise Lost*. Chapter 1, "The Talented Dr. Granger." http://teland.com/remember/hpebonychap6.html.

AngieJ. *Trouble in Paradise*. Chapter 6, "Curiouser and Curiouser." http://teland.com/remember/hpebonychap6.html.

Bacon, Katie. "An African Voice." *Atlantic*, August 2000. http://www.theatlantic.com/magazine/archive/2000/08/an-african-voice/306020/.

Barad, Karen. *Meeting the Universe Halfway: Quantum Physics and the Entanglement of Matter and Meaning*. Durham, NC: Duke University Press, 2007.

Bennett, Alanna. "What a 'Racebent' Hermione Granger Really Represents." BuzzFeed, February 1, 2015. http://www.buzzfeed.com/alannabennett/what-a-racebent-hermione-granger-really-represen-d2yp#.ltOxWdZmE.

Bond, Ernest L., and Nancy L. Michelson. "Writing Harry's World: Children Co-Authoring Hogwarts." In *Critical Perspectives on Harry Potter*, edited by Elizabeth E. Heilman, 309–27. New York: Routledge, 2009.

boyd, danah. "Why Youth (Heart) Social Network Sites: The Role of Networked Publics in Teenage Social Life." In *Youth, Identity, and Digital Media*, edited by David Buckingham, 119–42. Cambridge, MA: MIT Press, 2007.

Carrington, André M. *Speculative Blackness: The Future of Race in Science Fiction.* Minneapolis: University of Minnesota Press, 2016.

Dyson, Michael Eric, and Sohail Daulatzai. *Born to Use Mics: Reading Nas's "Illmatic."* New York: Basic Civitas Books, 2009.

Garcia, Antero, and Marcelle Haddix. "The Revolution Starts with Rue: Online Fandom and the Racial Politics of *The Hunger Games*." In *The Politics of Panem: Challenging Genres*, edited by Sean P. Connors, 203–17. Rotterdam: Sense Publishers, 2014.

Gay, Geneva. *Culturally Responsive Teaching: Theory, Research, and Practice.* New York: Teachers College Press, 2010.

Gee, James Paul, and Elisabeth R. Hayes. *Language and Learning in the Digital Age.* Abingdon, Oxon., England: Routledge, 2011.

Gonzalez, Robbie. "J. K. Rowling Says Hermione Should Have Married Harry, not Ron." Gizmodo, February 2, 2014. https://io9.gizmodo.com/j-k-rowling-says-hermione-should -have-married-harry-n-1514204695.

Green, John (@realjohngreen). "Books belong to their readers." Twitter, February 1, 2014. https://twitter.com/realjohngreen/status/429797089569439744.

Hamilton, Virginia. *The People Could Fly: American Black Folktales.* New York: Alfred A. Knopf, 1985.

Heavy D & Du Bois (@RelicUA). "I think poor non-white people." Twitter, December 6, 2016. https://twitter.com/relicUA/status/806323165798469633.

Holmes, Sarah. "Having Hermione Look Like Me Is Amazing." BBC News, December 23, 2015. http://www.bbc.com/news/world-us-canada-35156893.

Ireland, Andrew. "This Planet Has Four Walls: How Early *Doctor Who* Narrative Was Influenced by Techniques and Technology to Overcome the Confines of Studio Recording." Bournemouth University, Media School, 2008. http://eprints.bournemouth .ac.uk/12973/1/fourwalls5.pdf.

Jefferson, Thomas. *Notes on the State of Virginia.* PBS, n.d. https://www.pbs.org/wgbh/aia /part3/3h490t.html.

Jenkins, Henry, Sam Ford, and Joshua Green. *Spreadable Media: Creating Value and Meaning in a Networked Culture.* New York: New York University Press, 2013.

Keene, Adrienne. "'Magic in North America': The Harry Potter Franchise Veers Too Close to Home." *Native Appropriations* (blog), March 7, 2016. http://nativeappropriations.com /2016/03/magic-in-north-america-the-harry-potter-franchise-veers-too-close-to-home .html.

Kukkonen, Karin. "Navigating Infinite Earths: Readers, Mental Models, and the Multiverse of Superhero Comics." *Storyworlds* 2, no. 1 (2010): 39–58. doi:10.1353/stw.0.0009.

Ladson-Billings, Gloria, and William F. Tate IV. "Toward a Critical Race Theory of Education." *Teachers College Record* 97, no. 1 (Fall 1995): 47–68.

Larrick, Nancy. "The All-White World of Children's Books." *Saturday Review*, September 11, 1965, 63–65, 84–85.

Miranda, Lin-Manuel, and Frank DiGiacomo. "'Hamilton's' Lin-Manuel Miranda on Finding Originality, Racial Politics (and Why Trump Should See His Show)." *Hollywood Reporter*, August 12, 2015. http://www.hollywoodreporter.com/features/hamiltons -lin-manuel-miranda-finding-814657.

Ong, Walter J. *Orality and Literacy.* Abingdon, Oxon., England: Routledge, 2013.

Paris, Django. "Culturally Sustaining Pedagogy: A Needed Change in Stance, Terminology, and Practice." *Educational Researcher* 41, no. 3 (April 2012): 93–97.

Patterson, Orlando. *Slavery and Social Death*. Cambridge: MA, Harvard University Press, 1982.

Pettit, Tom. "Before the Gutenberg Parenthesis: Elizabethan-American Compatibilities." Paper presented at the Fifth Media in Transition conference, Cambridge, Massachusetts, April 27, 2007.

Philip, Thomas, and Antero Garcia. "The Importance of Still Teaching the iGeneration: New Technologies and the Centrality of Pedagogy." *Harvard Educational Review* 83, no. 2 (Summer 2013): 300–319.

Reese, Debbie. "Native People Respond to Rowling." *American Indians in Children's Literature* (blog), March 10, 2016. https://americanindiansinchildrensliterature.blogspot.com/2016/03/native-people-respond-to-rowling.html.

Rooks, Noliwe M. "Writing Themselves into Existence: The Intersection of History and Literature in Writings on Black Women." *Iowa Journal of Literary Studies* 10, no. 1 (Spring 1989): 51–63.

Rouse, Margaret. "Superposition." Tech Target, last updated October 2021. https://whatis.techtarget.com/definition/superposition.

Rowling, J. K. (@jk_rowling). "Canon: brown eyes, frizzy hair and very clever." Twitter, December 21, 2015. https://twitter.com/jk_rowling/status/678888094339366914?lang=en.

Sauerberg, Lars Ole. "The Encyclopedia and the Gutenberg Parenthesis." Paper presented at the Sixth Media in Transition conference, Cambridge, Massachusetts, April 24–26, 2009.

Sharpe, Christina. *In the Wake: On Blackness and Being*. Durham, NC: Duke University Press, 2016.

Sklar, Howard. "Narrative as Experience: The Pedagogical Implications of Sympathizing with Fictional Characters." *Partial Answers: Journal of Literature and the History of Ideas* 6, no. 2 (June 2008): 481–501.

Smagorinsky, Peter. "If Meaning Is Constructed, What Is It Made From? Toward a Cultural Theory of Reading." *Review of Educational Research* 71, no. 1 (2001): 133–69.

Sousanis, Nick. *Unflattening*. Cambridge, MA: Harvard University Press, 2015.

Thomas, Ebony Elizabeth. *The Dark Fantastic: Race and the Imagination from Harry Potter to the Hunger Games*. New York: New York University Press, 2019.

Thomas, Ebony Elizabeth, and Amy Stornaiuolo. "Restorying the Self: Bending toward Textual Justice." *Harvard Educational Review* 86, no. 3 (Fall 2016): 313–38.

Thompson, Clive. "Brave New World of Digital Intimacy." *New York Times*, September 7, 2008. http://individual.utoronto.ca/kreemy/proposal/07.pdf.

Tosenberger, Catherine. "'Oh My God, the Fanfiction!' Dumbledore's Outing and the Online Harry Potter Fandom." *Children's Literature Association Quarterly* 33, no. 2 (Summer 2008): 200–206.

Vasquez, Vivian. "Critical Ethnography and Pedagogy: Bridging the Audit Trail with Technology." Keynote address, presented at the Thirty-Fifth Annual Ethnography in Education Forum, University of Pennsylvania, March 2014.

Wanzo, Rebecca. "African American Acafandom and Other Strangers: New Genealogies of Fan Studies." *Transformative Works and Cultures* 20, no. 1 (2015). doi:10.3983/twc.2015.0699.

Wright, Michelle M. *Physics of Blackness: Beyond the Middle Passage Epistemology*. Minneapolis: University of Minneapolis Press, 2015.

Xie, Shaobo. "Rethinking the Identity of Cultural Otherness: The Discourse of Difference as Unfinished Project." In *Voices of the Other: Children's Literature and the Postcolonial Context*, edited by Roderick McGillis, 1–16. New York: Routledge, 1999.

#NotMyHermione

Authorship and Ownership in the *Harry Potter* and the *Cursed Child* Casting Controversy

Peter C. Kunze

On December 21, 2015, London's Palace Theatre announced the casting of *Harry Potter and the Cursed Child*, a new play by Jack Thorne based on a story by Thorne, John Tiffany, and Potter creator J. K. Rowling. Set nineteen years after *Deathly Hallows*, the play introduces the commercial theater into the Wizarding World franchise,[1] although the Wizarding World of Harry Potter–themed areas of Universal Parks and Resorts feature live performances. While news from the West End, London's theater district, rarely instigates an international cause célèbre, this announcement delighted and surprised many fans of Harry Potter in the casting of Noma Dumezweni as the headstrong female lead, Hermione Granger. An accomplished British actress born in Swaziland to South African parents, Dumezweni would become the second professional actress to portray Hermione following Emma Watson's star-making turn in the eight Harry Potter films produced by Warner Bros. between 2001 and 2011. Unlike Watson, however, Dumezweni is Black.

The ensuing controversy provides a productive inroad into examining race in the world of Harry Potter, not only for the questions it raises about the authorship and ownership of popular texts but also for the specific constraints and attendant cultures that come with media franchises. Adapting a media franchise for the stage means entering a new medium and, in the process, a new culture of common practices and expectations, both of artists and of audiences. This chapter explores these nuances not only to complicate our understanding of the decision to cast Dumezweni but also to further understand how race operates across the Harry Potter universe and youth media culture more broadly. Although I am a White critic, I ground my discussion of this controversy in the commentaries, critiques, and theories developed by scholars of color so that I might challenge received accounts of this illustrative moment in Harry Potter fandom while amplifying that important scholarly work. In so doing, I argue that a study of colorblind casting (hereafter, nontraditional casting) as an industrial practice lays bare racist and postracial logics at work within franchise storytelling and its fandoms through a focus on the Wizarding World.[2] Whereas Florence Maätita and Marcia Hernandez offer a rich analysis of the discourse around #BlackHermione on social media in the next chapter, I examine Dumezweni's casting via media industry studies, theater and performance studies, and critical race studies to contextualize and understand nontraditional casting as a tactic for social justice and cultural reform.

I will examine this case study through three different lenses: the cultural differences between film and theater as media and as entertainment industries; the enduring debate over nontraditional casting in the theater, in particular, but more recently across media culture; and the increasingly visible tension between authorship and ownership of popular texts that takes place online in what Henry Jenkins notably has called "convergence culture"—that is, to borrow from the subtitle of his influential book, "where old and new media collide."[3] Through a close analysis of nontraditional casting, I hope to further the critical examination of racial politics in the Harry Potter universe, in the entertainment industries, and in convergence culture.

The Casting Controversy

Casting Noma Dumezweni may have inspired little surprise among avid theatergoers in London. She earned an Olivier Award (the British equivalent of the Tony) for her portrayal of Ruth in a 2005 production of Lorraine Hansberry's *A Raisin in the Sun*, and her replacement of Kim Cattrall in Penelope Skinner's 2015 play *Linda* garnered rave reviews not only for her performance but for her professionalism in assuming the role at the last minute. Yet Dumezweni's impeccable credentials mattered little to a small contingent of fans who saw her casting in the role of Hermione Granger as an assault on a character whom they felt protective over, underscored by Harry Potter's status as a work of children's literature and therefore (presumably) a fundamental part of these fans' childhoods. In the previous chapter in this volume, Ebony Elizabeth Thomas asserts: "Changes like these ask audience participants to reimagine the narrative. But some changes are more acceptable than others." The comments online—many of them excited and supportive, while others were nasty and hateful—reveal the ownership fans often assume over popular culture as well as the complex network of stakeholders in these cultural products, including creators, corporations, producers, actors, and fans (both diehard and casual, open-minded and racist).

When discussing the professional practice of casting, one must acknowledge the essential differences between theater and film as production cultures. Both industries have long histories of structural racism, and the commercial logics that justify hiring the most well-known, the best-looking, and typically the White actor have been shamelessly espoused by theater and film producers as well as casting directors who maintain what George Lipsitz has called the "possessive investment in whiteness."[4] Broadway and the West End obviously remain geographically bound to New York City and London, respectively, and on any given day only a select number of people can see a stage show, whereas a film can hypothetically be played anytime and anywhere someone has a copy. (Touring productions somewhat complicate this fact, but the restricted access holds up, and there appears to be a somewhat lingering bias toward the original production over ancillary tours.) Intimacy, immediacy, spontaneity, and even ephemerality have long been selling points of the theater, especially as the threat of movies has siphoned off audiences, especially the working class and those attendees outside the metropolitan area.[5] In 2016, the Broadway League reported that 40.8 percent of the Broadway audience came from households whose income exceeds $150,000, although the same demographic makes up only 11.3 percent of the total US population.[6] While attending live theater in the West End is generally less expensive than on Broadway,[7] ticket prices for such shows remain cost prohibitive for many, leading to sporadic attendance rather than the more loyal patronage given to movies. Theater often prides itself on being more artistically daring and politically progressive than cinema; therefore, commercial theater producers may embrace nontraditional casting more often than their counterparts in the film industry.[8] Theater producers certainly have a good deal of money to lose in a failed production, but they serve a different audience and usually have much lower financial expectations than film producers. In the case of *Harry Potter and the Cursed Child*, first in the West End and later on Broadway and in Melbourne, San Francisco, Hamburg, and Toronto, the show's official affiliation with the Harry Potter universe and sizable presold audience offered a commercial potential that presumably helped to mitigate against any perceived financial risk in casting Hermione nontraditionally.

Nevertheless, a small but noticeable cohort voiced strong opposition to the casting, with responses ranging from skepticism and confusion to outright indignation. Two days after the announcement, one Twitter user exclaimed, "Hermione is not a [racial epithet]. She is a strong WHITE girl."[9] Another user, whose identity was concealed by an avatar, contended that Hermione could not be Black because she was "smart," "loyal," "has parents," and was "played by Emma Watson."[10] The line between wrath and insincere trolling remains unclear, though this ambiguity hardly excuses the undeniable racism of many of these comments. Some responses conceal liberal racism with sincerity and postracial logic: "I have nothing against Noma Dumezweni, it's not about her race, fans will get pissed too if a longtime black character was switched to white."[11] While we should not dismiss these tweets as innocent or exceptional, one might take comfort in their relative dearth when compared to tweets that applaud and celebrate this decision.

The casting controversy ably demonstrates how race and racism play out in and across fandoms of the Harry Potter universe. While the hateful backlash clearly represents a socially unacceptable reaction, it illuminates the complexity of fan experiences and responses, especially as they play out in spaces where anonymity is allowed and antagonism, even bullying, may be lauded. Yet we also should be wary of uncritical celebrations of nontraditional casting as well, for they conceal the ways in which liberal racism can simultaneously and unknowingly coexist alongside the more obvious racist vitriol. Close attention to the history and discourses around nontraditional casting in the theater help to contextualize the casting controversy while furthering the critical study of transmedia storytelling, its practices, and its fandoms.

Nontraditional Casting in the Theater

The issue of race and ethnicity in the US theater industry has a long tradition that continues to be relevant and complicated, including the enduring legacy of blackface minstrelsy in performance culture and in US popular culture more broadly. For the purposes of my discussion here, I am primarily focusing on theater in New York and London, although these conversations remain important across the performing arts, regional and local, commercial and nonprofit, professional and amateur. Three significant events continue to resonate in contemporary debates over casting practices: Joseph Papp's backing of nontraditional casting for the New York Shakespeare Festival (later Shakespeare in the Park);[12] the casting of White Welsh actor Jonathan Pryce as the Engineer, a character of Asian and European ancestry, in the West End and Broadway productions of *Miss Saigon*; and August Wilson's highly influential speech "The Ground on Which I Stand" at the 1996 Theatre Communications Group conference and the ensuing debate with critic Robert Brustein. Taken together, these events provide a cursory introduction to the rich discourse about race, ethnicity, and casting in US theater.

Joseph Papp was a highly influential theater director and producer who founded the nonprofit Public Theater in New York City. This theater has become a fixture of Off-Broadway—that is, theaters with 100 to 499 seats, often outside of the commercial theater district in midtown Manhattan— where it premiered some of the landmark musicals of past fifty years, including *Hair*; *A Chorus Line*; *Bring in 'da Noise, Bring in 'da Funk*; and *Hamilton*. Perhaps Papp's most enduring legacy remains the New York Shakespeare Festival, which produces free, open-air performances of plays (mostly Shakespeare, of course) and musicals in the Delacorte Theater in Central Park every summer. It was through these productions that Papp prominently advocated nontraditional casting, and the Public Theater staged and continues to produce plays that often star prominent actors of color in White and race-unspecified roles,[13] including James Earl Jones in *The Merchant of Venice* (1962), Raúl Juliá in *Two Gentlemen of Verona* (1971), Randall Duk Kim in *Pericles, Prince of Tyre* (1974), and Gloria Foster and Morgan Freeman in *Coriolanus* (1979). As Papp noted, "I always cast my plays with the best talent, but at the same time I'm aware that we live in a multi-cultural city. The performers on stage should mirror that fact."[14] Papp's comment reflects two ongoing concerns in the casting debate: the artistic, even commercial, need to award the role to the best actor and the aesthetic belief that art must reflect life as it is. These concerns have been wielded by champions and detractors of nontraditional casting, and they surface in the social media responses to the Dumezweni controversy as well. How quickly advocates deploy them reveals either the hegemonic or progressive intentions behind their respective arguments.

In 1990, the question of nontraditional casting caused major controversy when the producers of *Miss Saigon* cast Jonathan Pryce, a White British actor, to play the Engineer during the show's upcoming run on Broadway. (Pryce originated the role in the West End, where the actors' union had contested neither his casting nor the use of makeup and prosthetics to make White actors appear Asian.[15]) The musical, a lavish love story between a White American GI and a young Vietnamese entertainer set against the fall of Saigon, had proven a blockbuster success in London and was coming to Broadway with the largest ticket presale to date.[16] The Engineer is both White and Asian, and the makeup team modified Pryce's skin tone and eye shape to signify the character's Asian heritage by invoking corrosive stereotypes. Asian American theater professionals, led by David Henry Hwang and B. D. Wong, protested Pryce's casting, and Actors' Equity denied Pryce a visa. Helen Zia notes that the Equity leadership feared that their decision would not hold up in arbitration, but they took the stand on moral grounds.[17] Producer Cameron Mackintosh countered a perceived assault on his artistic freedom by staging a bold publicity stunt: he cancelled the US debut. As he later explained: "[I]f the show isn't going to come here with the performances that made it so fantastic in London, I'd rather it didn't move at all."[18] Here, Mackintosh states that only Pryce can do the character justice, and therefore his own artistic integrity will not allow him to bring an inferior production to Broadway since his detractors have "served only to create a poisonous atmosphere in which creativity and artistic freedom cannot function or survive."[19]

But Tisa Chang of the Pan Asian Repertory Theatre argues that this rhetoric distracted from the real issue behind Asian American actors' opposition: the perception that their talent was fundamentally inferior to that of their White counterparts.[20] The potential loss of a production—and therefore many jobs on stage and behind the scenes—led to a backlash from many Equity members, who put pressure on the leadership to reverse its decision. Ultimately it did, and *Miss Saigon* came to Broadway, though Pryce's prosthetics did not; actors who have played the Engineer on Broadway after

Pryce's tenure have been almost exclusively of Asian descent. The controversy over *Miss Saigon* inverts nontraditional casting, as a White actor portrays a mixed-race role, but it also reveals how the meritocracy argument can be exercised to exclude actors of color from mainstream productions on Broadway. Despite the disappointing conclusion, casting director Tara Rubin contends that the debacle "was the beginning of a huge shift in the way we think about casting."[21] Greater efforts are now made to cast actors of color in roles written for such actors in the theater, to forestall public criticism, while roles written for White actors are rarely, but occasionally, played by actors of color.[22] "Out of the turmoil that began as a protest over one role in a single play," Zia observes, "Asian Americans brought into the open the pernicious impact that deeply imbedded stereotypes have on all aspects of Asian American life."[23] The issue remains a central concern for Asian American arts and media activism, and scholars have drawn attention to the ongoing presence of yellowface performance in contemporary theater.[24]

Equally important to the debate over nontraditional casting was August Wilson's fiery speech before the Theatre Communications Group conference in June 1996. Wilson's speech decried the underfunding of Black theater in the United States in comparison to the majority of not-for-profit professional theaters: "If you do not know, I will tell you that black theatre in America is alive . . . it is vibrant . . . it is vital . . . it just isn't funded."[25] By Wilson's account, the League of Resident Theatres had sixty-six members—only one of which was a Black theater.[26] His critique of the practice of nontraditional casting remains paramount to his defense of the Black theater. In promoting the casting of Black actors in roles not written for Black actors, funders and administrators "have signaled not only their unwillingness to support black theatre but their willingness to fund dangerous and divisive assaults against it."[27] Wilson contends that nontraditional casting is a detrimental practice in which the White gatekeepers support Black art on their own terms—that is, by fitting it into White culture as convenience allows rather than actively supporting a distinctly Black theater:

> To mount an all-black production of [. . .] *Death of a Salesman* or any other
> play conceived for white actors as an investigation of the human condition
> through the specifics of white culture is to deny us our humanity, our own
> history, and the need to make our own investigations from the cultural ground
> on which we stand as black Americans. It is an assault on our presence, and

our difficult but honorable history in America; and it is an insult to our intelligence, our playwrights, and our many and varied contributions to society and the world at large. [. . .] We do not need colorblind casting; we need theatres. We need theatres to develop our playwrights.[28]

For Wilson, a Black actor cast as a White character renders the actor's race irrelevant. While Papp may argue that the actor's talent supersedes their physical embodiment, Wilson would contend such a casting dangerously decontextualizes the history of Black bodies while stifling the development of a Black theater that chronicles and celebrates the Black experience.

In his powerful assessment of contemporary US theater, Wilson also lambasted critic Robert Brustein, who had lamented in a 1993 *New Republic* article that sociological factors had trumped aesthetic concerns in arts funding.[29] Unsurprisingly, Brustein became Wilson's fiercest interlocutor in the debate that ensued, arguing in his article "Subsidized Separatism" that Wilson's "speech is melancholy testimony to the rabid identity politics and poisonous racial consciousness that have been infecting our country in recent years. Although Wilson would deny it, such sentiments represent a reverse form of the old politics of division, an appeal for socially approved and foundation-funded separatism."[30] One finds in their heated exchange a return of the ongoing debate among Black intellectuals, dating back to at least Booker T. Washington and W. E. B. Du Bois, over the appropriate political and economic strategies for Black liberation and self-actualization. Brustein himself saw the disagreement with Wilson as "a crucible for clarifying the conflict between the old methods of integration—Martin Luther King's position—and the separatism that's associated with black power."[31] Eventually, Wilson and Brustein met for a highly publicized debate in New York City, moderated by Anna Deavere Smith. Wilson openly acknowledged his political indebtedness to the Black Power movement, but he strongly opposed Brustein's reductive assessment of his argument as separatist: "If we choose not to assimilate, this does not mean we oppose the values of the dominant culture, but rather we wish to champion our own causes, our own celebrations, our own values."[32] Wilson's hardline approach on nontraditional casting reveals how a supposedly enlightened tactic actually may hinder true artistic progress—a silencing mechanism insidiously hidden behind the label of racial progress. And yet many Black theater artists did not find themselves aligned with Brustein's or Wilson's points of view, especially those producing commercial Black theater.[33]

Although Brustein supposedly champions "integration" against "separatism," in retrospect, his argument demands equality on the terms of the allegedly benevolent oppressor. Brandi Wilkins Catanese observes that "color blindness, through its efforts to dematerialize racial difference, offers itself as the structural vehicle through which racialized differences and discrimination will be overcome."[34] In so doing, it provides an alternative to multiculturalism that stages the tension between operative modes for dismantling structural racism. Similarly, Kristen J. Warner has argued that nontraditional casting on television "maintain[s] an idealistic but myopic view of the world based on normative (white) assumptions";[35] in so doing, it becomes a means of maintaining racial inequality. Nontraditional casting may seem like a means to productively reinvent the theater and the entertainment industries in general, but, at best, it is but one tactic en route to a truly radical revision. (In fact, it hinders such necessary reinvention.) As generative solutions, Wilson advocates funding and supporting Black artists and theaters, while in her discussion of television production practices, Warner argues that the casting of actors of color for roles where race is unspecified should lead to revisions that acknowledge the fundamental difference in lived experiences.[36] Not only do these efforts work to reject the centering of Whiteness, but they also pay dutiful respect to the distinctive histories and subjectivities of said races compared to their White counterparts.

Who Owns Harry?

Any casting decision for a narrative extension to a media franchise potentially raises concerns over who the character(s) "belong" to: the creator, the owner, or the fans. Unsurprisingly, many creators (or their estates) police their intellectual property to protect it not only from piracy and copyright infringement but also from interpretations that they may deem to be wrong, unflattering, or inflammatory. Ray Bradbury insisted that *Fahrenheit 451* was about the deleterious effect of television, not censorship, while S. E. Hinton has notoriously rejected queer readings of her novel *The Outsiders*. Lin-Manuel Miranda has capitalized on his fans' enthusiasm by expressing seemingly unending gratitude on social media, although *Hamilton*'s legal team quickly moved to shut down Canadian students' staging of three musical numbers from the show that they had posted to YouTube in an effort to obtain stage rights for a high school production. This is not to say authors do not have a right to engage with their fans or to protect their intellectual property; rather, social media platforms and fan sites reveal the long-standing tensions between creators and audiences over ownership of characters, plot lines, and narrative universes.

As the creator and custodian of the Wizarding World franchise, Rowling moved quickly to squash the casting controversy. In response to a fan's tweet inquiring how the author felt about the decision, Rowling tweeted the following on December 21, 2015: "Canon: brown eyes, frizzy hair and very clever. White skin was never specified. Rowling loves black Hermione [kiss emoji]." While Rowling's statement of support via Twitter is a worthy symbolic gesture, it is ultimately one that is somewhat disingenuous. In fact, Rowling's choice to address the fracas in this manner perpetuates what Jackie C. Horne identifies as the author's "decision [in the novels] to privilege a multicultural antiracism pedagogy over a social justice approach."[37] Consequently, Rowling presents racism as an isolated, rather than structural, phenomenon. While the print text of the novels mention Hermione's race only once,[38] her Whiteness clearly has been affirmed through paratextual elements and film adaptations, including book covers, illustrations, and, most obviously, Emma Watson's portrayal of Hermione in eight films. To suggest that Hermione could be non-White in a world where her race largely goes unacknowledged and poses no effect on her daily life is insensitive and inauthentic. Adaptations, by their very nature, can underscore certain readings, allow some variations, and shut down those readings that may be detrimental or simply erroneous. Rowling can claim final say over whose reading is correct (and she has), but whether readers agree and abide is another matter.

Well-intentioned liberal celebrations of nontraditional casting rarely acknowledge how such casting opens a text up to new meanings. For example, as Norm Lewis noted, when a Black actor portraying the Phantom of the Opera (as he has) romantically pursues a White actress playing Christine Daaé, his presence adds another layer of meaning, evoking the history of White anxieties over Black sexuality.[39] What does it mean for Hermione to not only be played by a skilled actor, but a skilled actor who is Black? How does the image of a Black-cast Hermione open up the play, even the entire franchise, to new, complex, and innovative readings? How do Black bodies demand a different kind of attention? As actress Lisa Gay Hamilton has observed, "To say to me you don't see color when I audition is bullshit. Of course you do. But the question is: What do you do with it? Do you make it an

asset or do you abuse it?"⁴⁰ Drama critics commenting on Dumezweni's performance rarely addressed her racial identity or the social media controversy
surrounding her casting. David Rooney, one of the few critics to mention the
uproar in his review, notes that "only the most bigoted idiot could find fault
with the brilliant Dumezweni's performance, her haughtiness, quicksilver
intellect and underlying warmth tracing a line way back to the precociously
clever girl Harry first met on the train all those years ago."⁴¹ What must be
underscored is that nontraditional casting may be well-intentioned gesture,
but it cannot be a solution in itself. Speaking of the film industry, Nancy
Wang Yuen has argued that such postracial logic "allows white decision makers and creative personnel to divest themselves of any social or moral responsibility while maintaining hegemonic control of the industry."⁴² In an age of
increasing conglomeration, in which theatrical divisions have become cogs
in a larger multinational corporate machine, the same rationales transcend
the film industry and resonate across the entertainment industries.

Furthermore, debates over race and Harry Potter are complicated by the
novel's genre status as a work of fantasy fiction. To what extent can—and
should—critics apply ideological and sociological realities onto an admittedly
imaginary context? While the text may never state Hermione's race, one could
argue that neglecting this fact renders race a nonfactor in her life, a privilege
almost exclusively afforded to Whites. Other fans have read her "Mudblood"
status to be reflective of a racial intolerance at Hogwarts and therefore a
metaphor for such injustice in the real world. Of course, the racial oversight
(intentional or otherwise) on Rowling's part allows readers to fill in the details,
thereby coauthoring the text with the author through the process of reading.⁴³
In a popular BuzzFeed article, Alanna Bennett, who describes herself as "a
biracial girl growing up in a very white city," discusses identifying with Hermione's struggle over her lineage, although Bennett says that she "related to her
deeply, but like with so much of what I watched and read, I couldn't *see* myself
in Hermione."⁴⁴ Later, while visiting fan sites, Bennett found that fans had
depicted Hermione as a person of color: "I was seeing parts of myself actually
spelled out in this character I'd always related to. [. . .] Hermione's story was
always one involving a young girl living in a world aggressive towards her for
her very existence."⁴⁵ Bennett's article draws attention to the "canon"—that
is, what the text says and the ways the text is used, revised, even abused by
readers. In what goes unsaid, women of color, and eventually Bennett herself,
can create a place for themselves within a franchise that has not. On Twitter,

Rowling sanctions this practice, but in many ways, previous renderings of Hermione that were not produced yet were presumably approved by Rowling shut down this reading as a preferred reading.

To be clear, I am not saying that Hermione must be portrayed as White. Rather, I am asserting that Rowling has long capitalized on representation of Hermione as White, so for her to dismiss the outcry against Dumezweni's casting as "idiotic" and "racist" is, ironically, both an accurate assessment of these critiques and a hypocritical posture from someone who has fostered and benefited from this indeterminacy. For example, on the British cover by Thomas Taylor for Bloomsbury and the American cover by Mary GrandPré for Scholastic of the first edition of *Harry Potter and the Prisoner of Azkaban*, Hermione is rendered White. Illustrations are textbook examples of what Gérard Genette calls "paratexts," accompanying material, apparatus, and adornments that help "to *make present*, to ensure the text's presence in the world, its 'reception' and consumption in the form (nowadays, at least) of a book."[46] While some may hastily dismiss illustrations as mere decorations, they actually help to shape readers' perceptions of the characters and, by extension, the text, making illustrators important collaborators. The first vision of Harry Potter, his classmates, and his instructors that readers encounter are the illustrations both on the book covers and in the books themselves, arguably before they even read the text's descriptions. Illustrations are interpretations, too, but they also model how readers should imagine the characters, especially if the illustrations are approved by the author.

Similarly, the casting of Emma Watson for the film series further reinforces the representation of Hermione as a White character. While Rowling neither illustrated her books nor cast the movies, she has undoubtedly advised Bloomsbury, Scholastic, and Warner Bros. and agreed to these elements, which have had a profound impact on the transmedia universe and the reading, viewing, and interpretation of it. One might argue that casting a Black actress as Hermione against previous representations of Hermione as White creates a more inclusive Potter universe, but this perspective is somewhat dissatisfying. To follow August Wilson's logic, to describe the casting of Dumezweni as progressive is misleading because the play has not been written with the experiences of a Black woman in mind. Here we face the tension between the unique experience of an individual and the historical and experiential injustice faced by Black bodies in particular. While Hermione's Muggle-born heritage may service the casting of an actress who is Black, the play ultimately avoids any attempt to engage or acknowledge the attendant nuances of Black subjectivity. Although *Harry Potter and the Cursed Child* is a British production, the critiques lodged by Wilson are not unique to the American context and can be applied to a study of artists and culture across the Black diaspora.

I agree with Florence Maätita and Marcia Hernandez's claim that casting Noma Dumezweni as Hermione is a necessary step toward dismantling racism and the racial contract.[47] The impact of the casting for communities of color, not to mention Black girls who saw Dumezweni's powerful performance, will be inestimable. But I worry that this single (yet important) decision's effect on improving systemic racism within the theater industry, popular culture, and society more broadly remains limited. For instance, how many other major Broadway and West End stage productions have followed this example? Rather than lauding the casting of Dumezweni as a progressive move by the theater industry, we might better serve the theater, the entertainment industries, and our society by considering how we can go further, sooner. This is not to say that Dumezweni should not have been cast—far from it. Instead, we must resist settling for such self-congratulatory gestures from content creators and entertainment conglomerates, who are capable of so much more, especially when they are so clearly commercializing provocation. Admittedly, in an age of spectacle-laden megamusicals and what Terry Teachout has called "commodity musicals" based on Hollywood movies, the cost of staging West End and Broadway shows has risen considerably, and with it, the price of tickets.[48] Yet shows such as *Rent, In the Heights, The Color Purple, Motown: The Musical,* and *Ain't Too Proud* have ably shown that the commercial theater can tell stories about people of color with diverse casts without sacrificing profit-earning potential. This reality, in turn, counters the insidious prejudice among creative talent and investors that casting actors of color undermines the possibility for financial success.[49] *Hamilton,* of course, has been one of Broadway's greatest critical and commercial successes ever, but its much-lauded embrace of hip-hop music and nontraditional casting has not protected it from necessary critiques about its exclusion of African American and Native American voices who also played an integral role in these historical events.[50] Until we demand that cowardly creators and conglomerates foster entertainment industries that are not only diverse but inclusive behind the scenes, on the stage, and in front of the camera, we will remain complicit in a mainstream culture that perpetuates White supremacy and the ongoing marginalization of people of color.

Notes

The author would like to thank Paul Ardoin and the editors for reading drafts of this chapter as well as the assistance of Aubrey Plourde and Leah Phillips on the research.

1. I use "Wizarding World franchise" to encompass the world of Harry Potter, which includes the seven books but also the subsequent books, films, online materials in Pottermore, theme park attractions, and other extensions that further develop the world in the spirit of transmedia storytelling, all under the supervision of J. K. Rowling.

2. Although the term "colorblind casting" is often used across the culture industries to discuss the practice of casting White roles or roles where race is not specified with actors of color, I will use "nontraditional casting" because not only does it encompass casting practices beyond questions of race, but it conscientiously avoids the casual ableism of the term. I will use the term hereafter only when quoting others.

3. Jenkins, *Convergence Culture.*

4. See Lipsitz, *The Possessive Investment in Whiteness.* For more on racial bias in casting, see Catanese, *The Problem of the Color[blind]*; and Yuen, *Reel Inequality.*

5. McLaughlin, *Broadway and Hollywood,* 97–98.

6. Broadway League, *The Demographics of the Broadway Audience,* 27.

7. Shapiro, "Why Are Theater Tickets Cheaper on the West End?"

8. For example, James Earl Jones has portrayed several roles on Broadway in recent years that have traditionally been cast as White: President Art Hockstader in Gore Vidal's *The Best Man* and Martin Vanderhof in Moss Hart and George S. Kaufman's *You Can't Take It with You.* Note that these shows were not Black-cast productions; instead, Jones's race was treated as negligible.

9. Kobold, "Hermione is not a [racial epithet]."

10. Rei AX2017, "Smart. Loyal."

11. Shang, "I have nothing against Noma Dumezweni."

12. Another important advocate was Rosetta LeNoire, who started the AMAS Repertory Theatre Company to stage productions with multiethnic casts. Actors' Equity has honored her important work with an award recognizing individuals and theaters who champion diverse casting.

13. I use the term "race-unspecified roles" apprehensively. My point here, as I hope will become clear, is that roles that do not specify race, especially those written by White playwrights and screenwriters, are often perceived as White, since race is treated as negligible in the descriptions.

14. Quoted in Horwitz, "Is Affirmative Action Coming to Broadway?," 25.

15. Lee, *A History of Asian American Theatre,* 177.

16. Sternfeld, *The Megamusical,* 296.

17. Zia, *Asian American Dreams,* 124.

18. Quoted in Paulson, "The Battle of *Miss Saigon.*"

19. Quoted in Horwitz, "Is Affirmative Action Coming to Broadway?," 25.

20. Horwitz, "Ever Since *Saigon,*" 19.

21. Quoted in Paulson, "The Battle of *Miss Saigon.*"

22. There are numerous exceptions to this practice, especially when estates become involved. For example, in 2017, the Edward Albee estate blocked a director from casting a Black actor as Nick in *Who's Afraid of Virginia Woolf?* Controversy ensued, and the estate

specified that while they do allow Black actors to play George and Martha or all-Black productions, casting a Black actor as Nick alone would introduce a subtext that Albee did not include in the original. Again, we see here how casting can inspire tensions over ownership between varying interests, in this case playwrights and directors. For more on this incident, see Tran, "When a Writer's Rights Aren't Right"; and Hetrick, "Albee Estate Clarifies Position."

23. Zia, *Asian American Dreams*, 135.

24. See, for example, Erin Quill's blog, *The Fairy Princess Diaries*; and Galella, "Feeling Yellow."

25. Wilson, "The Ground on Which I Stand," 16.

26. Wilson, "The Ground on Which I Stand."

27. Wilson, "The Ground on Which I Stand," 72.

28. Wilson, "The Ground on Which I Stand," 72.

29. Wilson, "The Ground on Which I Stand," 71; and Brustein, "Unity from Diversity."

30. Brustein, "Subsidized Separatism," 101.

31. Quoted in Goldberger, "From Page to Stage."

32. Quoted in Grimes, "Face-to-Face Encounter on Race."

33. Catanese, *The Problem of the Color[blind]*, 70.

34. Catanese, *The Problem of the Color[blind]*, 6-7.

35. Warner, *The Cultural Politics of Colorblind TV Casting*, 12.

36. Warner, *The Cultural Politics of Colorblind TV Casting*, 155.

37. Horne, "Harry and the Other," 76.

38. In *Harry Potter and the Prisoner of Azkaban*, Rowling writes, "Hermione's white face was sticking out from behind a tree" (401). I am inclined to agree with Jennifer Patrice Sims, who suggests that we can read "white face" as Hermione turning white (out of fear) rather than being identified as White racially. See Sims, "The Reality of Imaginary Whiteness."

39. *Playbill* Staff, "*The Great Comet's* Denée Benton."

40. Quoted in Raymond, "Indecent Proposal," 24.

41. Rooney, "*Harry Potter and the Cursed Child*: Theater Review."

42. Yuen, *Reel Inequality*, 50–51.

43. This idea, of course, has been well articulated by various scholars of reception and reader-response, including Louise Rosenblatt and Roman Ingarden.

44. Bennett, "What a 'Racebent' Hermione Granger Really Represents."

45. Bennett, "What a 'Racebent' Hermione Granger Really Represents."

46. Genette, *Paratexts*.

47. See Maätita and Hernandez's chapter in this volume, "Racism, Canon, and the Controversy Surrounding #BlackHermione."

48. Teachout, "The Broadway Musical Crisis."

49. Yuen, *Reel Inequality*, 61.

50. McMaster, "Why *Hamilton* Is Not the Revolution"; and Keene, "Where Are the Natives in *Hamilton*?"

Bibliography

Bennett, Alanna. "What a 'Racebent' Hermione Granger Really Represents." Buzzfeed, February 1, 2015. https://www.buzzfeed.com/alannabennett/what-a-racebent-hermione-granger-really-represen-d2yp?utm_term=.lveZ4Eon5#.wby5nyekL.

Broadway League. *The Demographics of the Broadway Audience, 2015–2016*. New York: Broadway League, 2016.

Brustein, Robert. "Subsidized Separatism." *American Theatre*, October 1996.

Brustein, Robert. "Unity from Diversity." *New Republic*, July 19–26, 1993.

Catanese, Brandi Wilkins. *The Problem of the Color[blind]: Racial Transgression and the Politics of Black Performance*. Ann Arbor: University of Michigan Press, 2011.

Galella, Donatella. "Feeling Yellow: Responding to Contemporary Yellowface in Musical Performance." *Journal of Dramatic Theory and Criticism* 32, no. 2 (Spring 2018): 67–77.

Genette, Gérard. *Paratexts: Thresholds of Interpretation*. Translated by Jane E. Lewin. Cambridge: Cambridge University Press, 1997.

Goldberger, Paul. "From Page to Stage: Race and the Theater." *New York Times*, January 22, 1997.

Grimes, William. "Face-to-Face Encounter on Race in the Theater." *New York Times*, January 29, 1997.

Hetrick, Adam. "Albee Estate Clarifies Position on Casting Controversy Surrounding *Who's Afraid of Virginia Woolf?*" *Playbill*, August 24, 2017. http://www.playbill.com/article/albee -estate-clarifies-position-on-casting-controversy-surrounding-whos-afraid-of-virginia -woolf.

Horne, Jackie C. "Harry and the Other: Answering the Race Question in J. K. Rowling's *Harry Potter*." *The Lion and the Unicorn* 34, no. 1 (January 2010): 76–104.

Horwitz, Simi. "Ever Since *Saigon*: A Non-Traditional Casting Update." *TheaterWeek*, February 13–19, 1995.

Horwitz, Simi. "Is Affirmative Action Coming to Broadway?" *TheaterWeek*, August 27– September 2, 1990.

Jenkins, Henry. *Convergence Culture: Where Old and New Media Collide*. New York: New York University Press, 2006.

Keene, Adrienne. "Where Are the Natives in *Hamilton*?" *Native Appropriations* (blog), August 5, 2016. https://nativeappropriations.com/2016/08/where-are-the-natives-in -hamilton.html.

Kobold, Samwise. "Hermione is not a [racial epithet]. She is a strong WHITE girl." Twitter, December 22, 2015. https://twitter.com/SamKbold/status/679410062322851841.

Lee, Esther Kim. *A History of Asian American Theatre*. Cambridge: Cambridge University Press, 2006.

Lipsitz, George. *The Possessive Investment in Whiteness: How White People Profit from Identity Politics*. Rev. ed. Philadelphia: Temple University Press, 2006.

McLaughlin, Robert. *Broadway and Hollywood: A History of Economic Interaction*. New York: Arno Press, 1974.

McMaster, James. "Why *Hamilton* Is Not the Revolution You Think It Is." *HowlRound*, February 23, 2016. howlround.com/why-hamilton-is-not-the-revolution-you-think-it-is.

Paulson, Michael. "The Battle of *Miss Saigon*: Yellowface, Art and Opportunity." *New York Times*, March 17, 2017.

Playbill Staff. "*The Great Comet*'s Denée Benton and *Sweeney Todd*'s Norm Lewis Have a Frank Chat about Race." *Playbill*, May 26, 2017.

Quill, Erin. *The Fairy Princess Diaries* (blog). https://fairyprincessdiaries.com/.

Raymond, Gerard. "Indecent Proposal." *TheaterWeek*, July 19–25, 1993.

Rei AX2017. "Smart. Loyal." Twitter, December 21, 2015. https://twitter.com/EyeAmStrongest /status/679021504474972160.

Rooney, David. "*Harry Potter and the Cursed Child*: Theater Review." *Hollywood Reporter*, April 22, 2018. https://www.hollywoodreporter.com/movies/movie-reviews/harry -potter-cursed-child-theater-review-1104812/.

Rowling, J. K. *Harry Potter and the Prisoner of Azkaban*. New York: Scholastic, 1999.

Shang (@shanglinlee). "I have nothing against Noma Dumezweni, it's not about her race."
    Twitter, January 14, 2016. https://twitter.com/shanglinlee/status/687519154824458240.

Shapiro, Ari. "Why Are Theater Tickets Cheaper on the West End Than on Broadway?" *All
    Things Considered.* NPR, July 30, 2014. www.npr.org/2014/07/30/336594091/why-are
    -theater-tickets-cheaper-on-the-west-end-than-on-broadway.

Sims, Jennifer Patrice. "The Reality of Imaginary Whiteness." *Black Perspectives,* July 24,
    2016. https://www.aaihs.org/the-reality-of-imaginary-whiteness/.

Sternfeld, Jessica. *The Megamusical.* Bloomington: Indiana University Press, 2006.

Teachout, Terry. "The Broadway Musical Crisis." *Commentary,* July–August, 2014. https://
    www.commentarymagazine.com/articles/the-broadway-musical-crisis/.

Tran, Diep. "When a Writer's Rights Aren't Right: The *Virginia Woolf* Casting Fight."
    American Theatre, May 22, 2017. https://www.americantheatre.org/2017/05/22/when-a
    -writers-rights-arent-right-the-virginia-woolf-casting-fight/.

Warner, Kristen J. *The Cultural Politics of Colorblind TV Casting.* New York: Routledge, 2015.

Wilson, August. "The Ground on Which I Stand." *American Theatre,* September 1996.

Yuen, Nancy Wang. *Reel Inequality: Hollywood Actors and Racism.* New Brunswick, NJ:
    Rutgers University Press, 2017.

Zia, Helen. *Asian American Dreams: The Emergence of an American People.* New York:
    Farrar, Straus and Giroux, 2000.

Racism, Canon, and the Controversy Surrounding #BlackHermione

Florence Maätita and Marcia Hernandez

Social media has affected how we talk about race, although it is doubtful the creators of this technology had any idea that it would become a platform for racial dialogue.[1] While different forms of social media allow for varying scale and scope of interaction, Twitter is unique in its format by giving "anyone with something to say a 'digital soapbox' where he or she can instantly express thoughts, values, and opinions on a variety of issues in 140 characters or less."[2] We examine the controversy on Twitter surrounding #BlackHermione upon the casting of Noma Dumezweni, a Swaziland-born Black English actor, as Hermione in the play *Harry Potter and the Cursed Child*. Two concepts, aggrieved entitlement and the racial contract, are central to our analysis of the flurry of tweets responding to the casting decision, which many fans contested as an undeniable break from Harry Potter canon. This study adds to the scholarship of colorblind ideology and racial representation in popular culture as well as discussions about challenges to and control over canon.[3]

Aja Romano defines canon as "simply the source narrative you're referring to when you talk about that thing you like."[4] Their definition acknowledges differences in opinion about what material constitutes canon. Romano continues: "[M]any *Harry Potter* fans don't consider anything but the published books to be canon, while other fans include the extra information author

J. K. Rowling has provided about the wizarding world on her Pottermore website and on Twitter."[5] Harry Potter fans around the world have inundated the internet with theories, fanfiction, and fanart. Collectively, these fans have added to and challenged the canon of Harry Potter, for instance by taking to the internet to present racebent interpretations of characters in the magical world, like Hermione Granger. Alanna Bennett, a biracial reporter, examines fanart on Tumblr that depicts Hermione as Black or biracial.[6] This interpretation of Hermione, which has often corresponded with the #BlackHermione designation, hinges on the absence of an explicit reference to her skin color in the books, although there are numerous mentions of her hair and her bossy personality. Moreover, fans consider her blood status a metaphor for her racial-ethnic identity: "Hermione's story was always one involving a young girl living in a world aggressive towards her for her very existence. . . . [P]ainting Hermione as a woman of color is an act of reclaiming her allegory at its roots."[7]

In the months between the announcement of the cast in December 2015 and the official London premiere in July 2016, social media was flooded with racist commentary and criticism about the actor and the character who came to be known as "Black Hermione." #BlackHermione exploded on December 20, 2015, upon the announcement of the cast of *Harry Potter and the Cursed Child*. Billed as the eighth installment of a tale created by Rowling, the play chronicles the contentious relationship between an adult Harry Potter and his youngest son, Albus, once the younger Potter goes off to Hogwarts School of Witchcraft and Wizardry. Rowling herself opined on June 29, 2015: "The story of #CursedChild should be considered canon, though. @jackthorne, John Tiffany (the director) and I developed it together."[8]

Fans were eager to reunite with beloved characters; this zeal was overshadowed as people learned that Noma Dumezweni had won the role of Hermione. Reactions to the casting of Dumezweni ran the gamut from pride and excitement to confusion, dislike, and even anger that the actor was defying canon. Peter C. Kunze notes that, although an adaptation from book or film to play typically means "a new culture of common practices and expectations, both of artists and of audiences," some reactions to the casting of Dumezweni illuminate the "possessive investment in whiteness" as well as questions about the ownership of popular texts.[9] Although there was a dispute over whether Rowling had ever specified Hermione's skin color, critics were quick to point out that Hermione is white because Emma Watson, a

French-born white English actor, played her in the eight movie adaptations that preceded *The Cursed Child*.

Here, we examine #BlackHermione as a multilayered controversy that is not just about the casting of Dumezweni as the beloved Hermione. This examination of fan response on Twitter illuminates a number of issues. First, exchanges on Twitter raise the question of who may claim control of the canon when it comes to the wizarding world. Second, critics use adherence to and continuity within canon (which they assert does not include a Black Hermione) as a way to dispute accusations of their own racism. We view debates over control of and continuity within canon through the lens of racism and aggrieved entitlement by fans who "object to the existence of black hashtags [that] epitomize mass majority narcissism, wherein not only do Whites believe that they should be the sole possessors of social goods, but of the social gaze as well."[10]

Finally, we are interested in why and how J. K. Rowling emerged as the prime target of her detractors' anger. These exchanges highlight the problems of racism and tension of racial representation among fans, as well as the cultural power that Rowling herself wields. We propose that fans who disagreed with Dumezweni's casting as Hermione were offended by Rowling's break with the racial contract, in which whiteness is privileged and unnamed as the norm.

The Canon of Hermione Granger

On December 21, 2015, J. K. Rowling reminded the Twitterverse of how she wrote Hermione Granger: "Canon: brown eyes, frizzy hair and very clever. White skin was never specified."[11] In fact, much of what we know (and love) about Hermione stems from her hair and her intelligence. For instance, when we first meet Hermione, all Rowling tells us is that she "had a bossy sort of voice, lots of bushy brown hair, and rather large front teeth" (*Harry Potter and the Sorcerer's Stone*, 105). We see no mention of Hermione's appearance again until just before she returns to Hogwarts for her second year: "Harry looked up and saw Hermione Granger standing at the top of the white flight of steps to Gringotts. She ran down to meet them, her bushy brown hair flying behind her" (*Harry Potter and the Chamber of Secrets*, 55). These two examples illustrate how Rowling does not devote much time to describing

Hermione's physical appearance, save for these fleeting references to her "bushy brown hair."

Audiences get another reference to Hermione's hair in *Harry Potter and the Cursed Child*, the play Jack Thorne wrote based on a story by Rowling. In one scene, Hermione, who is a mean Hogwarts teacher in an alternate reality, is talking to Ron, her estranged husband:

> Ron: Have you done something with your hair?
> Hermione: Just combed it, I suspect.
> Ron: Well . . . Combing it suits you.[12]

Even though nineteen years have passed since the Battle of Hogwarts and the trio are well into adulthood, Hermione's hair remains her defining physical characteristic.

Despite consistent mention of Hermione's hair, Rowling makes brief allusions to her skin color in *Harry Potter and the Prisoner of Azkaban*. First, when the trio meet in Diagon Alley before they return to Hogwarts, Rowling describes Hermione as "very brown" (*HP and the PA*, 55). Later on, Rowling writes, "Hermione's white face was sticking out from behind a tree" (*HP and the PA*, 401). Some readers interpret this description as proof of Hermione's whiteness, while others consider it an indication of the fright that she is experiencing at that moment. It is possible that Hermione's white face is a consequence of fear, although some critics point out that this change would only be possible if Hermione were white to begin with.[13] Regardless, these two passages are central to the controversy surrounding the eventual casting of a Black woman in *Harry Potter and the Cursed Child*.

While Rowling spends little time covering Hermione's physical appearance, she devotes more attention to Hermione's intellect. Throughout the series, Hermione is consistently the first to raise her hand to answer a professor's question, and she spends most of her time in the library doing research. She figured out the Potions test (*HP and the SS*, 285–87), brewed Polyjuice Potion (*HP and the CS*, 159–60, 214–26), and took extra classes with the use of a Time Turner (*HP and the PA*, 393–96); her spells and enchantments ensured the safety and survival of herself, Harry, and Ron in their quest to find the remaining Horcruxes (*Harry Potter and the Deathly Hallows*). Even Remus Lupin referred to Hermione as "the cleverest witch of her age" (*HP and the PA*, 346).[14] When we last see Hermione, she is the Minister of Magic.[15]

Hermione Granger is beloved, and her fans' adoration is evident in the fanfiction and fanart devoted to her. Moreover, she has inspired a great deal of attention from academics, who have examined, for example, whether she is a feminist, a role model, and a heroine.[16] The edited volume *Hermione Granger Saves the World: Essays on the Feminist Heroine of Hogwarts* goes so far as to argue that the full story truly hinges on her rather than just on Harry Potter.[17] Although scholars have scrutinized Hermione in reference to gender, sexism, and feminism, they have yet to examine her with regard to her race or ethnicity. Fans, however, have done so using her "bushy brown hair" as indicative of her Black or biracial identity. The politics of hair for Black girls and women is well documented. Many schools and workplaces have sought to ban or control Black girls' and women's hairstyles deemed distracting, unruly, or unprofessional through official policy that limits the range of acceptable styles.[18] Even if not official policy, these practices are routinely enforced through social interactions among peers, adding a layer of scrutiny for Black girls and young women to negotiate.[19]

Hermione is Muggle-born, which is why some characters refer to her as a Mudblood. Devotees have taken her hair combined with her blood status as evidence that Hermione is not white.[20] As Ron explains, "It's about the most insulting thing he could think of. . . . Mudblood's a really foul name for someone who is Muggle-born—you know, non-magic parents. . . . It's a disgusting thing to call someone" (*HP and the CS*, 115–16). While scholars have addressed blood status as an allegory for racial purity,[21] they have not addressed Hermione's own racial and ethnic identity. Given Hermione's advocacy of respect for all creatures and general concern for others, characteristics commonly applied to Black women as caregivers and leaders in social justice movements, solidified in the "strong Black woman trope," the popularity of racebending her character is understandable.[22] Although Rowling herself never specified Hermione's race, fans have claimed Hermione's racial and ethnic identity. As @aurorasaysyes tweeted, "Hermione was the brightest witch of her age, not the whitest."[23]

#BlackHermione on Twitter

For this project, we searched tweets that directly referenced #BlackHermione. Some of the tweets featured also include at least one additional hashtag referencing Harry Potter or Hermione including: #HermioneIsBlack, #Hermione, #HarryPotterAndTheCursedChild, and #HarryPotter. Twitter is an ideal platform to capture a flash point in pop culture from different perspectives, such as with the casting of Dumezweni as Hermione in *The Cursed Child*. This platform also offers the ability to collect qualitative data on a quantitative scale; to manage the volume of information, researchers must systematically organize and analyze data.[24] After omitting tweets that do not directly reference Harry Potter, Hermione, *Harry Potter and the Cursed Child*, or Noma Dumezweni, we were left with 1,056 tweets between November 8, 2012, and December 20, 2016.[25] Most #BlackHermione tweets (561) appeared on December 21, 2015, the day after the play's cast was announced, with a slight drop-off the following day with 206 #BlackHermione references. Here, we focus on tweets from these two days, although we do not completely ignore tweets from before or after this two-day period. The tweets cited in this study are from public accounts. We do not focus on the identity of Twitter users in this study, as the anonymity provided by social media makes identification logistically challenging. More importantly, our focus is on the racial discourse as illuminated by the range of fan reaction to #BlackHermione. As tweets provide unfiltered insight from fans before the media, theater critics, and researchers had a chance to analyze and theorize about Dumezweni's casting as Hermione, they are ripe for sociological analysis about race among Harry Potter fandom.

The fourteen #BlackHermione tweets we noted prior to the announcement of the cast referred to emergent theories, fanfiction, and artwork of a Black or biracial Hermione. #BlackHermione gained momentum on December 20, 2015, the day of the cast announcement, with thirty-six references. Most posts in support of Dumezweni pointed out that Rowling never specified Hermione's race and demonstrated that #BlackHermione was a source of pride. Perhaps the most poignant tweet that day was from @baerith_: "I AM CANON."[26] Meanwhile, ambivalent tweets pointed out that the color of Hermione's skin does not matter—or that it would not matter as long as Dumezweni did the role justice. Some tweets pointed out that people were arguing over a fictional character and that *The Cursed Child* is merely fanfiction rather than canon.

Who Controls the Canon?

On December 21, 2015, J. K. Rowling issued her official endorsement for Dumezweni as Hermione: "Rowling loves black Hermione (kissing face emoji)."[27] Many people retweeted Rowling's support with accompanying remarks such as "The Queen has spoken #suckithaters."[28] Still others used her tweet along with a screenshot of the scene from *The Prisoner of Azkaban* in which Hermione's white face peeks out from behind a tree. Rowling and her supporters responded by questioning how some observers could know the Harry Potter canon better than Rowling herself: "White dudes Mansplaining to JK Rowling about the race of her own character,"[29] and "Why do you question the queen?"[30]

All told, six Twitter accounts that used #BlackHermione referred to Rowling as a queen. This title speaks to the high regard in which some people hold Rowling and to the logical conclusion that, as the creator of Harry Potter, she has significant—if not total—control.[31] Many tweeters agreed by maintaining that Rowling's December 21, 2015, tweet quashed further discussion on the matter. Further, some tweeters claimed that she even had a hand in Dumezweni's casting. For instance, @BronzdBrownGirl exclaimed, "I love that ya'll think J. K. Rowling had NO say in Black Hermione. You will all be okay!"[32] Essentially, this camp of tweeters affirms that Rowling can do and say whatever she wants about the world she created.

Yet, as literary theorists have debated for decades, authors do not maintain ultimate control over their creations as fans debate canon among themselves, and the act of reading is a transaction between the audience and the text.[33] Meaning derives from the reader's mental and emotional reactions to this transaction. Moreover, not only have scholars examined the power the reader has in producing meaning, but they argue that relying on the author for interpretation limits us to only one meaning.[34] The proliferation of Harry Potter–inspired fanfiction, Black Hermione fanart, and the ongoing debates on social media about #BlackHermione are testaments to the complexity of the question of control over canon.

Some tweets focus on Rowling's limited control, claiming that she is prone to bow to "social pressure": for example, "devaluing your own work to appease political correctness, shame. #Hermione #BlackHermione #harrypotter."[35] These tweets suggest that Hermione is really white and that Rowling's tweet is a response to political correctness and the sociopolitical context of market forces. While she may have written the *Harry Potter* books, political and social pressure dictate the direction of canon. Tweeters spoke directly to this point by arguing that #BlackHermione is an economic move. As @BlogHogwarts tweeted, "One can be a fan but not a blind fanatic. You have to be clear that #BlackHermione looks more like a marketing decision than anything else."[36]

Tensions over who controls canon played out in different ways through #BlackHermione and racial representation. One perspective suggests that the fans, and not Rowling, created #BlackHermione. For example, @ngenerose wrote, "it was fans of color who wrote, drew, & created #blackhermione. it's them, not rowling, who deserve the praise and affirmation."[37] Other Twitter users cited Rowling's tweet that she "loves Black Hermione" as a reminder that the author does not need anyone to fansplain one of her characters to her.

Ultimately the tweets about Black Hermione highlight whiteness operating as an unmarked and universal racial category among fans who decry a racebent Hermione. The Harry Potter universe is largely white, with very few notable roles portrayed by people of color, although Cho Chang and Kingsley Shacklebolt are exceptions in that they receive multiple spoken lines in the films. Yet, given the connection of these characters to Harry's, Ron's, and Hermione's experiences at Hogwarts and beyond, they are largely underdeveloped relative to the white characters. People of color exist primarily in supportive roles, helping their white peers reach new personal and emotional milestones, such as with Cho and Harry's relationship. Or they are notable for their devotion to a group cause such as Kingsley's work with the Order of the Phoenix. In the following section, we examine how whiteness as a dominant racial category complicates claims of colorblindness for fans who are used to seeing only white characters as protagonists in fictional stories.

Racism and Continuity

Negative responses to #BlackHermione reveal cracks in the colorblind ideology of Harry Potter fandom. Those who opposed or questioned #BlackHermione declared that their criticisms were not a result of racism; rather, they desired continuity between the books, movies, and play.[38] As @CeceBearz94 wrote, "I'm not at all against #BlackHermione I just wish she would have been originally cast as such and not changed in the middle of things."[39] This tweet represents the view of many critics who argued that Hermione was white in the books *and* the movies; thus, continuity (and their interpretation of canon) dictates that she should also be white in the play.

Black Hermione is not the first occasion of discontinuity in the magical world, however. Rowling describes Dudley Dursley, Harry's cousin, as blond, although Harry Melling, who played him in the movies, has dark brown hair.

Jennifer Smith, a Black actor, played Lavender Brown, a Hogwarts student who is in the same year as Harry, Hermione, and Ron, although Jessie Cave, a white actor, took over when Lavender became Ron's love interest in the film adaptation of *Harry Potter and the Half-Blood Prince*. Yet, while such charges may have raised arguments about continuity, this discourse was neither as apparent nor as combative as the #BlackHermione discussion on social media.

The relative dearth of complaints about, for instance, Harry's eyes or Ron's stature prompted #BlackHermione users to identify critics as racists. While tweeters do not use the term "aggrieved entitlement," this process often played out in Twitter exchanges. Specifically, tweeters identified people's need for continuity as a thin veil for racism, as is evident in the following tweets:

> Honestly I don't see how you can justify having an exclusively white Hermione other than for racist reasons. #Blackhermione makes sense.[40]

> Here we go again. Racists whitesplaining their racism as simply being sticklers for detail & authenticity #HermioneIsBlack #BlackHermione.[41]

Not only was there a flurry of commentary on critics' racism, but people took to Twitter to challenge detractors' assumption that white is the default:

> If U default characters who race is never said as White, but nvr get mad about whitewashing canon POC ur part of the problem.[42]

These tweets signify how using colorblindness as an ideology, while holding whiteness in a privileged position in reality and fiction, underscores some of the frustration and controversy with the casting of Dumezweni.

Critics who cried for continuity between the books, the movie adaptations, and the play often used the disclaimer "I'm not racist, but . . ." We did not find anyone who made this claim while also using #BlackHermione, although we did see instances in which people who used the hashtag retweeted other posts or posted screenshots of racist commentary in letters to the British newspaper the *Daily Mail* and on Facebook. For example, @guiltyx references a Facebook discussion in which a user declared that people are not angry that Dumezweni is Black, but about "the lack of continuity to a story that has defined their childhoods and lives."[43] This user goes on to equate #BlackHermione to "remaking the fiction literature of *The Color Purple* with a white cast."

Collectively, the tweets comparing real people or intentionally racialized worlds with Harry Potter canon demonstrate aggrieved entitlement on behalf of the posters. Moreover, such commentary implies that critics cannot be racist if they are merely trying to play devil's advocate. That is, if characters from *The Color Purple* were white, for instance, then supporters of #BlackHermione would be pushing for continuity. Of course, this argument is flawed on many fronts. The characters in the book and later the cast members of the film and play in *The Color Purple* were explicitly conceived of as Black characters within a specific historical racial context. Moreover, detractors of #BlackHermione and Dumezweni's casting conveniently ignore the long history of white actors cast in roles originally written for people of color.

J. K. Rowling as the Target of Anger

The Facebook user we referenced above maintained that any discontinuity in the Harry Potter story violates people's "childhood and lives." For example, @adwipal wrote: "This is not about racism, bt about preserving what we grew up with! How would u react if Princess Leia was cast as black?"[44] Tweeters whose aim is to preserve their childhood have intentionally made serious indictments on J. K. Rowling.

There are a few ways to interpret Rowling as the primary target of critics' anger, as #BlackHermione users mentioned her name more than they mentioned Noma Dumezweni's.[45] First, people revere Harry Potter, and Rowling has significant power to make the sacred profane. This explanation concerns the amount of control she has over canon. Second, Rowling has never shied away from displaying her personal politics in her writings and on social media. For this reason, she is often a target of dissent. Plus, irrespective of her politics, she has political clout and can influence her fans in myriad ways. As @clariseamala tweeted, "Also, I'm glad J. K. Rowling didn't front on #BlackHermione. But all ya'll that needed a white woman to tell you it was okay are SEENT."[46] Third, Rowling is a woman, whose flaws are responsible for the fall of humankind (much like Eve in Christian theology), or the destruction of childhoods, in this case.[47]

There is another explanation as to why Rowling became the primary target of critics' racist anger: *she is white*. To explain, philosopher Charles W. Mills wrote about a "racial contract" that divides whites as people who matter and who belong from everyone else who neither matters nor belongs.[48] This contract works as long as white people endorse it, thus upholding their racial privilege. Hence, by supporting Noma Dumezweni and asserting control over canon, Rowling became a target because she violated that racial contract. Moreover, white detractors who claimed that a need for continuity—rather than racism— fueled their opposition to #BlackHermione were not only adhering to the racial contract, they were reminding Rowling (and other white supporters) of their obligation to do so as well. These two tweets illustrate this point:

> That's why #BlackHermione and @jk_rowling's response is so important. It's challenging the assumption of whiteness entrenched in our culture.[49]

> People fighting for Hermione's whiteness because they think she would be lesser if she were black. That's how racism works #blackhermione.[50]

Essentially, these tweeters have uncovered the racial contract in identifying how both racism and the notion of a Black Hermione as "lesser" are "entrenched in our culture." Moreover, some indicated that this backlash has mainly targeted J. K. Rowling.[51]

Making Sense of #BlackHermione

Harry Potter and the Cursed Child, which officially premiered in London on July 30, 2016, opened to positive reviews. Jack Shepherd of the *Independent* said that Dumezweni did a "tremendous job" as Hermione, Ben Brantley of the *New York Times* said that she was "perfect in the part," while Tufayel Ahmed of *Newsweek* lauded Dumezweni for the "precision and nuance" of her performance.[52] The play was nominated for eleven Olivier Awards, which recognize excellence in London theater, winning a record nine awards on April 9, 2017. Dumezweni won the award for Best Actress in a Supporting Role. She also won a WhatsOnStage Award for Best Supporting Actress in a Play, beating out her costar Poppy Miller, who played Ginny Weasley Potter. Some may wonder if Dumezweni's accolades are vindication for her rightful place in the Harry Potter canon; others are not as optimistic.

Controversies such as that which surrounded #BlackHermione are evidence that we, as global citizens and netizens, still have a long way to go to dismantle the structures that continue to support racism. The controversy that emerged upon Noma Dumezweni's landing the role of Hermione Granger is just one in a long series of public debates about canon, continuity, and racism. For instance, it was not that long ago that people were upset that Amandla Stenberg, an actor of African American, Danish, and Greenlandic Inuit descent, played Rue in the movie adaptation of Suzanne Collins's *The Hunger Games*. In the book, Collins describes Rue as having dark skin. As with #BlackHermione, fans took to social media to object to Stenberg as Rue, to challenge assumptions that Rue—a young woman whom *Hunger Games* protagonist Katniss Everdeen takes under wing—is white, and to question why race and representation are even issues in the fictional country of Panem.

More than one thousand #BlackHermione appearances on Twitter illuminated a controversy that is much deeper than objection to a Black actor playing a racially unspecified character. At one level, the posts we analyzed raised the question of who controls canon. Although J. K. Rowling created Harry Potter, it is difficult to see her outright control independent of social, political, and economic factors and/or fan support. Another level of examination suggested the inherent challenges in separating racism and the need for continuity. The convergence of these two justifications led us back to the question of control and social, political, economic, and fan pressures. Moreover, it led us to examine the severity of violating spoken and unspoken expectations about race and racism, a racial contract. This claim is especially noteworthy given that Rowling emerged as the prime target of her detractors' anger, even more than Dumezweni did.

As culture evolves, it is imperative that people of color—especially youth— see themselves at the center of the page, the screen, or the stage, rather than on the periphery. If the goal is to subvert the racial contract, white audiences must also see these very same representations more often. Increased racial-ethnic diversity in different types of art and literature are valuable steps to challenging the racial contract and white entitlement to dominance in cultural artifacts.[53]

The #BlackHermione Twitter debate highlights the important role that racial representation continues to play in popular culture. Casting Dumezweni as Hermione provided audiences with a rare glimpse of a Black actor in an artistic and theatrical space where she embodied a fully developed character with a story arc as a scholar, activist, and warrior as well as mother and (ex-)wife.[54] Conversations about #BlackHermione highlight the rarity of this phenomenon for Black women, and the anticipation that white women are expected to inhabit fully developed lives, even in a fictional world.

Continued conversation and reflection on race are also significant tools for disassembling racism. Such exchanges should not stop at "Who cares?" or "Why does it matter?" The point is that it—be it racism, canon, inequality, or lack of opportunity—matters to the people who make up a core of the Harry Potter fanbase. As Thomas writes, the "plurality of possible worlds might represent a crisis for some audiences, [while providing an] answer for emancipating the imagination for readers and fans who have for too long inhabited the margins—real and imagined."[55] Even if some people are not sure whether race matters in this fictional world, it is still evident that race matters to the fans of that world.

Notes

1. Chaudhry, "Not So Black and White."
2. Chaudhry, "Not So Black and White," 297.
3. See Thomas, *The Dark Fantastic.* See also Peter Kunze's chapter in this volume, "#NotMyHermione: Authorship and Ownership in the *Harry Potter and the Cursed Child* Casting Controversy."
4. Romano, "Canon, Fanon, Shipping and More."
5. Romano, "Canon, Fanon, Shipping and More."
6. Bennett, "What a 'Racebent' Hermione Granger Really Represents."
7. Bennett, "What a 'Racebent' Hermione Granger Really Represents."
8. Rowling, "The story of #CursedChild."
9. Lipsitz, *The Possessive Investment in Whiteness*; Thomas, *The Dark Fantastic*; and Kunze's chapter in this volume, "#NotMyHermione."
10. Sims and Pierce, "Black Twitter, White Tears."
11. Rowling, "Canon: brown eyes."
12. Thorne, *Harry Potter and the Cursed Child*, 146.
13. Kirchoff, "No J. K. Rowling."
14. In the movie adaptation of this book, Lupin refers to Hermione as the "brightest witch of [her] age." Sirius Black echoes this sentiment after Hermione and Harry save him from the West Tower. See Cuarón, *Harry Potter and the Prisoner of Azkaban.*
15. Thorne, *Harry Potter and the Cursed Child*, 31.
16. Zettel, "Hermione Granger and the Charge of Sexism"; Andrade, "Hermione Granger as Girl Sleuth"; and Heilman and Donaldson, "From Sexist to (Sort-of) Feminist."
17. Bell, *Hermione Granger Saves the World.*
18. For an in-depth discussion of the social, cultural, and political importance of hair for Black women, see Banks, *Hair Matters.* For contemporary examples of policies targeting Black girls' and women's natural hairstyles, see Jones and Meyer, "What's in a Hairstyle?"; Morris, *Pushout*; and Lattimore, "When Black Hair Violates the Dress Code."
19. Banks, *Hair Matters.*

20. There are characters in the books who are not white, such as the Patil twins, Cho Chang, Dean Thomas, and Lee Jordan. Rowling, however, does not show them as the targets of prejudice and discrimination. In fact, Dean Thomas is a Black half-blood wizard, but the only time anyone scoffs at him is when Ron sees Dean kissing his sister Ginny. See Rowling, *Harry Potter and the Half-Blood Prince.*

21. Horne, "Harry and the Other"; and Whited, "1492, 1942, 1992: The Theme of Race."

22. For an in-depth discussion of the "strong Black woman" trope, see P. H. Collins, *Black Feminist Thought*; and P. H. Collins, *Black Sexual Politics.*

23. Graduating in o assignments, "Hermione was the brightest witch." This tweet is a reference to Remus Lupin's and Sirius Black's acknowledgment of Hermione's intellect in the movie adaptation of *Harry Potter and the Prisoner of Azkaban.*

24. Chaudhry, "Not So Black and White," 297.

25. The overwhelming majority of tweets were in English, but we also included and translated tweets in ten other languages, including French, Spanish, and Finnish.

26. ☆ sephiroth's baby moms ☆, "I AM CANON."

27. Rowling, "Canon: brown eyes."

28. Librariana, "The Queen has spoken."

29. Librariana, "White dudes Mansplaining."

30. sensible shoes, "Also, most didn't know Dumbledore was gay."

31. Parry-Giles, "*Harry Potter* and the Paradoxical Critique."

32. Hickory, oak, pine and weed, "I love that ya'll think J. K. Rowling."

33. Rosenblatt, *Making Meaning with Texts.*

34. Barthes, "The Death of the Author."

35. Barbosa, "@jk_rowling devaluing your own work."

36. Harry Potter, BH!, "Uno puede ser fan." The authors translated this tweet from the original Spanish.

37. Nicki, "it was fans of color who wrote, drew, & created #blackhermione."

38. Kirchoff, "No J. K. Rowling."

39. Paye, "I'm not at all against #BlackHermione."

40. Mahoney, "Honestly I don't see."

41. Amira, "Here we go again."

42. Kyle, "If U default characters."

43. Black Lives Matter #BLM, "Reactions to a #BlackHermione."

44. Pal, "This is not about racism."

45. We would never deny that Noma Dumezweni was a target of racist criticism on social media. She addressed the backlash in an interview with the *Sunday Times*: "My name is being tagged into stuff that's not nice, that's not nice. . . . It's ignorance. It drives me crazy." Wise, "Noma Dumezweni Has Her Magic Moment."

46. Clarise, "Also, I'm glad J. K. Rowling didn't front on #BlackHermione."

47. Stephens, "Harry and Hierarchy." Lin-Manuel Miranda received similar types of criticism for his racebent casting of Alexander Hamilton and Aaron Burr in the musical *Hamilton.*

48. Mills, *The Racial Contract.*

49. Balakumar, "That's why #BlackHermione."

50. Magill, "People fighting for Hermione's whiteness."

51. Sevan, "It's fascinating to see the continuing #blackHermione backlash."

52. Shepherd, "Harry Potter and the Cursed Child, Review"; Brantley, "Review: *Harry Potter and the Cursed Child* Raises the Bar"; and Ahmed, "*Harry Potter and the Cursed Child* First Review."

53. Slater, "The Uncomfortable Truth."

54. For a detailed analysis of racial representation, body politics, and the challenges of portraying Black women as having complex lives due to gendered racism in popular culture, refer to Gammage, *Representations of Black Womanhood*; P. H. Collins, *Black Feminist Thought*; Springer, "Divas, Evil Black Bitches, and Bitter Black Women"; and Harris-Perry, *Sister Citizen*.

55. Thomas, *The Dark Fantastic*, 156.

Bibliography

Ahmed, Tufayel. "*Harry Potter and the Cursed Child* First Review." *Newsweek*, July 26, 2016. http://www.newsweek.com/harry-potter-and-cursed-child-first-review-484004.

Amira, Alahyo (@alahyo). "Here we go again. Racists whitesplaining their racism as simply being sticklers for detail & authenticity. #HermioneIsBlack #BlackHermione." Twitter, December 21, 2015. https://twitter.com/alahyo/status/678933282390712321.

Andrade, Glenna. "Hermione Granger as Girl Sleuth." In *Nancy Drew and Her Sister Sleuths: Essays on the Fiction of Girl Detectives*, edited by Michael G. Cornelius and Melanie E. Gregg, 165–78. Jefferson, NC: McFarland, 2008.

Balakumar, Aparna (@onceaparnatime). "That's why #BlackHermione and @jk_rowling's response is so important. It's challenging the assumption of whiteness entrenched in our culture." Twitter, December 21, 2015. https://twitter.com/onceaparnatime/status/679085406571266051.

Banks, Ingrid. *Hair Matters: Beauty, Power, and Black Women's Consciousness*. New York: New York University Press, 2000.

Barbosa, Alberto (@mortyhoward). "@jk_rowling devaluing your own work to appease political correctness, shame. #Hermione #BlackHermione #harrypotter." Twitter, December 21, 2015. https://twitter.com/search?f=tweets&q=%40mortyhoward%20%23blackhermione&src=typd.

Barthes, Roland. "The Death of the Author." In *Image, Music, Text*, by Roland Barthes, 142–48. Translated by Stephen Heath. London: Fontana Press, 1977.

Bell, Christopher E., ed. *Hermione Granger Saves the World: Essays on the Feminist Heroine of Hogwarts*. Jefferson, NC: McFarland, 2012.

Bennett, Alanna. "What a 'Racebent' Hermione Granger Really Represents." BuzzFeed, February 1, 2015. https://www.buzzfeed.com/alannabennett/what-a-racebent-hermione-granger-really-represen-d2yp?utm_term=.imGddY06J#.bk7AApG4k.

Black Lives Matter #BLM (@guiltyx). "Reactions to a #BlackHermione are predictably awful #headdesk." Twitter, December 21, 2015. https://twitter.com/guiltyx/status/679071914862579712.

Brantley, Ben. "Review: *Harry Potter and the Cursed Child* Raises the Bar for Broadway Magic." *New York Times*, April 22, 2018. https://www.nytimes.com/2018/04/22/theater/review-harry-potter-and-the-cursed-child-raises-the-bar-for-broadway-magic.html.

Chaudhry, Irfan. "'Not So Black and White': Discussions of Race and Twitter in the Aftermath of #Ferguson and the Shooting Death of Mike Brown." *Cultural Studies ↔ Critical Methodologies* 16, no. 3 (2016): 296–304.

Clarise (@clariseamala). "Also, I'm glad J. K. Rowling didn't front on #BlackHermione. But all ya'll that needed a white woman to tell you it was okay are SEENT." Twitter, December 21, 2015. https://twitter.com/clariseamala/status/679023237662121984.

Collins, Patricia Hill. *Black Feminist Thought: Knowledge, Consciousness, and the Politics of Empowerment*. New York: Routledge, 2008.

Collins, Patricia Hill. *Black Sexual Politics: African Americans, Gender, and the New Racism*. New York: Routledge, 2005.

Collins, Suzanne. *The Hunger Games*. New York: Scholastic, 2008.

Cuarón, Alfonso, dir. *Harry Potter and the Prisoner of Azkaban*. Warner Bros. Pictures, 2004.

Gammage, Marquita Marie. *Representations of Black Womanhood in the Media: The Damnation of Black Womanhood*. New York: Routledge, 2005.

Graduating in 0 assignments (@aurorasaysyes). "Hermione was the brightest witch of her age, not the whitest." Twitter, December 22, 2015. https://twitter.com/aurorasaysyes/status/679198595413762048.

Harris-Perry, Melissa V. *Sister Citizen: Shame, Stereotypes, and Black Women in America*. New Haven, CT: Yale University Press, 2011.

Harry Potter, BH! (@BlogHogwarts). "Uno puede ser fan pero no fanático ciego. Hay que estar claros de que #BlackHermione parece más una decisión de marketing que otra cosa." Twitter, December 21, 2015. https://twitter.com/BlogHogwarts/status/679018058963382272.

Heilman, Elizabeth E., and Trevor Donaldson. "From Sexist to (Sort-of) Feminist: Representations of Gender in the Harry Potter Series." In *Critical Perspectives on Harry Potter*, edited by Elizabeth E. Heilman, 139–61. New York: Routledge, 2009.

Hickory, oak, pine and weed (@BronzdBrownGirl). "I love that ya'll think J. K. Rowling had NO say in Black Hermione. You will all be okay! #HarryPotterAndTheCursedChild #BlackHermione." Twitter, December 21, 2015. https://twitter.com/BronzdBrownGirl/status/678969676135858177.

Horne, Jackie C. "Harry and the Other: Answering the Race Question in J. K. Rowling's *Harry Potter*." *The Lion and the Unicorn* 34, no. 1 (January 2010): 76–104. doi:10.1353/uni.0.0488.

Jones, Charisse, and Zlati Meyer. "What's in a Hairstyle? A Lot. New York City Bans Bias against Black Hair." *USA Today*, February 18, 2009. https://www.usatoday.com/story/money/2019/02/18/black-hair-protected-same-laws-ban-discrimination-nyc-says/2906013002/.

Jones, Trina, and Kimberly Jade Norwood. "Aggressive Encounters and White Fragility: Deconstructing the Trope of the Angry Black Woman." *Iowa Law Review* 102, no. 5 (July 2017): 2018–69.

Kirchoff, Courtney. "No J. K. Rowling, Not Everyone Who Thinks Hermione Is White Is a Racist." Louder with Crowder, June 7, 2016. https://www.louderwithcrowder.com/dear-j-k-rowling-sorry-not-everyone-who-thinks-hermione-is-white-is-a-racist/.

Kyle, Jasmine Leilani (@TolkienBlkGirl). "If U default characters who race is never said as White, but nvr get mad about whitewashing canon POC ur part of the problem. #BlackHermione." Twitter, December 21, 2015. https://twitter.com/JasmineLeiylani/status/678968677627203584.

Lattimore, Kayla. "When Black Hair Violates the Dress Code." NPR, July 17, 2017. https://www.npr.org/sections/ed/2017/07/17/534448313/when-black-hair-violates-the-dress-code.

Librariana (@thebilinguist). "The Queen has spoken #suckithaters #BlackHermione." Twitter, December 21, 2015. https://twitter.com/thebilinguist/status/678947786268655616.

Librariana (@thebilinguist). "White dudes Mansplaining to JK Rowling about the race of her own character #smh #BlackHermione #HarryPotterAndTheCursedChild." Twitter, December 21, 2015. https://twitter.com/thebilinguist/status/679044970892959744.

Lipsitz, George. *The Possessive Investment in Whiteness: How White People Profit from Identity Politics.* 3rd ed. Philadelphia: Temple University Press, 2018.

Magill, Jordan Robert (@JordanMagill). "People fighting for Hermione's whiteness because they think she would be lesser if she were black. That's how racism works #blackhermione." Twitter, December 21, 2015. https://twitter.com/JordanMagill/status /679025057750880256.

Mahoney, Neve (@Eve_Letters). "Honestly I don't see how you can justify having an exclusively white Hermione other than for racist reasons." Twitter, December 22, 2015. https://twitter.com/Eve_Letters/status/679167002297024512.

Mills, Charles W. *The Racial Contract.* Ithaca, NY: Cornell University Press, 1997.

Morris, Monique W. *Pushout: The Criminalization of Black Girls in School.* New York: New Press, 2016.

Nicki (@ngenerose). "it was fans of color who wrote, drew, & created #blackhermione. it's them, not rowling, who deserve the praise and affirmation." Twitter, December 22, 2015. https://twitter.com/ngenerose/status/679339378112466944.

Pal, Adwitiya (@adwipal). "This is not about racism, bt about preserving what we grew up with! How would u react if Princess Leia was cast as black? #BlackHermione." Twitter, December 22, 2015. https://twitter.com/adwipal/status/679119420644429824.

Parry-Giles, Trevor. "*Harry Potter* and the Paradoxical Critique of Celebrity Culture." *Celebrity Studies* 2, no. 3 (2011): 305–19. doi:10.1080/19392397.2011.609338.

Paye, Heather (@CeceBearz94). "I'm not at all against #BlackHermione I just wish she would have been originally cast as such and not changed in the middle of things." Twitter, December 21, 2015. https://twitter.com/CeceBearz/status/679043644460937216.

Romano, Aja. "Canon, Fanon, Shipping and More: A Glossary of the Tricky Terminology that Makes Up Fan Culture." *Vox,* June 7, 2016. https://www.vox.com/2016/6/7/11858680 /fandom-glossary-fanfiction-explained.

Rosenblatt, Louise. *Making Meaning with Texts: Selected Essays.* Portsmouth, NH: Heinemann, 2005.

Ross, Gary, dir. *The Hunger Games.* Lionsgate, 2012.

Rothstein, Edward. "Is Dumbledore Gay? Depends on Definitions of 'Is' and 'Gay.'" *New York Times,* October 29, 2007. https://www.nytimes.com/2007/10/29/arts/29conn.html.

Rowling, J. K. *Harry Potter and the Chamber of Secrets.* New York: Scholastic, 1999.

Rowling, J. K. *Harry Potter and the Deathly Hallows.* New York: Scholastic, 2007.

Rowling, J. K. *Harry Potter and the Goblet of Fire.* New York: Scholastic, 2000.

Rowling, J. K. *Harry Potter and the Half-Blood Prince.* New York: Scholastic, 2005.

Rowling, J. K. *Harry Potter and the Prisoner of Azkaban.* New York: Scholastic, 1999.

Rowling, J. K. *Harry Potter and the Sorcerer's Stone.* New York: Scholastic, 1998.

Rowling, J. K (@jk_rowling). "Canon: brown eyes, frizzy hair and very clever." Twitter, December 21, 2015. https://twitter.com/jk_rowling/status/678888094339366914.

Rowling, J. K. (@jk_rowling). "The story of #CursedChild should be considered canon, though." Twitter, June 29, 2015. https://twitter.com/jk_rowling/status/61549860180 9211393.

sensible shoes/ 🐦 🐦 🐦 🐦 🐦 🐦 🐦 💥 🐦 💀 ✊ (@THEYveGotAlist). "Also, most didn't
know Dumbledore was gay until she told you. Why do .you question the queen?!
#BlackHermione @jk_rowling, I LOVE YOUR GRACE." Twitter, December 22, 2015.
https://twitter.com/THEYveGotAlist/status/679090288040812544.

☆ sephiroth's baby moms ☆ (@baerith_). "I AM CANON https://T.co/PV9eRmIIXm
#blackhermione #Harrypotterandthecursedchild." Twitter, December 20, 2015. https://
twitter.com/baerith_/status/678755041839304707.

Sevan (@justSEVAN). "It's fascinating to see the continuing #blackHermione backlash for
@jk_rowling It is LUDICROUS and just proves racism is alive and healthy." Twitter,
June 11, 2016. https://twitter.com/justSEVAN/status/741691009357221888.

Shepherd, Jack. "Harry Potter and the Cursed Child, Review: A Magical Experience Tailor
Made for the Stage." *Independent*, August 5, 2016. http://www.independent.co.uk/arts
-entertainment/tv/reviews/harry-potter-and-the-cursed-child-review-palace-theatre-a
-magical-experience-tailor-made-for-the-a7155381.html.

Sims, Jennifer Patrice, and Vanisha Renée Pierce. "Black Twitter, White Tears." *Racism
Review: Scholarship and Activism Toward Racial Justice* (blog), January 14, 2016. http://
www.racismreview.com/blog/2016/01/14/black-twitter-white-tears/.

Slater, Dashka. "The Uncomfortable Truth about Children's Books." *Mother Jones*,
September–October 2016. http://www.motherjones.com/media/2016/08/
diversity-childrens-books-slavery-twitter.

Springer, Kimberly. "Divas, Evil Black Bitches, and Bitter Black Women: African-American
Women in Postfeminist and Post–Civil Rights Popular Culture." In *Feminist Television
Criticism: A Reader*, 2nd ed., edited by Charlotte Brunsdon and Lynn Spigel, 72–92.
Maidenhead, Berks., England: Open University Press, 2008.

Stephens, Rebecca. "Harry and Hierarchy: Book Banning as a Reaction to the Subversion of
Authority." In *Reading Harry Potter: Critical Essays*, edited by Giselle Liza Anatol, 51–65.
Westport, CT: Praeger, 2003.

Thomas, Ebony Elizabeth. *The Dark Fantastic: Race and the Imagination from Harry Potter
to the Hunger Games*. New York: New York University Press, 2019.

Thorne, Jack. *Harry Potter and the Cursed Child, parts 1 and 2*. New York: Scholastic, 2016.

Whited, Lana. "1492, 1942, 1992: The Theme of Race in the Harry Potter Series." *Looking
Glass* 10, no. 1 (2006). https://ojs.latrobe.edu.au/ojs/index.php/tlg/article/view/97.

Wise, Louis. "Noma Dumezweni Has Her Magic Moment." *Sunday
Times*, June 19, 2016. https://www.thetimes.co.uk/article/
noma-dumezweni-has-her-magic-moment-zrqg9nooh.

Zettel, Sarah. "Hermione Granger and the Charge of Sexism." In *Mapping the World of the
Sorcerer's Apprentice: An Unauthorized Exploration of the Harry Potter Series Complete
through Book Six*, edited by Mercedes Lackey, 83–100. Dallas: BenBella Books, 2006.

PART III

History, Pedagogy, and Liberation

Harry Potter and Black Liberation Movements

Addressing the Imagination Gap with History

Jasmine Wade

It is often in moments of rupture, when something breaks or snaps or turns, that one can gain new sight. This may be a "second sight" as W. E. B. Du Bois declared Black people received as a "gift" at the end of the Middle Passage.[1] It may be a widening of the "constricted eye" Minnie Bruce Pratt discusses.[2] It is a kind of expanded vision that comes from being "woke," as we might think of it in twenty-first-century terms.

The story of the moment Harry Potter's sight expanded is now a legend. In 1992, Harry's first year at Hogwarts, already so much had happened, including learning that he is a wizard, fighting a troll, and riding a broom. At the end of *Harry Potter and the Sorcerer's Stone*, Harry faces his nemesis, the Dark Lord, for the first time. Hermione and Ron help Harry get through a series of preventative measures the Hogwarts faculty so creatively and carefully created to guard the Sorcerer's Stone. When Harry gets past all those obstacles, he is surprised to find Professor Quirrell. Professor Quirrell unwraps his turban, and "where there should have been a back to Quirrell's head, there was a face, the most terrible face Harry had ever seen. It was chalk white with glaring red eyes and slits for nostrils, like a snake" (*HP and the SS*, 293). It is in this experience—meeting Voldemort and realizing that Voldemort cannot yet stand to touch him as well as the subsequent enlightening chat with Professor Dumbledore—that Harry gains another sight.[3] With each book, Harry's sight continues to expand until he is finally ready, in skill, in mind, and in heart, to defeat Voldemort. I'd like to think of the first book with Hermione, Ron, and Harry working together as a team as the actual beginning of Dumbledore's Army, the student-led movement that would ultimately thwart the Dark Lord.

Decades before Harry began his great adventure and J. K. Rowling penned her influential series, in early winter 1960, Ezell Blaire Jr., Franklin McCain, David Richmond, and Joseph McNeal, four North Carolina A&T freshmen, conferred on campus about the racial injustice of the time and what to do. Ultimately, they decided to sit at a segregated lunch counter in a Woolworth's Department Store in Greensboro. They refused to move until the counter closed. The Greensboro sit-in was not the first sit-in in the South; however, it was the one that caused the spark that eventually led to the creation of the Student Nonviolent Coordinating Committee or SNCC (pronounced "Snick").[4] Each of these young men, and the students who joined them in the days that followed the first sit-in, already had a second sight. However, when they chose to use that sight to challenge systemic racism, the "gift" Du Bois spoke of ignited, burning with a fire that fueled a movement.

The literature on Harry Potter and race tends to focus on two major areas. First, several scholars, including Steven Patterson and Amy Green, focus on the nonwizard "races" in the *Harry Potter* series.[5] This body of literature argues about the varying degrees to which Rowling addresses discrimination against goblins, centaurs, and other creatures. The house-elves, like Dobby and Winky, are particularly attractive for scholars thinking about race, as Rowling positions them as enslaved. However, as Farah Mendlesohn shows, Rowling relies on the stereotype of the happy darky to make a point with the house-elves that, in the end, falls flat.[6] As Jackie C. Horne further observes, "the humorous method by which house-elves can be set free—by a master giving them clothes—keeps all of the power in the hands of the oppressor, rather than allowing agency to the oppressed."[7] Hermione cannot get any traction with the Society for the Promotion of Elfish Welfare (S.P.E.W.), and in the final book, Rowling does not mention the Society at all, which seems to suggest that there is little room in the *Harry Potter* series for institutional change with regard to discrimination against house-elves; as Horne argues in her chapter in this volume, Rowling's dealings with race are limited to the personal. Harry makes personal, individual decisions regarding his treatment of and thoughts about house-elves and goblins. There is little motion, though, toward systemic change, and it is evident that Voldemort is not actually at the center of that discrimination.[8] Second, Horne is an example of another sector of Harry Potter scholarship: multicultural education. Horne specifically argues that there are two types of antiracist pedagogy: multicultural and social justice. The *Harry Potter* series is an example of multicultural antiracism, in which the focus is on individual decisions not to be racist, like when Harry decides to be nicer to the house-elf Kreacher.[9] Social justice antiracism operates on a systemic level rather than a personal one, and supports pedagogy that teaches young people about racism in a structural way.

Building on Horne's argument, I agree that one of the limitations of the *Harry Potter* series is that it focuses on the individual rather than the structural. For this reason, I argue here that when Harry Potter is paired with historical Black social movements, the pedagogical potential grows. Furthermore, in much of the Harry Potter literature, the reader is assumed to be a white young person. In this chapter, the hypothetical reader I consider is a young person of color. In the expansion of student movement literature to include Harry Potter and Dumbledore's Army, teachers and community members can reach their young people in a way that addresses both social justice and multicultural antiracism.

Moreover, as a secondary argument, I consider the role of historical stories in closing the imagination gap. Ebony Elizabeth Thomas speaks of a lack of diversity in children's and young adult literature, specifically in the genre of speculative fiction. She says that this lack of diversity partly contributes to an imagination gap. When young people only see single stories, their imaginations are affected.[10] This impacts not only their internal lives—for which creativity and imagination are crucial—but also their ability to see themselves in circumstances other than what is directly visible. Thomas writes that, when she herself was a child, she needed magic. It was fundamental to her internal and material well-being.[11] Thomas and others have argued that one way to combat the imagination gap is to create and publish more diverse literature.[12] Here, I suggest there is another way. While the *Harry Potter* series (both the books and the movies) contributes to the imagination gap in that it leaves out several groups, Black youth in particular can find similar themes, language, drama, and wisdom from studying historical Black resistance movements. I am in no way arguing that history is superior to fantasy (or vice versa). Rather, I am offering that history, particularly narratives that are infrequently told, has the power to impact the imagination gap in a way similar to fantastic novels and movies.[13] Considering history and literature together offers educators a way to reach students and teach the value of love and social justice in a way that the *Harry Potter* series cannot do alone. In the rest of this chapter, I consider links between the *Harry Potter* series, SNCC, the British Black Power movement, and Black feminist organizations in the United States.

Harry Potter and the Love Factor

SNCC was a student organization founded in April 1960 under the watchful eye of Ella Baker, a fierce and longtime activist. Throughout the 1960s, the young activists in SNCC fought for voting rights, desegregation, and increased political education. SNCC and the *Harry Potter* series intersect around one central concept: love. In both SNCC and the *Harry Potter* series, love is more than a feeling; it is an action and a force so powerful that it can severely wound, or even destroy, evil. In *Harry Potter and the Sorcerer's Stone*, a young, fresh, wide-eyed Harry encounters Voldemort for the first time.

> "But why couldn't Quirrell touch me?"
> "Your mother died to save you. If there is one thing Voldemort cannot understand, it is love. He didn't realize that love as powerful as your mother's for you leaves its own mark. Not a scar, no visible sign. . . . [T]o have been loved so deeply, even though the person who loved us is gone, will give us some protection forever. It is in your very skin. Quirrell, full of hatred, greed, and ambition, sharing his soul with Voldemort, could not touch you for this reason. It was agony to touch a person marked by something so good." (*HP and the SS*, 299)

From the beginning, Rowling, through Dumbledore, teaches young readers that love is not only a mark of goodness but a kind of magic in and of itself.

In *Harry Potter and the Half-Blood Prince*, when Dumbledore imparts as much knowledge as he can about Tom Riddle so Harry knows his opponent, Dumbledore offers a memory of when Riddle asked for a teaching position at Hogwarts. "'The old argument,' [Riddle/Voldemort] said softly. 'But nothing I have seen in the world has supported your famous pronouncements that love is more powerful than my kind of magic, Dumbledore'" (*HP and the HBP*, 444). Dumbledore retorts that perhaps Riddle is not looking in the right places.

Throughout the series, Dumbledore insists that Voldemort's greatest weakness is that he does not understand love, which is Harry's greatest weapon. What does this mean in terms of activism in the real world? It is tempting to take a more multicultural stance on the love philosophy and come away with the idea that Rowling is suggesting individual acts of kindness. However, this fails to capture the magnitude of Harry's (and Hermione's and Ron's) task: to defeat the greatest evil ever to plague the wizarding world. The multicultural stance also cannot account for the gravity of Lily and James Potter's sacrifice. Lily's love is, on one level, a mother's deep, unconditional love for her son; on another level, it is a resistance against the authoritarian regime Voldemort is attempting to establish.

In order to go beyond the multicultural understanding of love in Harry Potter, it can help to examine love in SNCC. The *Student Voice* was SNCC's official newspaper. In it, they declared their philosophy, gave updates on movement activity across the South, shared the opinions of members on relevant issues, and more. In one of the first issues of the *Student Voice*, SNCC leaders—formal and informal—write:

> We affirm the philosophical or religious ideal of nonviolence as the foundation of our purpose, the pre-supposition of our faith, and the manner of our action. Nonviolence as it grows from Judaic-Christian traditions seeks a social order of justice permeated by love. Integration of human endeavor represents the crucial first step towards such a society. Through nonviolence, courage displaces fear; love transforms hate. Acceptance dissipates prejudice; hope ends despair.[14]

SNCC makes it clear that the love that fuels the movement is rooted in action, specifically nonviolent action. Nonviolence can be mistaken for a lack of action. SNCC challenges this notion throughout issues of the *Student Voice* and argues that nonviolence not only means taking direct action that is separate from violence but also utilizing a transformative power (love).

> Love is the central motif of nonviolence. Love is the force by which God binds man to himself and man to man. Such love goes to the extreme; it

remains loving and forgiving even in the midst of hostility. It matches the capacity of evil to inflict suffering with an even more enduring capacity to absorb evil, all the while persisting in love.[15]

Furthermore, SNCC declares in a list of necessary factors to "win racial justice": "the non-violent resister [whose action is rooted in an extreme love] seeks to defeat the forces of evil."[16] Similarly, Dumbledore reminds Harry again and again that love is both his sword and his shield. "You are protected, in short, by your ability to love!" (*HP and the HBP*, 511).

All this considered, what does it mean, then, to connect fantasy with history? In terms of pedagogy, I see potential in grounding the *Harry Potter* series alongside the specific lineage of the civil rights movement. For young readers, Rowling's story ignites the imagination. It is a story that has led to two decades of fanfiction. These characters are beloved and their actions accessible. It is much easier to imagine and acknowledge evil in the form of Voldemort's sorcery of supremacy than it is to really conceive of and acknowledge the reaches of white supremacy. Perhaps, though, Rowling gives people, young and old, a door through which they can begin to understand systemic oppression in the United States.[17] To use the terms that Horne provides, on its own, the *Harry Potter* series only engages with antiracism on the multicultural level. This is not enough to lead to lasting change. In considering Harry Potter alongside SNCC and potentially other student movements, educators can engage students in social justice antiracism, which pushes students to think critically about the world they live in, not unlike Hermione. While Harry and his friends inspire passion, SNCC shows students how they might actually act.

Harry Potter, Power, and Political Economy

The iconic images of the Black Panther Party in black berets and guns have circulated for decades as monuments of their time. In the mid-1960s, the visual culture and philosophy of the US Black Panther Party traveled across the pond. Learning from Stokely Carmichael, Obi Egbuna considered the US Black Power movement's relevance to the British context.[18] This sparked what was known as the British Black Power movement from 1967 to 1968 and the British Black Panther Movement (BBPM) from 1968 to 1972, which is the focus of this section.[19] Under Egbuna, the BBPM were vying for a race and class revolution.[20]

Egbuna wrote a letter from prison titled "Destroy This Temple" in which he described some of his feelings about race relations in Britain.[21] He treated Black Britons as an economic class and argued that they were victims in two ways. First, Black Britons were victims of the lie not only that they could participate equally in a capitalist system but also that the system would benefit their communities in Africa and the Caribbean. Second, they were victims of "the biggest and most publicized myth in the world. It is generally believed that there is very little racialism in Britain. The English have succeeded in fooling the entire world that they are the least racist and most tolerant beings in the world."[22] Here, Egbuna brings together a fundamental principle of the BBPM: that race and class must be considered with equal power in any move toward justice.[23] In connection with Hermione's activism for the house-elves, the BBPM can give educators and their students a way to think about racial capitalism.

By way of a quick recap of Hermione's activist efforts, in *Harry Potter and the Goblet of Fire*, Hermione meets Winky, a house-elf who is forced to reserve a seat for her master even though she is terrified of heights. Then, Hermione learns that house-elves do the domestic tasks—cooking and cleaning—at Hogwarts. She is appalled that they do not receive wages or other benefits. She readily acknowledges these injustices as systemic, and she is so appalled that she starts the Society for the Promotion of Elfish Welfare. Hermione explains S.P.E.W.'s goals to the first two members, Harry and Ron: "Our short-term aims . . . are to secure house-elves fair wages and working conditions. Our long-term aims include changing the law about non-wand use, and trying to get an elf into the Department for the Regulation and Control of Magical Creatures, because they're shockingly underrepresented" (*HP and the GF*, 163). Hermione essentially wants house-elves to be able to participate in capitalism, with wages and the power to negotiate labor conditions, and in democracy, with representation. This analysis considers that Hermione's activism can be read as satire, or at the very least as ineffective because of her youth, ignorance, and misplaced idealism. With that in mind, within the framework I'm proposing here, the S.P.E.W. storyline acts as (a) an opening for understanding the political economy of the world, and (b) a moment of consciousness raising for Hermione.

The existence of S.P.E.W. speaks to the fact that the political economy of the wizarding world is racialized. Cedric Robinson's *Black Marxism* points out how capitalism has always been racialized, and this sparked a genealogy of scholarship in the field of racial capitalism.[24] In describing the term "racial capitalism," Robinson writes that, as "the development, organization, and expansion of capitalist society pursued essentially racial directions, so too did social ideology. As a material force . . . racialism would inevitably permeate the social structures emergent from capitalism."[25] Capitalism reigns in the wizarding world, and as Jodi Melamed proclaims, "capitalism is racial capitalism."[26] The situation with the house-elves can help students understand this.[27]

Hermione's S.P.E.W. efforts are radical in a sense, but not in the way the BBPM advocated. Hermione fights for house-elves to have rights as an economic class. The BBPM, however, argued that by understanding Black people globally as a racialized and oppressed class, the path to liberation requires an end to the capitalist system. In other words, S.P.E.W.'s demands fall more in line with SNCC's desire to be included in the system than with the BBPM's cries for the system's destruction.

This discussion points to recent literature that reads Hermione as Black. Alanna Bennett points out that Hermione is often described by her "bushy" hair, and once in *Harry Potter and the Prisoner of Azkaban*, she is described as "very brown."[28] Artists and fanfiction writers on Tumblr began to paint and write Hermione as a brown or Black young woman. This "racebending" of characters is another way to address the imagination gap.[29] As the racebending works to close the imagination gap in one way, it also connects Hermione to Black women throughout US and British history, thus addressing the imagination gap from a different direction. Hermione is potentially Black, a woman, and Muggle-born, and considering the multiplicity of her identity she can push students to think about oppression in a structural way.

The British Black Power movement was characterized as a movement of hatred. It may be surprising, then, to find that the first line of Egbuna's manifesto *Destroy This Temple* is: "This book is a love letter."[30] Egbuna continues: "To say you hate a murderer is only another way of saying you love the victim of his murder. At least, you love him enough to want him to live. In the same vein, a confession of disgust for the oppressor of a people is a declaration of love for the people who are at the receiving end of this oppression."[31] The BBPM grounded itself in the fury of the oppressed. That rage was mixed with an intense love for themselves and their communities. Out of love for all oppressed people, Egbuna called for an end to systemic oppression, which for him meant the end of the system.

A lack of understanding of love and other powers is Voldemort's biggest weakness. While Hermione believes that the house-elves deserve to participate in the political economy as equals because they are living creatures, and perhaps because of her own oppressed status, whether we consider her Black and Muggle-born or just Muggle-born, Dumbledore sees the house-elves in a different way. He gladly offers Dobby a weekly salary and weekends off, a deal Dobby does not take, but more than that, Dumbledore knows that the elves have power even he does not (*Harry Potter and the Order of the Phoenix*). In Harry's final conversation with Dumbledore (that we know of), in the supernatural scene at King's Cross, Dumbledore reveals to Harry that he was the final Horcrux and that Voldemort's ignorance is ultimately his downfall.

> That which Voldemort does not value, he takes no trouble to comprehend. Of house-elves and children's tales, of love, loyalty, and innocence, Voldemort knows and understands nothing. *Nothing.* That they all have a power beyond his own, a power beyond the reach of any magic, is a truth he has never grasped. (*Harry Potter and the Deathly Hallows*, 709–10)

One of Voldemort's biggest mistakes is allowing his pure-blood supremacy ideology to blind him from seeing the great and different power of goblins and house-elves. Egbuna and other Black Power activists would likely say that white supremacists make the same mistake. Even the term "Black Power" suggests that Black people have an agency and strength that the world does not acknowledge naturally. The movement is partly about harnessing that power for the betterment of oppressed peoples globally. The British Black Power movement can show young people how Voldemort's logic is replicated in the real world and help them imagine different paths forward.

Harry Potter and Women of the Margins

Harry Potter would never have defeated Voldemort without Hermione. In each of the seven books, young readers can point to several moments when Hermione has done an extraordinary amount of labor in order to help Harry on his heroic journey. The world of Harry Potter fandom has thoroughly memed and analyzed the depths of Hermione's contributions. She is, in many respects, positioned as a strong woman, a formidable mind, and a helpmate for Harry and Ron. On the surface, her position is one of support rather than leadership. However, I would like to offer two different ways of looking at Hermione here. First, looking at the *Harry Potter* series through a kind of intersectional lens allows young readers to consider Hermione with more depth.[32] Second, it is important to point out Hermione's shift to activism in the latter half of the series. Hermione, more than any other character, likely because of her identity, which I argue must be considered intersectionally, considers structural oppression in the wizarding world.[33] Third, in line with the central argument of this chapter, considering Black women activists through a similar intersectional lens, alongside an analysis of Hermione's identity and activism, allows young readers and their teachers to not only draw historical parallels to the lessons of the *Harry Potter* series but also to consider the series through a lens informed by Black feminism.

Hermione is best known for her love of books, her savvy research skills in the library, her high expectations of herself and her friends, and her ability to always come through whether Harry needs a spell to win the Triwizard Tournament, the location of the Chamber of Secrets, or a meal in the middle of the forest. However, alongside all those accomplishments, Hermione never forgets (and is never permitted to forget) one aspect of her identity: she is Muggle-born. The age of Voldemort's return, which is also the era of Dumbledore's Army, is a trying at best and fatal, at worst, time, especially for wizards who are Muggle-born. Rowling makes this apparent in *Harry Potter and the Chamber of Secrets* when Hermione is specifically targeted by Tom Riddle because of her parentage. In the final books, Harry, Hermione, and Ron hear stories about Muggle-born wizards who are targeted by Death Eaters. Of all the characters, Hermione is the only one targeted for her biological makeup. Bellatrix Lestrange tortures her—for information and for sport. Riddle attempts to kill her. Throughout the series, she is in danger in a particular way that Rowling does not address fully, as the focus is on Harry.

It is important to note that I do not consider the *Harry Potter* series to be a feminist text. By linking the series to Black feminist organizations, students can engage in a kind of critical thinking that they would not be able to do otherwise. For instance, an understanding of the Black feminist theory of intersectionality as well as the history of Black feminist movements can not only help young readers understand Hermione's character better but also add layers to an understanding of student movements. Kimberlé Crenshaw, who coined and defined the term "intersectionality," argues that identity-based politics are a consistent source of "strength, community, and intellectual development" for oppressed groups, including Black women, who are the focus of Crenshaw's piece "Mapping the Margins: Intersectionality, Identity Politics, and Violence against Women of Color."[34] Crenshaw points out that antiracist and feminist discourses cannot separately account for the intersecting power dynamics faced by women of color. She points to shortcomings in the law, specifically, to illustrate this point. In the tradition of Frances Beal's Double Jeopardy theory and the Combahee River Collective's manifesto, Crenshaw argues that feminism is limited if it does not include race, and antiracist discourse is limited if it does not include gender.[35]

The intersection of race and gender was crucial for the Black women of SNCC. Belinda Robnett, who takes a Black feminist approach to SNCC, notes that much of the literature on women in SNCC focuses on white women and reinforces stereotypes that Black men are sexist and sexually aggressive, white women are delicate and often victimized, and Black women are angry and ugly. The Black women in the group faced intense sexism. Stokely Carmichael famously said, "The only position for women in SNCC is prone."[36] They were also much less likely than others to take on leadership positions that had official titles. Even white women were more likely to have titles than Black women. Nevertheless, Black women did make valuable contributions to the movement, and in many circumstances they prioritized the movement and the circumstances of Black people at large over combating the sexism in the group. These women had an important perspective on racism because of their womanhood.[37] Ella Baker, for instance, is now often cited as the founder of SNCC. Her sharp critical lens as a Black woman was fundamental to the emergence and survival of the group. Understanding the intersection of white supremacy and patriarchy as interlocking forces in the lives of Black women helps us understand not only why they made the decisions they did at the time but also why, in the annals of history, they have been relegated to the role of sidekick.

Like the Black women of SNCC, Hermione never has a title that gives her power. She is not "The Boy Who Lived" or even a Weasley, a name often mocked but still associated with a notable pure-blood family. The steps she takes to keep Harry alive, whether it be on the Quidditch field or in the Triwizard Tournament, often go unrecognized publicly. Furthermore, her Muggle-born status alongside the patriarchy that is still very much present in the wizarding world make her particularly vulnerable. Despite this, she, more than any other character, approaches oppression in the wizarding world as structural. We see this when she creates S.P.E.W. While her activism may be misguided and ineffective, it is still important to consider as early moments of consciousness raising, impeded by untampered idealism. The fact that Hermione's idea remains in the realm of satire demonstrates the limitations of the Harry Potter narrative to address oppression in a structural, systemic way.[38] History, then, can pick up where the series leaves off. Hermione is able to make progress with Harry and Ron only on an individual level. Still, I argue that Hermione's vulnerable status and complex identity allow her to see the world through a lens that is unavailable to Harry and Ron, similar to the Black women of SNCC.

The *Harry Potter* series also offers students in high school and at the undergraduate level an entry point for understanding consciousness raising, a topic that could then be bolstered by an engagement with the histories of Black feminist organizations. The Combahee River Collective's history, writings, and ideology in particular are accessible to young people. This collective was one of several Black feminist organizations that operated during the late 1960s through the 1980s. It started in Boston with a few principal organizers, including Beverly and Barbara Smith. The Smith sisters' first consciousness-raising experiences were during the civil rights movement. Later, Barbara Smith got involved in the antiwar movement.[39] Consciousness raising, which I think of as increasing and deepening one's understanding of one's individual and communal position in society, became one of the central activities of Combahee.

Harry Potter can be useful in prompting students to understand how consciousness raising might work in their own lives. Imagine an assignment in which students must wonder what cause Hermione or Harry will decide to take up in their post-Voldemort world. When presented with this prompt, students might wonder if (and why) Hermione might return to S.P.E.W. with a different mind-set, especially if students themselves are approaching it with a better understanding of political economy. Students may also wonder how discrimination against Muggle-born wizards might continue and how Hermione, Harry, and Ron can live their lives fighting that discrimination. In other words, students can be prompted to read the fight against Voldemort as the young characters' first consciousness-raising moment—similar to how Barbara and Beverly Smith were shaped by the civil rights movement.

In the Combahee River Collective's statement, they describe how they came together:

> When we first started meeting early in 1974 after the NBFO [National Black Feminist Organization] first eastern regional conference, we did not have a strategy for organizing, or even a focus. We just wanted to see what we had. After a period of months of not meeting, we began to meet again late in the year and started doing an intense variety of consciousness-raising. The overwhelming feeling that we had is that after years and years we had finally found each other.[40]

The statement emphasizes that the people involved had found community. Many of the women in the group came to Combahee because they did not fit into other groups or movements. Having a tight-knit, like-minded community was critical to Combahee's work over the long term.[41]

The community found in Combahee and other feminist organizations, like the Third World Women's Alliance and the National Black Feminist Organization, can give students real-life examples of what youth organizations, like Dumbledore's Army, can grow into. Again, this is an instance in which the magic of the fantasy world can create an opening for students to better understand on-the-ground activism and concepts of structural inequity. The Combahee River Collective's statement and history complement the literary analysis and prompt students to do some consciousness raising of their own.

Black feminist organizations, SNCC, and the BBPM are not the only social movements with potential connections to the *Harry Potter* series. The Hogwarts faculty's struggles with Dolores Umbridge and the steps students take to resist may feel reminiscent of the student activism that fueled the Third World Liberation Front's work to create an ethnic studies curriculum. Hermione's S.P.E.W. could also connect to British labor movements. The White Rose group in Nazi Germany, the Soweto uprising in 1976 in South Africa, and the student activism during the Arab Spring are other examples of historical social movements that can close a bit of the imagination gap for students. Moreover, in the years since the Black Lives Matter movement began, Afrofuturist literature has made explicit ties to the movement. Victor LaValle's graphic novel *Destroyer*, Ta-Nehisi Coates's comic series *Black Panther and the Crew*, and Tomi Adeyemi's *Children of Blood and Bone* are all examples of science fiction and fantasy that make direct connections to the Black Lives Matter movement. This is to say, what I propose here is a framework, an interdisciplinary structure, that pulls fantasy and social movements together to strengthen each other's pedagogical power.

I have illustrated the compatibility between the *Harry Potter* series and SNCC as a historically specific example of a student movement powered by love, and between the *Harry Potter* series and the British Black Power movement, which equated race and class. I've rooted this argument in Black feminist principles about consciousness raising. SNCC sought to create a movement consciousness within the group and a consciousness of love outside of the group in order to combat their oppression. The BBPM sought to center radical thought and action in a Black consciousness. Black feminist organizations sought to push radical politics to be more intersectional. Rowling's *Harry Potter* series offers teachers a pathway to help students make the leap from love as individual, from person to person, to love as a movement, from group to systems.

Notes

1. Du Bois, *The Souls of Black Folk*.
2. Pratt, "Identity: Skin Blood Heart," 16.
3. The specific texts I mean here are: Du Bois, *The Souls of Black Folk*; Haraway, "Situated Knowledges"; and Pratt, "Identity: Skin Blood Heart."
4. SNCC Digital Gateway, "Sit-Ins in Greensboro."
5. Green, "Revealing Discrimination"; and Patterson, "Kreacher's Lament."
6. Mendlesohn, "Crowning the King."
7. Horne, "Harry and the Other," 81.
8. Horne, "Harry and the Other."
9. Horne, "Harry and the Other," 79.
10. Thomas, *The Dark Fantastic*; and Adichie, "The Danger of a Single Story."
11. Thomas, *The Dark Fantastic*, 8–9.
12. C. Myers, "The Apartheid of Children's Literature"; and W. D. Myers, "Where Are the People of Color in Children's Books?"
13. The We Need Diverse Books movement has taken up the challenge issued by Walter Dean Myers and has helped promote and fund the creation of a variety of diverse books for children and young adults.
14. Carson, *The Student Voice 1960–1965*, 2.
15. Carson, *The Student Voice 1960–1965*.
16. Carson, *The Student Voice 1960–1965*, 5.
17. Bishop, "Mirrors, Windows, and Sliding Glass Doors."
18. Blackness is different in the British context. In the United States, many of the Black liberation movements have centered the experiences of the descendants of slaves. Even when African and Caribbean immigrants are involved, the slavery narrative dominates. For the British, as Egbuna suggests, Black Britons are usually African and Caribbean immigrants, often from countries that Britain had colonized. Southeast Asians are also

sometimes considered Black in Britain. See Mirza, *Black British Feminism*; and Owusu, *Black British Culture and Society*.

19. Part of the history of the British Black Power movement has been dramatized in the Sky Atlantic television series *Guerrilla*.

20. Angelo, "The Black Panthers in London"; and Bunce and Field, "Obi B. Egbuna, C. L. R. James and the Birth of Black Power."

21. Egbuna, "Destroy This Temple."

22. Egbuna, "Destroy This Temple," 69.

23. Angelo, "The Black Panthers in London."

24. Robinson, *Black Marxism*.

25. Melamed, "Racial Capitalism," 77.

26. Melamed, "Racial Capitalism," 77.

27. For more readings on racial capitalism, see Davis, *Women, Race & Class*; S. Hall, "Cultural Studies and Its Theoretical Legacies"; and Kelley, *Race Rebels*.

28. Bennett, "What a 'Racebent' Hermione Granger Really Represents."

29. Bennett, "What a 'Racebent' Hermione Granger Really Represents"; and Thomas, *The Dark Fantastic*.

30. Egbuna, *Destroy This Temple*, 9.

31. Egbuna, *Destroy This Temple*, 9.

32. Combahee River Collective, "A Black Feminist Statement"; and Crenshaw, "Mapping the Margins."

33. Christina M. Chica's analysis in her chapter in this volume, "The Magical (Racial) Contract: Understanding the Wizarding World of Harry Potter through Whiteness," reinforces the idea of reading a kind of wizarding supremacy into the structures of the magical world of Harry Potter.

34. Crenshaw, "Mapping the Margins," 1242.

35. For more readings on intersectionality, see Bambara and Traylor, *The Black Woman*; Beal, "Double Jeopardy"; Collins and Bilge, *Intersectionality*; Nash, "Practicing Love," 1; and Nash, "Re-Thinking Intersectionality."

36. Lewis, Aydin, and Powell, *March*; and Robnett, *How Long? How Long?*

37. Crenshaw, "Mapping the Margins"; Ransby, *Ella Baker and the Black Freedom Movement*; and Robnett, *How Long? How Long?*

38. Similarly, Jackie C. Horne also questions the *Harry Potter* series' effectiveness in prompting antiracism in her chapter in this volume, "Harry and the Other: Multiculturalism and Social Justice Anti-Racism in J. K. Rowling's *Harry Potter* Series."

39. Springer, *Living for the Revolution*.

40. Combahee River Collective, "A Black Feminist Statement," 216.

41. Springer, *Living for the Revolution*.

Bibliography

Adichie, Chimamanda Ngozi. "The Danger of a Single Story." TED Talks, July 2009. https://www.ted.com/talks/chimamanda_adichie_the_danger_of_a_single_story.

Angelo, Anne-Marie. "'Black Oppressed People All over the World Are One': The British Black Panthers' Grassroots Internationalism, 1969–73." *Journal of Civil and Human Rights* 4, no. 1 (Spring–Summer 2018): 64–97. doi:10.5406/jcivihumarigh.4.1.0064.

Angelo, Anne-Marie. "The Black Panthers in London, 1967–1972: A Diasporic Struggle Navigates the Black Atlantic." *Radical History Review*, no. 103 (Winter 2009): 17–35. doi:10.1215/01636545-2008-030.

Baggett, David, and Shawn E. Klein, eds. *Harry Potter and Philosophy: If Aristotle Ran Hogwarts*. Chicago: Open Court, 2004.

Bambara, Toni Cade, and Eleanor W. Traylor, eds. *The Black Woman: An Anthology*. New York: Washington Square Press, 2005.

Beal, Frances M. "Double Jeopardy: To Be Black and Female." *Meridians: Feminism, Race, Transnationalism* 8, no. 2 (2008): 166–76.

Belcher, Catherine L., and Becky Herr Stephenson. *Teaching Harry Potter: The Power of Imagination in Multicultural Classrooms*. New York: Palgrave Macmillan, 2011.

Bennett, Alanna. "What a 'Racebent' Hermione Granger Really Represents." BuzzFeed, February 1, 2015. https://www.buzzfeed.com/alannabennett/what-a-racebent-hermione -granger-really-represen-d2yp.

Bishop, Rudine Sims. "Mirrors, Windows, and Sliding Glass Doors." *Perspectives: Choosing and Using Books for the Classroom* 6, no. 3 (Summer 1990).

Bunce, R. E. R., and Paul Field. "Obi B. Egbuna, C. L. R. James and the Birth of Black Power in Britain: Black Radicalism in Britain 1967–72." *Twentieth Century British History* 22, no. 3 (September 2011): 391–414. doi:10.1093/tcbh/hwq047.

Byrd, Jodi A. *The Transit of Empire: Indigenous Critiques of Colonialism*. Minneapolis: University of Minnesota Press, 2011.

Carson, Clayborne. *In Struggle: SNCC and the Black Awakening of the 1960s*. Cambridge, MA: Harvard University Press, 2001.

Carson, Clayborne, ed. *The Student Voice 1960–1965: Periodical of the Student Nonviolent Coordinating Committee*. Westport, CT: Meckler, 1990.

Cha-Jua, Sundiata Keita, and Clarence Lang. "The 'Long Movement' as Vampire: Temporal and Spatial Fallacies in Recent Black Freedom Studies." *Journal of African American History* 92, no. 2 (Spring 2007): 265–88. http://link.galegroup.com/apps/doc/A166016932 /LitRC?sid=googlescholar.

Collier-Thomas, Bettye, and V. P. Franklin, eds. *Sisters in the Struggle: African American Women in the Civil Rights–Black Power Movement*. New York: New York University Press, 2001.

Collins, Patricia Hill, and Sirma Bilge. *Intersectionality*. Cambridge: Polity Press, 2016.

Combahee River Collective. "A Black Feminist Statement." In *This Bridge Called My Back: Writings by Radical Women of Color*, edited by Cherríe Moraga and Gloria Anzaldua, 210–18. New York: Kitchen Table: Women of Color Press, 1983.

Cooper, Brittney. *Eloquent Rage: A Black Feminist Discovers Her Superpower*. New York: St. Martin's Press, 2019.

Crenshaw, Kimberlé. "Mapping the Margins: Intersectionality, Identity Politics, and Violence against Women of Color (1994)." In *Violence against Women: Classic Papers*, edited by Raquel Kennedy Bergen, Jeffrey L. Edleson, and Claire M. Renzetti, 282–313. Auckland: Pearson Education New Zealand, 2005.

Davis, Angela Y. *Women, Race & Class*. New York: Vintage Books, 1983.

Delp, Lorraine. "16 Hermione Memes Only True 'Harry Potter' Fans Will Appreciate." BookBub, September 18, 2017. https://www.bookbub.com/blog/hermione-memes.

Dowd Hall, Jacquelyn. "The Long Civil Rights Movement and the Political Uses of the Past." *Journal of American History* 91, no. 4 (March 2005): 1233–63. doi:10.2307/3660172.

Du Bois, W. E. B. *The Souls of Black Folk*. New York: Barnes and Noble, 2014.

Egbuna, Obi. *Destroy This Temple*. New York: William Morrow, 1971.

Egbuna, Obi. "Destroy This Temple." In *Black British Culture and Society: A Text Reader*, edited by Kwesi Owusu, 58–69. Abingdon, Oxon., England: Routledge, 2000.

Green, Amy M. "Revealing Discrimination: Social Hierarchy and the Exclusion/ Enslavement of the Other in the Harry Potter Novels." *Looking Glass* 13, no. 3 (2009). https://ojs.latrobe.edu.au/ojs/index.php/tlg/article/view/162.

Hall, Jordana. "Embracing the Abject Other: The Carnival Imagery of *Harry Potter*." *Children's Literature in Education* 42, no. 1 (March 2011): 70–89. doi:10.1007/s10583 -010-9123-y.

Hall, Stuart. "Cultural Studies and Its Theoretical Legacies." In *Stuart Hall: Critical Dialogues in Cultural Studies*, edited by David Morley and Kuan-Hsing Chen, 262–75. Abingdon, Oxon., England: Routledge, 1996.

Hall, Stuart. *The Fateful Triangle: Race, Ethnicity, Nation*. Cambridge, MA: Harvard University Press, 2017.

Hall, Stuart. "Gramsci's Relevance for the Study of Race and Ethnicity." *Journal of Communication Inquiry* 10, no. 2 (June 1986): 5–27. doi:10.1177/019685998601000202.

Haraway, Donna. "Situated Knowledges: The Science Question in Feminism and the Privilege of Partial Perspective." *Feminist Studies* 14, no. 3 (Autumn 1988): 575–99. doi:10.2307/3178066.

hooks, bell. *Killing Rage: Ending Racism*. New York: Henry Holt, 1996.

Horne, Jackie C. "Harry and the Other: Answering the Race Question in J. K. Rowling's *Harry Potter*." *The Lion and the Unicorn* 34, no. 1 (January 2010): 76–104. doi:10.1353 /uni.0.0488.

Huang, Viola H. "Between Protest, Compromise, and Education for Radical Change: Black Power Schools in Harlem in the Late 1960s." PhD diss., Columbia University, 2019.

Hughes, Sarah. "The Story of the British Black Panthers through Race, Politics, Love and Power." *Guardian*, April 9, 2017. https://www.theguardian.com/world/2017/apr/09/british -black-panthers-drama-photography-exhibition.

Jay, Michelle. "Critical Race Theory, Multicultural Education, and the Hidden Curriculum of Hegemony." *Multicultural Perspectives* 5, no. 4 (October 2003): 3–9. doi:10.1207 /S15327892MCP0504_2.

Kelley, Robin D. G. *Hammer and Hoe: Alabama Communists during the Great Depression*. Chapel Hill: University of North Carolina Press, 2015.

Kelley, Robin D. G. *Race Rebels: Culture, Politics, and the Black Working Class*. New York: Free Press, 1994.

Kellner, Rivka Temima. "J. K. Rowling's Ambivalence towards Feminism: House Elves— Women in Disguise—in the 'Harry Potter' Books." *Midwest Quarterly* 51, no. 4 (Summer 2010): 367–83.

Kendi, Ibram X. *How to Be an Antiracist*. New York: One World, 2019.

Lafferty, Karen. "'What Are You Reading?' How School Libraries Can Promote Racial Diversity in Multicultural Literature." *Multicultural Perspectives* 16, no. 4 (October 2014): 203–9.

Lewis, John, Andrew Aydin, and Nate Powell. *March*. Marietta, GA: Top Shelf Productions, 2013.

Littlechild, Chris. "Harry Potter: 25 Hilarious Hermione Memes That Make Us Want to Go Back to Hogwarts." The Gamer, May 31, 2018. https://www.thegamer.com/harry-potter -hermione-memes-hilarious-funny-go-hogwarts/.

Melamed, Jodi. "Racial Capitalism." *Critical Ethnic Studies* 1, no. 1 (Spring 2015): 76–85. doi:10.5749/jcritethnstud.1.1.0076.

Mendlesohn, Farah. "Crowning the King: Harry Potter and the Construction of Authority." *Journal of the Fantastic in the Arts* 12, no. 3 (2001): 287–308.

Mirza, Heidi Safia, ed. *Black British Feminism: A Reader*. London: Routledge, 1997.

Murray, Jonathan. "Greensboro Sit-In." North Carolina History Project, 2016. https://north carolinahistory.org/encyclopedia/greensboro-sit-in/.

Myers, Christopher. "The Apartheid of Children's Literature." *New York Times*, March 15, 2014. https://www.nytimes.com/2014/03/16/opinion/sunday/the-apartheid-of-childrens -literature.html.

Myers, Walter Dean. "Where Are the People of Color in Children's Books?" *New York Times*, March 15, 2014. https://www.nytimes.com/2014/03/16/opinion/sunday/where-are-the -people-of-color-in-childrens-books.html.

Nash, Jennifer C. "Practicing Love: Black Feminism, Love-Politics, and Post-Intersectionality." *Meridians: Feminism, Race, Transnationalism* 11, no. 2 (2011): 1–24.

Nash, Jennifer C. "Re-Thinking Intersectionality." *Feminist Review* 89, no. 1 (2008): 1–15.

Ostry, Elaine. "Accepting Mudbloods: The Ambivalent Social Vision of J. K. Rowling's Fairy Tales." In *Reading Harry Potter: Critical Essays*, edited by Giselle Liza Anatol, 89–102. Westport, CT: Praeger, 2003.

Owusu, Kwesi, ed. *Black British Culture and Society: A Text Reader*. Abingdon, Oxon., England: Routledge, 2000.

Patterson, Steven W. "Kreacher's Lament: S.P.E.W. as a Parable on Discrimination, Indifference, and Social Justice." In *Harry Potter and Philosophy: If Aristotle Ran Hogwarts*, edited by David Baggett and Shawn E. Klein, 105–18. Chicago: Open Court, 2004.

Perry, Phyllis Jean. *Teaching Fantasy Novels: From "The Hobbit" to "Harry Potter and the Goblet of Fire."* Portsmouth, NH: Teacher Ideas Press, 2003.

Pratt, Minnie Bruce. "Identity: Skin Blood Heart." *Women's Studies Quarterly* 11, no. 3 (Fall 1983): 16.

Raiford, Leigh. "'Come Let Us Build a New World Together': SNCC and Photography of the Civil Rights Movement." *American Quarterly* 59, no. 4 (December 2007): 1129–57. doi:10.1353/aq.2007.0085.

Ransby, Barbara. *Ella Baker and the Black Freedom Movement: A Radical Democratic Vision.* Chapel Hill: University of North Carolina Press, 2007.

Robinson, Cedric J. *Black Marxism: The Making of the Black Radical Tradition.* Chapel Hill: University of North Carolina Press, 2000.

Robnett, Belinda. *How Long? How Long? African-American Women in the Struggle for Civil Rights.* New York: Oxford University Press, 1997.

Rowling, J. K. *Harry Potter and the Chamber of Secrets.* New York: Scholastic, 1999.

Rowling, J. K. *Harry Potter and the Deathly Hallows.* New York: Scholastic, 2007.

Rowling, J. K. *Harry Potter and the Goblet of Fire.* New York: Scholastic, 2000.

Rowling, J. K. *Harry Potter and the Half-Blood Prince.* New York: Scholastic, 2005.

Rowling, J. K. *Harry Potter and the Order of the Phoenix.* New York: Scholastic, 2003.

Rowling, J. K. *Harry Potter and the Prisoner of Azkaban.* New York: Scholastic, 1999.

Rowling, J. K. *Harry Potter and the Sorcerer's Stone.* New York: Scholastic, 1998.

SNCC Digital Gateway. "Sit-Ins in Greensboro." SNCC Digital Gateway, 2015. https:// snccdigital.org/events/sit-ins-greensboro/.

Springer, Kimberly. *Living for the Revolution: Black Feminist Organizations, 1968–1980.* Durham, NC: Duke University Press, 2005.

Springer, Kimberly, ed. *Still Lifting, Still Climbing: Contemporary African American Women's Activism.* New York: New York University Press, 1999.

Stoper, Emily. *The Student Nonviolent Coordinating Committee: The Growth of Radicalism in a Civil Rights Organization.* Brooklyn: Carlson Publishing, 1989.

Stornaiuolo, Amy, and Ebony Elizabeth Thomas. "Restorying as Political Action: Authoring Resistance through Youth Media Arts." *Learning, Media and Technology* 43, no. 4 (October 2018): 345–58. doi:10.1080/17439884.2018.1498354.

Strimel, Courtney B. "The Politics of Terror: Rereading Harry Potter." *Children's Literature in Education* 35, no. 1 (March 2004): 35–52. doi:10.1023/B:CLID.0000018899.06267.11.

Thomas, Ebony Elizabeth. *The Dark Fantastic: Race and the Imagination from Harry Potter to the Hunger Games.* New York: New York University Press, 2019.

Whited, Lana. "1492, 1942, 1992: The Theme of Race in the Harry Potter Series." *Looking Glass* 10, no. 1 (2006). https://ojs.latrobe.edu.au/ojs/index.php/tlg/article/view/97.

Wild, Rosalind Eleanor. "'Black Was the Colour of Our Fight': Black Power in Britain, 1955–1976." PhD thesis, University of Sheffield, 2008.

Zinn, Howard. *SNCC: The New Abolitionists.* Boston: Beacon Press, 1965.

Teaching Harry Potter as an "Other"

An African American Professor's Journey in Teaching Harry Potter in the College Composition Classroom

Susan E. Howard

When approaching the teaching of any work of literature, I typically have a reader's response critical approach to the text. It is impossible to separate myself from who I am and where I come from with respect to the plots and character developments of any text, especially given my racial and sexual representations as an African American woman who also happens to be a college composition instructor for a diverse group of students at an open admissions college. What are the possible implications of the literature as it relates to my status as an "Other" in American society and culture? As an English professor teaching a themed composition course based on the *Harry Potter* books for three years in a statewide community college system, I am increasingly focusing on what the J. K. Rowling series insinuates about race, discrimination, and blood caste systems, and how the series can teach students to become agents of social change in a way that incorporates acceptance of differences. The good news is that the students do not mind this agenda one bit. Instead, they gravitate toward it as my content focus allows students to apply the events and lessons of one of their favorite book series to concepts that can affect their behavior toward "Others" in the real world. Teaching Harry Potter in the college composition classroom can be a tool for encouraging students to be agents of social change as they confront and modify their views about difference as it relates to the Other. This autoethnographic essay examines what it means to be an African American professor who uses the *Harry Potter* series in the classroom to encourage students to review their treatment and behavior toward stigmatized groups so they can become more inclusive—much like Harry Potter and his friends.

Teaching a Harry Potter–themed composition course was an experiment at first, but given the continued interest of students who want to take the course, it remains a popular course offering at Ivy Tech Community College in Fort Wayne, Indiana, much to the dismay of some faculty and staff such as academic advisers who frequently field questions from students interested in the course. Indeed, sometimes the Harry Potter class fills within a matter of days from the start of course registration. Given some of the themes about the treatment of stigmatized groups in Rowling's books, I realized that I had an opportunity to address the role of "the Other" in the series. After all, I had made presentations about the series at Harry Potter conferences in the United States and London and even written a scholarly article about how the enslavement of Rowling's house-elves matched up with the experience of African slaves, which appears in the book *Harry Potter's World Wide Influence*, edited by Diana Patterson. I was confident that I could tackle transforming the subject of otherness in the series into lessons suitable for a college composition class.

But I had encountered some problems using the *Harry Potter* books for students in some classrooms. I first attempted to use the books in a creative writing after-school program at Houston's Project Row Houses, located in the city's low-income and predominantly Black Third Ward district. My introduction of the series to the elementary school students met with disapproval from parents. Many parents expressed concerns about the use of witchcraft in the novels, and advocating the books in the face of that kind of opposition was not a challenge I wanted to take on at that time. But when I used the books to teach my creative writing classes to Latino youngsters via the Houston-based Writers in the Schools program, I faced no such protests. It did interest me that the Harry Potter craze had apparently not taken hold with any of the African American children I taught. Instead, they were more inspired by creative works with urban settings and mostly Black characters. When local children flooded the bookstores in Houston at midnight book sale parties on the release of the latest *Harry Potter* book, I was discouraged by the fact that there was rarely a Black child in view. Was there a reason why the Harry Potter phenomenon did not seem to impact Black youth? I became dedicated to a mission to familiarize student readers with the series' message about tolerance, especially as it related to stigmatized groups representative of the Other.

The seeming reluctance of the Black community's embrace of the *Harry Potter* series in the late twentieth and early twenty-first centuries was curious to me, as I thought that the plot of the first book at least was irresistible. I was always attracted to fantasies that featured other worlds, such as the Hogwarts School of Witchcraft and Wizardry. While reading the books, I was always on the lookout for any signs of multiculturalism, diversity, or inclusion. I savored every mention of Dean Thomas, Angelina Johnson, Lee Jordan, Cho Chang, Blaise Zabini, and the Patil twins. Such a racially diverse student body of "Others" is noticeably absent in Thomas Hughes's *Tom Brown's School Days* and other British boarding school tales. Rowling's most prominent characters may not be racial minorities, but each minority character plays a role in establishing that Hogwarts is not just for white students only. Even though it can be argued that the racial minorities in the *Harry Potter* series are mere tokens, I found their presence to be a necessity, as for any writing that seeks to reflect a twenty-first-century readership.

It did not take much effort to bring my specific interest in the multicultural aspects of the series into the classroom. Discussion about racial difference would take care of itself when discussing Mudbloods versus pure-bloods. But I would be lying if I did not admit to having my own personal interest in promoting an instructive agenda about race and difference as represented by the experiences of the Boy Who Lived. Harry Potter is an outcast within his own family. African Americans are outcasts within the "family" of Americans. He is mistreated, abused, and constantly on the defensive due to no fault of his own. Instead, his treatment, and that of many African Americans, is based on what they represent: the Other.

Before I could design a course around the *Harry Potter* books, I had to address the course objectives, which required the teaching of everything from communication theory to the use of argumentation. How would the Harry Potter–themed course offer students the same type of instruction that they might receive in a typical college freshman composition course? That was the most pressing question when the course was first advertised on our campus. Some instructors applauded the idea of the class, thinking it was a great way to arouse student interest and perhaps increase retention rates. Many professors, however, expressed skepticism and suggested that my course would lack academic rigor, considering the subject matter of Harry Potter alone. They argued that the series was juvenile at best and had questionable application in a college classroom. Peter Hunt maintains that "because children's books have been largely beneath the notice of intellectual and cultural gurus, they are (apparently) blissfully free of the 'oughts'—what we ought to think and say about them."[1] It was clear from the questions I received from some colleagues that Harry Potter was too lowbrow for a college audience, or at least not rigorous enough for a class designed to teach students how to write academic essays.

"How can you make sure they learn the same things as students in a regular freshman composition class?" That was the question I fielded the most from other faculty. It felt as though I was being interrogated by Harold Bloom, a notable literary critic of the *Harry Potter* series and someone who would no doubt bristle at the idea of the series being the fodder for a college-level composition course.[2] Yes, on the first day of class, I engage in activities meant to amuse my students. For instance, students inspect my Kingsley Shacklebolt replica wand (I have always liked this Black character's last name and what it represents—the bolt from shackles, a clear reference to the character's African slave ancestors), and they divide themselves into their respective Hogwarts Houses. Students are required to read Bloom's diatribe against the *Harry Potter* series and respond to it in their first assignment, the personal literacy narrative. The objective is not only to give them an exercise in critical reading and critical thinking but to introduce them to the prominent naysayers of the *Harry Potter* books and the books' success. For most students, not only is the introduction to Bloom the first time they have ever heard of the critic, but it also alerts them to those who view the series as unworthy as a college course offering.

Also at issue is the concept of fun. When some hear that word associated with a college course, they may conclude that the class in question is lightweight or lacks necessary rigor for a freshman composition course. I do not set out to make class *fun*. Instead, I like to think that while *engaging* students, fun may result from that process. "It's definitely not a fluff class," Hannah said.[3] "The thought going into it was, 'Oh, it should be pretty easy. I'm really familiar with the books,' but I'm being challenged in a whole new way." Hannah then went on to, well, complain about the fact that I required students to read all seven books in the course of a sixteen-week semester, which she noted as being overwhelming, especially when coupled with the scholarly articles I also assigned to read. I was later saddened when one student told me that my class took away her joy over the *Harry Potter* series. She noted that she had not expected the class to entail hard work, such as writing an informative paper about how Harry Potter had changed the world that required students to conduct an interview, to teach them how to do field research and create primary sources. Or that there would be so much reading of scholarly peer-reviewed articles, intended to establish the basis for their argument in their final persuasive paper.

The Harry Potter–themed composition course can challenge ideas associated with a discourse of the Other, as noted by Perry Nodelman in his essay "The Other: Orientalism, Colonialism, and Children's Literature." In this article, Nodelman criticizes the presence of Orientalism (as established by Edward Said) in children's literature and questions the inherently adult-centered aspect of much children's literature, in "the vast majority" of which "children share the message that, despite one's dislike of the constraints one feels there, home is still the best, the safest place to be."[4] This statement focuses on a topic—the symbolism of "home"—that is challenged by Rowling in the *Harry Potter* series because, apart from the homes of so-called blood traitors like the Weasleys, the private residences of other characters, such as Draco Malfoy and Harry, are places where prejudice and discrimination reign. In other words, "home" is where racism is taught and then spread through the actions of the children produced by such environments.

This idea of home as the point of hostility toward the Other is immediate in the *Harry Potter* series when the reader is introduced to the Dursleys, who, first and foremost, value normalcy above all else. But their "normal" existence is distinguished by a dislike for any form of difference in others, and this is made apparent by Professor McGonagall's observations of the Dursleys, specifically Vernon Dursley's dislike for and disapproval of anyone who seems to be out of step with the norm. But my emphasis on teaching the series' lessons about prejudice and the importance of accepting differences in others centers around the events portrayed in *Harry Potter and the Chamber of Secrets*.

> "No one asked your opinion, you filthy little Mudblood," he spat. (*HP and the CS*, 112)

This one statement from Draco to Hermione Granger dramatically changed my opinion of the series. Yes, I knew that Draco was an elitist and a bully based on his characterization in *Harry Potter and the Sorcerer's Stone*, but now I knew something about him that struck home for me as an African American woman. His verbal attack on Hermione was racist and discriminatory. While I had yet to understand what a "Mudblood" was at this point in the novel, I knew enough that it was a racial slur of some sort, especially given the immediate reaction from the surrounding members of the Gryffindor Quidditch team. This passage marks the point at which I argue that Rowling is addressing "the Other" in her work. There is no better way to strike at the heart of a racial minority than to create such a scenario, with which too many of us can relate. To call Hermione a "Mudblood" is tantamount to calling a Black person a n----r. This single sentence from Draco prompted me to identify the books as possible tools to encourage students to become agents of social change by attacking prejudicial behaviors; indeed, the series pointedly addresses issues of race through the portrayal of bloodline conflicts within the wizarding world of Harry Potter.

I argue to students that the *Harry Potter* book that has had the greatest impact on me as a member of a marginalized group is the second one. I use the method of dialogic teaching to entice students to present their own experiences or feelings about how *Harry Potter and the Chamber of Secrets*, in particular, can be a vehicle for advocating social change. I liken the sting of humiliation of Hermione being called a "Mudblood" to my own experience being called a n----r for the first time by a white classmate when I was a student in elementary school. The quotation hit me that hard. I also could not avoid comparing the treatment of Dobby, the house-elf, with that of African slaves. The *Harry Potter* series had changed for me from being a set of lively children's novels about the fight between good and evil to also being about racism, prejudice, and discrimination. While my students learn about the hero's quest and how the *Harry Potter* series follows that recipe, they also see that the fight against prejudice toward those who are "Other" is a part of a chivalric code for the protagonist and his friends. Draco is cast easily as the bully whose pure-blood belief and value system makes him synonymous with a white supremacist in the Muggle world. Students have no problem making that connection. Not only are the Malfoys akin to white supremacists but they are also slave owners, which gives instructors ways to discuss how the *Harry Potter* series is connected to themes of modern-day slavery.

As an African American woman in academia, I am obligated to address the concepts of racial inequality in our society, and the *Harry Potter* books are useful tools to teach such lessons.

I am a former journalist, and some of that background seeps into the objective of some assignments I hand out. In one exercise, my students must pretend to be reporters for the *Daily Prophet* and write reports about events that occurred in the book, such as writing a eulogy or an obituary for Albus Dumbledore. What is the academic value of that? It can teach students how to write in a different genre, for a specific audience, and how to appeal to a certain type of occasion. I tell them, God forbid, you may have to write a eulogy someday. Let's practice what that process is about for academic purposes. What does it mean to characterize someone's entire life in an informative tribute?

My students are dedicated fans of the *Harry Potter* series. Some have tattoos based on symbols from the series, like the one for the Deathly Hallows, while others wear Harry Potter–themed clothing. My students are aware that Harry Potter links them with other fans around the globe; while some have been at one of the movies, a Wizarding World theme park, or a Harry Potter convention, many have never been in a room full of Harry Potter fans. Most of the students have interacted with the Pottermore website and thus even have a Patronus based on what was assigned to them by the website. I establish myself as a Harry Potter nerd to ensure a certain comfort level with the class. I talk about the conventions I have attended in the United States and England, and the camaraderie achieved at an all-night reading party of *Harry Potter and the Deathly Hallows* at the University of Westminster in London when that book was released. I sometimes participate in a Harry Potter fan group on Facebook. I have been to the Harry Potter amusement park in Orlando, well, a few times. By the time I am finished detailing the Harry Potter–related activities I have participated in, my students appear comfortable in knowing that their instructor is just as much of a fan of the series as they are.

One topic for the literacy narrative, the first assignment in the course, is to write how one book or the whole series has had a significant impact on the student's life. The *Harry Potter* series is the focus for the Harry Potter course, but students in my standard composition courses also often write about Harry Potter. I have now read more than one hundred accounts from students about how they believe the *Harry Potter* series has affected their lives. I also purposely steer students into addressing how and why the series might be deemed didactic (which is usually a new word for the students). Frequently, students address how Harry seems to be a champion for equality and social justice. Many students' views are bolstered by the assigned scholarly readings for the course. Students are required to read one article with scholarly relevance per week, including a peer-reviewed article by Loris Vezzali and colleagues about how the *Harry Potter* novels reduce prejudice, given a reader's embrace of Harry's affinity for empathizing with stigmatized groups such as Mudbloods, house-elves, and the like.[5] The goal is to transform students from being passive about the issues Rowling presents in her *Harry Potter* novels to being active in challenging or acting against the discrimination of stigmatized groups in their own world. The *Harry Potter* books can inspire, instruct, and encourage students to speak up and take action about issues related to social inequalities. As Christina Lane Cappy notes in her article about how teachers in South Africa work as agents of social change: "[E]ducation should encourage students to *reflect* on social issues so that they become *responsible citizens* and leaders that uphold the values of *human rights*."[6]

My teaching style and philosophy challenge my current teaching standards to create new principles designed to engage students while also maintaining a commitment to "everyday advocacy." The latter term refers to a teaching strategy in which educators go beyond pedagogical content knowledge to become active change makers. No, I am not marching in the streets or going to my state capital, Indianapolis, to face the state legislature to pass specific laws that impact educators and their students. Instead, I have become an everyday advocate of diversity, social justice, social change, and even behavioral science. And I reach this goal primarily via a bespectacled orphan boy whose creator has produced a franchise worth more than a billion dollars: Harry Potter. Everyday advocacy is mostly teacher centered and driven, but I have taken the strategy of advocating for social change by using the *Harry Potter* series as fodder for course work that allows students to learn more about themselves and the world they live in, and how that can relate to something they have read. This is why one of the early assignments in the class is to reflect on how the *Harry Potter* series can be used as an agent for social change, which the students write about from their own first-person perspectives.

Perhaps the most challenging assignment for the students is the required essay test as one of the learning objectives for English composition. Students must select a chapter from *Harry Potter and the Prisoner of Azkaban* and consider it from a rhetorical perspective. Writing prompts like "What might different readers feel or think after reading this chapter? Why?"; "What does the writer want you think about the events of the chapter?"; "What is the theme of the chapter?"; "What is the writer's attitude toward the subject? How do you know this?"; and "What is the purpose of the chapter?" are some of the questions students can choose to respond to with their analysis. Students can easily narrate the events of a chapter, but it is challenging to engage in critical thinking about purpose, audience, content, and the writer's stance. A great deal of brainstorming for this assignment occurs during class discussions as students present their positions about the selected chapter. During the following week, they take the essay test, which includes a formal outline and which they must complete within three hours.

Other assignments that meet the course's learning objectives are a short book review of *Harry Potter and the Sorcerer's Stone*, which students must write as if the book had just been published, forcing them to engage in the process of evaluation and persuasion. They must determine the criteria for a good novel and then apply that to the book while endorsing or panning it. This assignment is excellent for helping students build a thesis statement as they learn how to establish a claim about why the book should or should not be read, along with good reasons to support their claim. Reading all of Rowling's first book is the primary reading requirement for the class, in which I teach lessons about the entire book along with fragments of the next two books in the series. The lighter load of reading the *Harry Potter* books is supplemented by reading scholarly articles as they approach their informative, research-based paper on how Harry Potter has changed the world.

Writing on this topic includes a required primary source, so students can learn how to craft questions and conduct a personal interview with someone who has the ethos to address the *Harry Potter* series. I encourage students to find an educator, librarian, or avid fan for their interview. The answers from their respondent revolve around the impact of the *Harry Potter* series on the topic or focus the student has established for their paper. These papers have examined how the *Harry Potter* series has influenced popular culture, the film industry, young adult and children's literature, literacy, fanfiction, the publishing industry, fandoms, and other categories the student may want to explore for their paper's theme. Another requirement for the assignment is finding scholarly articles via library databases including popular ones such as

EBSCOhost, ProQuest, and JSTOR. While the students learn the character-istics of scholarly peer-reviewed articles with this assignment, they also are instructed to utilize their newly learned knowledge by employing Aristotle's three arguments or appeals to evaluate sources based on ethos, pathos, and logos. Using Aristotle's three appeals and other techniques to evaluate sources helps students later write their argumentative paper according to the Classical Model, which also relies on the three appeals.

As far as rubrics are concerned, students produce about twenty-five pages of prose during the semester; about 60 percent of their final grade is based on this writing, including constructing a well-developed thesis statement and other higher-order concerns connected to their use of evidence or sup-porting details. Points are also awarded for following instructions, as I tell students that a paper failing to follow the assignment's directions dooms the writing project before the student even gets started drafting their essay. Lower-order concerns such as mechanics and documentation style are also featured in the rubrics. Evaluation of papers is based on not just how well the paper is written, but on the writer's stance and voice, and how the student has developed their ability to express their point of view as supported by evidence. The rubric is the same for my other English composition classes.

After writing various essays and exploring everything from Wizard Rock and Wizard Rap to Harry Potter fanfiction, an oral presentation delivered by each Hogwarts House concludes the students' activities for the course. Each Hogwarts House is assigned one of the last four books of the series for the presentation. Tasks range from leading a journal-writing exercise for the class based on close readings from the book to doing a mini-rhetorical analysis (in which students address the writer's argument, purpose, audi-ence, and content) of a scholarly peer-reviewed article about their assigned book. My primary request for the project is that students focus on parts of the books not featured in the movies. The logic is that most students have seen all the *Harry Potter* movies before the start of the course. Examining scenes depicted in the films is not allowed, unless the student points out the differences between the movie and the book. Exploring these differences requires students to speculate on why certain decisions were made, such as excluding characters like Winky. Or, why were the scenes in *Harry Potter and the Order of the Phoenix* in which Neville Longbottom visits his men-tally and emotionally damaged parents (remember, they had been tortured into a state of insanity by Death Eaters) at St. Mungo's Hospital for Magical

Maladies and Injuries, not included in the movie? In contrast, the film only briefly mentions Neville's parents, whereas the novel fully displays his mother in her altered state.

The oral presentation allows students to analyze the assigned *Harry Potter* novel on their own terms so long as it satisfies the ten different tasks or categories they have for the assignment. Creativity abounds. Some students arrive at their presentation dressed as their favorite Harry Potter character. This includes a Spectrespecs-wearing Luna Lovegood equipped with a copy of the *Quibbler* or a Dumbledore wearing a cloaked sheet and a knee-length gray beard. Culinary arts students taking the course have brought in chocolate cupcakes with handmade, edible Golden Snitches on top, and another group concocted a love potion made of sherbet. While PowerPoint presentations are the norm, students are given free rein to create multimodal elements. As a result, students have created portraits, Hogwarts House emblems for their group, and skits. Curiously, Ravenclaw House has consistently produced the best oral presentations. I attribute that to the scholarship associated with this particular Hogwarts House, as the more erudite students identified themselves as Ravenclaws when choosing their Hogwarts House at the beginning of the semester.

The final paper, an argumentative research-based essay, gives students the most freedom to create a topic on some aspect of the *Harry Potter* series. Motivated by the ability to devise their own topic, students are allowed to address almost any angle of the *Harry Potter* series, ranging from character analysis to themes. The main requirement besides argumentation is that students find scholarly sources for their research-based papers. Students have chosen a variety of topics over the years such as Harry Potter's impact on the moral development of children; how reading the books has impacted children's literacy by pushing them to read longer and more challenging books as they age;, how the books address bullying, government injustices, and social issues; teaching styles; the role of mentors like Dumbledore, Sirius Black, and Remus Lupin; and more than a few character analyses about the complexities of Severus Snape and Draco Malfoy as rounded characters. The goal is to encourage students to look at the *Harry Potter* series in a broader and more sophisticated context that takes them beyond their personal love for the series.

What follows are segments from student papers that illustrate how students have associated the material from the novel with their own viewpoints and behaviors. Kirsten writes: "The two weeks it took me to read all seven books set in motion an unwavering, lifetime love for reading and extreme gratitude for the impact J. K. Rowling had on my outlook on life, which was to choose to accept and embrace differences between people and live without judgment." Judy, an early childhood education major who was interested in the *Harry Potter* series and its impact on children, addresses how the series can impact one's behavior and thinking about stigmatized groups:

> The series does an amazing job of battling prejudices. Harry himself grew up being oppressed and judged, and this background served him well to not hold any prejudices himself.... [B]ecause readers have an affinity towards Harry, they can empathize with the hardships he endures. At the same time, they can feel empowered by his actions.... This series did not so much shape my views but instead reinforced them. I felt akin to the character traits that Harry demonstrated, such as being open-minded with people that seemed different, having an instinct to fight oppression, having the courage to be brave when the situation called for it. [The books] solidified my beliefs that one must question the things that do not seem right. One must have [the] courage to do the right thing even in the face of adversity.

And then there is the thesis by Iris, an African American student who chose to write her argumentative paper about Harry Potter and its lessons about prejudice: "The *Harry Potter* series is written with a sense of realism, engaging readers to focus on the seriousness of stereotypes and discrimination in both the real and wizarding world." In this paper, Iris chose to focus on S.P.E.W. and how Hermione's activism calls for others to fight against racial and social injustices.

Some readers are critical of the *Harry Potter* series for not being more inclusive, claiming that some characters represent the fulfillment of racial quotas, and I can agree with their argument to a point. The characters who represent various races, whether it be the Patil twins, Cho Chang, Lee Jordan, Angelina Johnson, Kingsley Shacklebolt, Dean Thomas, or Blaise Zabini (who is clearly identified as Black when Rowling introduces him on the train ride to Hogwarts in *Harry Potter and the Half-Blood Prince* and is thus portrayed by a Black actor in the last two *Harry Potter* films), have roles that show how they are embraced by a culture and a world that would stereotype them in the Muggle world. Kingsley later becomes a political leader and takes over the Ministry of Magic, perhaps becoming the first Black man to do so. Lee Jordan is a talented and funny broadcaster. Dean's story is given more layers as he is on the run from snatchers in *Harry Potter and the Deathly Hallows*. Cho is an accomplished Quidditch player, as is Angelina Johnson, who is brave and confident enough to put her name in the Goblet of Fire to compete in the Triwizard Tournament. The only "shady" racial minority character is Blaise, given his friendship with Draco. And, of course, it is through the portrayal of the house-elves that Rowling forces readers to learn about the horrors of slavery, oppression, and marginalization in society because of racial differences. Without these characters, the novels are not so accessible in teaching students about diversity. And when one considers the background of most of my students, who hail from rural northeastern Indiana, where their encounters with racial minorities are slim to none, the characters who happen to be racial minorities might be the first people of color whom the students come to know.

Currently, hate crimes in the United States are increasing. The rhetoric from our politicians is increasingly more divisive. White supremacist groups are becoming more vocal and prominent. These are the times in which my students live, and thus lessons about tolerance, diversity, and inclusion could not come at a better time. I cannot take credit for my students' observations and conclusions. However, I insist that sometimes just the presence of an African American professor automatically prompts some students to think about issues of race, especially when one considers that the vast majority of my students have never encountered a person of color as an instructor before. The credit for teaching students about how to appreciate differences in others rests on Rowling's shoulders and her apparent commitment to portraying ill-treatment of the Other in her *Harry Potter* book series. Her portrayal of the treatment of house-elves as slaves, the bloodline obsession exhibited by various characters in the series, and other themes in these books make it easy to teach concepts of the Other to college students in a freshman composition classroom. Sorry, Harold Bloom. Harry Potter is here to stay, largely because the series encourages students to transform themselves into agents of social change by challenging perceptions about racism, prejudice, and discrimination. I view myself as an agent of social change just by directing my students in thinking about issues of race, prejudice, discrimination, and how they view and treat others from stigmatized groups. That is one of the best lessons that one can learn from the series.

Notes

1. Hunt, "Introduction: The Expanding World," 1.
2. Bloom, "Can 35 Million Book Buyers Be Wrong?"
3. Hannah Huffman was a student in my very first Harry Potter class. *Inside Ivy Tech*, the campus monthly magazine, interviewed Hannah in 2018.
4. Nodelman, "The Other."
5. Vezzali et al., "The Greatest Magic of Harry Potter."
6. Cappy, "Shifting the Future?," 125.

Bibliography

Bloom, Harold. "Can 35 Million Book Buyers Be Wrong? Yes." *Wall Street Journal*, July 11, 2000. https://www.wsj.com/articles/SB963270836801555352.

Cappy, Christina Lane. "Shifting the Future? Teachers as Agents of Social Change in South African Secondary Schools." *Education as Change* 20, no. 3 (2016): 119–40.

Fisette, Jennifer L., and Theresa A. Walton. "'Beautiful You': Creating Contexts for Students to Become Agents of Social Change." *Journal of Educational Research* 108, no. 1 (2015): 62–76. doi:10.1080/00220671.2013.838537.

Hunt, Peter. "Introduction: The Expanding World of Children's Literature Studies." In *Understanding Children's Literature*, edited by Peter Hunt, 1–14. Abingdon, Oxon., England: Routledge, 1999.

Inside Ivy Tech. "Special Topics Classes Reach Students through Uncommon Means." *Inside Ivy Tech*, February 22, 2018. https://ivytechfortwaynenews.com/2018/02/.

Nodelman, Perry. "The Other: Orientalism, Colonialism, and Children's Literature." *Children's Literature Association Quarterly* 17, no. 1 (Spring 1992): 29–35.

Rowling, J. K. *Harry Potter and the Chamber of Secrets.* New York: Scholastic, 1999.

Vezzali, Loris, Sofia Stathi, Dino Giovannini, Dora Capozza, and Elena Trifiletti. "The Greatest Magic of Harry Potter: Reducing Prejudice." *Journal of Applied Social Psychology* 45, no. 2 (February 2015): 105–21. doi:10.1111/jasp.12279.

Is Dobby a Free Elf?

Sridevi Rao and Preethi Gorecki

In the magical wizarding world of Harry Potter there exists a hierarchy of power that privileges wizards while systematically oppressing nonhuman magical beings. Elves, goblins, and giants are similar to wizards in that they possess magical abilities, have the capacity to think, feel, and communicate, and are intellectually equivalent. However, they are treated as inherently inferior to wizards, and in the case of some elves are even enslaved by wizards. J. K. Rowling is careful to subtly highlight these inequities throughout the *Harry Potter* series to show the perceived normalcy of oppressive structures in the day-to-day workings of the wizarding world.

This chapter seeks to use a Foucauldian lens to analyze structures of power within the wizarding world of Harry Potter by reexamining the story of Dobby the house-elf and considering the question of whether or not Dobby truly dies a free elf. First, we discuss how government, policy, and education function as tools of oppression and subjugation in the wizarding world, which will serve as the recurring theme throughout the chapter. Next, we examine the role and treatment of elves in the wizarding world, mainly through Dobby's eyes. The chapter then wraps Dobby's story into a conversation about the strategic role "othering" plays in the systematic oppression of nonhuman magical beings. Finally, we conclude with a reflective analysis of how the exclusive nature of government, policy, and education in the wizarding world normalizes and enforces the subjugation of nonhuman magical beings.

The Ministry of Magic

"In modern society, law combines with power in various locations in ways that expand patterns of social control."[1] The Ministry of Magic serves several functions in the wizarding world, including the creation and enforcement of magical law, the sentencing of those in violation of magical law, and the regulation and control of magical creatures. In order to work for the Ministry of Magic one must be a witch or a wizard, meaning that nonhuman magical beings are excluded from creating and enforcing magical laws. Furthermore, the Ministry of Magic has an entire department devoted to the regulation and control of nonhuman magical beings.[2] By excluding nonhuman magical beings from government and extensively regulating their behavior, witches and wizards have complete power in the wizarding world to change and enforce laws, thereby exerting social control over all other magical beings.

In particular, the Ministry of Magic strictly enforces the Statute of Secrecy, which demands that all magical beings, human and nonhuman, safeguard the existence of magic from the "Muggle," or nonmagic, population.[3] For witches and wizards, it proves less difficult to abide by this set of laws, since witches and wizards are human by appearance and can thus hide themselves among Muggles. However, if nonhuman magic folk are spotted by a Muggle, they are immediately in direct violation of the Statute of Secrecy simply because of the way they look. For elves, goblins, giants, and other nonhuman magic folk, this leaves two options for spaces in which to legally exist: remote, often treacherous regions of the world that Muggles do not see fit to inhabit, or among the wizarding population. Given these options, many nonhuman magic folk choose to integrate into the wizarding world and live by wizards' laws, thereby relinquishing their right to exist on their own terms.

Similar to the Statute of Secrecy, the Code of Wand Use restricts the behavior of nonhuman magical creatures to a greater degree than that of wizards. Throughout the *Harry Potter* series, elves and goblins perform magic at the flick of their wrist or a snap of their fingers but never with a wand. In the wizarding world, Clause 3 of the Code of Wand Use states that "no non-human creature is permitted to carry or use a wand" (*Harry Potter and the Goblet of Fire*, 132). In *Harry Potter and the Deathly Hallows*, Griphook the goblin laments over goblins' exclusion from wand lore and explains that it has been a point of contention between goblins and wizards throughout the ages (488). There are a few mentions of the "Goblin Rebellions" scattered throughout the *Harry Potter* series, and given what we learn about the rebellions in addition to Griphook's commentary about wand lore, we can infer a bit about how the Code of Wand Use came to be and the purpose it serves.

According to the *Harry Potter* books, the first Goblin Rebellion took place in 1612, and similar goblin uprisings continued over the following centuries (*Harry Potter and the Prisoner of Azkaban*). Clause 3 of the Code of Wand Use, which makes it illegal for nonhuman magic folk to carry wands, was enacted by the Ministry of Magic sometime during the eighteenth century (*Harry Potter and the Order of the Phoenix*). From this timeline, it seems apparent that this section of the Code of Wand Use was at least partly the consequence of the goblin uprisings that took place just prior to its enactment. Although goblins may have been the catalyst for the law, they are not the only magical race negatively impacted by it, and this, too, is intentional. By privileging wizards with wands and excluding all others from that privilege, Clause 3 of the Code of Wand Use deliberately grants wizards more power and authority than anyone else in the wizarding world.

Elves and goblins are capable of sophisticated magic without wands, and giving them a wand through which to channel their magic could potentially enable them to match or surpass wizards' spellcasting abilities. Power is relational and becomes apparent when exercised,[4] and thereby legislation created by wizards that restricts the rights of those who are not wizards, such as Clause 3 of the Code of Wand Use, is an exercise of wizards' power over nonhuman magical races.

The Wizarding Schools

"It is not possible for power to be exercised without knowledge, it is impossible for knowledge not to engender power."[5] In the wizarding world, young witches and wizards are invited to attend a wizarding school, at which they are taught various aspects of magic. Globally, there are eleven such schools, which vary in their admission standards and curricula.[6] Interestingly, none of these schools admit nonhumans as students despite that there does not appear to be a specific law limiting enrollment to only witches and wizards.

The Code of Wand Use does pose challenges for nonhuman magical beings participating in classes or activities requiring wands, but the law in and of itself is an inadequate explanation for why they are excluded from the wizarding schools. It is probable that all of the wizarding schools teach at least one subject that does not require wand use, and in fact, the Uagadou Wizarding School exclusively taught only wandless magic until the present century.[7] It may seem fair to argue that other magical beings are excluded from schools for witchcraft and wizardry because these schools are customized to fit the educational needs of only witches and wizards, but this begs the question of why there do not appear to be any schools for goblins or elves. Throughout the *Harry Potter* series, there is no mention of schools or formal education structures targeted to any nonhuman magical race. Without receiving education on how to use magic, how to read, and how to write, nonhuman magic folk are unable to rise to the same level of achievement that wizards can.

While it is unclear whether half-giants are considered humans or non-humans in the wizarding world, both Madame Maxime and Rubeus Hagrid have wizard blood and appear to be human, which seems to be adequate criteria for legally possessing a wand and attending wizarding school. Rubeus Hagrid, who is vocally half-giant, was expelled from wizarding school for a crime he did not commit (*Harry Potter and the Chamber of Secrets*), while Madame Maxime adamantly denies that she is half-giant, instead claiming to be "big-boned" (*HP and the GF*). Taken together, these characters' experiences highlight their ability to pass as fully human and the prejudice they face should they choose to identify as anything other than human in a wizard-dominated education system. Being a part of the wizarding race comes with extra privileges. This is similar to the idea Gloria Ladson-Billings and William F. Tate discuss about property, that a ruling race possesses a type of property just by belonging to that race.[8] In the case of the wizarding world, the more similar one is to the ruling race, the witches and wizards, or whether one can "pass" and sufficiently fit in with them, determines if one can also benefit from some of the advantages they possess, including the right to an education and the right to use a wand. In his book *Racism without Racists*, Eduardo Bonilla-Silva discusses this idea of "passing" enough to fit into the most powerful race and gain more power, although not as much power as the ruling class. Bonilla-Silva explains how a hierarchical racial order shapes all aspects of life, and occasionally allowing members of nonprivileged groups who can fit in enough to "pass" to become part of the most privileged race ensures that the dominant race stays in power.

The purpose of education is to empower, enrich, and enable individuals; however, the wizarding institutions of education perpetuate inequity by reproducing those policies, like educating only witches and wizards, that maintain inequities. Michel Foucault describes education as a machine for supervising, hierarchizing, and rewarding.[9] Even within the powerful wizarding race's educational institutions, there are multiple levels of power in different contexts. At school, the rewards go to those who conform to the instruction of the professors and headmasters, and even among the students there are those who are deemed head boy and head girl as well as prefects. These titles are usually given to students who follow the rules.

The wizarding world, by not providing equal access to education for all the races (wizards, witches, and magical creatures alike), maintains this power hierarchy that continually places nonhumans at the bottom and humans at the top. Witches and wizards are essentially in charge, and nonhuman creatures like house-elves must obey their wizard masters. Excluding other magical races from the existing education system helps wizards maintain the illusion of superiority over nonhuman magic folk, lending to the inherent sense of inferiority that many of these folk (especially house-elves) feel. By ensuring that nonhuman magic folk continue to lack the knowledge, skills, and self-worth necessary to protest wizard-biased policies, participate in government, or otherwise evoke nonviolent change, wizards perpetuate the cycle of oppression without much threat of retribution. Elves continually find themselves on the bottom of this hierarchical society. This next section will discuss the plight of house-elves, using Dobby's story as the focus.

The Elves' Tale: The Ugly Face of Slavery

Children's literature has formative power on the development of young minds.[10] Philip Nel states that literature for young people is one of the places where racism hides, and ironically also one of the places where racism can be opposed.[11] One topic of current debate is whether white children's innocence should be risked in teaching them about racism and racial violence.[12] White people have the privilege to ignore this question, whereas Black children need to understand the histories of their ancestors for their own safety and survival.[13] In a way, Rowling indirectly uses house-elves as a metaphor for the institution of slavery. By casting house-elves instead of humans as the enslaved, it may be easier for children to digest and potentially even overlook the historical reality of slavery. This decision still begs the question of why

Rowling chose to dance around the idea of the house-elf as a slave when she describes them and their position in the wizarding world.

Slavery is a race-based system of oppression.[14] House-elves are never explicitly called slaves in the books; however, they are servants who are bound to a wizarding family until they are freed by the receipt of a piece of clothing from a member of that family. The plight of the house-elves clearly parallels that of human slaves being owned by a master. Although elves have many wizard-like characteristics, they are viewed as inferior to witches and wizards and treated as property owned by wizarding families. One character who plays an integral role in Harry Potter's adventures is a house-elf named Dobby. Dobby's interactions with the other characters as well as his various, sometimes alarming impulses offer insight into the psyche of the house-elves of Harry Potter's world. Dobby is an enslaved and mistreated magical creature who belonged to three generations of the Malfoy family, at whose hands he endured much emotional and physical abuse.

Encounters between Lucius Malfoy and Dobby showcase the Malfoys' abusive behavior toward Dobby in the form of physical blows and emotional abuse. This family has never considered that Dobby may have feelings, or deserve to be treated differently. To the Malfoy family, Dobby is a possession, and they treat him as just that: a thing, not a living being. While the Malfoys appear to be more abusive than others who employ house-elves, their treatment of Dobby is still considered perfectly normal in the wizarding world. On the other hand, Dobby's behavior in response is described by Shira Wolosky's Foucauldian analysis as an effect of discipline in which one knows and takes their place in society as a result of ingrained power structures and begins to discipline themselves without the need for subjugation from those in power, as when Dobby punishes himself for speaking ill of his master. There is a pervasive belief among the wizarding community that house-elves prefer a life of servitude over freedom; however, house-elves have never experienced agency or freedom. Even Ron Weasley, who is portrayed as one of the heroes in the Harry Potter epic, said: "[House-elves]. Like. It. They like being enslaved!" (*HP and the GF*, 224). However, Hermione refuses to accept this as the status quo and fights for elves' rights, stating: "[D]on't you see . . . how sick it is, the way they've got to obey?" (*HP and the DH*, 162). The *Harry Potter* books both allow and critique these hierarchies and Foucauldian views of power.[15]

The story of Dobby steadily disproves the myth that house-elves enjoy being enslaved, revealing that house-elves' attachment to servitude is partially due to fear of the uncertainty that comes with being free. The depth of Dobby's unhappiness is first made apparent by how he is affected by acts of kindness. During their initial encounter, Harry asks Dobby, who is agitated over some matter, if he wants to sit down, to keep him calm. Dobby is so taken aback by this simple gesture that he bursts into tears and replies:"Dobby has never been asked to sit down by a wizard—like an equal" (*HP and the CS*, 13). He then goes on to say that he has not met many decent wizards such as Harry, and then immediately jumps up and starts banging his head on the window and chastising himself.

When Harry questions this behavior, Dobby explains that he has to punish himself for speaking ill of the Malfoys. Discipline is so ingrained in the house-elves that it almost completely defines their will.[16] A. S. Neill, the founder of Summerhill School, describes two types of discipline—one in which a violinist obeys a conductor, and the outcome is a good performance, and one in which, if someone disobeys, they will be punished, thereby inciting fear.[17] The latter is what is present in the lives of many house-elves. Dobby is rebellious, especially for an elf, but even so, he has internalized his treatment as inferior and believes that disrespecting the wizard family he serves is the greatest sin he can commit. Wolosky states that one becomes accustomed to norms that are socially determined, and eventually these norms become internalized through psychological processes. On the surface, it seems that this behavior stems from loyalty to one's masters; however, it becomes apparent that Dobby's behavior stems from his understanding of the norms and hierarchies present in the wizarding world in addition to an extreme lack of self-worth ingrained by years of oppression and abuse.

The friendship that develops between Harry Potter and Dobby is built upon mutual respect and loyalty. At the end of the second book, Harry tricks Lucius Malfoy into freeing Dobby, and Dobby is immediately thrilled by the prospect of life as a free elf. Dobby eventually finds work in the Hogwarts kitchens, and as a result of Hermione Granger advocating for social change, he gets paid a small wage for doing so. In contrast to Dobby's misery while serving the Malfoy family at the start of the *Harry Potter* series, it is apparent how much happier he is as a free elf, although some of the other house-elves still see his new status as disgraceful, since they have been socialized to serve without any type of compensation. Harry understands the pride and happiness Dobby takes from being free, and when Dobby dies in the act of rescuing Harry and his friends, Harry marks Dobby's gravestone with the words: "Here lies Dobby, a free elf" (*HP and the DH*, 481).

Discussion

The idea that Dobby dies a "free elf" is certainly a powerful one that merits further exploration. First, let us define what "free" even means in this context. "Freedom" can be conceptualized in one of two ways: as freedom *from* something, or freedom *to do* something. Given that Dobby's freedom is discussed in the context of being freed from a life of servitude, we can assume that it falls into the category of "freedom from." Dobby's freedom from serving the Malfoy family allows him to choose where he works and what clothing he wears; he can now label himself a "free elf" rather than a "house-elf." Beyond those freedoms, Dobby is quite limited in his choices for how to carry out his life. The limitations on Dobby's "freedom" are often obscured by his contentment with being a "free elf" and Harry Potter's pride in having helped free Dobby from the Malfoy family. However, if we frame Dobby's postslavery existence within the context of what we know about the wizard-dominated magical world, we can get a much more objective perspective of his standing as a "free elf."

Dobby is considered a traitor by most wizards for leaving the Malfoys and an outcast by house-elves. The Foucauldian ideas of discipline are so pervasive that the other house-elves cannot even see an alternative to their own servitude, and they look down upon efforts to formulate such alternatives. While Dobby is far from experiencing the world as a wizard does, he does have more freedom than house-elves, which gives him a sense of ambiguity about his life's purpose. In order to survive and continue wearing the clothes he enjoys so much, he needs money. Dobby spent the bulk of his life serving wizards, and he does not have any skills or education beyond cleaning, cooking, and otherwise existing within the bleak walls of Malfoy Manor. His lack of education limits his opportunities and his power.[18] Given that he is an elf, he cannot work at the Ministry of Magic, nor can he enroll in classes at any magical educational institution. Due to his lack of skills and education, he cannot realistically compete with wizards for positions in retail, business, or most jobs in the service industry. Additionally, because he is viewed as untrustworthy by wizards, it seems unlikely that he would be hired by one in any meaningful capacity. This leaves Dobby with very few options: he can either disguise himself and live among the Muggles, live outside both the Muggle and wizarding communities in exile, or find another wizard to serve who is willing to pay him. Although Dobby is free from the Malfoys whom he used to serve, he is not necessarily free to do whatever he pleases; he is limited and bound by his status as an elf.

The societal norms, expectations, and laws governing house-elves, compounded by Dobby's lack of education, continue to oppress him and limit the level of freedom he can experience. Although power relations among individuals in the wizarding world can shift to some degree, the overarching relations and power structures stay the same. Upon exploring the limitations of what "freedom" really means and the role it plays in Dobby's new life as a free elf, it becomes apparent that Dobby's sense of freedom is completely relative to his prior enslavement. So: is Dobby a free elf?

Conclusion

Although he is no longer enslaved, Dobby is not a free elf. Being free from enslavement does not give him the freedom or privilege to express true agency or free will. Dobby is inevitably governed by the same wizard-biased laws as all other nonhuman magical folk. Through systematic exclusion from wands, education, and government representation, nonhuman magical folk are oppressed by the ruling class: wizards. The carefully crafted and reinforced laws regulating nonhuman magic folk put parameters around their existence such that their experiences within the wizarding world are completely divorced from the experiences of their human magical counterparts. The life of a nonhuman magical being is highly regulated, devoid of purpose beyond either serving or escaping from wizards, and generally regarded as having less value than that of a wizard. Wizards rarely perceive the disparity inherent in the society their laws helped shape, choosing instead to believe that nonhuman magic folk are simply inferior to them, thereby continuing the cycle of oppression.

Notes

1. Turkel, "Michel Foucault: Law, Power, and Knowledge," 170.
2. Rowling, "Ministers for Magic."
3. Rowling, "Ministers for Magic."
4. Foucault, *Power/Knowledge*.
5. Foucault, *Power/Knowledge*, 52.
6. Rowling, "Wizarding Schools."
7. Rowling, "Wizarding Schools."
8. Ladson-Billings and Tate, "Toward a Critical Race Theory of Education."
9. Foucault, *Discipline and Punish*.
10. Wolosky, "Foucault at School."
11. Nel, *Was the Cat in the Hat Black?*
12. Fielder, "Black Girls, White Girls, American Girls."
13. Fielder, "Black Girls, White Girls, American Girls."
14. Fielder, "Black Girls, White Girls, American Girls."
15. Wolosky, "Foucault at School."
16. Wolosky, "Foucault at School."
17. Neill, *Summerhill*.
18. Foucault, *Power/Knowledge*.

Bibliography

Bonilla-Silva, Eduardo. *Racism without Racists: Color-Blind Racism and Racial Inequality in the United States*. 2nd ed. Lanham, MD: Rowman and Littlefield, 2006.

Fielder, Brigitte. "Black Girls, White Girls, American Girls: Slavery and Racialized Perspectives in Abolitionist and Neoabolitionist Children's Literature." *Tulsa Studies in Women's Literature* 36, no. 2 (2017): 323–52.

Foucault, Michel. *Discipline and Punish: The Birth of the Prison*. Translated by Alan Sheridan. New York: Vintage Books, 1995.

Foucault, Michel. *Power/Knowledge: Selected Interviews and Other Writings, 1972–1977*. Edited by Colin Gordon. New York: Pantheon Books, 1980.

Ladson-Billings, Gloria, and William F. Tate IV. "Toward a Critical Race Theory of Education." *Teachers College Record* 97, no. 1 (Fall 1995): 47–68.

Neill, A. S. *Summerhill: A Radical Approach to Child Rearing*. New York: Hart Publishing, 1960.

Nel, Philip. *Was the Cat in the Hat Black? The Hidden Racism of Children's Literature and the Need for Diverse Books*. New York: Oxford University Press, 2017.

Rowling, J. K. "5 Friendship Lessons We Learned from Dobby the House-Elf." Pottermore, September 22, 2015. https://www.pottermore.com/explore-the-story/dobby.

Rowling, J. K. *Harry Potter and the Chamber of Secrets*. New York: Scholastic, 1999.

Rowling, J. K. *Harry Potter and the Deathly Hallows*. New York: Scholastic, 2007.

Rowling, J. K. *Harry Potter and the Goblet of Fire*. New York: Scholastic, 2000.

Rowling, J. K. *Harry Potter and the Half-Blood Prince*. New York: Scholastic, 2005.

Rowling, J. K. *Harry Potter and the Order of the Phoenix*. New York: Scholastic, 2003.

Rowling, J. K. *Harry Potter and the Prisoner of Azkaban*. New York: Scholastic, 1999.

Rowling, J. K. *Harry Potter and the Sorcerer's Stone*. New York: Scholastic, 1998.

Rowling, J. K. "Ministers for Magic." Wizarding World (Pottermore, August 10, 2015). https://www.wizardingworld.com/writing-by-jk-rowling/ministers-for-magic.

Rowling, J. K. "Wizarding Schools." Pottermore, January 29, 2016. https://www.pottermore.com/collection-episodic/wizarding-schools.

Townley, Barbara. "Foucault, Power/Knowledge, and Its Relevance for Human Resource Management." *Academy of Management Review* 18, no. 3 (July 1993): 518–45.

Turkel, Gerald. "Michel Foucault: Law, Power, and Knowledge." *Journal of Law and Society* 17, no. 2 (Summer 1990): 170–93.

Wolosky, Shira. "Foucault at School: Discipline, Education, and Agency in *Harry Potter*." *Children's Literature in Education* 45 (December 2014): 285–97.

The Failed Wizard Justice System

Race and Access to Justice in Harry Potter

Charles D. Wilson

The witches and wizards in J. K. Rowling's *Harry Potter* books consider themselves superior to other beings. This world view is encapsulated in the golden fountain of magical brethren in the Ministry of Magic.

> Halfway down the hall was a fountain. A group of golden statues, larger than life-size, stood in the middle of a circular pool. Tallest of them all was a noble-looking wizard with his wand pointing straight up in the air. Grouped around him were a beautiful witch, a centaur, a goblin, and a house-elf. The last three were all looking adoringly up at the witch and wizard. (*Harry Potter and the Order of the Phoenix*, 127)

The bias in favor of witches and wizards permeates the legal system, rendering it all but useless for goblins, house-elves, Muggles, Squibs, sentient magical creatures, and even wizards of lower social standing. These marginalized groups don't have "access to justice," a term that is generally understood to mean they don't have the ability to seek and obtain a remedy through formal means like the courts or informal institutions such as mediation.[1] The wizard justice system functions as a form of social control dictating who can use magic, what magic they can use, and under what circumstances.

The failed legal wizard system perpetuates injustice and contributes to the rise of Voldemort by allowing his crimes to go unpunished. Throughout the books, Voldemort exploits the flaws in the wizard legal system by using, scapegoating, and even killing marginal figures who don't have access to the justice system. He further takes advantage of the system's failure by persuading the subject races of magical creatures including giants, werewolves, and others to join him by promising them what the legal system has failed to deliver. In Harry Potter, access to justice issues have major implications for wizard society. Rowling uses systemic failings drawn from recognizable real-world legal and political conflicts to illustrate racial and social injustice in the wizard legal system. However, this is more of world-building exercise than a focal point of the series. The main plot line is a struggle between two factions of the wizard elite, not a revolutionary struggle for change in the social order. Rowling's approach to the wizard justice system is deeply cynical, illustrating the consequences when the participants act in self-interested or politically expedient ways. This chapter sheds light on the importance of a functioning legal system, the risks that accompany the misuse of legal authority, and the consequences of denying disfavored groups access to justice in Harry Potter and beyond.

As Aaron Schwabach observes: "[L]iterature shapes law."[2] Harry Potter references abound in legal texts. As early as 2005, the Court of Appeals of Ohio was interpreting the trial court's use of the word "Potteresque."[3] For readers of Harry Potter, the flaws in the justice system will inform their judgments about real-world issues:

> Harry's story is a story about law. Harry's world is governed by a detailed and deeply flawed legal regime. Law, laws and legal structures appear in nearly every chapter. Conflicts and imperfections abound, providing Harry and his companions with the opportunity to ponder moral choices and readers with the opportunity to ponder the nature of law. For millions of readers, especially younger readers, the legal regime of Harry's world will form expectations about legal regimes in Mugglespace.[4]

Readers readily recognize the parallels between injustice in the wizarding world and real-world examples of racial and class conflict. Jackie C. Horne observes that the reader "is asked to condemn the racism of the wizarding world—not only the distinction between 'Mudbloods' and 'pure-bloods' voiced by its extreme members, but also its limitations of the rights of sentient others and its foundation on the enslavement of house-elves."[5] Rowling regularly describes the different types of sentient magical creatures as "races" (*Harry Potter and the Deathly Hallows*, 296). American readers will see parallels with segregation and the civil rights movement. Wizard law contains parallels with both the de jure racial discrimination that existed by law in the United States in the Jim Crow era and the de facto discrimination that followed after the Civil Rights Act of 1964 and numerous court rulings attempted to put an end to it. Rowling, who worked at Amnesty International in the 1980s,[6] may have had South Africa's apartheid or British political conflicts in mind. African Caribbean immigrants and South Asians were victims of racist violence in Britain in the 1970s and 1980s.[7] This period was marked by a series of riots spurred by racism, poverty, oppressive policing, and perceptions of powerlessness.[8]

Rowling's fictional wizard justice system exists within the framework of the modern United Kingdom, and its structures are familiar to those who live in countries with similar legal systems. Frequent references are made to recognizable components of the government, statutes, laws, and even the Muggle Prime Minister. However, the precise relationship between the Muggle government, and the Ministry of Magic and the wizard justice system, is never made explicit.

The Minister of Magic is elected, as Rowling clarified via Pottermore.[9] However, Rowling describes Cornelius Fudge's departure from the role as being "sacked" and Rufus Scrimgeour as being "appointed," but there is no indication who has the authority to do this (*Harry Potter and the Half-Blood Prince*, 15, 60, 40–41).[10] In *Sorcerer's Stone*, Rowling mentions that Dumbledore was offered the post of Minister of Magic (*HP and the SS*, 64–65). On Pottermore, Rowling clarified that in times of crisis the post has simply been offered to an individual without a public vote.[11] This is significant because the Ministry of Magic controls both the courts and law enforcement, and the possibility of public accountability has significant consequences.

The presence of a democratic process, albeit somewhat limited, explains the shifting attitudes of the Minister of Magic, Cornelius Fudge, toward Harry Potter throughout the series. When Harry "blows up" the Dursley's Aunt Margaret, Fudge tells Harry that he won't be punished at all. When queried by Harry, the minister replies: "Circumstances change, Harry. . . . [W]e have to take into account . . . the present climate" (*Harry Potter and the Prisoner of Azkaban*, 45). Two books later, in *Order of the Phoenix*, the Ministry unsuccessfully prosecutes Harry on the same charge. According to Ron, Harry is let off in the first instance because he is something of a celebrity in the wizarding world (*HP and the PA*, 56). However, in *Order of the Phoenix*, the Ministry of Magic pressures the wizard newspaper, the *Daily Prophet*, to disparage Harry and Dumbledore (73–75, 94, 306–8). This helps make Harry's subsequent prosecution politically palatable.

There are very few checks on the power of the Ministry of Magic. In *Order of the Phoenix*, the Ministry seizes control of Hogwarts in an effort to control public opinion and curtail academic freedom. Benjamin Barton outlines the absence of checks on the power of the Ministry, the lack of democratic accountability, the lack of oversight by other governmental or nongovernmental entities, the lack of judicial oversight, the lack of a free press, and the lack of public-minded bureaucrats in the Ministry.[12] In short, Barton concludes, the Ministry of Magic lacks governmental legitimacy.[13] Generally speaking, the concept of the rule of law requires political restraints on the exercise of public power, procedural fairness or due process, the recognition of the societal need for order over disorder and chaos, and respect for rights and dignity.[14] The wizard justice system is deficient on each count.

The books refer to statutes and codes governing magical subjects, but no reference is made to a wizard legislative body. Danaya Wright characterizes Rowling's depiction as conflating "government and bureaucracy to the point that in the wizarding world there is no government outside bureaucracy."[15] Rowling offers a few glimpses into the civil law of the wizarding world, but her focus is almost exclusively on criminal law and the power of the state.

As Professor Binns tells his magical history class, Hogwarts was founded in the tenth century, and Rowling seems to have borrowed from the real-world Anglo-Saxon legal tradition that prevailed in that era (*HP and the HBP*, 150), perhaps suggesting that the wizard justice system predates the common law system established after the Norman invasion of 1066.[16] The name of the wizard high court, the Wizengamot, derives from the Witenagemot, an Anglo-Saxon council of nobles and officials.[17] The name consists of a combination of the words Witan, a term for nobles, and Gamot or moot, meaning court or council.[18]

The two courts share more than an etymological origin. Like its historical analog, the Wizengamot is staffed by the wizarding world's elite. Dolores Umbridge attempts to improve her social standing by claiming that her father was a member of the Wizengamot instead of his true occupation as a maintenance man.[19] During the series, both Albus Dumbledore and Cornelius Fudge take a turn as Chief Warlock of the Court (*HP and the OP*, 138, 143).[20] The Wizengamot, like the Witenagemot, has a distinctly political role dealing with rebels and disaffected individuals.[21]

The wizarding world has other courts and commissions that serve a variety of functions. Death Eater Pius Thicknesse's Ministry of Magic established the Muggle-Born Registration Commission headed by the former Hogwarts Inquisitor, the sadistic Dolores Umbridge.[22] The sinister nature of this commission is highlighted by its similarity to South Africa's Population Registration Act, a pillar of the apartheid system, which required everyone to register from birth as belonging to one of four racial classifications.[23] The Ministry of Magic keeps records on all wizards and requires Animagi to register so that it can be sure they don't commit crimes in animal form, even though they are still considered wizards.[24] The Ministry of Magic administers justice differently to wizards, and three categories of magical creatures: beings, beasts, and spirits.[25] Magical creatures are dealt with through a separate system. Buckbeak the Hippogriff is tried, convicted, and sentenced to death by the Committee for the Disposal of Dangerous Creatures rather than by the Wizengamot.

Aurors, the wizarding world's police officers, enforce the laws, by lethal force if necessary. According to Ron Weasley, Aurors have killed "loads" of giants (*HP and the OP*, 430). Several Death Eaters, including Rosier and Wilkes, have been killed by Aurors (*Harry Potter and the Goblet of Fire*, 531). Sirius Black strongly implies to Harry that Aurors do not always use restraint before killing by contrasting the restraint shown by "Mad-Eye" Moody, who "never killed if he could help it" (*HP and the GF*, 532). Wizarding law appears to be enforced through force and terror rather than due process, especially toward nonhumans, and there seems to be little recourse for those falsely accused. British and American readers alike would recognize the parallels between the Aurors' oppressive misconduct and real-world conflicts between law enforcement and communities of color in their home countries. Examples of misconduct abound in the books; Rubeus Hagrid, the Hogwarts gamekeeper, is sent to the wizard prison of Azkaban without a trial, and Stan Shunpike and two others are detained there merely to make it appear that the Ministry of Magic is making progress in their investigation of Death Eaters (*HP and the HBP*, 331).

There don't seem to be any limits to the Ministry of Magic's surveillance of law-abiding wizards. In *Chamber of Secrets*, Harry receives a letter from the Ministry after it detects magic being used at Privet Drive (21). Paul Joseph and Lynn Wolf observe that this surveillance is conducted without any knowledge or consent on Harry's part and that Harry is found guilty without any opportunity to plead his case or confront his accusers.[26] In fact, it was not Harry who used magic at Privet Drive but the house-elf, Dobby. Nevertheless, the Ministry concludes that Harry has violated the "Decree for the Reasonable Restriction of Underage Sorcery, 1875, paragraph C," and puts him on probation (*HP and the CS*, 21).

Punishment in the wizarding world can range from having one's wand broken to incarceration in Azkaban. The prison of Azkaban, under the control of its Dementor jailers, is nearly a death sentence. The Dementor's Kiss is a particularly cruel punishment in which the victim's soul is said to be sucked out by the Dementors. Professor Remus Lupin describes the Dementor's Kiss to Harry in *Prisoner of Azkaban*: "You can exist without your soul, you know, as long as your brain and heart are still working. But you'll have no sense of self anymore, no memory, no . . . anything. There's no chance at all of recovery. You'll just—exist. As an empty shell. And your soul is gone forever . . . lost" (247). The Dementor's Kiss is used on Barty Crouch Jr. after his escape from the prison is discovered (*HP and the GF*, 703). The Dementors are given permission to do the same to Sirius Black upon capture, even though he was incarcerated without a trial (*HP and the PA*, 247).

While having one's wand broken might seem like a minor punishment in comparison to being handed over to the Dementors, it is in fact a serious matter. It not only disarms the convicted individual, but it marks them as being outside the community of witches and wizards. Wands are a particularly important symbol in Rowling's wizarding world. The wand chooses the wizard rather than the other way around. Not surprisingly, wizard law and the wizard justice system are greatly concerned with wands. Possession of a wand is synonymous with membership in the wizarding world and possession of full rights in that community. Wizard children do not possess wands, nor do Muggles, Squibs, goblins, house-elves, or other sentient magical creatures. Wand lore is a closely guarded prerogative of wizards, one they refuse to share with other magical races (*HP and the SS*, 488–89).

Among wizards, the punishment for misuse of magic is having one's wand broken. Hagrid suffers this fate after he is framed by the future Voldemort,

Tom Riddle. Harry escapes this punishment when Dumbledore successfully defends him in front of the Wizengamot in *Order of the Phoenix* (137–51). This is the only instance of legal representation in the books, and there doesn't seem to be any formal legal profession in the wizarding world or any right to an attorney. The accused are left to fend for themselves.

When a witch or wizard's wand is broken, they lose the right to perform magic. When they first meet in *Sorcerer's Stone*, Hagrid tells Harry that he was expelled from Hogwarts and had his wand snapped: "I'm not supposed ter do magic strictly speaking" (*HP and the SS*, 59). There is a corresponding loss of status. Hagrid is kept on as an employee at Hogwarts, but it is clear that his job as gamekeeper is a low-status position akin to that of the Squib caretaker, Filch. Hagrid is eventually cleared of the charges and becomes a teacher at Hogwarts, but he still isn't considered "a fully qualified wizard" (*HP and the PA*, 94).

Elevated social status is crucial to getting access to justice in the wizarding world. Magical creatures, lower-status wizards, and nonmagical creatures suffer from a justice gap. Throughout the series, the Malfoys demonstrate influence over the justice system and the Ministry of Magic. By comparison, the Weasleys, though pure-blooded wizards, are comparably disadvantaged because of their lower socioeconomic status. Draco Malfoy repeatedly invokes his father in situations where he, as a student, does not have the power to effect an outcome (*HP and the PA*, 113; *HP and the SS*, 250; *HP and the GF*, 206). He does this as both a boast and a threat; and it is not an idle threat. In *Prisoner of Azkaban*, Draco and his father, Lucius Malfoy, cause Hagrid's hippogriff to get tried and convicted by the Ministry of Magic's Committee for the Disposal of Dangerous Creatures. Harry believes that the committee "had had its mind made up for it by Mr. Malfoy" (*HP and the PA*, 316). Lucius Malfoy repeatedly demonstrates a powerful influence on the government. He is acquitted in his trial after the First Wizarding War, he serves on Hogwarts's influential Board of Governors, and he appears at the Quidditch World Cup as the Minister of Magic's guest.[27] When Cornelius Fudge, the Minister of Magic, declines to go after Death Eaters named by Harry, including Lucius Malfoy, he justifies it saying: "Malfoy was cleared . . . A very old Family—donations to excellent causes—" (*HP and the GF*, 706). Dumbledore rebukes Fudge, saying: "You place too much importance, and you always have done, on the so-called purity of the blood! You fail to recognize that it matters not what someone is born but what they grow to be!" (*HP and the GF*, 708).

Wright finds that "Rowling has created strong families and a weak state which seems to be subsumed into a series of family dynasties."²⁸ These families wield an unseen influence on the law and politics of the wizarding world, further reducing the access to justice of marginal or disaffected members of the magical world. These families are in some ways a law unto themselves, using enchantments and spells to enforce their will. Wright explains that "wizarding families exist as autonomous institutions that, in many respects, make their own rules and solve their own problems without oversight by a bureaucratic or therapeutic state."²⁹ Dumbledore explains to Harry that if Sirius Black's magical will had not worked, the house would have passed according to Black family tradition (*HP and the HBP*, 50). Apparently, family tradition trumps any form of intestacy law.

The status of each wizard as pure-blood, half-blood, or Muggle-born is considered very important by other wizards. The wizarding world's hierarchy is reinforced by wizards' education at Hogwarts, where students are served by house-elves and sorted into appropriate houses.³⁰ Ancestral differences are embedded in the Hogwarts house system and exacerbated by the process of sorting the students. This sorting divides the Hogwarts community and makes interhouse alliances difficult—another weakness exploited by Voldemort.³¹ Voldemort's supporters come predominately from Slytherin. Gryffindors dominate the opposing faction. In *Order of the Phoenix*, the sorting hat warns the students about these divisions:

> Though condemned I am to split you
> Still I worry that it's wrong,
> Though I must fulfill my duty
> And must quarter every year
> Still I wonder whether sorting
> May not bring the end I fear.
> Oh, know the perils, read the signs,
> The warning history shows,
> For our Hogwarts is in danger
> From external, deadly foes
> And we must unite inside her
> Or we'll crumble from within
> I have told you, I have warned you. . . .
> Let the sorting now begin. (*HP and the OP*, 206–7)

The issue, in the primary conflict, is who among human magic users may be considered a witch or a wizard. The Malfoy family and their Slytherin House peers are the series' most vocal exponents of the theory that pure-blood wizards are superior to their Muggle-born or mixed peers. In their allegiance to Voldemort, they are joined by the Black family, with the notable exception of Sirius, the lone member of the family to be sorted into Gryffindor. The Black family motto is "Toujours Pur"—always pure (*HP and the OP*, 111). Hogwarts cofounder Salazar Slytherin felt strongly enough about the issue to leave behind a basilisk concealed in Hogwarts to kill future students of Muggle parentage (*HP and the CS*, 151, 290).

In another example of the wizarding world's apartheid-like registration system, the official records in the Ministry of Magic do not document the Squibs (*HP and the OP*, 143). They are thus unenrolled in the community of wizards, and their memory is officially expunged from the records. In *Half-Blood Prince*, Marvolo Gaunt says to his own daughter: "You disgusting little Squib, you filthy little blood traitor!" (210). Her offense, other than exhibiting a limited talent for magic, was a romantic interest in a Muggle, Tom Riddle Senior. "Blood traitor" is one of several terms used to disparage pure-blood wizards who associate with Muggles, Muggle-borns, or magical creatures. The Black family goes so far as to remove Squibs and blood traitors from the family tree at no. 12 Grimmauld Place (*HP and the OP*, 111–14). Sirius Black explains that, even though he is related to the Weasleys, they don't appear on the family tree: "[T]here's no point in looking for them on here—if ever a family was a bunch of blood traitors it's the Weasleys" (*HP and the OP*, 113).

When Dolores Umbridge arrests Muggle-borns for their unauthorized use of magic, she demands to know from which wizard or witch they stole their wand (*HP and the DH*, 260). Umbridge knows that they did not steal the wands. This form of interrogation is solely to put the Muggle-borns in their place. Umbridge is not trying to gather information about how they obtained their wand; her line of questioning, rather, is designed to drive home their change in status under the new regime by retroactively imposing a new legal reality on them. That status places them on a reduced level, akin to that of the goblins or other subject races of magical creatures.

Prejudices about the bloodlines of wizards are not confined to Death Eaters; they seem to be widely shared by many wizards. This bias is carried over into the wizard justice system. In Harry's trial in *Order of the Phoenix*, it becomes clear that Muggles and Squibs are not considered to be credible witnesses. His only defense witnesses are a Muggle, Dudley Dursley, and a Squib, Arabella Figg. It is only with great difficulty that Dumbledore is able to get Figg's testimony admitted, and it is clear that there is great skepticism that a Squib can even see a Dementor (*HP and the OP*, 143). The Muggle is not allowed to testify; Dumbledore does not even bother to call him as a witness. Rowling likely had in mind US laws that banned African Americans from testifying against whites or serving on juries. Such laws were common, even in the northern United States. Muggles are similarly excluded from the wizard justice system. The Ministry of Magic is charged with keeping the magical world secret, and the memories of Muggles who witness magic are regularly altered by the Ministry's employees. Voldemort murders at least three Muggles to create his Horcruxes,[32] but in another echo of real-world racism, the Ministry of Magic shows scant interest in investigating crimes against Muggles.

Even stronger than their views about Squibs and mixed-blood wizards are the prejudices wizards hold against magical creatures. These prejudices are enshrined in wizard law. Unlike the institutional racism employed against other wizards, magical creatures are subject to explicit laws that discriminate by race. This regime is closer to South African apartheid or the segregation era in the United States. Tom Riddle is able to scapegoat an elderly house-elf for his theft of Helga Hufflepuff's cup and the murder of its owner, Hepzibah Smith, because of elves' diminished status and credibility. Magical creatures such as Buckbeak do not even have access to the Wizengamot, being tried instead by the Committee for the Disposal of Dangerous Creatures.

In spite of the struggle between Voldemort's Death Eaters and the Order of the Phoenix, neither faction constitutes a reform movement with respect to the justice system and magical creatures. Both factions consider witches and wizards superior to their magical brethren; the primary difference between them is that Voldemort's Death Eaters have an even narrower definition of witch or wizard than the wizarding establishment. However, they also have fewer scruples about making deals with magical creatures, who have ample reason to resent their treatment by the current regime. This is an important advantage. The goblin Griphook makes it clear that nonhumans see the struggle in the context of their desire to vindicate their rights even if the wizards don't (*HP and the DH*, 488–89).

Perhaps no group suffers more legal disadvantages or is portrayed more sympathetically than the house-elves. House-elves are essentially enslaved, and they are forbidden to carry wands. Winky, the Crouch family's house-elf, is dismissed after being discovered unconscious and holding a wand in violation of the Code of Wand Use (*HP and the GF*, 131–38). Voldemort uses at least two house-elves as scapegoats or test subjects while creating his Horcruxes. Hokey, the house-elf of Helga Hufflepuff's descendant, is framed for her murder by Tom Riddle. Kreature, the Black family's house-elf, is abandoned by Voldemort with the locket Horcrux. Hermione campaigns for a change in the status of the house-elves. She recognizes this as a legal issue in her manifesto "Stop the Outrageous Abuse of Our Fellow Magical Creatures and Campaign for a Change in Their Legal Status" (*HP and the GF*, 224–25). Hermione wants to get elves' wand rights restored and an elf into the Department for the Regulation and Control of Magical Creatures. Unfortunately, there doesn't seem to be any legal avenue available to vindicate the rights of house-elves, even if Hermione could persuade them to pursue it. Jackie C. Horne recognizes that although Rowling points to the institutional roots of racism in the wizarding world, she doesn't provide a model of an institutionally based solution.[33]

Werewolves are another group that suffers from discrimination and legal oppression. Werewolves are subject to anti-werewolf legislation, drafted by Dolores Umbridge, that makes it nearly impossible for them to hold a job (*HP and the OP*, 302). Many are forced to live on the margins stealing or even killing in order to eat (*HP and the HBP*, 334). Other werewolves, including Hogwarts professor Remus Lupin, choose to conceal their condition when possible. This is one of several instances in the books when characters engage in a form of racial passing, a technique employed by African Americans to escape slavery and avoid discrimination by assimilating into the white majority. Nearly all of the werewolves join Voldemort in the Second Wizarding War because they believe that they would have a better life under his rule (*HP and the HBP*, 334).

Although no specific legal status for giants is outlined in the series, it is clear that they are considered to be lower status and are therefore denied full rights. Ron Weasley indicates that all giants have been driven from Britain (*HP and the GF*, 430). Madame Olympe Maxime, in an unsuccessful attempt at racial passing, denies being half-giant in spite of her obvious heritage (*HP and the GF*, 429). Her denials do her no good; she immediately falls under suspicion after the disappearance of Barty Crouch as a result of anti-giant prejudice (*HP and the GF*, 606). Hagrid, a half-giant, suffers a regular string of insults, especially at the hands of the pure-blood Draco Malfoy. He is also framed by Tom Riddle along with the giant spider, Aragog, for the death of Moaning Myrtle (*HP and the CS*, 311–12).

The giants side with Voldemort in the First Wizarding War, and Dumbledore urges the Minister of Magic, Cornelius Fudge, to reach out to them before the Second:

> "Extend them the hand of friendship, now, before it is too late," said Dumbledore, "or Voldemort will persuade them, as he did before, that he alone among wizards will give them their rights and their freedom!"
>
> "You—you cannot be serious!" Fudge gasped retreating further from Dumbledore. "If the magical community got wind that I had approached the giants—people hate them, Dumbledore—end of my career—" (*HP and the GF*, 708)

Fudge does not approach the giants, and Voldemort successfully recruits some of them to join him in the Second Wizarding War.

Although the goblins have a long history of rebellions, they don't side with Voldemort, perhaps concluding that they would fare no better, and perhaps worse, under a Death Eater regime. The goblins don't side with the Order of the Phoenix, either. When Bill Weasley tries to recruit the goblin Ragnok to the Order of the Phoenix, Ragnok declines in part because he believes that the Ministry of Magic conspired to cover up a debt owed by Ludo Bagman (*HP and the OP*, 85–86).

Goblins interact with wizards more than any other group, other than house-elves. Unlike centaurs and Merpeople, who shun wizards and manage their own affairs,[34] goblins are actively engaged in a long-term struggle to vindicate their rights. This periodically violent history resembles the numerous Irish and Scottish rebellions of past centuries. Although they have more rights than house-elves, goblins are subject to serious legal disadvantages. Like other nonhumans, goblins are forbidden to carry wands. Harry Potter skips an exam question in his History of Magic class about whether wand legislation contributed to one of the seemingly innumerable goblin rebellions (*HP and the OP*, 725); Harry and Ron both fail the exam (*HP and the HBP*, 100). Their ignorance of this legislation and the goblins' point of view comes back to haunt them when they need help from Griphook (*HP and the DH*, 488).

The goblins' views on property rights aren't respected under wizard law, and they are rightfully suspicious of the Ministry of Magic. Goblins have a distinctive view of property rights with respect to artistic items, believing that the creator retains the right to have the item revert to the creator after the purchaser dies. This belief has parallels in Muggle intellectual property law.[35] However, wizards reject this view, leaving goblin creators with no path to vindicate their rights. Bill Weasley explains to Harry that goblins consider passing a goblin-made item from wizard to wizard instead of returning it to be a form of theft (*HP and the DH*, 517). It is for this reason that Griphook demands the goblin-made Sword of Gryffindor as payment for assisting Harry. Griphook agrees to help Harry and his friends for the limited purpose of breaking into Gringotts Bank. Griphook makes it clear that he dislikes wizards in general but agrees to help, in part because of the respect that Harry showed for Dobby the house-elf, but he demands the Sword of Gryffindor as payment (*HP and the DH*, 488–89).

Although the Dementors have long worked with the Ministry of Magic, they defect and join Voldemort. The Dementors are among the most valuable allies recruited by Voldemort. The Ministry of Magic has made a Faustian bargain with the Dementors—they rely on them to keep order—but they cannot control them. They also can't offer the Dementors full scope to use their powers, a privilege Voldemort has no problem offering them (*HP and the GF*, 707). Dementors help Voldemort arrange the mass breakout from Azkaban of Bellatrix Lestrange and other Death Eaters (*HP and the OP*, 544–45). They later join Voldemort in the Second Wizarding War.

It is not surprising that much of the magical world turns its back on the wizards. The wizard judiciary is far from impartial; judicial bias seems to permeate their proceedings.[36] When Harry is tried for the underage use of magic, there seems little doubt that he would have been convicted, and his wand broken, but for the intervention of Dumbledore. The trial of Ludo Bagman, which Harry views through the Pensieve in *Goblet of Fire*, is another instance of favoritism. Ludo, a famous Quidditch player and Ministry of Magic employee, is cleared of all charges, just as the influential Lucius Malfoy is also cleared of all charges after the First Wizarding War (*HP and the GF*, 592–93, 706). This stands in stark contrast to the lack of any due process Rubeus Hagrid, Sirius Black, and Stan Shunpike receive from the same judiciary when public opinion is against them.

From the perspective of nonwizards, even more sinister are the show trials of Death Eaters after the First Wizarding War, which are both a show of force by the Ministry of Magic and an act of revenge by a frightened wizarding community.[37] Barty Crouch Sr., the head of the Department of Magical Law Enforcement, even puts his own son on trial. According to Sirius Black, the trial "wasn't much more than an excuse for Crouch to show how much he hated the boy. . . . [T]hen he sent him straight to Azkaban" (*HP and the GF*, 528). Crouch Senior's concern, in large part, was the protection of his own career.

The wizard justice system, which was never very sound to begin with, never seems to regain its equilibrium after the First Wizarding War. As Sirius Black explains to Harry, Ron, and Hermione:

> The Aurors were given new powers—powers to kill rather than capture, for instance. And I wasn't the only one who was handed straight to the Dementors without trial. Crouch fought violence with violence, and authorized the use of the Unforgivable Curses against suspects. I would say he became as ruthless and cruel as many on the Dark Side. (HP and the GF, 527)

Once the strictures against these practices were lifted, the Ministry lacked the checks and balances to rein in such abuses.

The wizards live in fear of Voldemort and the Death Eaters and therefore tolerate or even support the extreme measures of the Ministry of Magic. The wizarding public goes around armed with wands at all times, learns to duel in school, and has a long history of violence. The Ministry of Magic and its Aurors seem to exist in a perpetual state of violent conflict. Before the Death Eaters, the wizarding community's fear of goblins, giants, werewolves, and other magical creatures contributed to the creation of a legal system that valued order over concerns about access, fairness, or due process.

As the crisis with Voldemort escalates over the course of the series, the characters and the wizarding community lose faith in the Ministry's ability to handle it. The Ministry's lack of legitimacy now comes back to haunt it. The factions resort to forming extralegal groups and alliances to deal with the crisis without the sanction of law behind them. The Ministry's oppression of magical creatures and their harsh, arbitrary, and occasionally incompetent enforcement methods drive some groups into Voldemort's camp and rob the wizards of potentially valuable allies.

Horne detects a shift in Rowling's treatment of subordinated groups as the series progresses. Initially, the house-elves are a form of comic relief, but cultural and institutional structures and policies that oppress the subject races are treated with greater seriousness as the series reaches its conclusion.[38]

This shift brings the Ministry of Magic and justice system into focus. The oppression of other races is not merely the product of individual bigotry but is inherent in the system of justice itself.

Wright notes that in the absence of a competent government, "the only way to protect one's family is through private action and personal courage."[39] The later books describe the scramble to organize the factions and recruit allies for the inevitable conflict. The final battle takes place between Voldemort's forces and the Order of the Phoenix and their allies. The Ministry of Magic is conspicuously absent during this process and the final battle. It is telling that Voldemort in his quest for power does not seek to become the Minister of Magic.

Rowling's wizard justice system is a plot device created to fail. It is a cynical version of the real-world justice system with the self-interest of the participants laid bare. It cannot even competently serve its core group of insiders, to say nothing of those it victimizes or excludes in its quest to maintain the social order. In the end, the wizard justice system doesn't produce stability, order, or justice. Disappointingly, the defeat of Voldemort doesn't result in any fundamental change to the power structure. At most, Rowling offers her readers a partial reform. After the story's conclusion, Rowling clarified in an interview that the cynical, self-interested leaders of the justice system have been removed and replaced by more reform-minded enforcers, including Harry, Ron, and Hermione.[40] Readers are left to contemplate its flaws and those in the Muggle justice system.

Notes

1. Salem and Saini, "A Survey of Beliefs," 668.

2. Schwabach, "Harry Potter and the Unforgivable Curses," 311.

3. State v Kuykendall (2005 WL 3527022), 12th Dist. Clermont No. CA2004-12-11, 2005-Ohio-6872, ¶ 24–25. The term was used to analogize the statutorily necessary words at a sentencing hearing to the precise words necessary to perform a spell.

4. Schwabach, "Harry Potter and the Unforgivable Curses," 310.

5. Horne, "Harry and the Other," 77.

6. Rowling, "About."

7. Taylor, Holbrook, and Currie, *Extreme Right Wing Political Violence*, 40–43.

8. Newburn, Lewis, and Metcalf, "A New Kind of Riot?"; and BBC News, "Q&A: The Scarman Report."

9. Rowling, "Ministers for Magic."

10. Barton, "Harry Potter and the Half-Crazed Bureaucracy," 1532.

11. Rowling, "Ministers for Magic."

12. Barton, "Harry Potter and the Half-Crazed Bureaucracy," 1532–35.
13. Barton, "Harry Potter and the Half-Crazed Bureaucracy," 1532–35.
14. Liston, "The Rule of Law," 45.
15. Wright, "Collapsing Liberalism's Public/Private Divide," 442.
16. Pfander and Birk, "Article III Judicial Power," 1410, n. 309.
17. Garner, *Black's Law Dictionary*, s.v. "Witan," 1836.
18. Garner, *Black's Law Dictionary*, s.v. "Witenagemot," 1836; and Vinogradoff, "Transfer of Land," 544–48.
19. Rowling, "Dolores Umbridge."
20. Rowling, "Ministers for Magic."
21. *Encyclopaedia Britannica Online*, s.v. "Witan," https://www.britannica.com/topic/witan.
22. Rowling, "Dolores Umbridge."
23. Population Registration Act, Act no. 30 of the 1950 Parliament of South Africa.
24. Rowling, *The Tales of Beedle the Bard*, 81.
25. Rowling, *Fantastic Beasts*, xii, n. 2.
26. Joseph and Wolf, "The Law in Harry Potter," 195.
27. Barton, "Harry Potter and the Half-Crazed Bureaucracy," 1524.
28. Wright, "Collapsing Liberalism's Public/Private Divide," 235.
29. Wright, "Collapsing Liberalism's Public/Private Divide," 438.
30. MacNeil, "'Kidlit' as 'Law-and-Lit,'" 551–58; and Horne, "Harry and the Other," 83.
31. Spitz, "Wands Away," 316.
32. Rowling, "Bloomsbury Live Chat."
33. Horne, "Harry and the Other," 86.
34. Rowling, *Fantastic Beasts*, xiii.
35. Pulsinelli, "Harry Potter and the (Re)Order of the Artists," 1102.
36. MacNeil, "'Kidlit' as 'Law-and-Lit,'" 450.
37. MacNeil, "'Kidlit' as 'Law-and-Lit,'" 549–50.
38. Horne, "Harry and the Other," 88.
39. Wright, "Collapsing Liberalism's Public/Private Divide," 440.
40. Vieira, "Exclusive: J. K. Rowling on Final 'Potter.'"

Bibliography

Barton, Benjamin H. "Harry Potter and the Half-Crazed Bureaucracy." *Michigan Law Review* 104, no. 6 (May 2006): 1523–38.
BBC News. "Q&A: The Scarman Report." April 27, 2004. http://news.bbc.co.uk/2/hi/programmes/bbc_parliament/3631579.stm.
Garner, Bryan, ed. *Black's Law Dictionary*. Saint Paul, MN: Thomson Reuters, 2014.
Horne, Jackie H. "Harry and the Other: Answering the Race Question in J. K. Rowling's *Harry Potter*." *The Lion and the Unicorn* 34, no. 1 (January 2010): 76–104.
Joseph, Paul R., and Lynn E. Wolf. "The Law in *Harry Potter*: A System Not Even a Muggle Could Love." *University of Toledo Law Review* 34, no. 2 (Winter 2003): 193–202.
Liston, Mary. "The Rule of Law through the Looking Glass." *Law and Literature* 21, no. 1 (Spring 2009): 42–75.
MacNeil, William P. "'Kidlit' as 'Law-and-Lit': Harry Potter and the Scales of Justice." *Law and Literature* 14, no. 3 (Fall 2002): 545–64.

Newburn, Tim, Paul Lewis, and Josephine Metcalf. "A New Kind of Riot? From Brixton 1981 to Tottenham 2011." *Guardian*, December 9, 2011. https://www.theguardian.com/uk/2011 /dec/09/riots-1981-2011-differences.

Pfander, James E., and Daniel D. Birk. "Article III Judicial Power, the Adverse-Party Requirement, and Non-Contentious Jurisdiction." *Yale Law Journal* 124, no. 5 (March 2015): 1346–447.

Pulsinelli, Gary. "Harry Potter and the (Re)Order of the Artists: Are We Muggles or Goblins?" *Oregon Law Review* 87, no. 4 (2008): 1101–32.

Rowling, J. K. "About." *J. K. Rowling* (blog), n.d. https://www.jkrowling.com/about/.

Rowling J. K. "Bloomsbury Live Chat." Harry Potter Wiki, July 30, 2007. http://harrypotter .wikia.com/wiki/Bloomsbury_Live_Chat.

Rowling, J. K. "Dolores Umbridge." Pottermore, August 10, 2015. https://www.pottermore .com/writing-by-jk-rowling/dolores-umbridge.

Rowling, J. K. *Fantastic Beasts and Where to Find Them*. New York: Scholastic, 2001.

Rowling, J. K. *Harry Potter and the Chamber of Secrets*. New York: Scholastic, 1999.

Rowling, J. K. *Harry Potter and the Deathly Hallows*. New York: Scholastic, 2007.

Rowling, J. K. *Harry Potter and the Goblet of Fire*. New York: Scholastic, 2000.

Rowling, J. K. *Harry Potter and the Half-Blood Prince*. New York: Scholastic, 2005.

Rowling, J. K. *Harry Potter and the Order of the Phoenix*. New York: Scholastic, 2003.

Rowling, J. K. *Harry Potter and the Prisoner of Azkaban*. New York: Scholastic, 1999.

Rowling, J. K. *Harry Potter and the Sorcerer's Stone*. New York: Scholastic, 1998.

Rowling, J. K. "Ministers for Magic." Pottermore, August 10, 2015. https://www.pottermore .com/writing-by-jk-rowling/ministers-for-magic.

Rowling, J. K. *The Tales of Beedle the Bard*. New York: Children's High Level Group, 2008.

Salem, Peter, and Michael Saini. "A Survey of Beliefs and Priorities about Access to Justice of Family Law: The Search for a Multidisciplinary Perspective." *Cardozo Journal of Conflict Resolution* 17, no. 3 (Spring 2016): 661–89.

Schwabach, Aaron. "Harry Potter and the Unforgivable Curses: Norm-Formation, Inconsistency, and the Rule of Law in the Wizarding World." *Roger Williams University Law Review* 11, no. 2 (Winter 2006): 309–51.

Spitz, Laura. "Wands Away (or Preaching to Infidels Who Wear Earplugs)." *Law Teacher* 41, no. 3 (2007): 314–29.

Taylor, Max, Donald Holbrook, and P. M. Currie, eds. *Extreme Right Wing Political Violence and Terrorism*. New York: Bloomsbury Academic, 2013.

Vieira, Meredith. "Exclusive: J. K. Rowling on Final 'Potter'" (video interview). *Today*, July 26, 2007. https://www.today.com/video/exclusive-j-k-rowling-on-final-potter -48760899952.

Vinogradoff, Paul. "Transfer of Land in Old English Law." *Harvard Law Review* 20, no. 7 (1907): 532–48.

Wright, Danaya. "Collapsing Liberalism's Public/Private Divide: Voldemort's War on the Family." *Texas Wesleyan Law Review* 12, no. 1 (Fall 2005): 434–41.

About the Contributors

Christina M. Chica is a doctoral candidate in sociology at the University of California, Los Angeles, and the daughter of immigrants from Mexico and El Salvador. She is a mixed-methods researcher, writer, and creator who grew up reading fantasy fiction in Los Angeles. Christina primarily focuses on placemaking across time, space, and genre as an interdisciplinary sociologist. She is currently working on a COVID-related project examining the LGBT+ community's social, spatial, and technological adaptations to the pandemic in Mexico City. This work is part of a larger project that investigates the relationship between urban change and LGBT+ placemaking in Mexico City. Please visit christinachica.com for more information.

Kathryn Coto is a fan studies and children's and young adult literature scholar. She is particularly interested in LGBTQIA+ young adult lit and sees queer fan works as an expansion of the genre that creatively and critically responds to, revises, and evolves the products of mainstream media. Her scholarship examines the ways in which fandom is a potentially cosmopolitan space, which often provides the first platform for marginalized voices, these voices intersecting and gaining the power to change our cultural narrative.

Sarah Park Dahlen is an associate professor at the School of Information Sciences at the University of Illinois at Urbana-Champaign. A graduate of the University of California, Los Angeles's Asian American Studies Department, she earned her PhD and MS in library and information science from the University of Illinois at Urbana-Champaign. She cofounded *Research on Diversity in Youth Literature* and coedits that journal with Sonia Alejandra Rodríguez, coedited *Diversity in Youth Literature* with Jamie Campbell Naidoo, and coedited the *Children's Literature Association Quarterly*'s special issue on Orphanhood and Adoption in Children's Literature with Lies Wesseling. Her next book addresses Asian American youth literature with Paul Lai. She can be reached at sarahpark.com and @readingspark.

Preethi Gorecki is the communications librarian at MacEwan University. Prior to that, she was a student engagement librarian at Florida State University and a library faculty diversity fellow at Grand Valley State University. Preethi holds a bachelor of arts degree in sociology from Concordia University in Montreal and a master of library and information science degree from the University of Western Ontario in London, Ontario. Her research interests include practices for diversifying librarianship, project and task management tools and techniques for everyday academic librarianship, and student engagement as related to student wellness.

Tolonda Henderson is a PhD student in the English Department of the University of Connecticut. They study the intersection of disability and adolescence in young adult literature with particular focus on how race is inflected in how we understand that intersection. These questions have led Mx. Henderson to pursue a certificate in American studies. In addition to numerous presentations at academic conferences focused on Harry Potter, Mx. Henderson has previously published Harry Potter scholarship on the themes of visual culture and fatness and has a forthcoming book chapter on the trauma aesthetic in the series.

Marcia Hernandez is a professor of sociology at the University of the Pacific. Her primary research areas are intersectionality in popular culture and higher education, with an emphasis on the experiences and representations of Black women. She teaches sociological theory, race and ethnicity, gender, and family courses. Along with Florence Maätita, she has written about the use of space in the magical world of Harry Potter in *The Sociology of Harry Potter*, edited by Jenn Sims (2012). She is currently working on a project exploring women's experiences in graduate chapters of historically Black sororities, and an article examining the role of race and gender in political participation.

Jackie C. Horne worked for a decade in children's book publishing before returning to academia to earn an MA in children's literature from Simmons College and a PhD in eighteenth- and nineteenth-century British literature from Brandeis University. As an assistant professor at the Center for the Study of Children's Literature at Simmons College, she taught courses on fantasy and science fiction for children and young adults, multicultural literature, and writing pedagogy. She is the author of *History and the Construction of the Child in Early British Children's Literature*, as well as the coeditor of two essay collections in the Children's Literature Association's Centennial series and editor of *Conversations with Madeleine L'Engle*.

Susan E. Howard was an associate professor and assistant program chair of English at Ivy Tech Community College in Fort Wayne, Indiana. An avid fan of the *Harry Potter* series since the publication of the first book, she wrote about the series as a postcolonial slave narrative in the book *Harry Potter's World Wide Influence*, edited by Diana Patterson. She also presented papers on the series at Harry Potter conferences at Oxford University's Magdalen College and the University of Westminster. Her Harry Potter–themed English composition class was a popular course option for students at Ivy Tech for three years. (Editors' note: Dr. Howard passed away as this book was being prepared for publication. We greatly value her contribution to this volume.)

Peter C. Kunze is a visiting professor of communication at Tulane University. His research and teaching interests include media history, media industry studies, and children's culture. He edited *The Films of Wes Anderson: Critical Essays on an Indiewood Icon* and *Conversations with Maurice Sendak*, and he coedited *American-Australian Cinema: Transnational Connections*. His book project, *Staging a Comeback: Broadway, Hollywood, and the Disney Renaissance*, examines the creative and industrial relationships between Broadway and Hollywood in the late twentieth century.

Florence Maätita is a professor of sociology at Southern Illinois University Edwardsville. She teaches various courses, such as race and ethnic relations, social inequality, immigration, and the sociology of Harry Potter. Her research has focused on safe spaces in the wizarding world, immigration and motherhood, and tokenism among women of color in academia. In addition to teaching and promoting sustained conversations and actions toward ending racism, sexism, xenophobia, heterosexism, and transphobia, she loves to do Pilates, dream of travel, drink hazelnut lattes, and look out the windows with her two cats, Sani and Bellatrix (yes, she is named after that character).

Sridevi Rao is a recent graduate from Pennsylvania State University, where she earned her PhD in higher education and comparative and international education. She is currently working on a new student success program called UT for Me at the University of Texas at Austin. The goal of this holistic program is to increase persistence, retention, and graduation rates for low-income students while helping them achieve their goals. Her research interests include the identity negotiations of underrepresented college students, women and underrepresented students in STEM, and creating more equitable educational pipelines and opportunities in higher education.

Kallie Schell received her master's degree in library and information science from St. Catherine University. Currently she works as a children's librarian at the Oshkosh Public Library in Oshkosh, Wisconsin. She can be found at @kallschell.

Jennifer Patrice Sims, PhD, is a US-based sociologist whose work examines racial construction, perception, and identity. She is the coauthor of *Mixed-Race in the US and UK* (Emerald Publishing, 2020) and the editor of *The Sociology of Harry Potter* (Zossima Press, 2012). Her research and teaching have been covered by BBC World News, the *Washington Post*, and the *Chronicle of Higher Education*. In 2016, she was the featured speaker at Edinboro University's Potterfest. Dr. Sims is an assistant professor of sociology at the University of Alabama in Huntsville and a member of Ravenclaw House.

Paul Spickard is a distinguished professor of history, Black studies, Asian American studies, and Chicana/o studies at the University of California, Santa Barbara. He has taught at fifteen universities in the United States and abroad. He is the author or editor of twenty books and eightyish articles on race, mixed race, and related topics, including: *Red and Yellow, Black and Brown: Decentering Whiteness in Mixed Race Studies* (2017); *Race in Mind* (2015); *Global Mixed Race* (2014); *Almost All Aliens: Immigration, Race, and Colonialism in American History and Identity* (2007); *Is Lighter Better?*

Skin-Tone Discrimination among Asian Americans (2007); and *Mixed Blood: Intermarriage and Ethnic Identity in Twentieth-Century America* (1989).

Lily Anne Welty Tamai is an assistant professor of history at California State University Sacramento. She earned a doctorate in history from the University of California Santa Barbara. Dr. Tamai conducted research in Japan and in Okinawa as a Fulbright Graduate Research Fellow and is also a Ford Foundation Fellow. Her forthcoming book is titled, *Military Industrial Intimacy: Mixed-race American Japanese, Eugenics and Transnational Identities*, which documents the history of mixed-race American Japanese born after World War II and raised during the postwar period. She coedited *Shape Shifters: Journeys across Terrains of Race and Identity* (University of Nebraska Press, 2020).

Ebony Elizabeth Thomas is an associate professor in the Joint Program in English and Education at the University of Michigan's School of Education. Previously, she was an associate professor in the Literacy, Culture, and International Education Division at the University of Pennsylvania Graduate School of Education. A former Detroit public schools teacher and National Academy of Education/Spencer Foundation Postdoctoral Fellow, she serves as coeditor of *Research in the Teaching of English,* and her most recent book is *The Dark Fantastic: Race and the Imagination from Harry Potter to the Hunger Games* (New York University Press, 2019). Her expertise on race and representation in children's and young adult literature has been sought after nationally and internationally. She has been interviewed by MSNBC, the BBC, the *New York Times*, the *Philadelphia Inquirer*, and the *Chicago Tribune*, to name a few. She is a former reviewer for *Kirkus*'s children's book section and has written book reviews for the *Los Angeles Times*. She is a past National Book Award for Young People's Literature judge and is a current member of the United States Board on Books for Young People.

Jasmine Wade is a doctoral candidate in cultural studies at the University of California, Davis, with designated emphases in feminist theory and research and Native American studies. Her dissertation, "Healing/Encountering: Black and Indigenous Radical Aesthetic Practices," is an interdisciplinary project that looks at Black and Indigenous speculative aesthetics, including the manifestos of Black Lives Matter and Idle No More, in relation. Her work engages Black studies, Native American and Indigenous studies, Black and Native feminisms, queer studies, and speculative futures studies. In addition to her work as a lecturer at Sacramento State University, Jasmine is also a freelance curriculum writer. In this capacity, she writes inclusive, critical teaching guides for educators and reviews educational materials with a culturally responsive education lens. Jasmine is also a speculative fiction writer whose work has appeared in *Drunken Boat*, *Trouble the Waters: Tales of the Deep Blue*, *Lunch Ticket*, and more.

Karin E. Westman serves as an associate professor and department head of English at Kansas State University, where she also teaches and conducts research on twentieth- and twenty-first-century British literature, including children's and young adult literatures and women's literature. Her next book will be *Harry Potter in Context: J. K. Rowling's Library*. With Naomi Wood and David Russell, she has served as the coeditor of the journal *The Lion and the Unicorn* (Johns Hopkins University Press) since 2008.

Charles D. Wilson is an attorney and librarian who manages Knowledge Management and Competitive Intelligence at Ballard Spahr LLP. His work is focused on the use of legal technology to help the firm's lawyers and their clients gain insights into legal trends and work together efficiently. Prior to becoming a librarian, Charlie practiced law for more than ten years. He is the author of several articles and book reviews in legal publications including the *Legal Information Review* and *Law Library Journal*.

Index

CPSIA information can be obtained
at www.ICGtesting.com
Printed in the USA
BVHW040023210722
642638BV00007B/97